MW00989821

Eds. Paul Duncan & Jürgen Müller
With texts by Jonathan Penner, Steven Jay Schneider, et al.

HORROR CINEMA

TASCHEN
Bibliotheca Universalis

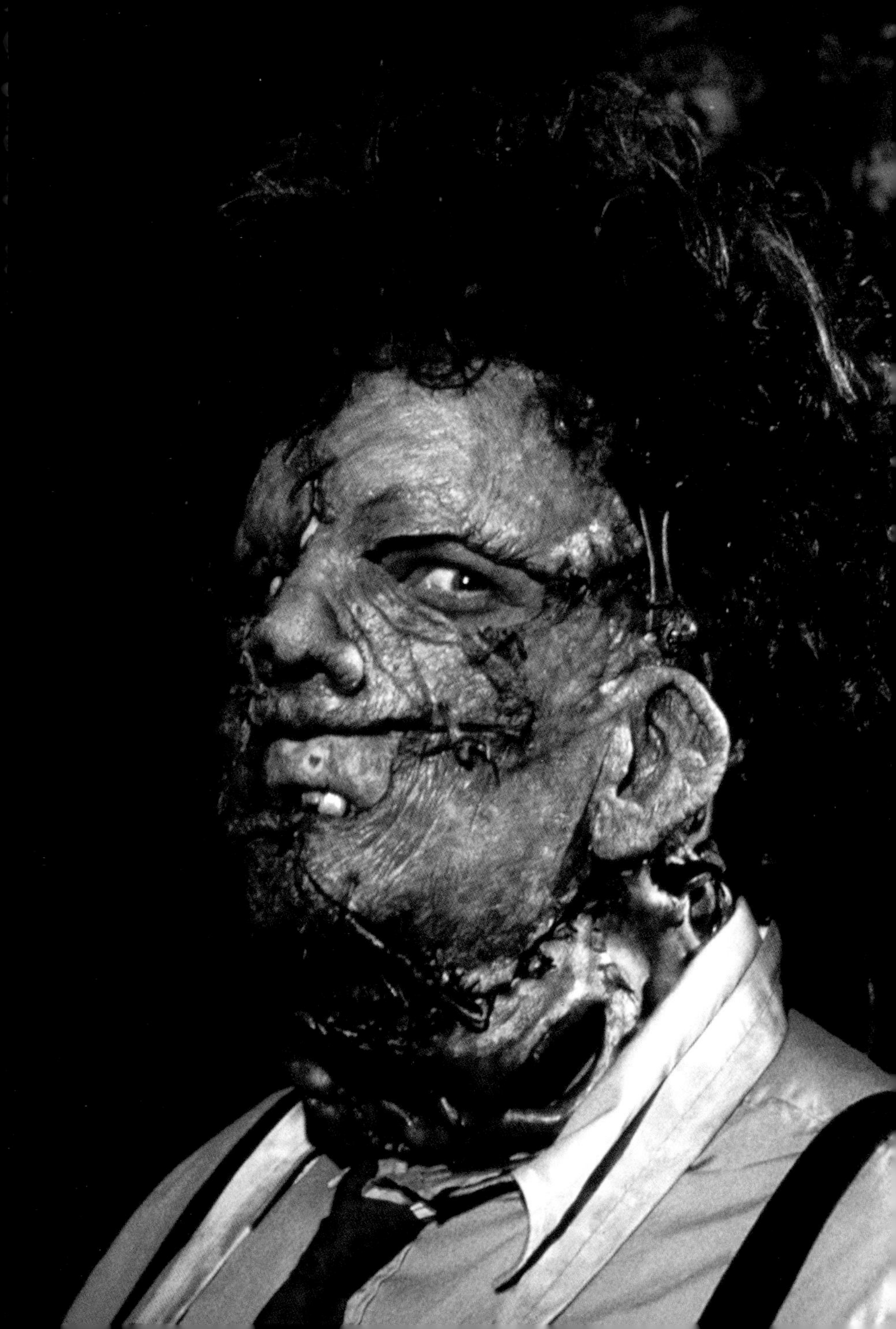

1

INTRODUCTION

What is "Horror"?

Horror is the real. The realization. It's the fact you have to face; the killer before you, teeth bared, knife raised. The dead spouse on the floor. It's the sagging flesh in the mirror and the kid running for the ball, oblivious to the truck you see coming. It's the bug crawling out of your ear. It's the Nazis in power.

What's the difference between "horror" and "terror"? Horror comes after. Terror is the suspense, the fear. You worry about something awful that could happen. "What's that sound?" "Where's my baby?" "My boyfriend?" "What's that itch?" "What's that bump?" These things terrify you. The panic starts, the dread. Terror is what's lurking behind the door—the promise of the pain. And the horror is your fear realized. Horror is the promise fulfilled.

Horror as art and entertainment has been with us since the beginning. Since cave paintings of the lions and tigers and bears. What are the last days of Christ but a horror tale? One of carnage, injustice, brutality, and, finally, the afterlife. The Bible, the Koran, the texts of ancient China and Japan—all have elements of the horrific and the spiritual. Of man's most painful endings and worst fears made manifest. They are reminders that the very real, very tangible end is always just around the corner. As a film genre, horror has its roots in the English Gothic novels of the 18th and 19th centuries. Key examples like Horace Walpole's *The Castle of Otranto* (1764), Ann Radcliffe's *The Mysteries of Udolpho* (1794), and Matthew Lewis's *The Monk* (1796) contain mystery, doom, decay, old buildings filled with ghosts, madness, monsters, and hereditary curses, all of which find ample expression in horror cinema. And Gothic literary classics such as Mary Shelley's *Frankenstein* (1818), Bram Stoker's *Dracula* (1897), and Robert Louis Stevenson's *The Strange Case of Dr. Jekyll and Mr. Hyde* (1886) considerably advanced the form before being adapted for the silver screen on numerous occasions.

"He who fights with monsters might take care lest he thereby becomes a monster. And if you gaze for long into an abyss, the abyss gazes also into you."

Friedrich Nietzsche, Beyond Good and Evil

After the Selig Polyscope Company produced a brief adaptation of *Dr. Jekyll and Mr. Hyde* in 1908 and Edison Studios released a 15-minute version of *Frankenstein* two years later, the stage was set for Robert Wiene's masterpiece of German Expressionist cinema, *The Cabinet of Dr. Caligari* (1920). *Nosferatu*, F. W. Murnau's silent magnum opus starring Max Schreck as the decidedly unglamorous, unromantic count, followed in 1922. Over the rest of the decade, the genre continued in silent dribs and drabs, thanks largely to the extraordinary acting and contortionist abilities of Lon Chaney, who played the armless, legless, and hunchbacked through the roaring 1920s.

The next wave of horror began when Universal Pictures, looking to stave off bankruptcy and heavily influenced by the shadowy German style of Murnau, Paul Leni, Fritz Lang, and others, staked a claim on Hollywood's cinematic dark side. The strategy worked wonders, and in just a few years Universal became king of the sound horror movie. *Dracula* (1931), *Frankenstein* (1931), and *Bride of Frankenstein* (1935)—the first directed by Tod Browning, the latter two by James Whale—made household names out of their larger-than-life monster stars, Bela Lugosi and Boris Karloff, respectively. These pictures were exceedingly popular, not least because audiences of the time were desperate for entertaining diversions amidst the Great Depression. The source of threat was nearly always supernatural, and, as if to further reassure viewers that things would turn out all right, the monster was always soundly defeated in the end. In those "innocent" days, even horror stories ended with hope.

"O woe, woe,/People are born and die,/We shall also be dead pretty soon/Therefore let us act as if we were dead already."

Ezra Pound

Universal's reign was superseded during the Second World War by independent-minded RKO producer Val Lewton, who understood that huge budgets weren't necessary for scares when talent was available. Encouraging his directors to avoid the straightforward depiction of violence, he attempted instead to make viewers conjure up images of horror by means of suggestion and innuendo. Although Jacques Tourneur's *Cat People* (1942) is the most highly acclaimed Lewton production, the influence of his cinematic approach and techniques extended well into the 1960s with *The Haunting* (1963), Robert Wise's masterful adaptation of the Shirley Jackson novella, which brilliantly plays up the ambiguity between supernatural and psychological horror.

In the 1950s, Cold War anxieties, coupled with advancements in special-effects technology, gave rise to a cycle of highly successful science-fiction horror movies. Some of them, such as *The Thing from Another World* (1951) and *Invasion of the Body Snatchers* (1956), focus on man's brave (read: "patriotic") battle against a hostile alien threat; others, such as *Them!* and *Godzilla* (both 1954), reflect worldwide fears of the deadly Atomic Age.

Creatures, monsters, and outer-space baddies remained all the rage until England's Hammer Studios went back to the bloody Gothic with their own star players, Christopher Lee and Peter Cushing. Taking full advantage of the industry's greater permissiveness with respect to the depiction of sex and violence, Hammer released *The Curse of Frankenstein* in 1957 and followed this success with a string of colorful, gruesomely detailed versions of the Universal classics. American International Pictures quickly followed suit, churning out its own series of campy horror-comedies, beginning with *I Was a Teenage Werewolf* (1957). AIP also distributed Mario Bava's atmospheric Italian Gothic masterpiece, *Mask of the Demon* (aka *Black*

1 ON THE SET OF "THE BIRDS" (1963) Tippi Hedren and technicians create a terrifying avian set piece on the Universal backlot.

2 PUBLICITY STILL FROM "DRACULA" (1931) Hungarian actor Bela Lugosi never escaped his iconic portrayal of pop culture's most famous monster.

3 PORTRAIT FOR "CRIME & PUNISHMENT" (1935) Peter Lorre became a star playing a killer of little children in Fritz Lang's masterful *M* (1931). Like a dangerous child himself, Lorre could be both mischievous and murderous.

Sunday, 1960), along with Roger Corman's popular cycle of Edgar Allan Poe adaptations, most of which starred Vincent Price as a mentally unstable aristocrat. Price also starred in some of marketing maven-cum-director William Castle's "gimmick horror" movies, such as 1959's *The Tingler*, which made use of "Percepto" technology (really just theater seats equipped with electric buzzers) to literally shock audience members during key scenes.

In 1960, two films—Alfred Hitchcock's *Psycho* and Michael Powell's *Peeping Tom*—initiated a whole new era in cinematic horror by making their monsters not just human, but psychologically real. The killers in these movies, both normal enough on the surface, are driven by instinctual drives and irresistible compulsions to commit murder against sexually transgressive women. Making disturbing connections between male-on-female voyeurism and the objectification of women, between gender confusion and murder as substitute for sex, these two pictures showed that monstrosity is as likely to be located *within* as without.

As the decade progressed, an increasing number of independent-minded producers and directors assumed the reins of horror cinema and moved it—as society had moved—into darker, yet more youthful, terrain. 1968, the year of the assassinations of Robert Kennedy and Martin Luther King Jr., was also the year of Roman Polanski's paranoid urban Gothic *Rosemary's Baby* and George A. Romero's no-frills black-and-white zombie classic *Night of the Living Dead.* Though this one-two punch marked the rise of both studio gloss and independent gore, both films presented visceral mirrors on the state of things. "Innocence" was lost, and the genre (and society) would never be the same again.

Generic horror conventions were put to use in the service of social statement. If *Psycho* and *Peeping Tom* made the monstrous human, many of the films that followed brought the monstrous *home*, making it not so much human as familiar. In Wes Craven's notorious *Last House on the Left* (1972), the parents of a murdered girl exact brutal revenge on the disaffected youths who killed her. In Bob Clark's *Deathdream* (1974), a young soldier killed in combat in Vietnam is temporarily brought back to life—unfortunately as a vampiric zombie—by his mother's prayers. And in Larry Cohen's *It's Alive* (1974), the Frankenstein legend is retold in distinctly modern terms, with the role of ambivalent creator given to the father of a grotesquely deformed baby on a rampage.

Not all of these films were low-budget, independently produced affairs. Stripped of its demonic-possession theme, William Friedkin's Oscar-winning *The Exorcist* (1973) provides commentary on the uselessness of modern medicine when confronted with unknown illnesses, the crises of guilt and responsibility faced by single mothers, and the difficulty parents have comprehending the generation gap and their often hostile, hormonal children. And in his masterful *The Shining* (1980), Stanley Kubrick uses haunted-house conventions as a means of exploring the real-life horrors of America's legacy in the west: alcoholism, child abuse, and domestic violence. Even the plethora of "revenge of nature" movies that appeared after Hitchcock's *The Birds* (1963) and Steven Spielberg's *Jaws* (1975) were mostly family horror movies at heart: externalizing the manifest source of horror while insinuating that what should be most feared is something lying within the individual, the family, or the community at large.

In *Halloween* (1978), John Carpenter's slasher-movie exemplar, the *Psycho*/*Peeping Tom* elements are finally overshadowed by an intense, life-or-death game of terror waged between the masked, superhuman psycho killer Michael Myers and the one surviving female (the so-called Final Girl). Partly to create space for sequels, partly to exploit the insecurity of modern viewers, and partly out of deference to the audience's growing sophistication, open-ended narratives became the order of the

4 STILL FROM "FRANKENSTEIN AND THE MONSTER FROM HELL" (1973)
This hirsute creature rightly spelled the end of Hammer Studios' Frankenstein series, which began with *The Curse of Frankenstein* in 1957 and always focused on the human monster—Peter Cushing's heartless Doctor Frankenstein.

day. Following on *Halloween*'s heels came the campier, bloodier *Friday the 13th* (1980), the outer-space slasher *Alien* (1979), and a host of less original, less successful slasher variants. Though the best of the 1980s—David Cronenberg's body-horror classics *Videodrome* (1983) and *The Fly* (1986); Sam Raimi's "splatstick" cult faves *The Evil Dead* (1981) and *Evil Dead II* (1987); Wes

"It's as much fun to scare as to be scared." *Vincent Price*

Craven's hallucinatory dream-killer flick *A Nightmare on Elm Street* (1984); Clive Barker's splatterpunk classic *Hellraiser* (1987); and John Landis's special-effects bonanza *An American Werewolf in London* (1981)—flew in the face of horror conventions, by the end of the decade most horror films had grown stale and derivative, and the genre suffered a decline in viewer interest. But with Jonathan Demme's *The Silence of the Lambs* (1991) selling the mystique of the serial killer to mainstream audiences, the horror/thriller/suspense hybrid gave the genre a massive boost in popularity. By the mid-1990s, glossy, big-budgeted, star-powered films such as *Se7en* (1995) focused on the gruesome handiwork of charismatic, creative serial killers and reflected public fascination with those who commit mass murder on principle (or so they would have us believe), not merely because of some underlying psychosexual disorder.

A sleeper hit in 1996, Wes Craven's *Scream* was the first in a wave of "neo-slashers"—highly self-reflexive works that contrive to satirize slasher-film conventions while still providing genuine scares. Three years later, *The Blair Witch Project* and *The Sixth Sense* breathed new life into the cinematic ghost story, the former cleverly exploiting mock-documentary conventions and the latter delivering a killer third-act twist. The beginning of the 21st century heralded the discovery of Japanese horror (or "J-horror") by much of the world. Hollywood remakes of hits *Ringu* (1999; remade as *The Ring*, 2002) and *Ju-on* (2003; remade as *The Grudge*, 2004) each broke the $100 million mark in the United States. More political and more subversive are the Iraq War era, Abu Ghraib–inspired "torture porn" of the *Saw* (2004) and *Hostel* (2005) series and their imitators.

All of these movies and many more are discussed in the chapters that follow, but the underlying question books like this always feel compelled to answer, as if to justify a guilty pleasure, is *why*. Why do we want to hear these stories over and over, to see them again and again? Why be reminded of our own mortality and the many faces of death we know from our collective unconscious? There's some part of us—call it morbid curiosity, call it the dark side, call it the safely sinful—that wants to explore all those aspects of life that scare us, without actually having to face death or (maybe worse) face ourselves as killers, rapists, and ghouls.

By experiencing the visceral thrills afforded by film, we can do just that: taunt death; sneer at and sympathize with victims (our own victimization); experience as delicious treats the horrors that once were the daily pitfalls of humanity. Film was invented at the turn of the 20th century, just a few generations into the industrial revolution. Life expectancy in the western world still hovered at an average age of 40. Everything could kill you, and the fact of death was a simple yet profound part of life.

Our technologies and our culture have evolved much faster than we have, and we *need* death in our daily lives—it's an essential part of the human experience. That is why horror and film have grown together. Because as technology has allowed us to live longer, and

5 STILL FROM "HOUSE ON HAUNTED HILL" (1959) Vincent Price does what is necessary to lure audiences in. Rightly or wrongly, director William Castle was always known more for his outlandish and innovative marketing ploys than for his actual filmmaking.

has taken the facts of death out of our everyday lives, so too has it allowed us to manifest those deaths on screen and with extraordinary realism. We are *wired* to experience the bloody aspects of life. And those that claim not to like horror are in denial. They are denying themselves, and they are denying their own humanity. *Because they are afraid.* Of how they feel. Of how wet and sticky and bloody fucking good horror makes us feel at its best and most horrifying.

This book celebrates the morbid impulse. The pulse. The sexual darkness. The primal pleasure of fear presented in all its sound and fury. Horror movies. A universal expression for over a century. A (not-really-so-very) guilty pleasure. A mostly surefire box-office winner. An ever-growing drugstore of mainline-able antibody psychedelia, cut, shot, and hawked hard by pushers of the unconscious and the unconscionable. Buyer beware. This is art that demands audience responsibility. Horror filmmakers have made the same sexy pitch for over 100 years. They say, "We'll give it to you good. We'll give you your money's worth." But you know the message is really this: "We're going to fuck with you, kid. And if we don't, then we ripped you off. But if we succeed, then you get brought to a place you've never gone to before. We'll take you further, harder, better than you've ever been, and we'll spoil you for the next one, who'll have to do it even harder. Even faster." Step right up. We're going to take you around the world. As hard and as fast as we can. Just the way you like it. That *is* why you're reading this, right?

"Maybe this world is another planet's hell." *Aldous Huxley*

6 STILL FROM "NEAR DARK" (1987)
Severen (Bill Paxton), a smiling psychopath in Kathryn Bigelow's cult favorite. Though often called a tale of modern-day vampires, Bigelow and screenwriting partner Eric Red assiduously avoided using the term in the picture.

1

SLASHERS & SERIAL KILLERS

PART ONE

Slashers & Serial Killers

Faced with such literally stiff competition as vampires, werewolves, zombies, body-snatching aliens, giant bugs, haunted houses, and a cornucopia of vengeful ghosts, malevolent demons, and all manner of evil spirits, it is all too easy to overlook the central role of serial killers and their psycho-slashing brethren in the history of horror cinema. In part, this is because such baddies pose something of a challenge when it comes to drawing the boundaries of the genre. If you believe that monsters are an essential ingredient of any horror movie, and if you believe moreover that monsters are by definition nonhuman (unless the term is used metaphorically), then human psychopaths belong to a closely related but nevertheless distinct genre, perhaps the "psychological thriller" or even the conveniently named "serial-killer flick." Certainly the latter term has been elevated to at least sub-genre status since the arrival of Jonathan Demme's 1991 Oscar winner, *The Silence of the Lambs*. For various reasons, however, including obvious counterexamples and the fluidity of genre labels and definitions, it seems only fair to take a more liberal view of what constitutes a horror film... and what constitutes a monster.

In fact, the inherently sensational yet all-too-real tales of serial murderers have always proven grist for the cinematic mill. Long before the term *serial killer* was coined by FBI profilers in the 1970s, Peter Lorre disturbed audiences with his brilliant, dangerous portrayal of the perverse—and perversely sympathetic—child murderer Hans Beckert in Fritz Lang's 1931 German classic, *M*. The Beckert character was based on Peter Kürten, a real-life killer in the 1920s dubbed the "Vampire of Düsseldorf" by the press. Four years earlier, Alfred Hitchcock had made *The Lodger*, a silent riff on the Jack the Ripper murders. In 1943, Hitchcock directed Joseph Cotten as a deceptively genial psychopath in *Shadow of a Doubt*; the next year saw *Arsenic and Old Lace*, a lighthearted affair about a pair of sweet old biddies who kill vagrants and bury their bodies in the cellar, and *Bluebeard*, featuring John Carradine as the infamous turn-of-the-century strangler of women. In 1947, Charlie Chaplin directed and starred in *Monsieur Verdoux*, a black "comedy of murders" about a modern-day Parisian Bluebeard who murders his wives for their money. Widely rejected by both critics and audiences upon its initial release, *Monsieur Verdoux* has subsequently been acclaimed as a masterpiece.

"There is no happiness without tears; no life without death. Beware, I will give you cause to weep." *Lucian Staniak, serial killer*

It wasn't until 1960 and the dual appearance of Alfred Hitchcock's *Psycho* in the United States and Michael Powell's *Peeping Tom* in the United Kingdom that the serial-killer film truly came into its own. Arguably, however, these twin masterpieces did more to set the stage for the "slasher" subgenre of the 1980s than to codify an authentic serial-killer cinema. It took Clint

Eastwood's series of edgy cop thrillers, including *Dirty Harry* (1972), *Magnum Force* (1973), and *Tightrope* (1984), together with William Friedkin's controversial Al Pacino vehicle *Cruising* (1980), to shift the serial-killer film into procedural territory. With Michael Mann's highly stylized *Manhunter* in 1986 (the first film appearance of Thomas Harris's genius psychopath, Hannibal Lecter, here portrayed by Brian Cox rather than Anthony Hopkins), and, of course, *The Silence of the Lambs*, FBI profiling techniques were introduced to the mix, blurring even further the fact/fiction divide so often exploited in subsequent serial-killer pictures.

"We serial killers are your sons, we are your husbands, we are everywhere. And there will be more of your dead tomorrow."

Ted Bundy, serial killer

Besides the slasher film and the cat-and-mouse investigative thriller—the latter epitomized by David Fincher's *Se7en* in 1995—non-slasher movies featuring human serial murderers have come mainly in the form of mock documentaries (e.g., *Man Bites Dog*, 1992; *The Last Horror Movie*, 2003; *Behind the Mask: The Rise of Leslie Vernon*, 2006; *The Poughkeepsie Tapes*, 2007); dark character studies of real-life serial killers (e.g., *The Boston Strangler*, 1968; *10 Rillington Place*, 1971; *Henry: Portrait of a Serial Killer*, 1986; *Angst*, 1983; *Dahmer*, 2002); auteurist one-offs (e.g., Hitchcock's *Frenzy*, 1972; Brian De Palma's *Dressed To Kill*, 1980; Donald Cammell's *White of the Eye*, 1987; Oliver Stone's *Natural Born Killers*, 1994); and the series of Italian *"giallo"* thrillers made famous by Mario Bava and Dario Argento (e.g., *The Girl Who Knew Too Much/La ragazza che sapeva troppo*, 1963; *Blood and Black Lace/Sei donne per l'assassino*, 1964; *The Bird with the Crystal Plumage/L'uccello dalle piume di cristallo*, 1970; *Four Flies on Grey Velvet/4 mosche di velluto grigio*, 1971; *Deep Red/Profondo rosso*, 1975). These *gialli*, so named for the yellow-backed mystery novels that inspired them, typically feature a black-gloved, knife-wielding killer; an amateur sleuth as protagonist; and a preference for stylish, graphic murders over narrative cohesion.

With the possible exception of the hardcore porn flick, no modern film genre has managed to achieve quite the level of commercial success in spite (or because) of its inherently controversial nature as the slasher movie. The "slasher" label has been adopted by most fans and critics to designate a voluminous collection of remarkably similar post-1960 horror films. In these movies, isolated psychotic males—occasionally you get a female psychopath, but usually only to allow for a twist ending—typically masked or at least hidden from view, are pitted against young men and women (especially the latter) whose looks, personalities, or promiscuous ways serve to trigger recollections of some past trauma in the killer's mind, thereby unleashing his seemingly boundless psychosexual fury.

Although the precise formula of the slasher movie varies depending on one's initial characterization, the genre's exploration (at times, its exploitation) of some or all of the following themes has remained strikingly consistent through the years: male-upon-female voyeurism, gender confusion and sexual perversion, the spectacle of murder, the efficacy of female self-defense, the substitution of violent killing for sexual gratification, and the utter inability of traditional authority figures to eliminate a communal threat. Vilified by feminists for supposedly promoting misogynistic messages and targeted for censorship by

1 STILL FROM "PSYCHO" (1960) Norman Bates (Anthony Perkins) heads home to mother.

2 PUBLICITY STILL FOR "THE SILENCE OF THE LAMBS" (1991) Jodie Foster was probably too American Gothic in this unused poster art. The film won five Academy Awards, including Best Actress for Foster and Best Director for Jonathan Demme.

3 STILL FROM "THE LODGER" (1927) In Hitchcock's English silent classic, the hand-cuffed lodger (Ivor Novello) is trapped in a railing whilst escaping from the mob, who believe him to be Jack the Ripper.

4

5

4 STILL FROM "PEEPING TOM" (1960) Mark Lewis (Karlheinz Böhm) and his phallic killing camera. Released the same year as Hitchcock's *Psycho*, this study of a damaged son's voyeurism and homicidal mania was equally influential but was not a critical or commercial success.

5 ON THE SET OF "PEEPING TOM" (1960) Writer/director Michael Powell talks his own son through a scene. In the film, the young boy plays the child of a perverse psychologist (Powell himself, in a cameo) whose camera records him in moments of abject terror—created by the father. Not surprisingly, psychosis results.

outraged parents and lawmakers, the slasher movie has nevertheless been treated as unworthy of critical discussion by most mainstream academics, presumably because of its "low-culture" status. In recent years, however, the progressive potential of a genre once dismissed as "violent pornography" has been examined by film theorists as well as pop-cultural historians.

As suggested above, *Psycho* and *Peeping Tom* are jointly responsible for establishing many of the slasher's primary generic elements, including an explanation (or pseudo-explanation) of the killer's motive in quasi-psychoanalytic terms; a figuring of the main victim as a sexually transgressive female; and a focus on intimate assault with sharp, phallic, penetrating implements. One might read the subsequent history of the slasher as little more than elaborations on the themes introduced in these two films.

Based on a 1959 novel by mystery/fantasy/sci-fi author Robert Bloch, *Psycho* was shot in black and white on a shoestring budget of $80,000 by the crew of Hitchcock's TV show. Groundbreaking in its canny manipulation and overturning of narrative conventions; its brilliant execution of suspense, tension, and outright horror through the application of formal technique—along with Anthony Perkins's unforgettably chilling performance as Norman Bates—and its unblinking focus on psychosexual perversion and homicidal mania, the picture was successfully marketed at the time of its release as an endurance test for audiences.

"A boy's best friend is his mother."

Norman Bates, Psycho (1960)

Bloch's novel was loosely based on the real-life case of necrophilic serial murderer Ed Gein. It tells of a lonely, mother-obsessed innkeeper named Norman Bates. Norman and his mom are the sole owners of the Bates Motel, a seedy establishment patronized by Mary Crane, an attractive young office worker who has impulsively stolen $40,000 of her chauvinistic boss's money. After an awkward but enlightening chat with Norman in which he discusses his apparently unbalanced mother, Mary resolves to return the stolen loot before anyone knows it has gone missing. But in a shocking turn, Mary is cut down in her motel-room shower by a butcher knife wielded by someone with "the face of a crazy old woman." Shortly thereafter, Mary's sister initiates an investigation into her sibling's disappearance, which eventually reveals that Norman killed his mother years earlier and has now become a homicidal split personality of Norman/Mother.

It was screenwriter Joseph Stefano who decided to begin the story with the office worker (now Marion Crane) instead of with Norman and his mother. By telling the story from Marion's point of view and engaging audience sympathy for her, he could shock viewers by killing her off before the film was barely half over. To add to this impact, Hitchcock cast well-known actress Janet Leigh in the role. To garner sympathy for Norman Bates, the director chose Anthony Perkins, known for his portrayal of sensitive men in such films as *Fear Strikes Out* (1957) and *Friendly Persuasion* (1956). After *Psycho*'s release, public perception of Perkins was forever altered, leading to a career of weird roles, including reprises of his Norman Bates character in several belated and disappointing sequels. (Part homage, part experiment, *Psycho* was unfortunately remade shot for shot by Gus Van Sant in 1998 with Vince Vaughn in the Norman role, proving once and for all that Hitchcock's original is a singular work that needs no updating or improving.)

Shooting on *Psycho* went quickly, but an entire week was lavished on the sequence widely considered the most terrifying movie murder in cinema history: the shower

6 ON THE SET OF "PSYCHO" (1960) Alfred Hitchcock directs Janet Leigh to take the most famous shower in cinema history. *Psycho* killed off its heroine in a mere 47 minutes, gleefully violating the audience's expectations and setting a new bar for the film thriller.

6

7

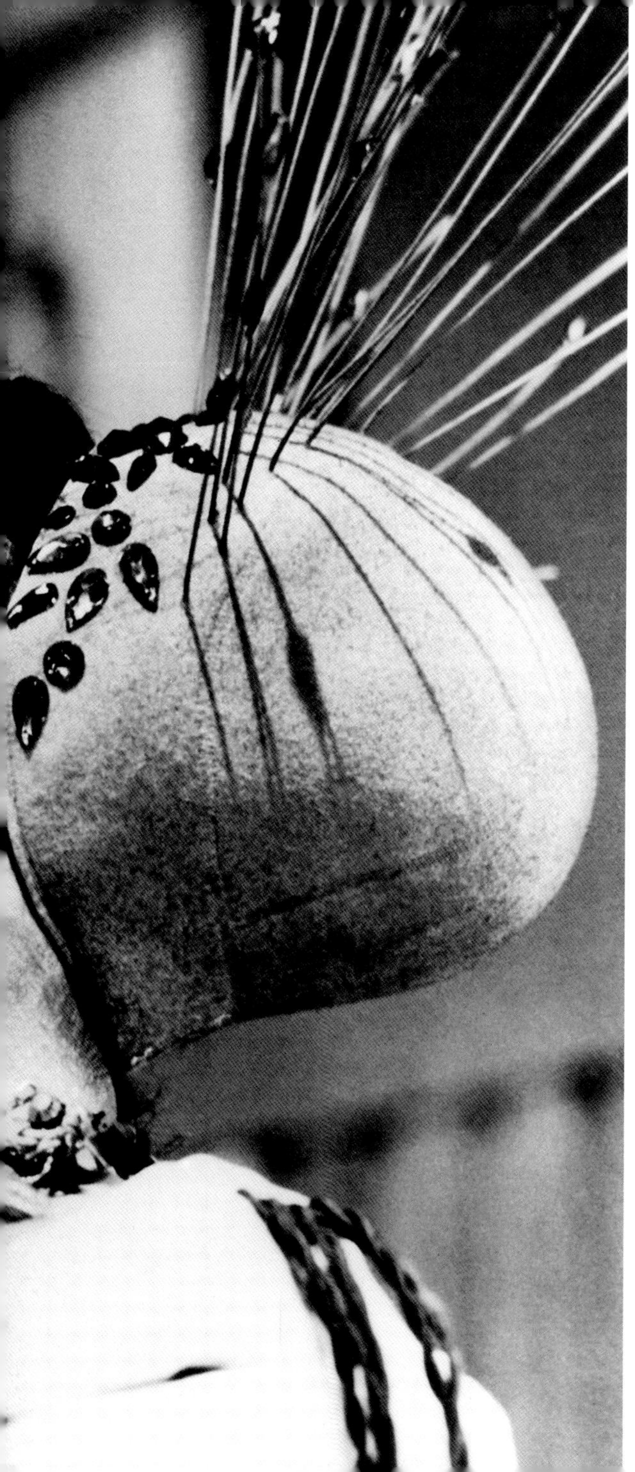

7 STILL FROM "THE ABOMINABLE DR. PHIBES" (1971) Dr. Anton Phibes (Vincent Price) and Vulnavia (Virginia North) share a kiss. A campy revenge tale filled with Grand Guignol set pieces, this almost-comedy was straight from the *Tales from the Crypt* school of "ick." (That's a compliment.)

8 ON THE SET OF "THE ABOMINABLE DR. PHIBES" (1971) Director Robert Fuest (center), a set designer on *The Avengers* TV Show, brought a sense of fun villainy and bloodless death to the big screen.

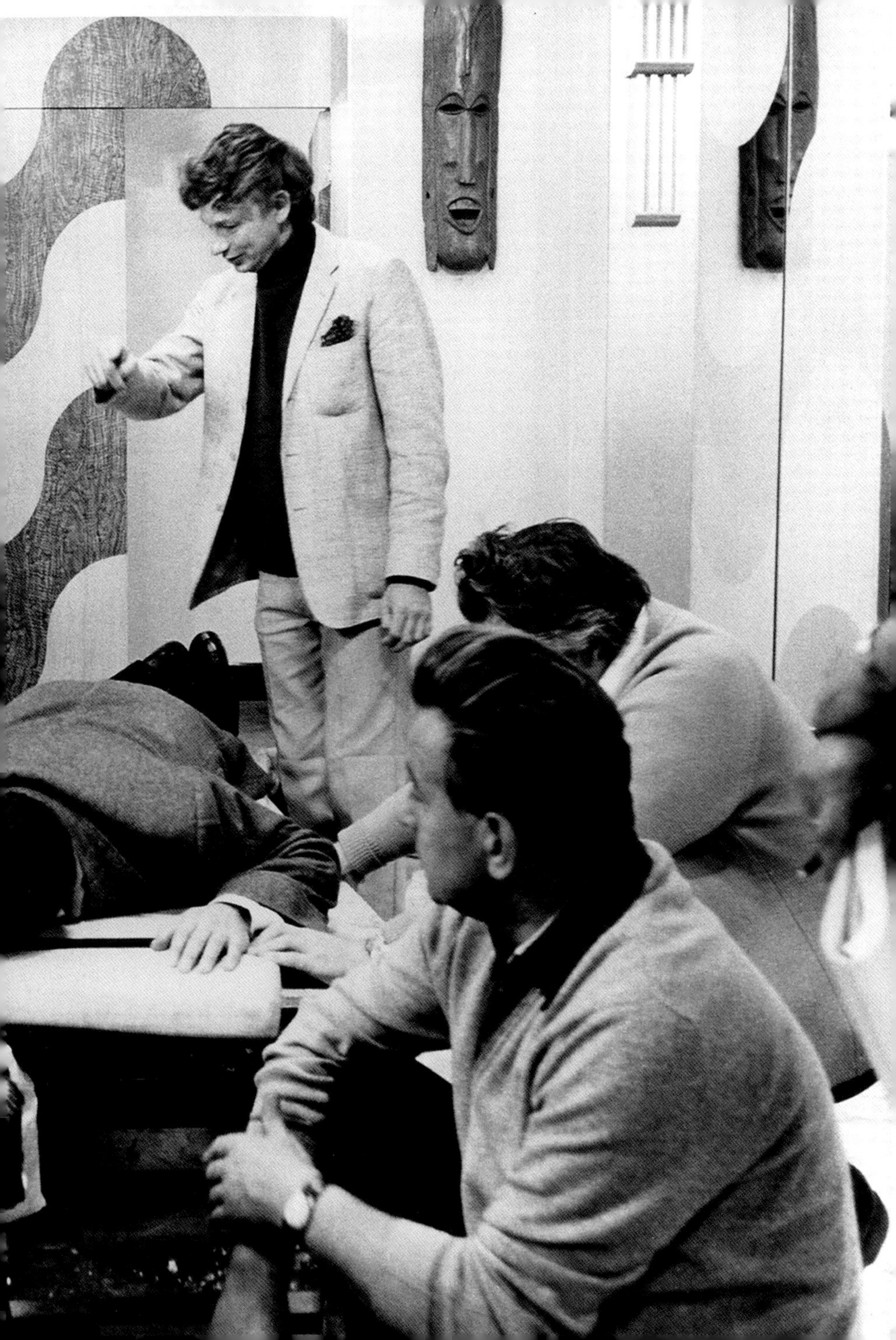

9

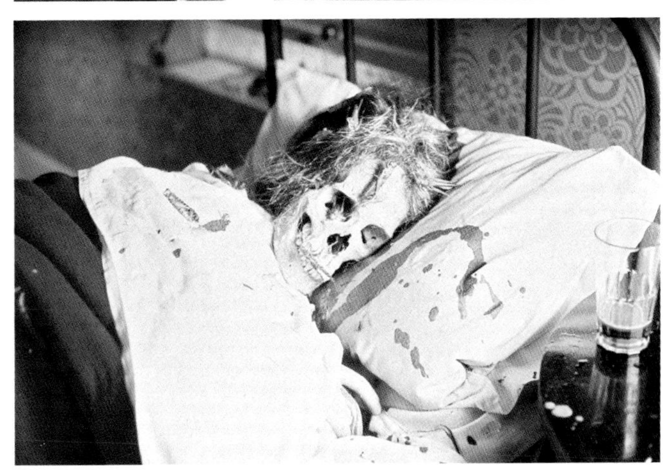

scene. Working from storyboards provided by *Psycho* title designer Saul Bass, Hitchcock shot the scene from numerous angles, which, when edited into a rapid montage—and underscored by the piercing strings of Bernard Herrmann's score—had the desired effect of shocking the audience on a primal level. Along with the stairway murder of private investigator Milton Arbogast (Martin Balsam) and the dual reveals of Mrs. Bates's skeletal remains and Norman dressed in drag at the film's climax, the shower scene has maintained its efficacy through the years—and it provides a master class in the achievement of cinematic terror through formal means. Compared to the host of horror movies to follow in its wake, *Psycho* was surprisingly circumspect in its handling of gore; Hitchcock could have shown the knife actually entering Marion's belly in the shower, but he wisely decided to achieve his effects through sheer montage editing instead.

Hitchcock's clever ad campaign, coupled with the stricture against seating anyone after the film had begun, was tongue in cheek: "Don't give away the ending—it's the only one we have!" The director always claimed that the film was a black-humored joke, but there was no denying its impact on the moviegoers who flocked to the film and subsequently swore off taking showers. *Psycho* proved to be the pinnacle of Hitchcock's career, earning him one of his too-few Oscar nominations.

Like *Psycho* before it (and *The Silence of the Lambs* after it), Tobe Hooper's *The Texas Chain Saw Massacre* took for inspiration the monstrous crimes of Ed Gein. Unlike *Psycho*, however, Hooper's film put an emphasis on gore and bodily carnage, thereby situating itself within the tradition of Herschell Gordon Lewis's notorious "splatter" films, notably *Blood Feast* (1963), *Two Thousand Maniacs!* (1964), and *The Wizard of Gore* (1970). *The Texas Chain Saw Massacre* also contributed two important elements of its own to the slasher-movie formula: a group of adolescent victims who are picked off one by one, and a "Final Girl" who undergoes a lengthy, terrifying ordeal in the film's second half, only to come out alive at the end. (For a detailed discussion of this film, see the next chapter herein.)

John Carpenter's *Halloween* (1978) eschewed the gore of *Texas Chain Saw Massacre* in favor of impressively subtle startle effects; it kept the latter film's youthful victims, however, and made its Final Girl (Jamie Lee Curtis, daughter of *Psycho* star Janet Leigh) even more aggressive and self-reliant. *Halloween*'s incredible commercial success ensured its place at the head of the "Stalker Cycle" class; between 1978 and 1981, no fewer than eleven *Halloween*-inspired slashers were made (including *Friday the 13th*, 1980; *Prom Night*, 1980; *Terror Train*, 1980; and *Graduation Day*, 1981), all structural, if not quite stylistic, copies of the original. In these movies, the predator-prey theme takes on unprecedented importance, as does the emphasis on "creative" murders and a reliance on camera shots taken from the killer's point of view. To what extent this camerawork forces viewer identification with the killer, however, remains an open question.

Despite the Final Girl's ever-increasing strength and ferocity—as exemplified by Lieutenant Ellen Ripley (Sigourney Weaver) in the *Alien* series of outer-space slashers—public debate over the genre's antisocial consequences only intensified in the 1980s. Representatives from numerous states, citing hastily acquired and somewhat dubious "empirical evidence" for support, complained of a direct cause-and-effect relationship between the depiction of graphic violence in films such as *Friday the 13th* and the increase in violent crimes perpetrated by youths. In 1984, the Video Recordings Bill passed through Britain's Parliament on the heels of an effort to restrict the consumption of arbitrarily designated "video nasties" (the

9 STILLS FROM "THE ABOMINABLE DR. PHIBES" (1971) Almost 25 years before *Se7en* (1995), Dr. Phibes uses insane variations on the ten Biblical plagues to kill his victims. For instance, he drips honey onto the face of a sleeping victim and then lets voracious locusts finish the job. In America, these fun murder movies were rated suitable for all ages.

vast majority of which were slashers). By 1989, bills were passed in Colorado, Missouri, Ohio, and Texas granting local prosecutors the power to decide which videos cross the line of "excessive violence" and so cannot be rented to persons under 18 without parental permission.

It is arguable that at least some of this negative attention was unnecessary, even self-defeating. Notwithstanding Wes Craven's high-concept supernatural variant on the genre, 1984's *A Nightmare on Elm Street*, the slasher movie was in a state of decline by the mid-1980s, primarily because of an over-reliance on convention and a glut of predictable entries. But just like its most popular monsters, Michael Myers and Jason Voorhees (from the *Friday the 13th* series), the slasher would rise from the dead. With the appearance of screenwriter Kevin Williamson's quartet of self-consciously reflexive "neo-slashers"—*Scream* (1996), *Scream 2* (1997), *I Know What You Did Last Summer* (1997), and *Halloween H20* (1998)—came a whole new range of convention-bending possibilities.

"What scares me is what scares you. We're all afraid of the same things. That's why horror is such a powerful genre. All you have to do is ask yourself what frightens you and you'll know what frightens me." *John Carpenter*

One thing is clear: No easy answer to the question why slasher movies have proven so popular currently exists. Whether they enforce conservative values by demonstrating "the inefficacy of sexual freedom" (Vera Dika), promote tolerance by "constituting a visible adjustment in the terms of gender representations" (Carol Clover), or further a feminist agenda by "articulating the legitimacy of female rage in the face of male aggression" (Isabel Pinedo), it can hardly be denied that these films appeal to different audiences at different times and for different reasons, and that they will continue to engender heated debate in homes, classrooms, and courtrooms.

10 STILL FROM "HALLOWEEN" (1971)
John Carpenter echoes a central image from *Psycho* (see pages 20–21).

11 STILL FROM "HALLOWEEN" (1971)
Annie Brackett (Nancy Kyes) and Michael Meyers (Nick Castle, credited as "The Shape") in this classic tale of suburban unrest. Only promiscuous teens die here, adhering to the traditional narrative strategy of never killing true innocents.

10

11

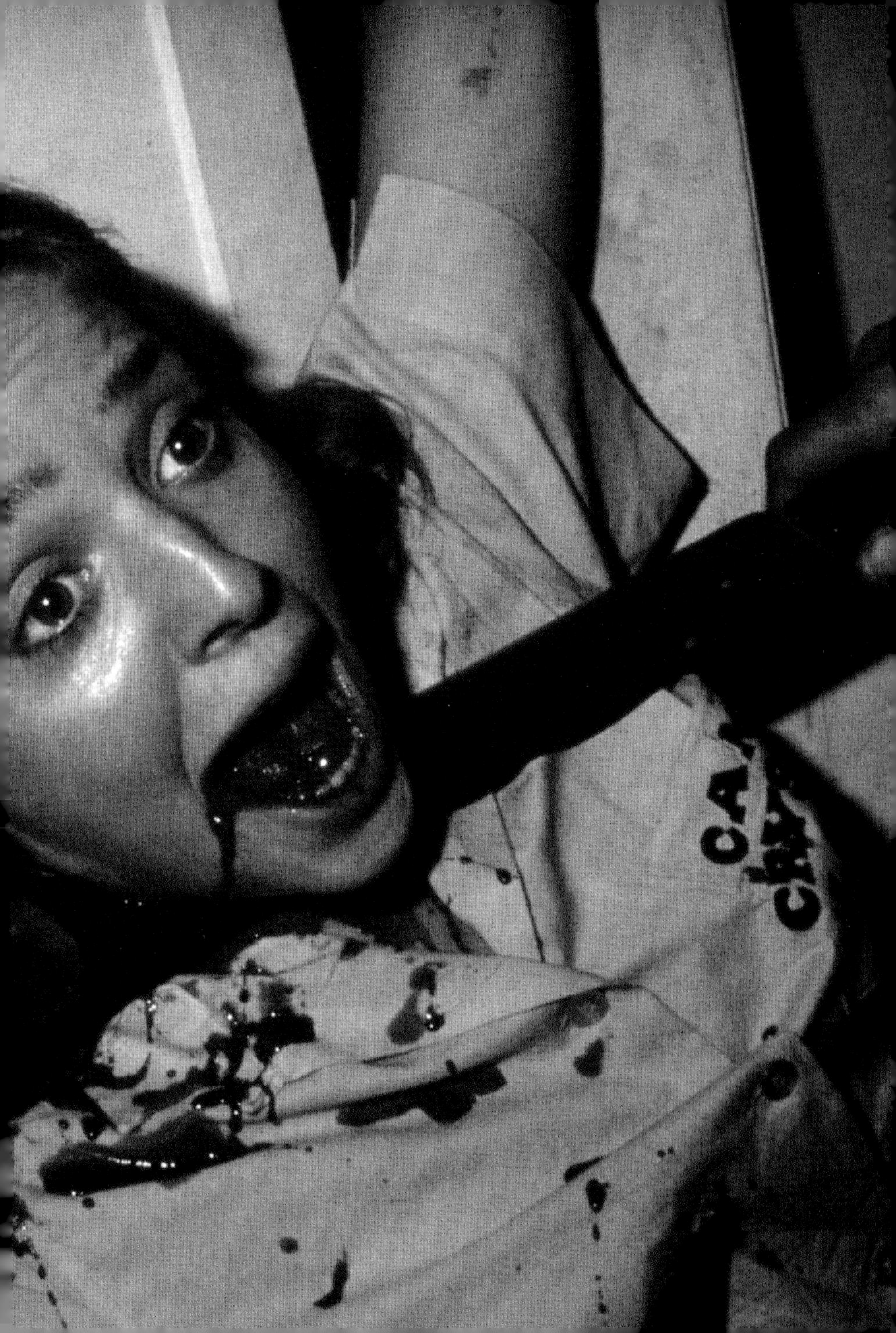

13
14

12–15 STILLS FROM "FRIDAY THE 13TH" (1980) Jack Burrell (Kevin Bacon) and his lady friend cuddle and contemplate a future that is not to be. Bacon is one of many stars who got their start in horror flicks. Johnny Depp, Tom Hanks, Renée Zellweger, and Matthew McConaughey are among the others.

16 ON THE SET OF "FRIDAY THE 13TH" (1980) Vietnam vet Tom Savini created the film's amazingly realistic makeup and gore effects. Here director Sean S. Cunningham shares a moment with Jason Voorhees (Ari Lehman).

17 STILL FROM "THE VANISHING" (1988) One of the great horror-thrillers of the 1980s, George Sluizer's film follows one man's obsessive quest to find out what happened to his missing girlfriend.

18 STILL FROM "DRESSED TO KILL" (1980) Do reflections reveal the truth? Nancy Allen sees Angie Dickinson dying in the elevator, but will she see the tall blonde woman lurking inside?

19 STILL FROM "MAN BITES DOG" (1992) Like *Cannibal Holocaust* (1980), *Henry: Portrait of a Serial Killer* (1986), and *The Last Horror Movie* (2003), *Man Bites Dog* uses documentary conventions to make us question the violence we pay to watch on screen.

20 STILL FROM "MAN BITES DOG" (1992) Ben (Benoît Poelvoorde) dispatches his latest victim in this sardonic—and brilliant—horror mockumentary.

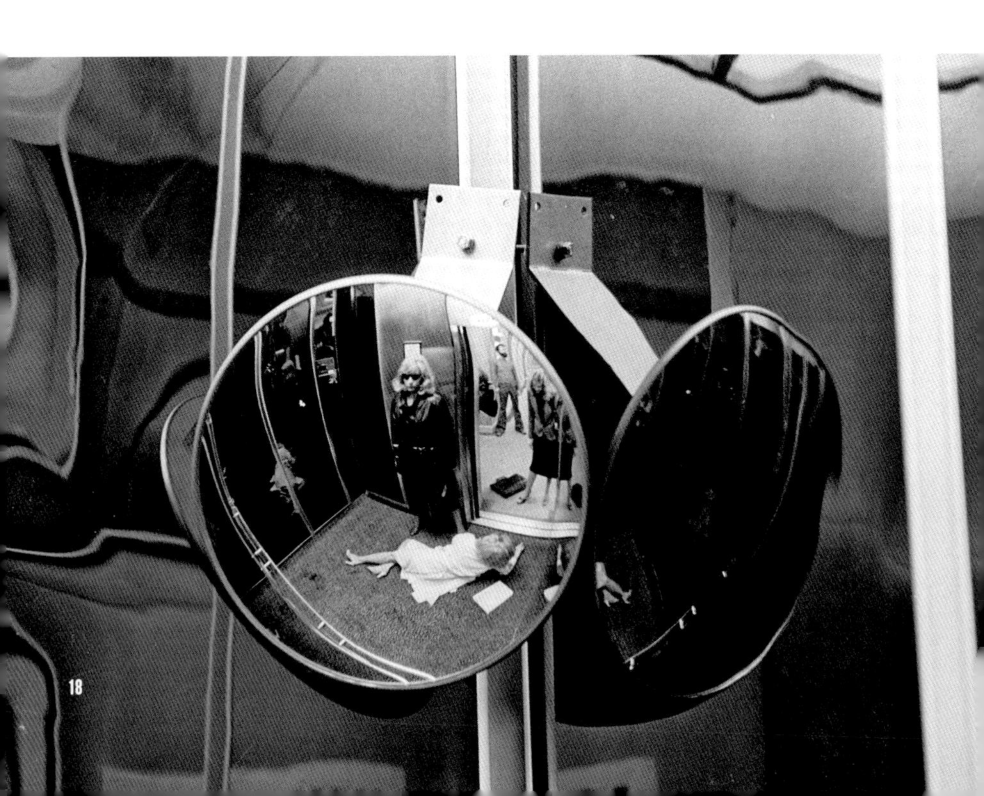

18

19
20

21 STILL FROM "DEEP RED" (1975) Marcus Daly (David Hemmings) arrives too late to save a life in Dario Argento's highly stylized *giallo*, where the logic of the unconscious creates one of cinema's most distinctive and operatically gory fever dreams.

22 STILL FROM "THE STEPFATHER" (1987) Terry O'Quinn as the eponymous stepfather, tries to find his place in the family. A stellar script by Donald E. Westlake gives him a pessimistic answer.

23 STILL FROM "M" (1931) Hans Beckert (Peter Lorre), killer of children. "Is this the face of a monster?" he seems to be asking himself.

"If I wanted a victim, I'd just go get one... I didn't even consider a person a human being."

Henry Lee Lucas, serial killer

WHO
AM I
HERE
?

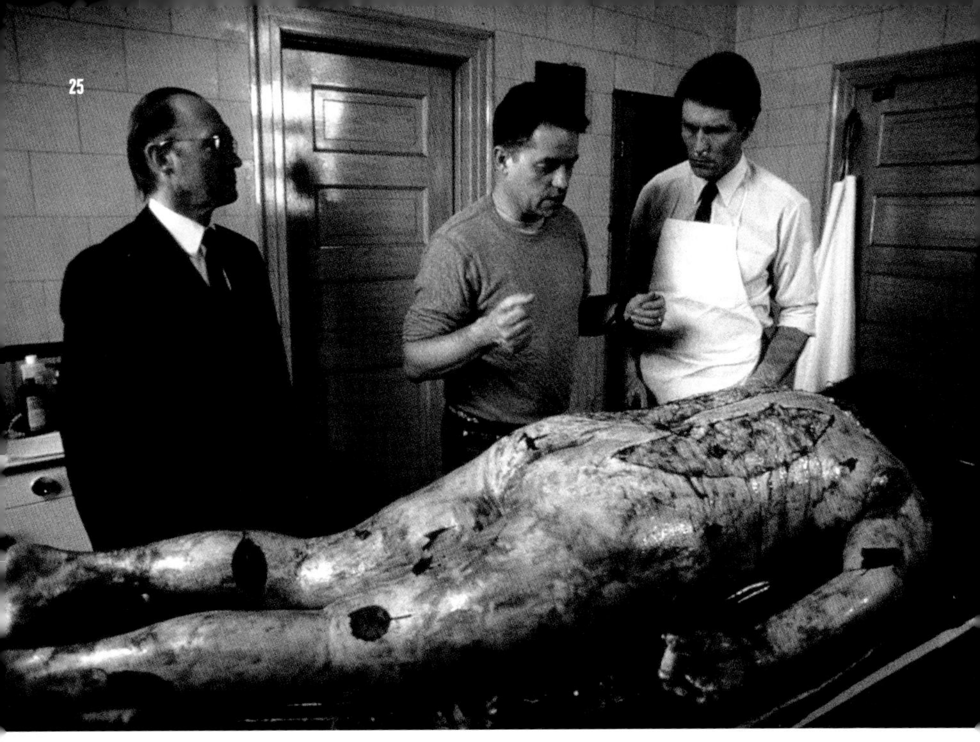

24 STILL FROM "THE SILENCE OF THE LAMBS" (1991) An archetypal horror image: Clarice Starling (Jodie Foster) and a clutching hand, the proverbial damsel in distress. Starling, with an FBI-issued handgun, spends the whole movie trying to prove her worth in a man's world.

25 ON THE SET OF "THE SILENCE OF THE LAMBS" (1991) Demme at work—the scene is a small-town autopsy. In the film, killer Jame Gumb is nicknamed "Buffalo Bill" by the authorities because he skins his humps.

26 ON THE SET OF "THE SILENCE OF THE LAMBS" (1991) Director Jonathan Demme mugging with Anthony Hopkins. Hopkins won the Best Actor Oscar for a role that enjoyed only 16 minutes of screen time.

27 STILL FROM "THE SILENCE OF THE LAMBS" (1991) Lecter's synthesis of high culture and basest impulse made him one of the screen's most beloved villains. Killing with a truncheon's akin to conducting a symphony. Murder as high art. Genius as madness.

"I ate his liver with some fava beans and a nice chianti."

Hannibal Lecter, The Silence of the Lambs (1991)

B5160-8

CANNIBALS, FREAKS & HILLBILLIES

1

PART TWO

Cannibals, Freaks & Hillbillies

What do cannibals, freaks, and hillbillies have in common? (No, this isn't a horror version of one of those "A priest, a rabbi, and a minister walk into a bar..." jokes, though we're open to funny punch lines if you know any.) In genre terms, what they have in common are the facts that (1) they are all human, and (2) though they may kill multiple victims in a relatively serialized fashion, they don't neatly fit the standard serial-killer profile of the repressed, compulsive nut driven to commit murder as a result of psychosexual trauma.

Aside from these two admittedly general qualities, not a lot holds these characters together as a unified group. They are not all, or always, villains (consider *Freaks*, 1932; *The Man Who Laughs*, 1928; and *The Hunchback of Notre Dame*, 1923). They are not all physically deformed, although they tend not to look like you, me, or the "average" audience member. They are not all from the backwoods (to the contrary, they make appearances all across the globe, often in exotic locales). But it is fair to say that they are all manifestly *different* from the rest of us, not just on the inside but on the outside; even those who live in the most rural of American communities can safely distance themselves from the hyperbolic, occasionally humorous fashion in which horror's homicidal hillbillies are depicted in movies such as *Two Thousand Maniacs!* (1964), *The Texas Chain Saw Massacre* (1974), *Eaten Alive* (1977), *Just Before Dawn* (1981), *Wrong Turn* (2003), *House of 1000 Corpses* (2003), and *The Devil's Rejects* (2005).

"The first monster you have to scare the audience with is yourself." *Wes Craven*

If anything, the stories of cannibals, freaks, and hillbillies appeal because they can take us down the end of the lane where the weirdos live in their old, dark house. They take us to visit the cultish families with the disgusting

1 STILL FROM "THE PHANTOM OF THE OPERA" (1925) The deep, dark dungeon of love: for a while the Phantom can control Christine (Mary Philbin) by hypnosis, as we see from the faraway look in the singer's eyes.

2 PUBLICITY STILL FOR "THE HILLS HAVE EYES" (1977) Michael Berryman as Pluto, a cannibal god who exists as part of his own "nuclear" family—one that has been mutated by U. S. atomic testing. Writer/director Wes Craven strikes hard at the hypocrisy in the American dream, and how little it takes to turn the civilized into savages. Craven's *The Last House on the Left* (1972), *A Nightmare on Elm Street* (1984), and *The People under the Stairs* (1991) are all variations on that theme.

3

habits, the unschoolable kids, and the serious lack of regard for the ways of us normal upstanding citizens. Or they take us into the desert or jungle, where those untouched by "civilization" practice their awful barbarities and their horrible rites. Those are the kinds of stories these films share, but perhaps more significantly, there is something inherently exploitative about these movies,

"We make up horrors to help us cope with the real ones." *Stephen King*

because they inevitably center on "folks" who are classically considered less than us or beneath us—and any story dealing with them is by its very existence exploitative. These tales are ultimately about the basest parts of the horror genre: the sideshow-barker part where we're invited in to witness the tragic and traumatic—and to enjoy something we all secretly crave: the guilty (twin) pleasures of superiority and pity.

The first cinematic freaks were a pair of titans from the silent-film era, Conrad Veidt and Lon Chaney. The German-born Veidt (1893–1943) was featured in two of the darkest and most famous silent films ever made: He played the somnambulist servant of the homicidal title character in Germany's Expressionist masterpiece, *The Cabinet of Dr. Caligari* (1920), and later the facially disfigured circus performer in Universal's adventure-horror classic, *The Man Who Laughs* (1928). Beyond the Expressionistic set designs featured in *Caligari*, it is Veidt's brilliantly modulated body language that enables him to become one with those sets, resulting in the first and one of the best examples of psychological horror on the big screen. And in *The Man Who Laughs*, Paul Leni's adaptation of the Victor Hugo novel, Veidt plays a tragic hero with a hideous grin carved into his sometimes half-covered face; here he trades body language for incredibly expressive eye movements to convey the subtlest of emotions.

Lon Chaney (1883–1930), meanwhile, succeeded in doing Veidt one better (at the very least) when it came to manipulating his visage on camera. Nicknamed "The Man of a Thousand Faces," Chaney is best remembered for his characterizations of tortured, often grotesque and afflicted characters, and for his groundbreaking artistry with film makeup. After traveling with popular vaudeville and theater acts, he transitioned to film and eventually

3 STILL FROM "THE CABINET OF DR. CALIGARI" (1920) Cesare (Conrad Veidt) pursued by the mob. This film is perhaps the greatest example of German Expressionist cinema, in which the physical environment reflects the warped psyche of Dr. Caligari.

4 PRODUCTION SKETCH FOR "THE CABINET OF DR. CALIGARI" (1920) The film used flashbacks and a very unreliable narrator. By making the story a dream, the studio tried to remove the teeth from a biting political allegory, but the timeless power of the film rests in its aesthetic accomplishments.

hooked up with director Tod Browning. It was a match made in freak heaven.

Chaney appeared in ten Browning pictures, usually playing disguised and/or mutilated characters, including carnival knife-thrower Alonzo the Armless in *The Unknown* (1927) and *London After Midnight* (1927), one of the most infamous lost films of all time. His last picture was a sound remake of the 1925 silent classic *The Unholy Three* (1930); it was the only time he ever got to display his versatile voice on the big screen.

"I always like less gore, I've always liked the idea of implied gore. I think when you can put something in the mind, the unconscious mind of the audience, they can create in their own mind something far more frightening than anything you can put on the screen." *Roger Corman*

Although lauded for his highly eccentric Browning roles, Chaney is chiefly remembered today as a pioneer in such silent horror classics as *The Hunchback of Notre Dame* (1923) and, most notably, *The Phantom of the Opera* (1925). His ability to transform himself using self-invented makeup techniques became legendary; in an autobiographical 1925 article published in *Movie* magazine that gave a rare glimpse into his life, Chaney referred to his specialty as "extreme characterization." In Quasimodo, the bell-ringer of Notre Dame, and Erik, "The Phantom" of the Paris Opera House, Chaney created two of the most grotesquely deformed characters in film history. But his portrayals sought to elicit a degree of sympathy and pathos among viewers who were not overwhelmingly terrified or repulsed by these characters' monstrous disfigurements, seeing them instead as mere victims of fate. As Chaney wrote in the *Movie* magazine article: "I wanted to remind people that the lowest types of humanity may have within them the capacity for supreme self-sacrifice. The dwarfed, misshapen beggar of the streets may have the noblest ideals. Most of my roles since *The Hunchback*, such as *The Phantom of the Opera*, *He Who Gets Slapped*, *The Unholy Three*, etc., have carried the theme of self-sacrifice or renunciation. These are the stories which I wish to do." And he did them like no one else, before or since.

Perhaps surprisingly, Browning's number-one freak-show film did *not* feature Chaney. Instead, his 1932 oddity *Freaks* starred a bevy of actual "freaks," including dwarves, midgets, Siamese twins, bearded ladies, thin men, pinheads, a boy (Johnny Eck) who only exists from the waist up, and, perhaps most spectacularly, the aptly named "Human Torso," Prince Randian. The picture virtually ended Browning's career just one year after *Dracula* (1931) made it; pleasing neither critics nor audiences, it was banned in the United Kingdom, led MGM to remove its logo from all the prints, and disappeared for decades. It wasn't until the rise of the midnight movie and "cult film" phenomenon of the 1960s and 1970s that the movie enjoyed a resurgence of attention and popularity. However, for the most part, *Freaks* isn't really a horror film. Browning takes pains to create pathos for the picture's parade of undesirables, and several scenes in which they engage in normal day-to-day activities—an armless girl drinking wine, Eck scuttling about on his hands, the Human Torso lighting a cigarette—are fascinating rather than frightening to watch.

The use of actors with real human deformities has continued in other horror films, notably those featuring

5 STILL FROM "THE PHANTOM OF THE OPERA" (1925) Erik, The Phantom (Lon Chaney), leads Christine Daaé (Mary Philbin) into the depths of his watery lair.

6 PRODUCTION SKETCH FOR "THE PHANTOM OF THE OPERA" (1925) In this, the greatest screen treatment of the Gaston Leroux novel, Lon Chaney was not simply a horror star like Karloff and Lugosi, but a major character actor—one of the biggest during Hollywood's silent era.

5
6

Rondo Hatton (1894–1946), whose acromegaly (a disorder of the pituitary gland) gradually but consistently distorted the shape of his head, face, and extremities. Universal saw him as a new horror star after he played the role of the Hoxton Creeper in one of the studio's Sherlock Holmes movies, 1944's *The Pearl of Death*; he went on to play variations of the Creeper character in a half dozen B-grade horror flicks until he died of a heart attack as a direct result of his acromegaly. In the 1970s, films like *The Mutations* (1974), *The Hills Have Eyes* (1977), and *The Sentinel* (1977) also went a similar route, although in most of these cases the effect lacks the pathos Browning engendered in *Freaks*, threatening instead to leave viewers with an unpleasant feeling at the exploitation of genuine human tragedies. More effective during this period were movies like Larry Cohen's *It's Alive* trilogy (1974, 1978, 1987), David Lynch's *Eraserhead* (1977), and Frank Henenlotter's *Basket Case* trilogy (1982, 1990, 1992), in which horribly deformed babies or aborted Siamese twins seek revenge, solace, or just plain sustenance. Here, the freaks in question are clearly exaggerations: real enough to repulse and frighten viewers, but not so real as to repulse them morally. Instead these films explicated how deformed children can be genetic daggers to the hearts of families. A cause of pain, shame, and, of course, horror.

Ahead of its time in so many ways, *Freaks* can be seen as, among other things, a precursor to the "mondo film" (or "shockumentary") subgenre initiated by *Mondo cane* in 1962. *Mondo cane* was an immensely popular and influential compilation documentary that played with the boundaries separating fiction from nonfiction film-making practices. It purports to subscribe to the adage that "truth can be stranger than fiction," all the while betraying its own principles by presenting often misleading voice-over commentary and manipulated (if not wholly faked) footage. Gualtiero Jacopetti's sensationalist travelogue-cum-nature film set out to shock viewers with its exposé of bizarre cultural behavior, which fluctuates "from the exotic to the erotic to the undeniably repellant." A one-time journalist and war correspondent, Jacopetti was hired to write the voice-over narration for two celebratory compilation films of popular nightclub acts. This gave him the initial idea for *Mondo cane*; only *his* documentary would showcase—and exploit, whenever possible—all that was lurid and sensational by contemporary western standards. Jacopetti traveled across Europe, Asia, North America, and Africa with his associates, collecting assorted footage of tribal ceremonies, extreme cruelty to animals, religious rituals involving cross-dressing and self-flagellation, and environmental catastrophes. This more-or-less random material was then assembled into a 105-minute episodic whole, the various segments connected by the thinnest of associative links (one cut, for example, takes the viewer from a dog cemetery in California to a restaurant in Taiwan that specializes in fresh dog meat).

The opening words of *Mondo cane* were both spoken and shown as text on the screen: "All the scenes you will see in this film are true and are taken only from life. If often they are shocking, it is because there are many shocking things in this world. Besides, the duty of

7 PUBLICITY STILL FOR "THE PHANTOM OF THE OPERA" (1925) Chaney always did his own makeup, creating the monstrous and the tragic with a variety of state-of-the-art tools including dentures, greasepaint, puddy, wigs, and wires. "Be careful what you step on," went a national joke in the 1920s, "it might be Lon Chaney!"

8 STILL FROM "THE PHANTOM OF THE OPERA" (1925) For the masque sequence, color tinting was used, typical for a Hollywood superproduction of its time.

9

"If *Freaks* has caused a furor in certain censorship circles, the fault lies with the manner in which it was campaigned to the public. I found it to be an interesting and entertaining picture, and I did not have nightmares, nor did I attempt to murder any of my relatives."

Charles E. Lewis, review, Motion Picture Herald (July 23, 1932)

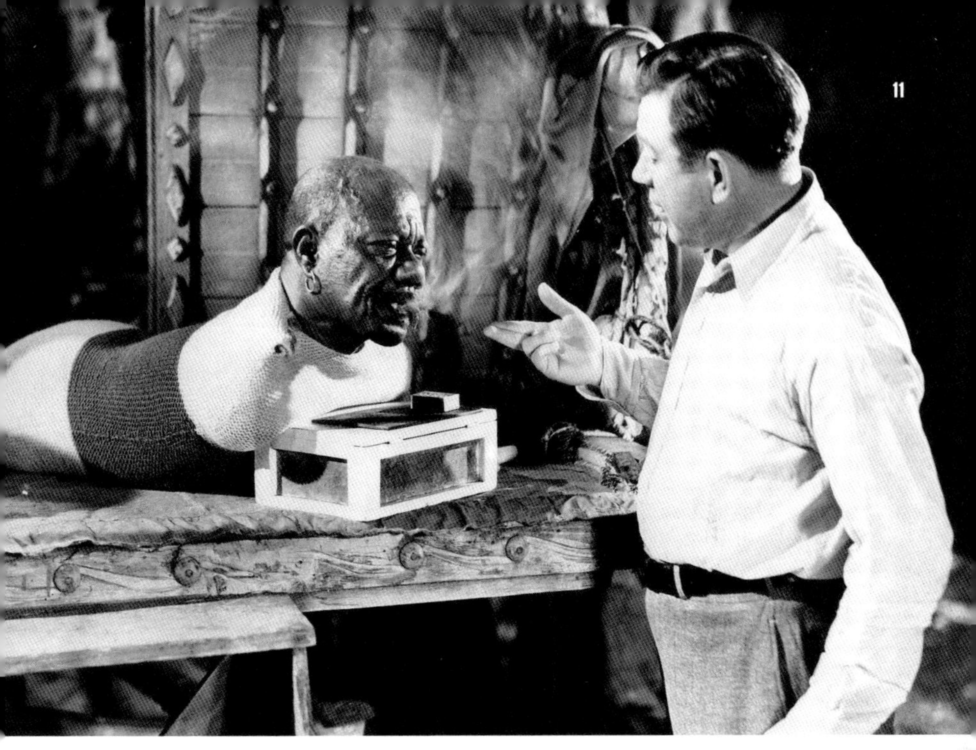

9 ON THE SET OF "FREAKS" (1932) Tod Browning (far right) directs his performers. His taste was called into question and his career never recovered.

10 STILL FROM "FREAKS" (1932) Cleopatra (Olga Baclanova) has married Hans (Harry Earles, on her shoulders) for his money. By the end, she's the one who pays. Although much more disturbing than director Tod Browning's hit *Dracula*, *Freaks* was a financial disaster.

11 STILL FROM "FREAKS" (1932) Prince Randian as "The Living Torso." Browning's picture tried to walk the line between entertainment and exploitation, but the tragic realities of his performers' lives put off even the most thrill-seeking audiences.

12 STILL FROM "THE UNKNOWN" (1927) Alonzo the Armless (Lon Chaney) sips tea. The actor's murderous, tragic performance is matched in intensity by a then-teenage Joan Crawford's volcanic sexuality. One of the great shockers of silent cinema.

the chronicler is not to sweeten the truth but to report it objectively." Even if it *was* the case that the scenes then presented were "true" in the sense of being detached and unbiased recordings of actual events—which they clearly are *not* (the only question concerns precisely which footage is real, which is reconstructed, and which is com-

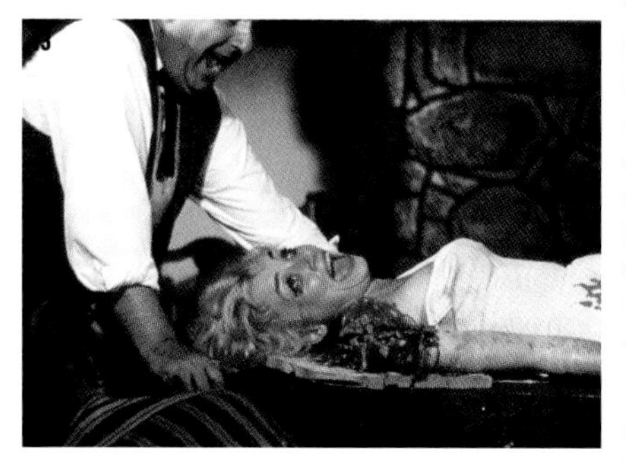

pletely staged)—*Mondo cane* still breaks its promise, as the film's reportage is anything but "objective." It's an exploitation sideshow film of the highest (read: lowest) quality, and as such begat a wave of imitators and has proven formative for such diverse pop- and pseudodocumentary traditions as the snuff film, the horror mockumentary, hardcore pornography, execution videos... even reality television.

If *Freaks* presaged the mondo film, Ruggero Deodato's *Cannibal Holocaust* (1979) took its disturbing and exploitative possibilities to a whole new level. Filmed largely on the border between Brazil and Colombia, Deodato's picture combines tropes from popular Italian horror traditions, such as the zombie and cannibal film, with mock-documentary aesthetic and narrative motifs. In its use of found footage, including archival newsreel depictions of executions by African dictators, *Cannibal Holocaust* recalls the content of *Mondo cane* while anticipating the "pseudosnuff" iconography made infamous in the *Faces of Death* series (1978–96).

As a direct descendant of the mondo film, the Italian cannibal cycle drew explicitly on morbid western fascination with the customs of ancient tribal communities in the third world. The cycle was launched in 1972 with Umberto Lenzi's *Man from Deep River*, and was followed by titles like *Last Cannibal World* (1977), *Trap Them and Kill Them* (1977), and *The Mountain of the Cannibal God* (1978). In all of these films, cannibalism is practiced by primitives deep inside the Asian or South American rainforests. Replete with imagery of the actual slaughter of jungle wildlife, as well as various forms of shocking, graphic violence—including torture, rape, and occasionally castration—the so-called cannibal boom reached its peak with *Cannibal Holocaust*, only to swiftly erode in the hands of Lenzi, whose *Eaten Alive* (1980) and *Cannibal ferox* (1981) effectively marked the end of the cycle.

But the Italians weren't the only ones into cannibal cinema. In 1972, Gary Sherman delivered the British cult horror film *Death Line* (aka *Raw Meat*), about the last descendant of a tunnel collapse in the British underground 80 years previous, who has survived by living on the flesh of his dead brethren... until now. And two years later, Tobe Hooper's ultra-low-budget hillbilly/cannibal classic *The Texas Chain Saw Massacre* opened to a firestorm of controversy that has continued to generate heated debate over its aesthetic merits and potentially damaging effects on viewers.

Loosely inspired by the real-life story of Wisconsin serial killer Ed Gein—as was *Psycho* before it and *The Silence of the Lambs* after it—Hooper's film (which begins with some voice-over narration by a young and then-unknown John Larroquette) follows five hippieish teens on a road trip through 1970s Texas who have the misfortune

13 STILL FROM "TWO THOUSAND MANIACS!" (1964) Herschell Gordon Lewis knew that Dixie sadists were always good for a laugh. Northerners laughed at them; Southerners laughed with them.

14 STILL FROM "BLOOD FEAST" (1963) Director Herschell Gordon Lewis and producer David Friedman designed their movies for drive-in theaters. Every ten minutes or so you had to provide something that warranted breaking away from a make-out session. Simple cute nudity was already de rigueur, so they added the novelty of extreme gore. The kids certainly took notice. At least for a little while.

15 STILL FROM "BLOOD FEAST" (1963) Audiences loved the movie's obvious fakery; it was so outrageous, everyone felt like they were in on the joke.

14

15

16

of bunking down next to an all-male clan of cannibalistic ex-slaughterhouse workers. The most memorable baddie is Leatherface (Gunnar Hansen, in the role of a lifetime), he of the eponymous chain saw and gruesome mask made of several of his victims' sewn-together facial epidermis. After an unforgettable family dinner in which she is served as desert to the ancient, vampiric patriarch who can barely move his lips enough to suck the blood from her finger, Sally Hardesty (Marilyn Burns)—the one teen still alive—manages an escape from this chamber of horrors by jumping through a second-story window. After a seemingly endless run through the woods, with Leatherface's motorized saw (which incredibly never runs out of gas) literally inches away from her back, Sally finally hops on the back of a conveniently situated pickup truck and drives away as Leatherface angrily waves his phallic weapon in the morning light.

Upon viewing this intense picture, with its relentless pace and quasi-documentary style, well-known critic Rex Reed declared it one of the most frightening movies ever made. Shortly after its release, The Museum of Modern Art purchased a print for its permanent collection, and the film was honored in the Directors' Fortnight at Cannes. The accolades continued to pour in; the prestigious London Film Festival even went so far as to name *The Texas Chain Saw Massacre* "Outstanding Film of the Year" in 1974. Eventually grossing close to $31 million at U.S. box offices alone, and spawning three sequels (plus a successful remake by Marcus Nispel in 2003, which led to its own "prequel" in 2006), Hooper's warped labor of love stands as, among other things, one of the most profitable independent films in cinema history.

An adjunct series of pictures, the horrors of exploitation champ Herschell Gordon Lewis also featured cannibalism, hillbillies, and sideshow ghouls. Lewis, a filmmaker with more talent for the ballyhoo than the director's chair, helped create such memorable features as *Blood Feast* (1963), with an Egyptian cannibal, *Two Thousand Maniacs!* (1964), with its hillbilly psychos from the past, and *The Wizard of Gore* (1970), with its magician who performs murder on stage as part of his performances. All showcased outsiders eating insiders and were notable for their technical incompetence and great enthusiasm.

On the heels of *The Texas Chain Saw Massacre* came 1980's *Motel Hell*, notable primarily for its tagline, "It takes all kinds of critters to make Farmer Vincent's fritters." 'Nuff said. 1986 saw the bigger, bloodier, zanier *Texas Chainsaw Massacre 2*, starring Dennis Hopper as a former Texas marshal on the trail of Leatherface and his kin. But perhaps the most notorious cannibal movie in the early 1990s is *The Untold Story* (1993), featuring Hong Kong "Category III" horror icon Anthony Wong. The film tells of a heinous (again, true) crime that took place in Macau in the 1980s, wherein an entire family was slaughtered, their bodies dismembered, the bones dumped into the trash, and their flesh used as fillings in roasted meat

16, 17 STILLS FROM "CANNIBAL HOLOCAUST" (1980) Ruggero Deodato's notorious movie, which led to his arrest when first screened for the public, is a gory and bruising mindfuck. Rape, torture, murder, and, of course, cannibalism are portrayed in documentary-style footage, while actual animal vivisection and human executions are shown. An indictment of "civilized" man's perverse nature, and a clear example of it.

18 STILL FROM "DELIVERANCE" (1972) Burt Reynolds as a city slicker forced to discover his inner savage.

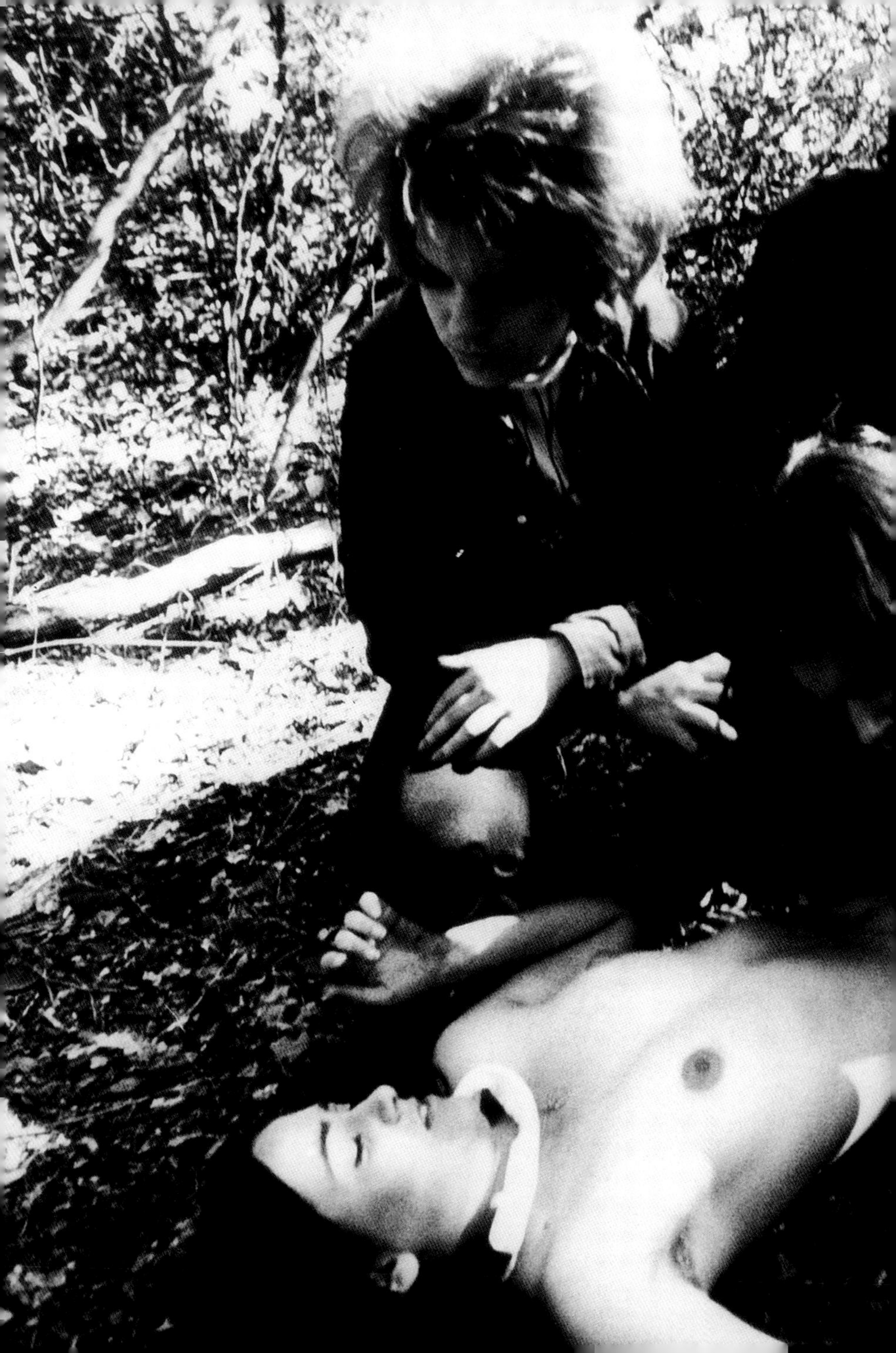

“The ‘art’ of horror film is a ludicrous notion, since horror, even in its most commercially exploitative, is genuinely subcultural like the wild child that can never be tamed, or the half-human mutant who appeals to our secret fascination with deformity and the grotesque.” *Morris Dickstein*

21

19 STILL FROM "THE LAST HOUSE ON THE LEFT" (1972) Rape, murder, addiction, and despair—the tatters of America's idealism of the 1950s and 1960s.

20 ON THE SET OF "THE TEXAS CHAIN SAW MASSACRE" (1974) Director Tobe Hooper (left) helps hook one of his actors. Hooper's second feature has an authentic look, a freewheeling style, and refreshingly quirky monsters, not to mention arguably the greatest title in horror movie history.

21 STILL FROM "THE TEXAS CHAIN SAW MASSACRE" (1974) As the sun comes up on his night of fun, Leatherface (Gunnar Hansen) gives his partner one last spin. The film ends on this note—as delirious and exuberant as any movie musical.

buns. Wong plays the insane baddie Wong Chi Hang, giving one of his typically inspired performances as a dangerous, calculating criminal hiding behind a pair of nerdy-looking eyeglasses.

Less obviously "horror" than some of these others, John Boorman's *Deliverance* (1972) featured the ultimate

"One of the obvious things at stake in the city/country split of horror films, in short, is social class—the confrontation between haves and have-nots, or even more directly, between exploiters and their victims." *Carol C. Clover*

killer hillbillies preying on and emasculating the soft and civilized. (It was released the same year as the similarly violent and similarly themed *Straw Dogs* and *A Clockwork Orange*, from Sam Peckinpah and Stanley Kubrick, respectively. These were two other major studio pictures featuring rape and packs of attacking thugs. All three films were critical and commercial hits.)

Sandwiched between his notorious debut, *The Last House on the Left* (1972), and his supernatural slasher film, *A Nightmare on Elm Street* (1984), Wes Craven's *The Hills Have Eyes* tends to get lost in critical discussion of America's reigning horror auteur. This may be truer than ever today, considering Craven's rise to mainstream respectability after the staggering box-office success of his *Scream* tetralogy (1996, 1997, 2000, 2011), followed by the silly but effective thriller *Red Eye* (2005). A relentless chronicle of violence against and within the bourgeois family unit, *The Hills Have Eyes* usually occupies the role of Craven's "cult classic": celebrated by the director's hardcore fans, appreciated for its low-budget aesthetic, generating semi-ironic readings that praise its archetypal allusions as well as its exploitation themes. Arguably, however, *The Hills Have Eyes* warrants consideration as one of the richest and best-executed pictures of Craven's career to date.

The plot moves inexorably towards establishing a structural correspondence between two superficially opposed families who face off in a battle to the death on the desolate site of a U.S. Air Force bomb-testing range. In one corner are the suburban middle-class Carters, headed for Los Angeles by car but making an unwise detour through the Yucca desert to locate a silver mine willed to Ethel (Virginia Vincent) and her husband, "Big Bob" (Russ Grieve), by a deceased aunt. In the other corner is a clan of primitive scavengers who live in the surrounding hills and are ruled with an iron fist by a mutated monster-patriarch named Jupiter (James Whitworth). This group of cannibalistic guerrillas—standing in for any number of oppressed, embattled, and downtrodden minority/social/ethnic groups—manages to eke out a squalid existence by using discarded army-surplus tools and weapons for the purpose of committing petty thievery.

When their car crashes in Jupiter's neck of the desert, the members of the Carter family reveal the extent of their ideologically inherited arrogance, repression, and capacity for denial, all of which makes them prime targets for victimization by their ruthless, unscrupulous enemies. Big Bob is crucified and eventually immolated by his counterpart, Papa Jupiter, in a highly symbolic act signifying utter repudiation of Judeo-Christian values—values that Big Bob himself has hypocritically denounced in an earlier racist diatribe. Two of Jupiter's sons later raid the Carters' RV trailer, where they rape younger daughter Brenda (Susan Lanier) and murder her sister and mother. Stripped of all pretensions, desperate for survival, the remaining members of the Carter clan finally find within themselves the courage, craftiness, and rage to kill off their enemies. The film closes with a powerful red-filtered freeze-frame

22 STILL FROM "HOUSE OF 1000 CORPSES" (2002) Rob Zombie's directorial debut features red-blooded rednecks in a rock-'n'-roll carnival of death. A true homage to 1970s horror films, in the style of a contemporary music video.

23
24

of son-in-law Doug (Martin Speer) in full fury, set to stab Jupiter's son Mars (Lance Gordon) in the chest—though Mars is surely already dead.

Craven's creativity is especially evident in his mixing and matching of different genres, including the horror film, the western, the road movie, and the siege film. Stylistically, he makes innovative use of shock tactics and startle effects to keep the anxiety level high throughout. And the varied employment of handheld camerawork, masked point-of-view shots, night photography, and rapid-fire editing is all endowed with a strong sense of purpose, serving to sustain pace and tension in the narrative. Arriving three years after its sort-of companion piece, *The Texas Chain Saw Massacre*, *The Hills Have Eyes* was poorly sequelized by Craven himself in 1985 but then was eventually remade by stylish European director Alexandre Aja in 2006, three years after the *Texas Chain Saw Massacre* remake; and again, like *The Texas Chain Saw Massacre*, the remake of *The Hills Have Eyes* was itself franchised in 2007.

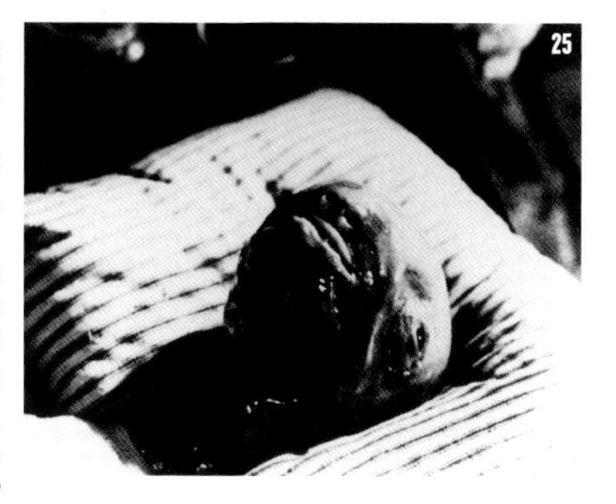

These are truly the guiltiest of pleasures—stories of backwater clans who fuck each other and produce violent, cannibalistic freaks. "Step right up and see the two-headed baby," says the carnival barker. And we step. Still, we step lively, wanting to see what tragedies befall *other* families, and thanking God it's not us, right? Please, God, not us.

23–25 STILLS FROM "IT'S ALIVE!" (1974), "BASKET CASE" (1982) & "ERASERHEAD" (1977) Expectant parents always fear their babies will consume their lives in a monsterous manner. This fear, and a national anxiety over the U. S. Supreme Court's legalization of abortion in 1973, helped deliver these unholy cinematic triplets.

REVENGE OF NATURE & ENVIRONMENTAL HORROR

1

2

PART THREE

Revenge of Nature & Environmental Horror

Often overlooked and insufficiently appreciated by fans and historians of horror alike, the so-called revenge-of-nature film consistently explores "the ways in which humankind has engaged with the processes of natural order" (Paul Wells, *The Horror Genre: From Beelzebub to Blair Witch*). And by "engaged," of course, we mean seriously screwed with. These are the pictures that gladly, even gleefully, illustrate just what's in store for "civilization" if it doesn't clean up its act.

Thirty years before Alfred Hitchcock's *The Birds* (1963) began codifying the revenge-of-nature formula for subsequent films in the genre, Merian C. Cooper and Ernest B. Schoedsack's *King Kong* (1933; remade 1976, 2005) delivered the most archetypal, unforgettable collision between (animal) nature and (human) culture ever seen on screen. In *Tracking King Kong: A Hollywood Icon in World Culture*, Cynthia Erb shows how the movie creates a remarkable mirroring system between the worlds of New York and Skull Island, which stand respectively as orders of "civilization" and "nature"; she also discusses how the first part of *King Kong* presents the modern world of civilization as both orderly and dull, "providing ample incentive for escape into another world."

After this "order of culture" is established in the opening scenes of New York, we travel to primitive Skull Island, where the giant ape resides and the "order of nature" is in full effect. And during the film's third and final section, in which Kong is brought to New York in chains, only to break free and go on his tragic rampage, we are witness to nature's devastating (both physically and emotionally) revenge on culture. Schoedsack and Cooper make perfectly clear what side *they're* on: King Kong has our sympathy throughout the picture, and his fight with aircraft while atop the Empire State Building

serves as a metaphor for the ruin of the natural order in a broader sense.

Despite Atomic Age sci-fi/horror precursors like *Them!* (1954) and *Tarantula* (1955), and the occasional one-off such as *The Naked Jungle* (1954), produced by George Pal, in which Charlton Heston and Eleanor Parker try to resist an army of devouring marabunta ants deep in the South American jungle, the revenge-of-nature movie didn't come into its own as a subgenre until the arrival of *The Birds*. Loosely basing their script on the Daphne du Maurier novella, Hitchcock and his screenwriter Evan Hunter (better known as crime novelist Ed McBain) do something extraordinary in removing *context* from their scenario: The never-answered question of *why* this rampage is occurring endows the picture with as much anxiety and discomfort as any of the specific avian attacks. Even when the characters themselves suggest explanations, be it pollution or The Bomb, Hitchcock and Hunter refuse to either confirm or contradict what is being put out there. The film works as a fable—and so allows itself innumerable interpretations. Moreover, the film's ending is shockingly anticlimactic and open-ended: After a night's sustained onslaught, there is no resolution. The morning light simply finds an infinity of birds watching and waiting. The human survivors are allowed to leave the farmhouse unmolested, but where are they going to go? The birds (i.e., the problems the characters face) are everywhere. Rather than offering a conclusive "thriller" ending with the birds either triumphant or vanquished, the movie just fades away into an anxiety-inducing state of unease. A horror ending, to be sure, perfectly in tune with the tensions of 1963.

What *The Birds* willfully lacks in *context*, however, it more than makes up for in *subtext*—pop-Freudian psychosexual subtext in particular. Here, too, Hitchcock's picture set the stage for the rash of revenge-of-nature movies to follow. As esteemed film scholar Robin Wood has noted

"It wasn't the airplanes.
It was Beauty killed the Beast."

Carl Denham, King Kong (1933)

in *Hollywood from Vietnam to Reagan*, "the struggle for recognition of all that our civilization represses or oppresses" may be the true subject of modern horror cinema. And at the heart of civilization in our society is, of course, the nuclear family. In Wood's view, although "the connection (to the family) is most tenuous and intermittent in... the revenge of nature films, even there... the attacks are linked to, or seem triggered by, familial or sexual tensions." And while its raison d'être may be birds from hell, Hitchcock's movie is actually "about" the unlocking of icy Tippi Hedren's sexuality by suave he-man Mitch Brenner (Rod Taylor) while her mother (Jessica Tandy), sister (Veronica Cartwright), and rival (Suzanne Pleshette) all circle the pair. Without a single other male character of import, Mitch finds himself hen-pecked indeed. And the suspense builds even when the birds are nowhere to be seen.

1 STILL FROM "KING KONG" (1933) Some say directors Merian C. Cooper and Ernest B. Schoedsack, together with visual effects supervisor Willis H. O'Brien, created the ultimate vision of technology beating down nature. Others call it cinema's ultimate lynching of a black man who dares love a white woman. The picture's big enough to take on all interpretations.

2 STILL FROM "THEM!" (1954) Joan Weldon tries to hide from one of "Them." Radiation turns ants into monsters; one more cost of science meddling with the laws of nature, in one of the creepiest manifestations of our atomic neurosis during the Cold War.

3 ADVERT FOR "THE INNOCENT AND THE BEAST" (1929) This ballet, which was performed at the Folies Bergère, inspired Edgar Wallace to write *King Kong*.

4 PRODUCTION SKETCH FOR "KING KONG" (1933) An artist's sketch of Kong's titanic battle with the T. rex.

5 STILL FROM "KING KONG" (1933) The battle as it appeared in the film. A combination of miniatures, mattes, glass paintings, rear projections, and other effects were used. The inimitable Fay Wray starred as Ann Darrow.

6
7

Unfortunately there is only one Hitchcock, and the revenge-of-nature pictures that followed *The Birds* have often concentrated on the genre aspects over the humane. The bulk of these also centered on the usually meek inheriting the Earth, while placing more obviously "frightening" creatures front and center. There were plenty of bee movies (no pun intended), including *The Deadly Bees* (1967), *The Killer Bees* (1974), *The Bees* (1979), and Irwin Allen's *The Swarm* (1978), the latter of which featured a bevy of distinguished actors (including Michael Caine, Richard Widmark, José Ferrer, Olivia de Havilland, and Henry Fonda) but made hardly any sense and flopped spectacularly at the box office. There were also wasps (*The Food of the Gods*, 1976), flaming cockroaches (*Bug*, 1975), earthworms (*Squirm,* 1976), ants (*Phase IV*, 1974; *It Happened at Lakewood Manor*, 1977; *Empire of the Ants*, 1977), *Ticks* (1993), and spiders (*Kingdom of the Spiders*, 1977). One of the most distinctive and disturbing entries of the decade was Walon Green's 1971 Oscar-winning documentary, *The Hellstrom Chronicle*, in which a fictional entomologist—Dr. Nils Hellstrom (Lawrence Pressman)—demonstrates through amazing microphotography how the brutality and efficiency of the insect world could result in their taking over the planet.

Unlike the U.S. giant bug and Japanese Toho monster movies of the 1950s and 1960s, the 1970s revenge-of-nature cycle tended to feature normal-sized or only mildly exaggerated members of the insect world or animal kingdom, whose attacks are often "prompted by (man's) unthinking abuse of his environment, and of the very ecological system of which we are a part" (Bridget Brown, *They Know Us Better than We Know Ourselves: The History and Politics of Alien Abduction*). The films in question thus gave expression in genre terms to the era's "collective anxieties about the earth's exacting revenge for industrial excess." Besides the hordes of insects and arachnids cited above, the decade saw killer felines (*Eye of the Cat*, 1969), canines (*Dogs*, 1976; *The Pack*, 1977), frogs (*Frogs*, 1972), rabbits (*Night of the Lepus*, 1972), rats (*Willard*, 1971; *Ben*, 1972), bears (*Grizzly*, 1976; *Prophecy*, 1979), bats (*Nightwing*, 1979), and pretty much the entire goddamn zoo in *Day of the Animals* (1977). And while none of these pictures come close to matching Hitchcock's for subtlety or ambiguity of explanation, they all hold firm to the central tenet of revenge-of-nature cinema: it's never the animal's fault that it kills people—it's always the fault of man. Among the "explanations" offered for the attacks: pesticides; insecticides; fluorocarbons that damage the ozone layer; hormones that interrupt breeding cycles; and pollution, pollution, and more pollution.

Despite anomalies like *Godzilla vs. the Smog Monster* (1971) and *Blood Beach* (1981), most of the aquatic beasties that made their presence felt on screen in the 1970s, including entries like *Tentacles* (1977),

6 STILL FROM "CREATURE FROM THE BLACK LAGOON" (1954) Man or fish? A lot of both. The creature attacks as effectively out of the water as he does in it.

7 ON THE SET OF "CREATURE FROM THE BLACK LAGOON" (1954) The Gill Man (Ricou Browning) watches Kay Lawrence (Julie Adams). Underwater cameras gave audiences the first real swimming monster. It was unique enough to turn the picture into a hit during the 1950s animal cycle of horrors.

8 ON THE SET OF "THE ALLIGATOR PEOPLE" (1959) Beverly Garland shares an intimate moment with a friend. 20th Century Fox followed their far superior *The Fly* (1958) with this effort. A more accurate title would have been "The Alligator Person."

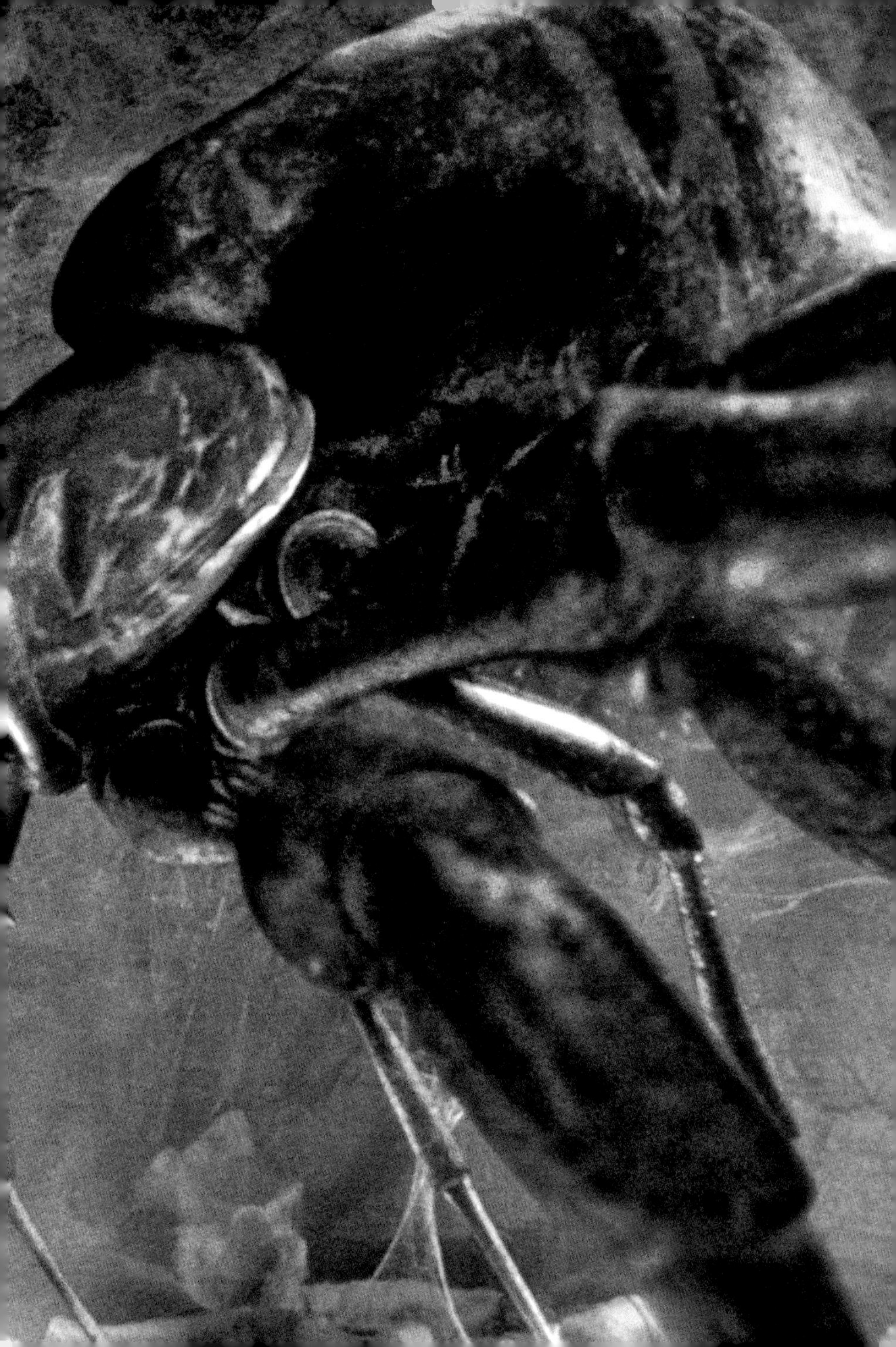

Orca: Killer Whale (1977), and *Piranha* (1978), came directly in the wake of Steven Spielberg's 1975 revenge-of-nature blockbuster, *Jaws* (as did *Jaws*'s own trio of disappointing sequels in 1978, 1983, and 1987). The previously unknown filmmaker was only 28 when *Jaws* was released, but that changed forever when the movie became the number-one box-office champion in history in under a month. Equally adept at crafting brilliant suspense scenes and drawing complex, relatable characters, Spielberg—like Hitchcock with his winged killers—managed to make his giant shark represent different things to different people. Of course, it also represented really big, really sharp teeth... and gave a generation of moviegoers a complex about swimming in the ocean.

"I don't believe in evil, I believe only in horror. In nature there is no evil, only an abundance of horror: the plagues and the blights and the ants and the maggots." *Karen Blixen*

It should be noted that Americans weren't the only ones making revenge-of-nature movies during this period. In Australian cinema, too, themes of man's alienation from nature—and from man—were particularly striking in the 1970s. Perhaps the best example is the still shamefully obscure thriller *Long Weekend* (1979), directed by Colin Eggleston, in which a vacationing married couple, careless and dismissive in their attitude toward the pristine forest they head to for a weekend getaway, are destroyed psychologically and then physically by their environs. Much like Peter Weir's *Picnic at Hanging Rock* (1975), *Long Weekend* works "not through direct narrative statement, but through the juxtaposition of image and event. It represents an unusual approach to the revenge of nature theme insofar as the couple's assailants are not some barely-natural monster... but rather the less insistent menaces of ants, birds, a possum, the thick undergrowth—all acting in a way which, in a less intense context, we would consider 'ordinary'" (Jonathan Rayner, "'Terror Australis': Areas of Horror in the Australian Cinema" in *Horror International*). *The Last Wave* (1977)—another masterpiece by top Australian auteur Peter Weir—is even more ambiguous in its narrative, although its set pieces of hail, frogs, storms, and floods make it arguably the most apocalyptic (certainly the most biblical) revenge-of-nature film in history. To quote Jonathan Rayner, "the revenge that the natural world wreaks upon the empty and immoral suburbanites (in *The Last Wave*) articulates an abhorrence of the spiritual vacuum within western civilization."

One of the most satisfying horror movies to come out of Oz is *Razorback* (1984), directed by rock-video maker Russell Mulcahy and written by *Long Weekend* (as well as *Patrick*, 1978, and *Roadgames*, 1981) scribe Everett De Roche. *Razorback* exploits the outback paranoia theme present in so many Australian pictures (e.g., *Wake in Fright*, 1970; *Walkabout*, 1970; *Encounter at Raven's Gate*, 1988). The desolation is oppressive, with civilization only in evidence as desert debris, a community that is struggling to survive, a sinister pet-food plant, and an environment that conjures postapocalyptic thoughts of *Mad Max* (1979). A strong feeling of otherworldliness abounds, and that other world is really unpleasant—it's a place where the human population frankly doesn't give a shit and individuals can be as arbitrarily violent as the huge razorback boar of the movie's title.

Having burnt itself out like so many other horror cycles due to derivative premises and oversaturation in the marketplace (cf. the decline of the slasher movie in the late 1980s), revenge-of-nature films were few and far

9 STILL FROM "EIGHT LEGGED FREAKS" (2002) David Arquette, ill-prepared in this comic rehash of *Tarantula* (1955) and the other giant bug movies of the 1950s.

10 STILL FROM "THE RETURN OF GODZILLA" (1984) The original was a dark and serious horror film, Japan's version of the atomic aftermath and the return of a very angry superpower. Over time, Godzilla has become kid-friendly, action-packed and one of Japan's most enduring cultural exports.

10

11
12

between after John Frankenheimer's highly anticipated *Prophecy* fell flat in 1979. But again, as with so many other horror cycles (cf. the return of the slasher movie initiated by *Scream* in 1996), revenge-of-nature films returned with a vengeance in the late 1990s. This was thanks to both a renewed focus on environmental issues in American society (consider the impact of 2006's *An Inconvenient Truth* in the documentary field) and advances in special effects and CGI technology. Unfortunately, none of them—save perhaps the *Mimic* franchise (1997, 2001, 2003), and these killer-cockroach movies are as much *Alien*-inspired creature features as anything else—made any noise with either critics or viewers. Nevertheless, all of a sudden audiences were bombarded with a slew of B-grade revenge-of-nature fare along the lines of *Anaconda* (1997), *Bees* (1998), *Bats* (1999), *Lake Placid* (1999), *Deep Blue Sea* (1999), *Eight-Legged Freaks* (2002), *Anacondas: The Hunt For the Blood Orchid* (2004), *Swarmed* (2005), *The Breed* (2006), *Black Sheep* (New Zealand, 2006), and a pair of giant-crocodile films, *Primeval* (2007) and *Rogue* (Australia, 2007). Three films have managed to rise well above the pack, however, using very different approaches and very different monsters. *Open Water* (2003), made by the husband-and-wife team of Chris Kentis and Laura Lau, is *Jaws* by way of *The Blair Witch Project* (1999); a micro-budgeted shark-attack movie, it shows little blood or guts but generates incredible suspense as an abandoned scuba-diving couple awaits its oceanic demise. Cult maestro Larry Fessenden's *The Last Winter* (2006) sees a primeval force unleashed from beneath the melting Arctic permafrost, with ghostly and deadly results. And Bong Joon-ho's Korean box-office smash *The Host* (2006) seamlessly blends CGI wizardry with a quirky sensibility, all-too-human characters, and an overtly political context.

From *King Kong* to *The Birds* to *Jaws* to *The Host*—a pretty bumpy ride over the depths of civilization's collective guilt. And collective unconscious.

11 STILL FROM "SQUIRM" (1976)
Downed power lines turn everyday earthworms into rabid killers. Most of the so-called revenge-of-nature films that followed directly in the wake of *Jaws* pretty much sucked.

12 STILL FROM "PHASE IV" (1974)
Saul Bass directed this thriller about normal-sized, superintelligent ants.

13

14

13 **STILL FROM “PIRANHA” (1978)**
This savvy B movie combines elements of *Jaws* (1975) with evil military scientists tampering with nature. The result, written by John Sayles and directed by Joe Dante, is both muscular and knowing.

14 **ON THE SET OF “PIRANHA” (1978)**
A hungry piranha has a little finger food between takes.

15 **STILL FROM “GREMLINS” (1984)**
Billy Peltzer (Zach Galligan) fights Stripe, the malignant offspring of his cute and cuddly pet Mogwai.

16 **STILL FROM “PROPHECY” (1979)**
Directing great John Frankenheimer was brought on board this studio “eco-horror” film, which arrived too late to capitalize on the environmental horror films that came before it.

“Of course it would be an awful thing if somebody actually did die in the theater. The publicity would be terrific though!”

William Castle

1

SCIENCE-FICTION-HORROR

PART FOUR

Science-Fiction-Horror

Whether it's jumping off from the basic science of cable TV as in David Cronenberg's *Videodrome* (1983) or the vast technologies of space exploration as in *Alien* (1979) and its progeny, sci-fi horror uses the realities of our world today to suppose terrifying worlds of tomorrow. Some of these films put our nervous relationship with technology front and center, while others just use a scientific setting to explore horrific aspects of human society. The two richest subgenres are "The Mad Scientist" and those films that make it clear that "We Are Not Alone."

Technology is fun. It's cool. Everyone likes gadgets and everyone appreciates "advances" in science. But in these movies the scientists who want to advance things are always "mad." Never calm, rational professionals, but madmen who refuse to listen to reason. They want to go further. They tempt fate to explore and discover. And they believe in their causes to the exclusion of all others. Strangely, this kind of single-minded determination is usually called "heroism" in fiction. But in these dark tales, human fallibility always rears its ugly head, turning heroism into villainy or tragedy.

In many of these stories, the scientists are unable to resist the corrupting nature of the power their scientific knowledge lends them. In 1932's *Island of Lost Souls,* brilliant Dr. Moreau surgically transforms animals into men, subverting evolution. But his God-like abilities, first to create and then to dictate over his own private-island food chain, inevitably bring out his sadism and megalomania. In the end, his creations, enslaved and betrayed by their maker, use his medical instruments to finish him off in the surgical "House of Pain," where his agonizing screams are anything but God-like. This early shocker starred the extraordinary Charles Laughton as Moreau, a rotund chameleon of an actor in a notorious performance of breathtaking intelligence, verve, and depravity.

Another early mad-scientist talkie from an H. G. Wells source was *The Invisible Man*, made a year after *Island of Lost Souls.* In this James Whale adaptation, it's the God-like power to go anywhere and see anything that drives Claude Rains, an otherwise high-minded scientist, to robbery, madness, and murder. The sad implication is that man, no matter how bright, is mentally incapable of safely harboring too much knowledge without going insane. Like Whale's other horror films, this one is fast-paced, often funny, and features state-of-the-art special effects.

"In space, no one can hear you scream." *Alien (1979)*

In Georges Franju's extraordinary *Eyes Without a Face* (*Les yeux sans visage,* 1959), Pierre Brasseur plays a doctor whose daughter has lost her looks in a terrible accident. He provides her with many replacements—via brutally stolen skin grafts—driven by his need to succeed as a surgeon and to provide as a father. But the surgeries never seem to work out, and in the end it is as much his inability to accept his own fallibility as any willingness he displays to kidnap and murder that leads to his deserved doom. This French masterpiece, with its raw medical footage and fairy tale-meets-*giallo* narrative, is both poetic and disturbingly graphic. Once again technological advances are nothing when held up against even the most basic human emotions.

Ken Russell's troubled *Altered States* (1980) hinges as much on mad scientist Eddie Jessup's (William Hurt) inability to appreciate his "mundane" existence and caring spouse, Emily (Blair Brown), as it does on his wild quest to understand the origins and meaning of life. Though he tries seemingly everything, from mushrooms to sensory deprivation, to get to the bottom of life's greatest mysteries, he only finds the answers in the embrace of the woman who loves him. Humanity, we are told here (as in countless other films), has less to do with our accomplishments or advances than with our capacities for connection and understanding. The film was seen by Warner Bros. as another potential high-tech throwback blockbuster like *Alien* and *Close Encounters of the Third Kind* (1977). Unfortunately, screenwriter Paddy Chayefsky and director Russell fought constantly over control of the picture. Chayefsky ultimately removed his name from the film—marking it for death before it ever had a chance to connect with its audience.

A much happier result was produced by *The Fly* (1986). That film's clear auteur, David Cronenberg, has spent much of his cinematic career exploring ill-fated scientists and the societies they affect with their passions; and this, his only remake, is one of his best. In it, Jeff Goldblum portrays Seth Brundle, a young genius who has solved the riddles of matter, time, and space. But Brundle is such a realistically cerebral nerd that his inability to marry his mind and his emotions causes the inevitable and tragic misstep. Drunk with champagne and his desire for beautiful journalist Veronica Quaife (Geena Davis), Brundle loses his laserlike concentration and boldly (read: stupidly) experiments on himself, failing to realize the titular insect has entered his apparatus with him. He emerges from his mechanical cocoon as something quite unique. Over the course of the picture his character evolves brilliantly—first enjoying the physical prowess his new "fly-ness" provides and then desperately embracing the changes occurring within him from a rational, scientific point of view. Much pathos, comedy, sex, violence, and terror follow in an almost operatic study of human foibles and fluids. Ultimately, however, as Brundle transforms into Brundlefly and beyond, his desire to remain as "human" as possible leads to a wonderfully tragic conclusion.

"A clever horror movie that plays with suppressed irrationality and wraps it up in a somber genre story."

Lexikon des internationalen Films, on: Altered States

Canada's best (and best-known) director, David Cronenberg was born in Toronto in 1943, and his fascination with photography, philosophy, and medicine led him to the most technical of art forms: film. His early and mid-

1 STILL FROM "THE INVISIBLE MAN RETURNS" (1940) Convict Vincent Price (right) is injected with Jack Griffin's invisibility serum to save him from the gallows and allow him to find the real murderer (Sir Cedric Hardwicke, center).

2 STILL FROM "ALIENS" (1986) James Cameron's ferocious sequel, with the classic monster designed by H. R. Giger: a machine-bug-animal-bitch.

3 STILL FROM "THE INVISIBLE MAN" (1933) It's not easy to show an invisible man in publicity stills, so they simply drew an outline on the photos.

4 STILL FROM "THE INVISIBLE MAN" (1933) Jack Griffin (Claude Rains) unwraps his bandages and promptly disappears. Director James Whale cast the English actor for his extraordinary speaking voice.

3
4

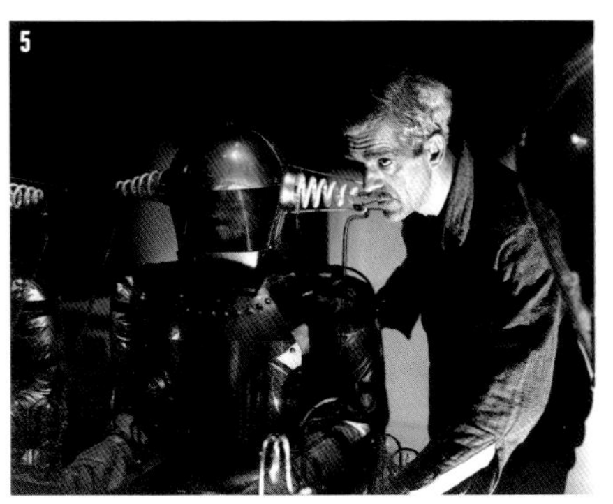

career pictures make for fascinating explications of the effects of technology on both the individual and society at large. They are explicitly Cartesian explorations of both mind and body—and Cronenberg is known for the consistency of his interest in making physical what's mental. These films are bloody, gooey, and brilliantly unique. In *Shivers* (1975) he posits a venereal disease with a mind of its own—driving its carriers to have sex so it may live and spread. *Rabid* (1976) surgically placed a killer phallus in Marilyn Chambers's armpit, and *The Brood* (1979) takes the extreme-therapy movement of the late 1970s and plays up the monstrous ramifications of all the sublimated rage it brought out into society. *Scanners* (1980) is a conspiracy thriller about the power of the mind over matter; *Videodrome* explores what the ubiquitous presence of TV may be doing to us all; and *eXistenZ* (1998) vividly explores the new technologies of gaming and the rapidly closing gap between reality and virtual reality. These science-minded films, along with the literary adaptations *Spider* (2002), *Crash* (1996), *Naked Lunch* (1991), *Dead Ringers* (1988), and *The Dead Zone* (1983), have made Cronenberg the most singular auteur in the annals of horror cinema.

The Thing that Couldn't Die (1958), *The Incredible 2-Headed Transplant* (1971), and *The Thing with Two Heads* (1972) all study mad doctors who want to keep heads alive. *Scream and Scream Again* (1970), *—And Now the Screaming Starts!* (1973), *Coma* (1978), *The Awful Dr. Orloff* (1962), and (unofficial *Eyes Without a Face* remake) *Mansion of the Doomed* (1976) all feature transplantations and medical experiments gone evil. And Boris Karloff, always able to play passion, evil, and intelligence, spent much of the 1930s and 1940s as various mad guys in pictures like *The Devil Commands* (1941), *The Invisible Ray* (1936), and *The Mask of Fu Manchu* (1932).

But not all sci-fi horror is about the madness of the scientists themselves. Since the United States started the space race with the Russians in 1950, stories of aliens visiting us and of our exploration of other worlds have captured the cinema's imagination. Within a year of the then-U.S.S.R's terrifying launch of Sputnik in 1950, Howard Hawks had sent *The Thing from Another World* (1951) into theaters. Here, a group of soldiers and scientists, isolated from the rest of the world by miles of snow and ice, uncover a spaceship long buried in the permafrost. Inside they find a space creep played by James Arness… and when they defrost him, his truly antagonistic intentions are made clear. Basically an old-fashioned monster show smashingly gussied up for the frightened Cold War/Nuclear Age audience, *The Thing* spawned an entire genre. It was immediately followed by such titles as *It! The Terror from Beyond Space* (1958), *It Conquered the World* (1956), the H.G. Wells-inspired *The War of the Worlds* (1953; remade 2005), *Invaders from Mars* (1953; remade 1986), *Invasion of the Saucer Men* (1957), and Don Siegel's truly thrilling *Invasion of the Body Snatchers* (1956; remade 1978, 1993, 2007). This last is another classic, a simple, fast-paced analogy decrying the mind-

5 STILL FROM "THE DEVIL COMMANDS" (1941) Dr. Julian Blair (Boris Karloff) tries to contact the dead in one of the many mad scientist roles he'd play over the course of a career spanning over 50 years and more than 150 films.

6 ON THE SET OF "ISLAND OF LOST SOULS" (1932) Director Erle C. Kenton (left) on the set with star Charles Laughton and Kathleen Burke. This first and arguably best screen version of H. G. Wells's novel "The Island of Dr. Moreau" deals with animal experiments and human torture. It was banned in the United Kingdom for a quarter-century.

6

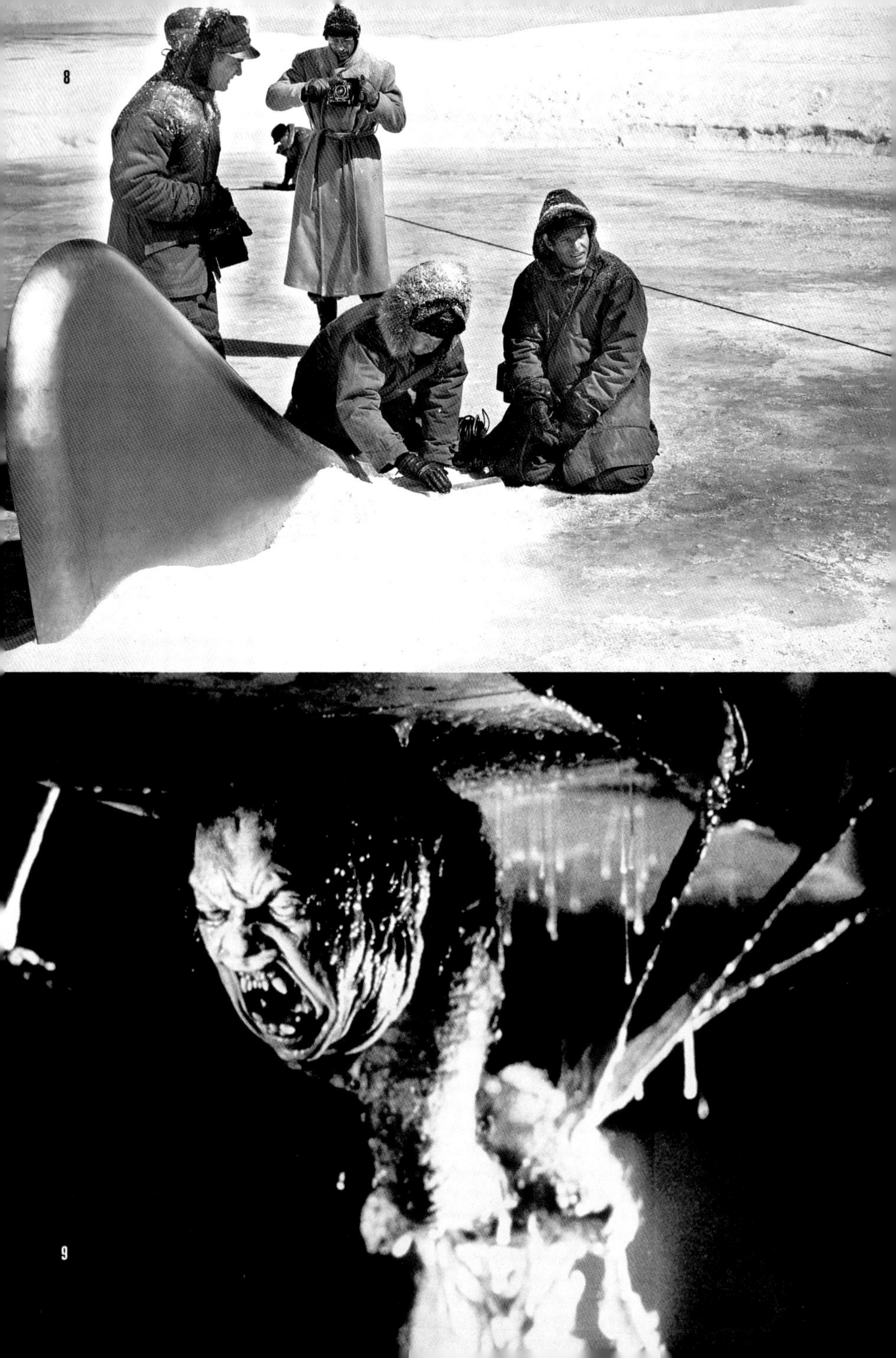

8

9

7 STILL FROM "PUMPKINHEAD" (1988) The directiorial debut of make-up and effects maestro Stan Winston, best known for his design and fabrication work on such classics as *The Terminator*, *Predator*, *Jurassic Parc* and *Edward Scissorhands*.

8 STILL FROM "THE THING FROM ANOTHER WORLD" (1951) Scientists and soldiers find what appears to be a massive ship buried in the Arctic ice. The snowy setting was timely in 1951, when Alaska was pushing hard to become America's 49th State.

9 STILL FROM "THE THING" (1982) Makeup and special effects master Rob Bottin tried to always stay one step ahead of the audience with his Thing's outrageous manifestations. After 1979's *Alien*, it became de rigueur for monsters to transform multiple times in multiple ways over the course of a single movie.

10 STILL FROM "THE THING FROM ANOTHER WORLD" (1951) The Thing (James Arness) meets its end. Once it is determined that the monster is essentially vegetable in composition, the survivors set a course for its destruction. "What do you do with a carrot?" one asks rhetorically. Obvious. "You cook it."

"No passion so effectually robs the mind of all its powers of acting and reasoning as fear." *Edmund Burke*

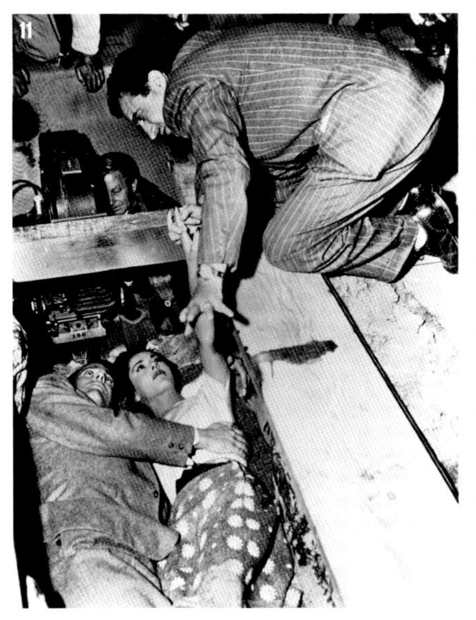

rotted "group think" of mid-1950s America: perfect on the outside, decayed and soulless beneath the skin. In *Invasion of the Body Snatchers*, "pod people" replace real folks overnight, leaving unfeeling replicas to populate a small town and, ultimately, if their spread is not halted, the Earth itself. Of course almost no one believes the menace is real—it is this willful oblivion to the obvious that makes the takeover so easy. In fact, much of the population seems half-pod already. This theme, of how dangerous human alienation can be, plays beautifully, but it's a simpler, even more devastating fear that truly gives the oft-remade *Body Snatchers* its incredible staying power: the dark notion that our way of life will end—not with a nuclear bang, but with our somehow waking up enslaved and debased, without identity or safety. That someday *we* could be colonized. That in an unknown future, ours will be the Old World, and we will be the innocent natives enslaved by a technologically superior race or civilization...

The last, and one of the very best, of these Cold War/"aliens among us" movies is *The Village of the Damned* (1960; remade 1995), which supposes that on one afternoon, a small town in rural England is taken over by some unseen alien force. When the episode is over, the town awakens to find many of its women pregnant. Betrayals and wantonness are blamed, until the children are born and a slow realization dawns. All of the children are alike, related in some mysterious way. They are brilliant, cold, and united—clearly intent on (and capable of) taking over the world. Both a precursor to the already nascent youth movement of the British 1960s, and a bitter acknowledgment of the still-open wounds the empire suffered during and immediately after the Second World War, *Village of the Damned* also plays to this fear of waking up under the thumb of a power whose agenda we cannot comprehend. The children also share a group mind, and, in the end, a simple, even artistic solution is presented—only individuality protects from group think; unique thoughts and actions are unpredictable and so dangerous to the monolith. This rebelliousness, of course, is at the center of much of the countercultural movements of the 1950s, and these horror films provided both chills and hopeful solutions to the guys sitting there in the dark believing their world might be gone by the morning light. Out of fear comes anger or destruction. "Fight," they said. "Fight for your rights. And for your individuality."

A later, less socially conscious version of this story was Robert Wise's *The Andromeda Strain* (1971), adapted from Michael Crichton's breakthrough novel of the same name. In it, the future-shock notion of viruses from space was introduced. Again science and government must try to work together at an isolated military base, but instead of a

11 ON THE SET OF "INVASION OF THE BODY SNATCHERS" (1956) Director Don Siegel, an acknowledged genre master, later mentored Clint Eastwood's career behind the camera.

12, 13 STILLS FROM "INVASION OF THE BODY SNATCHERS" (1956) The classic paranoid thriller from the Red Scare of the 1950s. Small-town normalcy under siege... from within. Dr. Miles Binnell (Kevin McCarthy, right) discovers that alien pods are replicating and replacing humans as they sleep.

12
13

stalking alien killer or a faceless cadre of single-minded malevolence, our heroes, who are initially wary of each other, have to fight a new version of an old colonial threat: a disease from outer space for which we have no antibodies. At the time Crichton was positing the unthinkable—that no matter how technologically advanced we may become, viruses may ultimately inherit the Earth. And not surprisingly, his narrative solution was not that individuality is the key to winning, but that the team must pull together and muster their collective brainpower to defeat an enemy unable to think at all. Interestingly, from a cinematic point of view, the attackers remain virtually unseen; it's the alienating and omnipresent technologies needed to defeat them that Wise puts on screen to scare us.

Other versions of these "we are not alone" stories take *us* into the void as the colonialists. Invariably, the natives we meet out there are restless… to say the least. Films like *Alien* and its antecedents *It! The Terror from Beyond Space* and *Planet of the Vampires* (Italy/Spain, 1965) turn the technological marvels of spaceships and space stations into modern haunted houses or Cretan mazes. The hostility of space itself forces protagonists into highly designed enclosed settings from which there is neither escape nor relief—perfect for scares and visuals.

Alien is a wonderful case of exactly the right movie appearing at exactly the right time. In the four years preceding it, audiences had embraced *Jaws* (1975), *Halloween* (1978), *Star Wars* (1977), and *Close Encounters*. Here was a picture that synthesized all that was successful about these four hits while providing viewers with its own unique pleasures. It featured a superb cast of distinguished actors, including Sigourney Weaver, Ian Holm, John Hurt, and Yaphet Kotto. And commercial director Ridley Scott, who had made a minor impact with his visually splendid *The Duellists* in 1977, brought tremendous verve and visual punch to a film that hit as hard as any horror film, but had the look and scope of a huge-budgeted sci-fi extravaganza. And the alien of the title was an amazing creation, a monster whose evolving look and abilities kept the audience riveted. What can it do? What will it look like next? And how the hell do our heroes stop it?

In *Alien*, the crew of the industrial space freighter *Nostromo*—seven working stiffs of varying talents and mental capacities—sail their battered ship through dis-

14 STILL FROM "GOKE, BODY SNATCHER FROM HELL" (1968) This Japanese alien-vampire B movie is also a surprisingly effective anti-Vietnam War fable.

15 STILL FROM "INVADERS FROM MARS" (1953) The looming power of the authority figure; the frightening insignificance of the innocent individual.

16 STILL FROM "PLANET OF THE VAMPIRES" (1965) Mario Bava wasn't the first filmmaker to use science-fiction trappings to "modernize" a haunted-house tale. Nor the last. This film, along with *It! The Terror from Beyond Space* (1958), were obvious inspirations for Ridley Scott's *Alien*. (Note the monster design.)

17

tant galaxies light-years from home. They pick up a distress signal from a seemingly barren planet and of course they go to help. But they find nothing left alive on the surface, until a strange, crablike "face-hugger" flies out of an eerie egg and lodges itself into a crew member. After carrying the unconscious man back to the ship, they realize that the creature has inserted itself deep into the man's throat. It looks grim for him. But when the alien dies, and dislodges, the man comes to and seems no worse for wear. That's when the tiny infant incubated in the man's stomach is born, bursting out of his chest in one of the most famous sequences in horror-film history. The amount of blood and viscera is so shocking that even the cast screamed in actual fear. The alien hides away somewhere in the ship; from there it's kill or be killed. The crew tries to track and analyze this creature's weaknesses, while the creature continues to grow and pick them off one by one in a series of beautifully orchestrated, booladen set pieces. And, further humanizing our heroes, an evil robot and a corporate (greed-based) conspiracy are thrown into the plot, tightening the already excruciatingly tight screws. In the end, only beautiful Ripley (Sigourney Weaver) is left to defeat the beast. Which she does, ingeniously launching it into the cold depths of space. *Alien* was so successful, and so influential, that its sequels attracted top directors like James Cameron (*Aliens*, 1986), David Fincher (*Alien³*, 1992), and Jean-Pierre Jeunet (*Alien: Resurrection*, 1997). The science-fiction aspects made the picture more widely acceptable. The horror aspects made it a classic.

As a direct result of *Alien*'s success, a huge-budgeted remake of *The Thing* (not coincidentally one of *Alien*'s clear antecedents) was put into production for release in the summer of 1982. The original was John Carpenter's favorite movie, and the savvy creator of *Halloween* and the Hawks-inspired *Assault on Precinct 13* (1976; remade 2005) asked for and was given the chance to remake it. Collaborating with effects master Rob Bottin—hot off his lauded work for *The Howling* (1981)—the two men tried to out-*Alien Alien* with amazingly gory on-screen transformations and mucho macho intercharacter fireworks. But audiences felt they had already seen this film, and turned instead to that summer's ostensibly more original *Poltergeist* (1982), the first ghost story for the blockbuster generation, and *E.T.: The Extra-Terrestrial* (1982), essentially *Alien* for a family audience, in which affection was substituted for fear. This left Carpenter's extremely ambitious but coldly calculated picture to collect box-office crumbs.

Of course there are other sci-fi horror films of merit and import. *The Incredible Shrinking Man* (1957),

17, 18 STILLS FROM "VILLAGE OF THE DAMNED" (1960) Shades of the Hitler Youth? This tale of an alien über-race, born of common Earth women, showed the power of the collective mind to force others to do its bidding, even to commit suicide.

19 ON THE SET OF "VILLAGE OF THE DAMNED" (1960) Facing us is young David Zellaby (Martin Stephens), leader of the precocious brood that caused the car crash in the background.

18
19

20, 21, 23, 24 STILLS FROM "THE ANDROMEDA STRAIN" (1971) An alien virus hits a small town, with an infant and an old man the only survivors. Dr. Mark Hall (James Olson) is one of a group of scientists working underground to neutralize the virus, but when the virus escapes he must race against time to save them.

22 STILL FROM "QUARTERMASS AND THE PIT" (1967) This British picture, like *The Thing from Another World* (1951), imagined aliens buried here for eons… just waiting for us to dig them out.

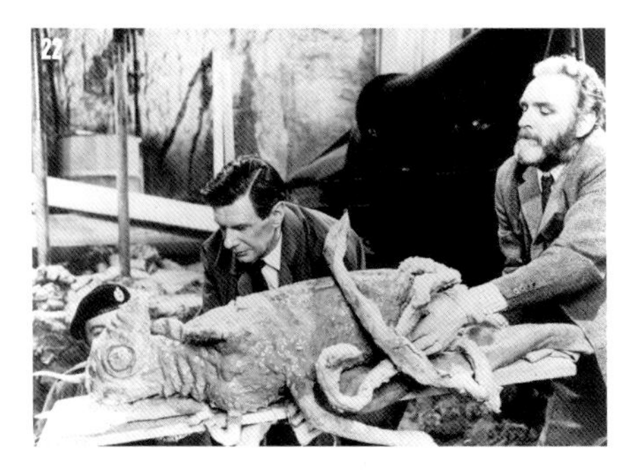

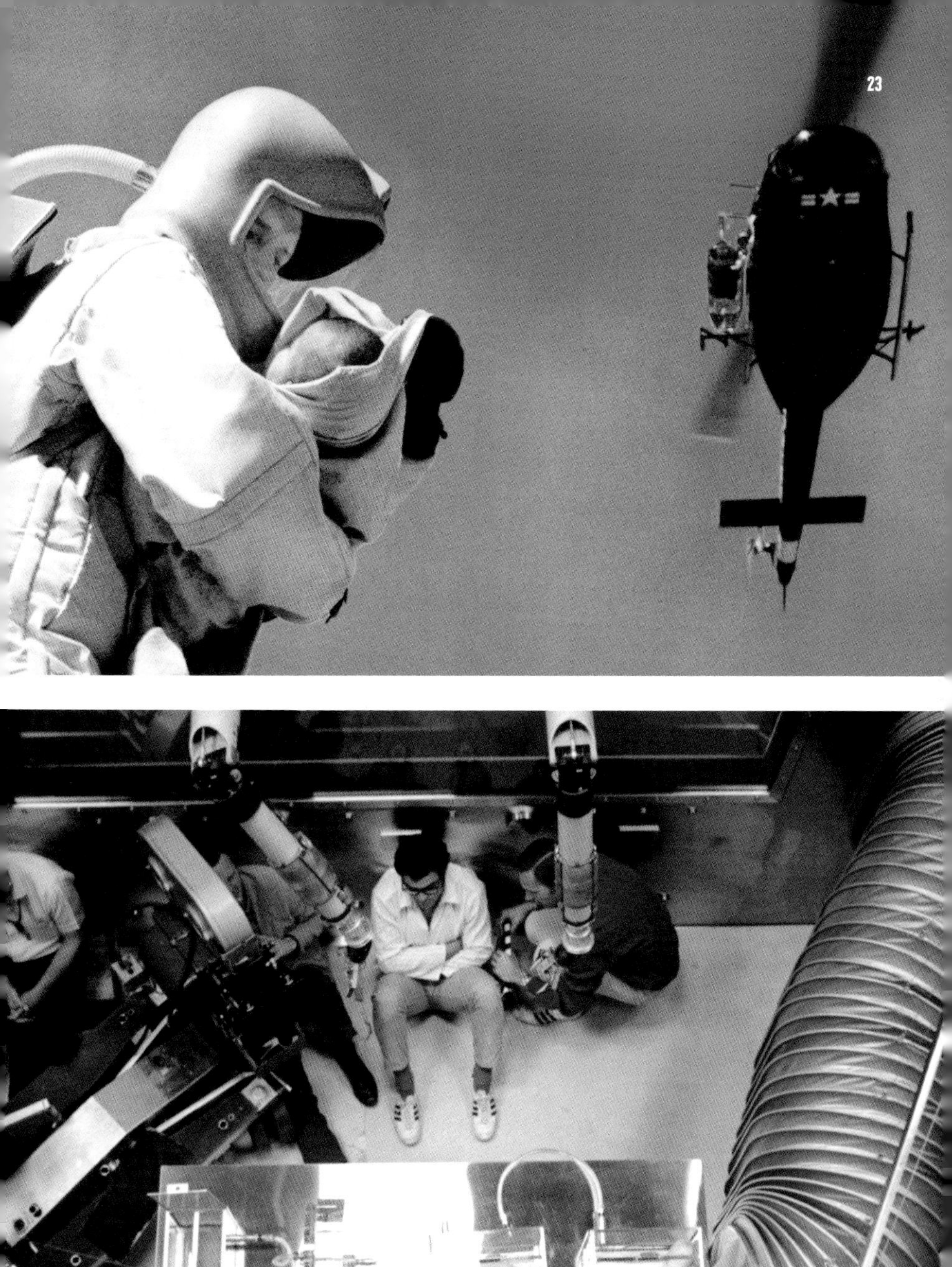
23
24

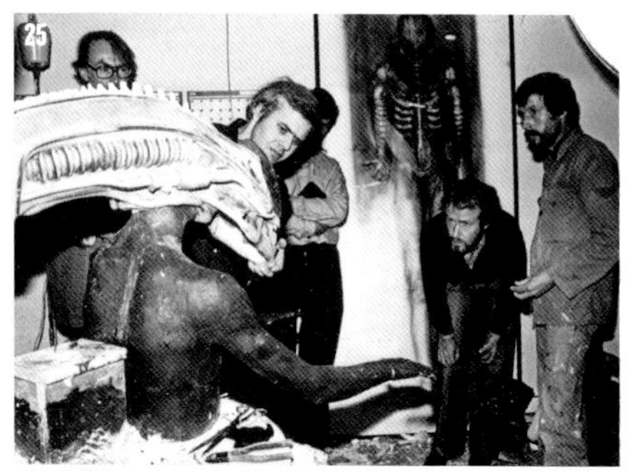

with its literal analogy to the state of American manhood in the monolithic American 1950s, is unsurpassingly strange and foreboding, while *Tetsuo: The Iron Man* (1989) and its sequel, *Tetsuo II: Body Hammer* (1992), offer similarly scathing indictments of the dehumanized Japanese manhood of the 1980s. Hammer's *Quatermass* series was suitably science-minded, taking more sober approaches to the technological marvels of the 1950s and 1960s. And the long-running *Godzilla* series always threw "science" into its fantasy mix. Aliens, spaceships, and "experimental rays" constantly pop up, but usually only in the most gee-whiz way. These films understand that science is just another venue for the extraordinary in the movies. Another shiny mirror for exploring our surfaces and depths.

In all, these films concentrate our attention on the technologies that surround us, fill us, and have overtaken our lives. They are dehumanizing, they are enabling, they are evolving faster than we are. Scary stuff, indeed.

25 ON THE SET OF "ALIEN" (1979)
H. R. Giger explains the design as Ridley Scott looks on. Subsequent films in the series liberated the alien's movements with more elaborate animated, puppet, robotic, and CGI effects.

26 ON THE SET OF "ALIEN" (1979)
Filming at Shepperton Studios. Small actors were used to make the sets look larger.

27 STILL FROM "ALIEN" (1979) Giger's designs extended to all aspects of the production, including the crashed alien ship.

28 STILL FROM "ALIEN" (1979)
A penis, a train, a monster, a foetus. Giger and Scott create one of the most famous birth/death sequences in horror film history.

29 ON THE SET OF "ALIEN" (1979)
The Swiss surrealist H. R. Giger with egg. His designs are at once sexual and funereal. Director Ridley Scott hired him after seeing his book *Necronomicon.*

26
27

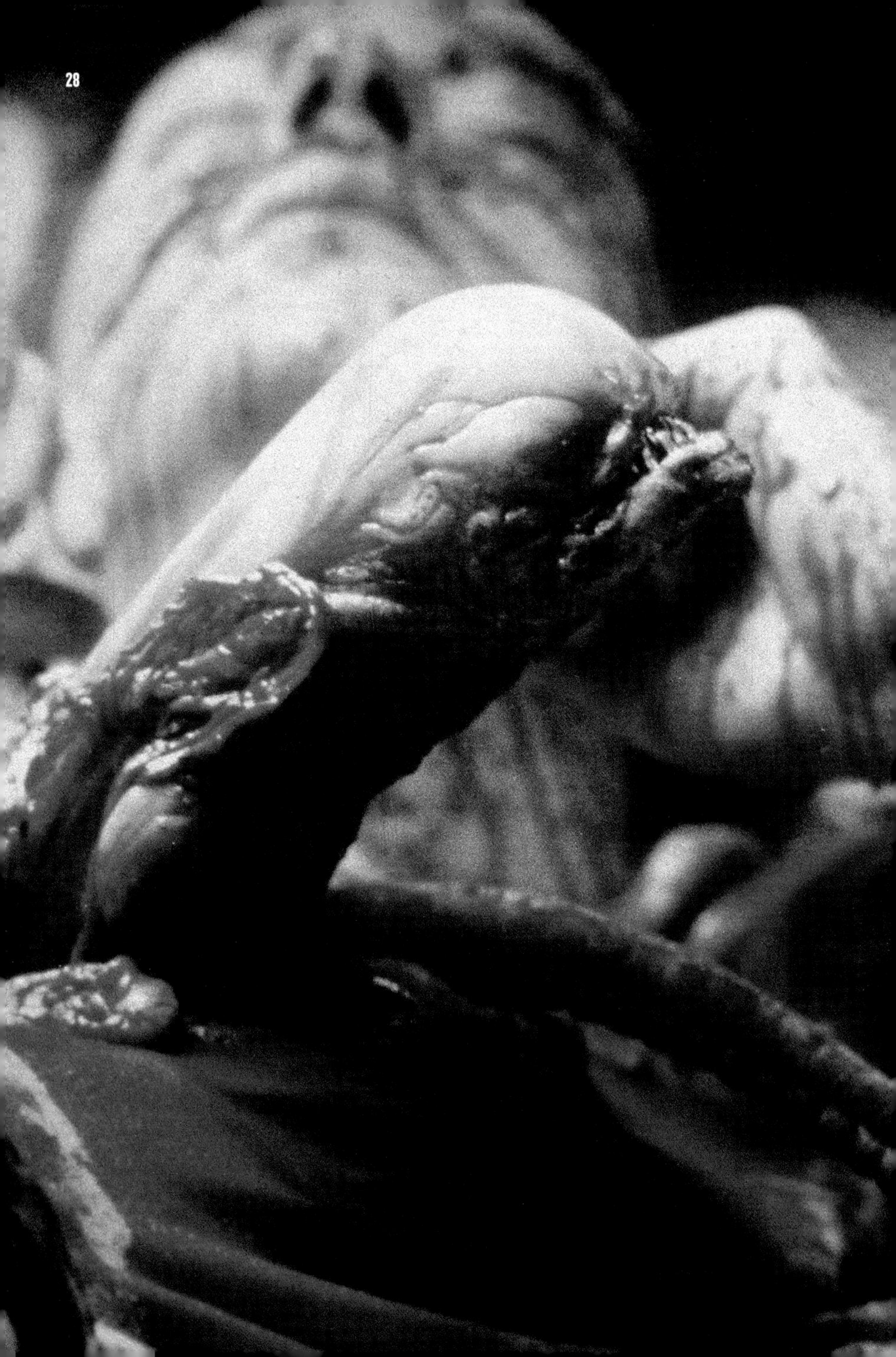

30
31

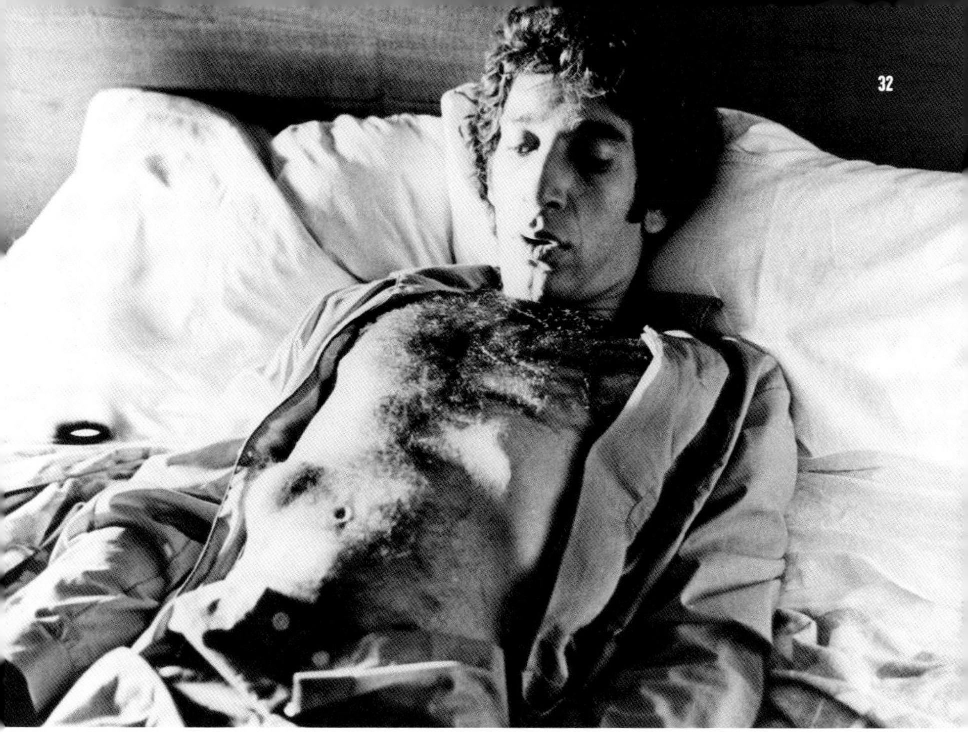

30 STILL FROM "TETSUO II: BODYHAMMER" (1992) Tomorowo Taguchi is changing into a weapon… and he seems to like it. The two Tetsuo films, handmade by Japanese auteur Shinya Tsukamoto, are among the first industrial punk-rock horror movies.

31 STILL FROM "THE FLY" (1986) Part man, part fly, part machine. The tragic end of Cronenberg's reimagining of the 1958 film. This version is so perfectly distilled there are fewer than ten speaking roles. Jeff Goldblum and Geena Davis star.

32 STILL FROM "SHIVERS" (1975) Sex and death encapsulated: Roger St Luc (Paul Hampton) and a venereal disease with a mind of its own. Writer and director David Cronenberg literally burst onto the scene here with his first commercial film.

33 ON THE SET OF "EYES WITHOUT A FACE" (1959) Director Georges Franju and the incomparable Edith Scob. Franju was a cofounder (along with Henri Langlois) of the Cinémathèque Française. With this, his most famous film, he created a one-of-a-kind medico-horror fairytale.

34 STILL FROM "THEY LIVE" (1988) How did we become so apathetic in the TV age? John Carpenter explains it all to us in this underrated alien invasion thriller, based on a short story by Ray Nelson.

35 STILL FROM "NAKED LUNCH" (1991) Even imaginary creatures need to take the edge off. Here is a mugwump in Cronenberg's semi-biographical adaptation of William S. Burroughs' psychedelic novel.

36 STILL FROM "ALTERED STATES" (1980) If the history of our evolution is stored in our DNA, how might we unlock its secrets? Director Ken Russell and writer Paddy Chayefsky present a far-out solution, while actor William Hurt and makeup artist Dick Smith help us take the trip.

37 STILL FROM "VIDEODROME" (1983) David Cronenberg's unforgettable take on the addictive, transforming monster that is television. Max Renn (James Woods) tries to get a little closer to Nicki Brand (Deborah Harry).

36
37

THE LIVING DEAD

PART FIVE

The Living Dead

True, death is a horrible thing. What with the loss of life for the dead themselves, and the loss of loved ones or colleagues for those left behind. But the *return* of the dead would be worse. It is almost the ultimate arena for horror. Because the reanimation of a body, and the awful miracle required to do it, would imply nothing less than the end of the world as we know it.

The greatest of all these reanimation tales is, of course, the extraordinary *Frankenstein or, The Modern Prometheus*. Written in 1816 by 19-year-old Mary Wollstonecraft Shelley, this complexly structured novel features a man of science, Dr. Frankenstein, whose quest for knowledge leads him to stitch together a man from dead bodies and give it the spark of life. Awfulness follows. The man he creates is a shambling mess, and Frankenstein's journey of creation carries him beyond the

"It's alive! It's alive!"

Doctor Frankenstein, Frankenstein (1931)

realm of human understanding and into the realm of the gods. A place where no man dare tread without dire consequences… (Ironically, while many narratives encourage us to "reach for the stars" and "be all that we can be," when characters somehow overreach, it registers as hubris and tragedy occurs, turning the story into horror. How are people, fictional or real, supposed to know when their reach is perfectly extended? When what they are reaching for is neither too much nor too little?)

One of the reasons for the continued success of *Frankenstein* and its progeny is the notable fact that since Shelley wrote her novel, global life expectancy has risen from 30 years of age in 1800 to 67 years of age in 2000 (jumping to 75 years of age in favored countries). This extraordinary achievement is not so far from the mastering of death and the creating of life she herself prophesized, and as we continue to push the boundaries of life expectancy and healthy living, the stories in question indicate some subconscious push back. That is, our fears that all this extra life, all this lessening of death, is some-

1 STILL FROM "FRANKENSTEIN" (1931) The ending of this scene, showing the girl's inadvertant drowning at the hands of The Monster, was originally cut for being too horrible. The resulting edit, though, implied a much more shocking defilment and desecration.

2 STILL FROM "FRANKENSTEIN" (1931) Boris Karloff as The Monster. The set design matched the makeup. We share his Expressionist prison.

3 STILL FROM "FRANKENSTEIN" (1910) Charles Ogle in the 15-minute silent version produced by Thomas Edison's film company.

4 ON THE SET OF "BRIDE OF FRANKENSTEIN" (1935) Director James Whale puts some finishing touches on Karloff. Seated directly behind is makeup artist Jack Pierce, who created the iconic square-headed look of the Universal monster.

5 STILL FROM "THE GOLEM" (1920) A top director and star in Germany during the 1920s, Paul Wegener made two Golem pictures before this one. Unfortunately, they have been lost. This story has a man of clay created by a rabbi to protect a Jewish ghetto. How fine the line between protector and monster.

5

how unnatural and ultimately costly in ways we can't begin to anticipate.

First filmed in 1910 by Thomas Edison's company, *Frankenstein* was most famously brought to the screen in 1931 by Englishman James Whale (the gay director portrayed by Ian McKellen in Bill Condon's 1998 film, *Gods and Monsters*). Under contract to Universal, the theater-trained Whale updated the Frankenstein tale to contemporary England and created a smash hit, gorgeous to look at and tremendously frightening for its time. (The unveiling of the monster was said to have caused fainting in the theaters.) But the picture also succeeded in capturing much of the thematic power of *Frankenstein* the novel. Not only does it crackle with a pyrotechnical version of the classic "overreaching scientist whose experiment goes awry" story, but it holds at its heart one of the real questions of the cinema of the living dead; that is: which option is better—to live as a monster, as something less than human, or not to live at all? To manifest this dilemma, Whale hired Boris Karloff, a fellow expat Englishman, and together they created one of the most iconic characters of the 20th century: the square-headed Frankenstein's Monster—a figure pitiable and terrifying enough for the audience to ask itself whether sometimes "dead isn't better."

"The monster was the best friend I ever had." *Boris Karloff*

The role made Karloff a star, and though the monster was destroyed at the film's conclusion, *Frankenstein*'s great success, based on its wonderful mixture of the canny and the uncanny, led to an even better sequel, *The Bride of Frankenstein*, in 1935. The monster is revived, and the dilemma of his painful existence (aka the human condition) comes front and center. Karloff's scenes with O.P. Heggie's blind hermit and Ernest Thesiger's Dr. Pretorious (a scientist even madder than Frankenstein) are especially effective, at once touching and frightening. The audience totally "feels" for the poor guy, and throughout the picture Whale packs in more humor, pathos, action, and visual splendor than in the original. His coup de grâce was casting petite young Elsa Lanchester, who, in an amazing turn, playing both Mary Shelley and the shock-haired Bride of the Monster, creates a character almost as iconic as Karloff's.

Many other effective science-of-the-living-dead pictures have followed the Whale films, including the wonderfully awful *The Thing That Couldn't Die* (a decapitated head) in 1958 and the six-picture Peter Cushing *Frankenstein* cycle from Hammer Studios that began with 1957's *The Curse of Frankenstein* and ended with 1974's *Frankenstein and the Monster from Hell*. But the most successful is arguably Stuart Gordon's *Re-Animator* (1985). Gordon, a theater-trained director like Whale, based his script on the public-domain H. P. Lovecraft story *Herbert West: Re-Animator*. Like Whale, he too uses high comedy to offset the chills, but also pours on the outrageous gore and genuine sexual tension. Not only are people attacked by the living dead, but by their mobile, reanimated intestines as well. Gordon, like George A. Romero in *Dawn of the Dead* (1978; remade 2004) before him and Peter Jackson in *Braindead* (1992) after, understands the literally visceral comic possibilities in these outrageous scenarios. In *Re-Animator*'s most famous sequence, a lascivious older professor takes his own decapitated head and, holding it in his hands before him, "goes down" on the nubile young daughter of his rival. She's tied spread-eagle to a surgical gurney, fully nude and frantically writhing. (The audience writhed right along with her. There was no fainting, but in one theater a female patron was heard to scream, "For God's sake! Please, somebody HELP that woman!!!")

6 ON THE SET OF "BRIDE OF FRANKENSTEIN" (1935) The movie soundstage as laboratory: bringing something new and extraordinary to life. Part science, part art, part industry.

7 STILL FROM "BRIDE OF FRANKENSTEIN" (1935) The Monster (Boris Karloff) and his mate (Elsa Lanchester) in one of those rare sequels that actually tops the original.

7

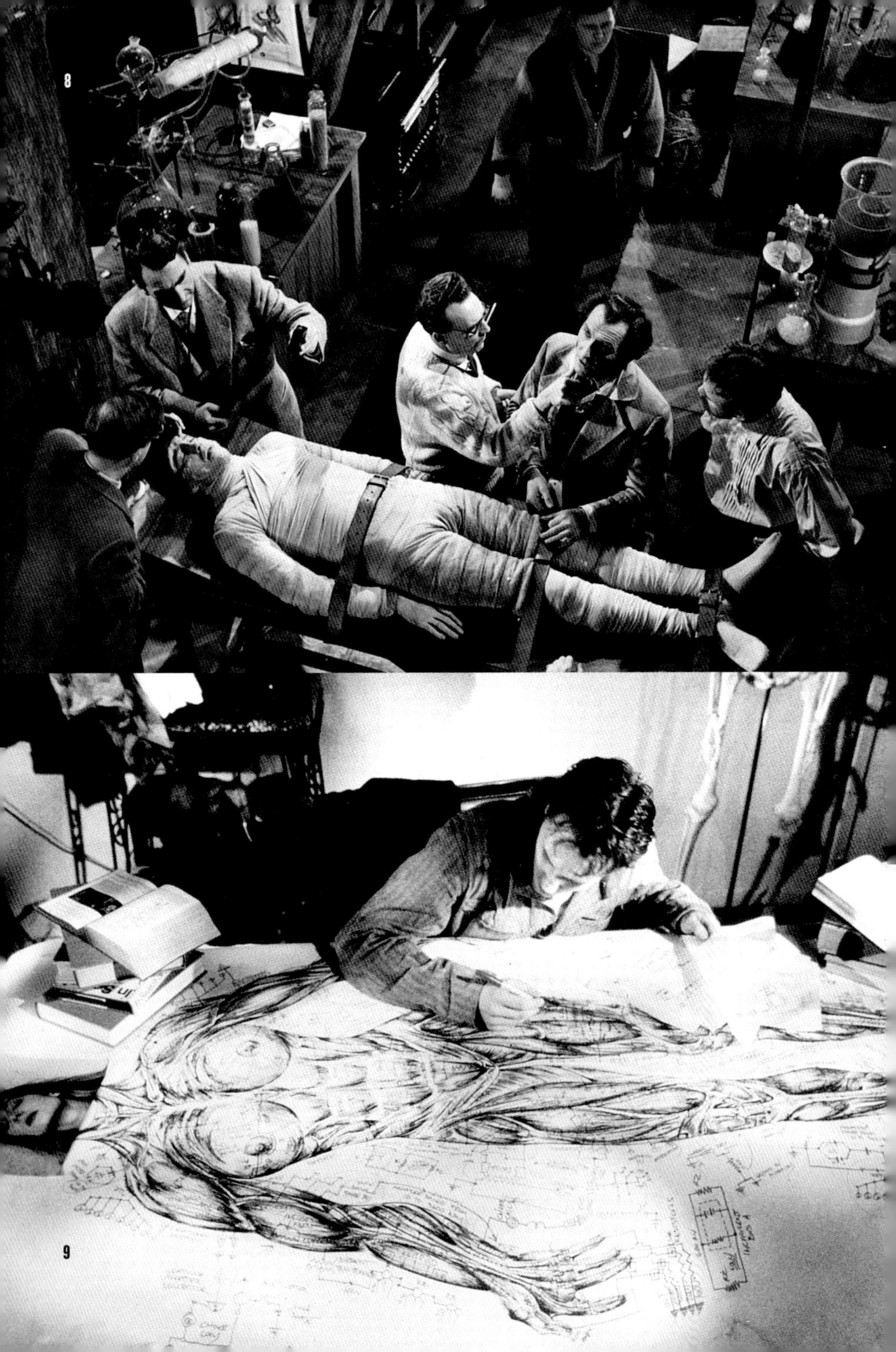

8

9

8 ON THE SET OF "CURSE OF FRANKENSTEIN" (1957) Christopher Lee and Peter Cushing prepare for filming. After this picture, both men would forever be associated with horror, the fantastic… and each other.

9 STILL FROM "FRANKENHOOKER" (1990) This comic update, like Henenlotter's equally transgressive *Basket Case* trilogy and *Brain Damage*, was a cerebral sleaze-fest, gleefully reveling in sex, drugs and rock'n'roll. A victim of changing tastes and economics, but a true student of the underbelly of film, New York based Henenlotter turned from directing to rescuing older exploitation titles from the garbage heap, rediscovering and releasing many *Frank Henenlotter's Sexy Shockers* on video before returning in 2008 with an amazing throwback/comeback film, *Bad Biology*.

10 STILL FROM "FLESH FOR FRANKENSTEIN" (1973) Baron Frankenstein (Udo Kier) takes obvious pleasure in his work. Paul Morrissey's X-rated gorefest was released in 3-D under the auspices of Andy Warhol.

11 PUBLICITY STILL FOR "THE BRAIN THAT WOULDN'T DIE" (1959) Eddie Carmel, who suffered from a pituitary gland tumor and plays The Monster beautifully here, is probably best known as the subject of a famous Diane Arbus photograph, *A Jewish Giant at Home with His Parents* (1970).

12 ON THE SET OF "THE MUMMY" (1932) Billed on screen as "?" for his role as The Monster in Frankenstein (1931), just one year later Karloff saw his name above the title in *The Mummy*.

13 STILL FROM "THE MUMMY" (1932) Boris Karloff just before waking in Karl Freund's chiller. Makeup, again, courtesy of Jack Pierce.

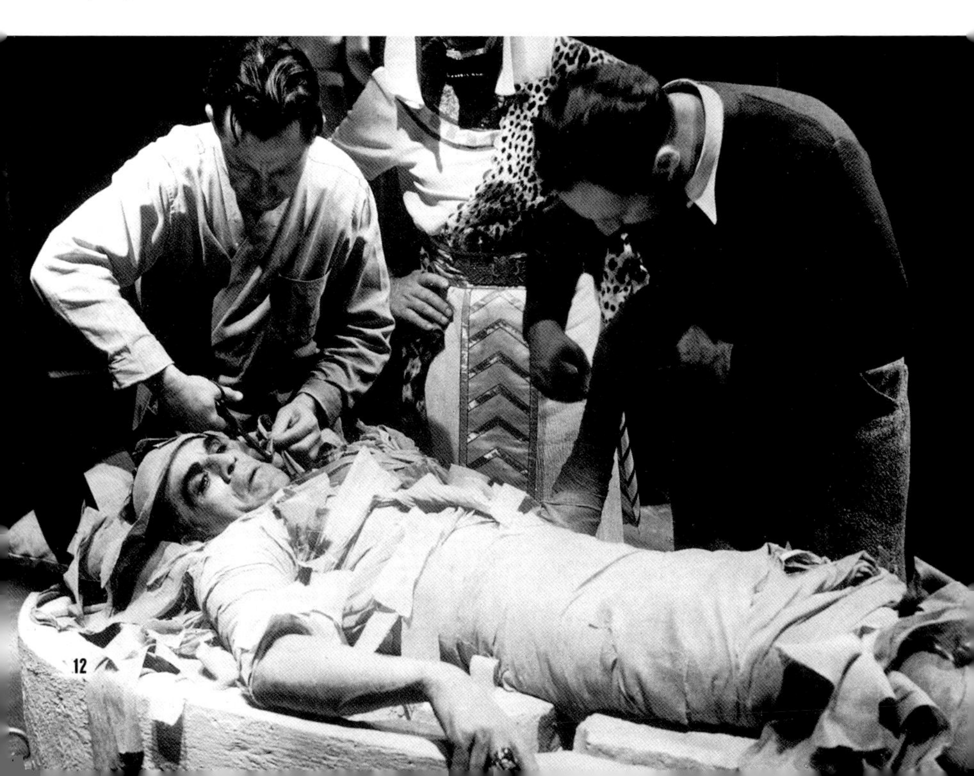

Before the scientific method brought rational explanations to our world, magic and ritual lived and breathed in every culture. Numerous films tap back into those times and those ways, using religious beliefs and rites to bring about the return of the dead. "The Golem" is a biblical creature brought to life by rabbinical incantations of Hebrew kabbalistic texts. Most of the "Mummy" movies have centered on Egyptian ritual and focus on curses, reincarnation, and reanimation. Implicit of course in all these tales is the notion of Christian primacy—the rituals involved are invariably from older, "darker" religions, and the implication is that only the rising up of Christ Himself could be a good (Godly) resurrection of the dead. The cinematic problems with these two classic undead monsters are relatively simple. The Golem was a Jewish legend and so has been virtually untouched since the 1930s. (First because Jews were vilified in Germany and so deemed unworthy of depiction, and later because their near destruction at the hands of the Nazis somehow protected them on moral grounds from ever being vilified on film.) And as for mummies, though they were used by Universal in the 1930s and 1940s in films like *The Mummy*, (1932), *The Mummy's Curse* (1944), and *The Mummy's Hand* (1940), and then by Hammer in the 1950s and 1960s (e.g., 1959's *The Mummy*, with Christopher Lee and Peter Cushing, and 1964's *Curse of the Mummy's Tomb*), their scariness came from some supposed curse on the archeologists behind the discovery of King Tut's tomb in 1923. The problem was always that mummies are really just slow, ponderous, and boring (at least, they were until Stephen Sommers took a stab at directing an action-oriented mummy movie in 1999, and then again in 2001).

"It's funny. The world is so different in the daylight. But at night, your fantasies get out of hand. But in the daylight, everything falls back into place again." *Mary Henry, Carnival of Souls (1962)*

Many films of the living dead are really not interested in science or ritual or any of the imaginary ways our universe can be rent apart. Viruses, sunspots, toxic waste spills; the ostensible rationales of these more modern takes on the subject are largely interchangeable and are usually dismissed in one line of dialogue or less. Instead, blood, guts, and sheer terror drive the narratives. Whether it's the various adaptations of Richard Matheson's novel *I Am Legend* (*The Last Man on Earth*, 1964; *The Omega Man*, 1971; *I Am Legend*, 2007), *28 Days Later...* (2002; and its sequel, *28 Weeks Later*, 2007), the Italian zombie pictures of Fulci and company (*Zombie,* 1979; *The Gates of Hell,* 1980; *The Beyond*, 1981; etc.), or the numerous additions to the Romero canon of zombie classics (*Night of the Living Dead*, 1968, remade 1990; *Dawn of the Dead*, 1978, remade 2004; *Day of the Dead,* 1985, remade 2008; *Land of the Dead*, 2005; and *Diary of the Dead*, 2008), these films use their horror narratives to explore deeper themes of society under pressure from

"I've always felt that the real horror is next door to us, that the scariest monsters are our neighbors." *George A. Romero*

14 STILL FROM "CARNIVAL OF SOULS" **(1962)** Director Herk Harvey makes a cameo as the most sinister of the apparitions.

15 STILL FROM "CARNIVAL OF SOULS" **(1962)** Mary Henry (Candace Hilligoss) in the car accident that begins her haunting journey. The only feature made by writer/producer/director Herk Harvey, who spent the rest of his career in commercials and industrial film.

14

15

within. Overnight the world simply tips into nightmare and, upon waking, the "survivors" face new, unclear delineations between themselves and "the others." Suddenly it is a not-so-brave new world where nothing they've learned or prepared for is worth a damn. These films are violent in the extreme—violating bodies gleefully, tearing people apart as they tear apart all sense of normalcy. Nothing is sacred, as there obviously is no God. These are worlds that provide filmmakers high stakes, technical challenges, disgusting visceral set pieces, and exciting ways to explore deeply human themes without seeming to be too artsy. They ask us to face ourselves at our worst—not just metaphorically as decaying, undead cannibals, but literally as a society decaying and cannibalizing itself. A society that thinks movies about undead cannibal zombies are entertaining...

16 STILL FROM "DAY OF THE DEAD" (1985) Following his indictment of rampant consumerism, *Dawn of the Dead* (1978), George A. Romero turned the genre on its head yet again—this time making the living dead oppressed and misunderstood.

17 STILL FROM "NIGHT OF THE LIVING DEAD" (1968) Released the year of the Martin Luther King Jr. and Robert Kennedy assassinations, Romero's downbeat film struck audiences as an almost (and too) true depiction of their suddenly dehumanized society.

18 STILL FROM "BOWERY AT MIDNIGHT" (1942) The Bowery was Manhattan's skid row. After using a soup kitchen as a front for his nefarious deeds, Karl Wagner (Bela Lugosi) winds up getting his just desserts.

19 STILL FROM "PET SEMATARY" (1989) Gage Creed (Miko Hughes) puts the bite on Jud Crandall (Fred Gwynne) in Stephen King's screen adaptation of his own novel.

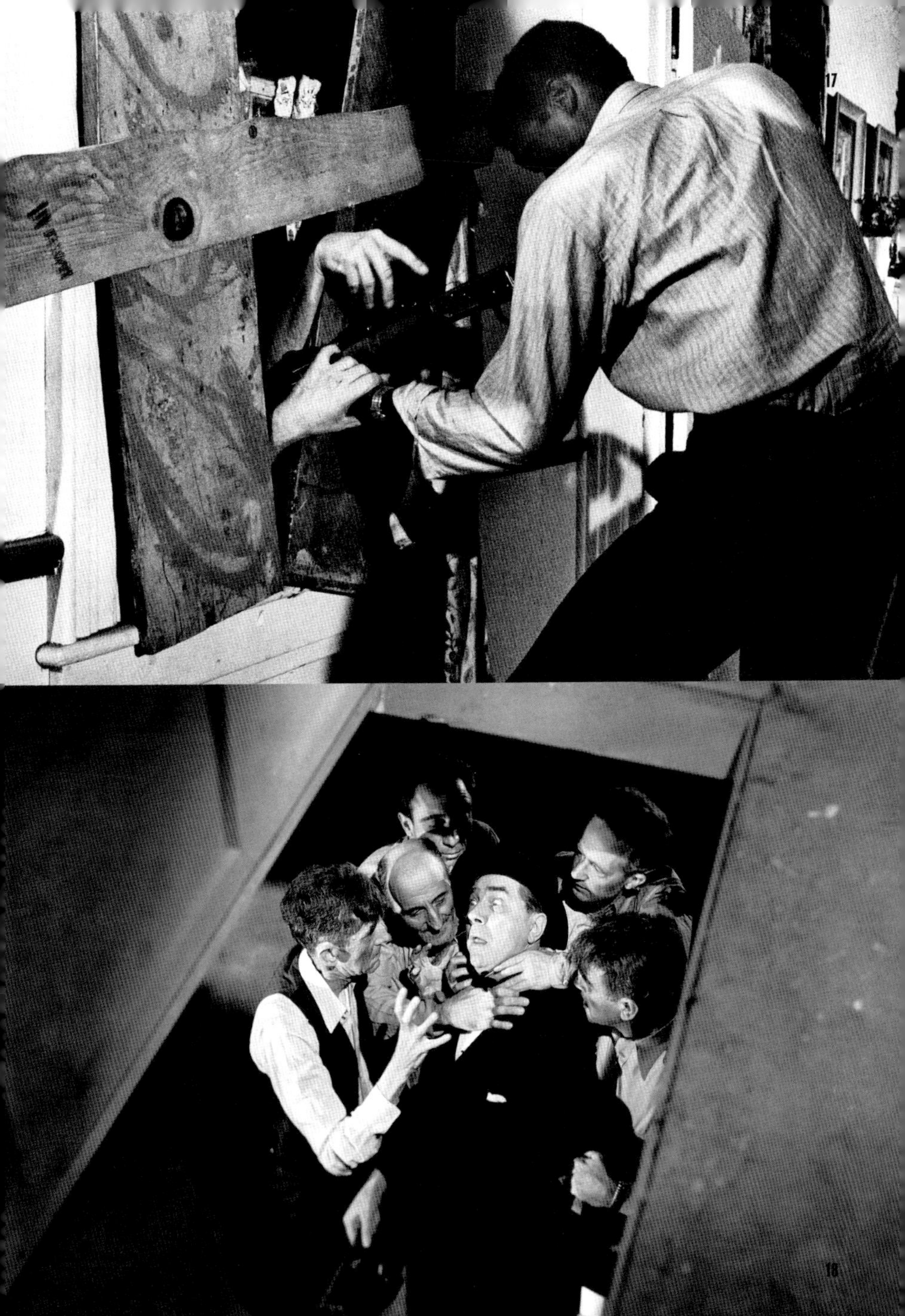
17
18

“Zombies are the blue-collar monsters.”

George A. Romero

20, 21 STILLS FROM "28 DAYS LATER..." (2002) Jim (Cillian Murphy, right) comes out of a coma, only to find himself in a nightmare world where people are infected with the "Rage Virus."

22 STILL FROM "BRAINDEAD" (1992) Lionel Cosgrove (Timothy Balme) is near the end of his rope in Peter Jackson's breakthrough horror-comedy. Ambitious, malicious, delicious. This climatic sequence reportedly took six weeks to film.

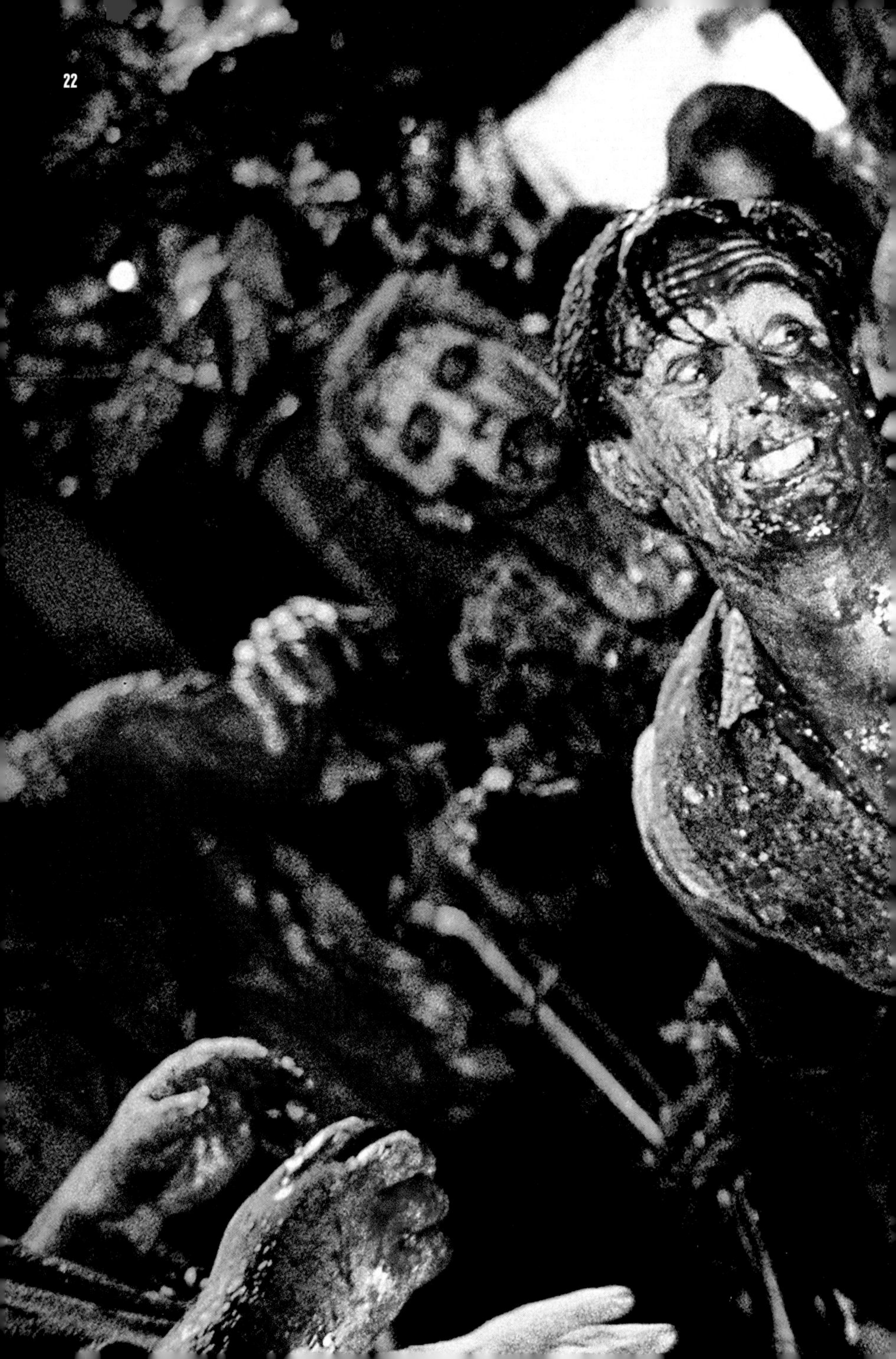

1

GHOSTS & HAUNTED HOUSES

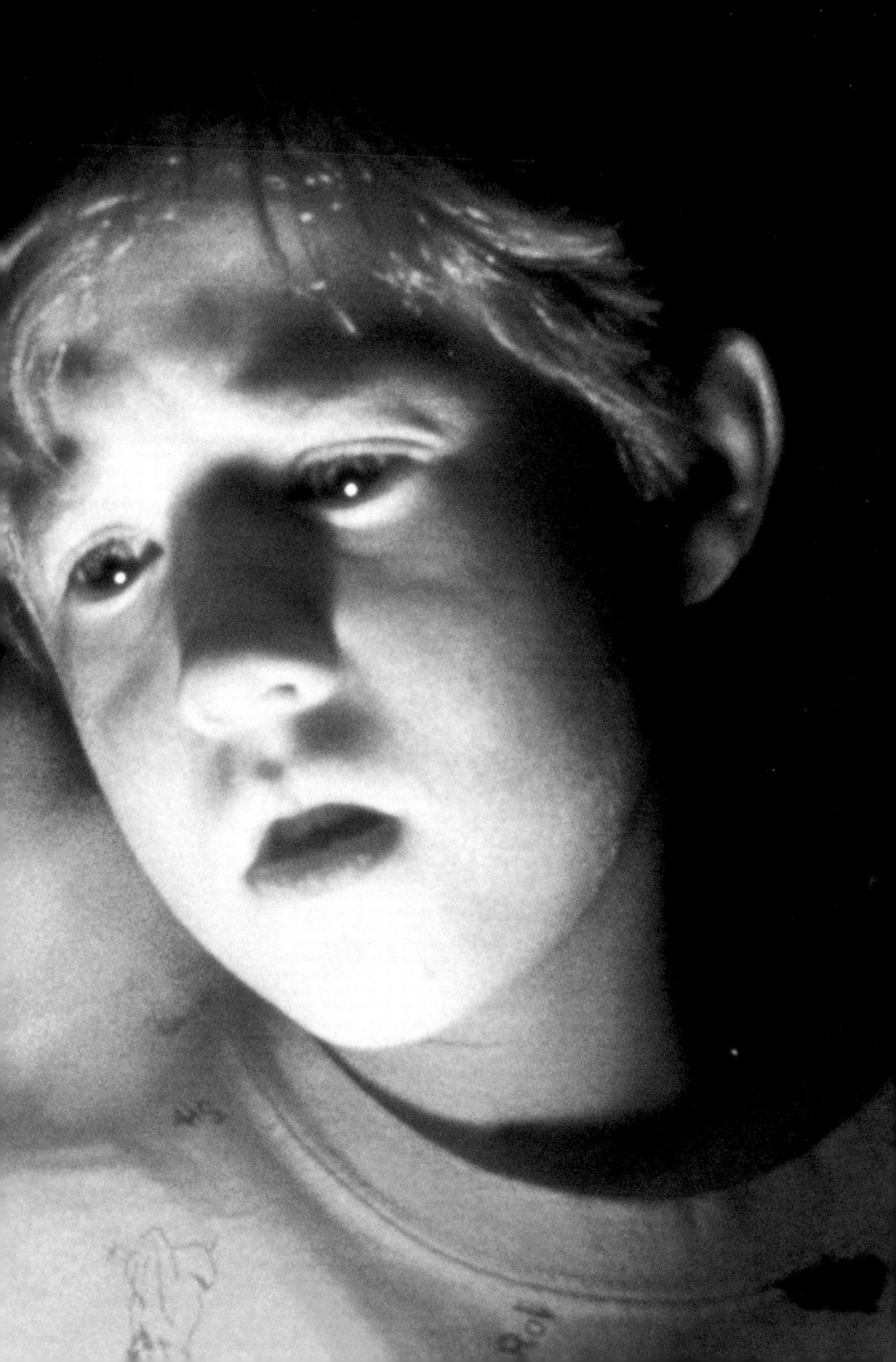

PART SIX

Ghosts & Haunted Houses

Ghosts haunt for a living. And, more often than not, they haunt houses, since that's where they tend to find a relatively captive audience. In fact, one of the biggest creative challenges endemic to any haunted-house tale is how to plausibly keep the inhabitants of the residence in question from getting the hell out at the first sign of supernatural trouble. In William Castle's *House on Haunted Hill* (1959; remade 1999), for example, an eccentric millionaire (Vincent Price) offers five strangers $10,000 if they can last the night in his haunted manse. In Robert Wise's *The Haunting* (1963; remade 1999), anthropologist John Markway (Richard Johnson) has "been looking for an honestly haunted house all his life," and so arranges an experiment for himself and two women with documented psychic abilities to stay at the notorious "Hill House" precisely to see what will transpire there. In Mikael Håfström's *1408* (2007), John Cusack plays a debunker of apparent supernatural sightings; he starts out by adamantly refusing to exit his ghost-infected motel room, only to find—once his skepticism gives way to belief and terror—that his spectral roommates simply won't let him leave. And in Oren Peli's *Paranormal Activity* (2007), we learn that the malevolent entity harassing Katie Featherston and her boyfriend, Micah Sloat, has been stalking her since she was a child, so leaving her current abode, sadly, won't accomplish a damn thing.

But though ghosts and haunted houses are closely connected in a survey of horror cinema, the presence of one does not automatically imply the presence of the other. There are plenty of haunted-house movies in which the haunter is no ghost, such as *The Cat and the Canary* (1927), *The Old Dark House* (1932), *Crawlspace* (1972), *Bad Ronald* (1974), and *Hider in the House* (1989). Similarly, there are numerous supernatural horror films in which the ghosts aren't restricted to a single address; key examples include *Carnival of Souls* (1962), *Don't Look Now* (1973), *The Fog* (1980; remade 2006), *Ringu* (Japan, 1998), and *The Sixth Sense* (1999). Nevertheless, for many reasons—not least the opportunity to engender uncanny effects by transforming a domestic, safe, and/or familiar space into one reeking of death, decay, and, above all, danger—most horror films featuring paranormal phenomena situate the source of the trouble in a contained location, be it a house (*The Innocents*, 1961; *The Legend of Hell House*, 1973; *The Amityville Horror*, 1979, remade 2005; *Poltergeist*, 1982; *The Others*, 2001); hotel (*The Shining*, 1980); motel (*1408*, 2007); apartment complex (*Dark Water/Honogurai mizu no soko kara*, Japan, 2002, remade in the United States, 2005; *At the End of the Spectra*, Spain, 2006); spacecraft (*Event Horizon*, 1997); submarine (*Below*, 2002); ocean liner (*Ghost Ship*, 1952, remade 2002); or automobile (*Christine*, 1983; *Mr. Wrong*, New Zealand, 1985).

"The oldest and strongest emotion of mankind is fear. And the oldest and strongest kind of fear is fear of the unknown." *H. P. Lovecraft*

The modern haunted-house tale finds its origins in the Gothic literature of the late 18th and early 19th centuries, when novelists such as Ann Radcliffe, Horace Walpole, and Matthew Lewis delivered sexually charged, eerily dreamlike bestsellers, including *The Castle of Otranto*, *The Mysteries of Udolpho*, and *The Monk*. These and many other Gothic novels of the time served to reveal—and to revel in—our darkest, most perverse fantasies and longings, our innate belief that crimes of the past will inevitably resurface in the present and evil will persist across time (if not across space).

Eventually, the old dark castles of Gothic literature transformed into the old dark houses of rural, suburban,

"Now death is the most terrible of things; for it is the end, and nothing is thought to be any longer either good or bad for the dead." *Aristotle*

even urban America. A direct lineage can be traced from the haunted castles of Europe all the way to the ghost-plagued residences of *The Uninvited* (1944), *The Changeling* (1980), *The Woman in Black* (1989), *Stir of Echoes* (1999), *What Lies Beneath* (2000), *Ju-on* (2000), and *An American Haunting* (2005).

What makes the ghost story, and the haunted house tale in particular, so appealing to filmmakers (and not just filmmakers who specialize in horror), is its reliance on atmospherics, sound design, special-effects trickery, and the like—quite literally all the tools of the cinematic trade—in order to startle, shock, creep out, and, above all, terrify audiences. Arguably the greatest haunted-house movie in the history of the genre, the 1963 version of *The Haunting* offers an excellent case study of how to render those proverbial "things that go bump in the night" on the big screen.

Between his two most famous films, *West Side Story* (1961) and *The Sound of Music* (1965), director Robert Wise chose to adapt Shirley Jackson's novella, *The Haunting of Hill House*, lauded by numerous scholars (not to mention Stephen King) as one of the greatest modern tales of supernatural horror. Unlike Jan de Bont in his misguided remake, Wise succeeds in providing audiovisual analogues for Jackson's literary horror effects, such as her personification/demonization of Hill House. Jackson has her characters describe the house in psychological terms; she even has them address it directly on occasion, as if the house could hear them... and perhaps respond. Moreover, Jackson uses impersonal narration to endow the house with physical characteristics typically reserved for living creatures: "The face of Hill House seemed awake, with a watchfulness from the blank windows and a touch of glee in the eyebrow of a cornice." Following Jackson's lead, Wise digs deeply into his bag of cinematographic and editing tricks to endow Hill House with life. By visually disorienting his audience, he supports the novella's claims that the house is psychologically unstable. This disorientation is achieved through mise-en-scène (the framing inside Hill House is frequently canted from a variety of angles); the use of a prototype 30mm wide-angle lens for distortion purposes; and rapidly edited montage sequences. All of this, along with multispeed camerawork, makes it nearly impossible to get a handle on spatial relations.

In addition, Wise bestows on Hill House a kind of protoconsciousness by (1) alternating between shots of the human protagonist, Eleanor (Julie Harris), and location shots of the house itself, thereby establishing a virtual (visual) dialogue between them; (2) cutting to close-ups of wall patterns resembling faces and statues with eyes that

1 STILL FROM "THE SIXTH SENSE" (1999) Enough to take your breath away: horrific visions from the realm of the dead.

2 STILL FROM "THE INNOCENTS" (1961) By turning Miss Giddens (Deborah Kerr), the young governess of Henry James's *The Turn of the Screw*, into a dowager, director Jack Clayton was able to heighten the story's theme of sexual repression for a modern audience.

3 STILL FROM "THE OLD DARK HOUSE" (1932) Margaret Waverton (Gloria Stuart) is menaced by Boris Karloff's hand in James Whale's follow-up to *Frankenstein*. (Note the similarity to the still of Jodie Foster on pages 50–51.) The house wasn't actually haunted in the movie, but it was certainly old and dark.

4 STILL FROM "THE CAT AND THE CANARY" (1927) The cliché images of the old-dark-house genre—secret doors opening behind people, clawed hands reaching out to grab stunned victims, and the like—are employed to great shock effect by director Paul Leni.

3
4

5
6

hum with life; (3) providing high overhead shots of Eleanor that turn into unclaimed points of view that swoop down and threaten her; and (4) situating mirrors throughout the house that function as eyes, reflecting images of the unwelcome tenants back to them when least expected.

One of the most frightening aspects of Jackson's novella is her description of strange, hostile noises—so precise and detailed that readers are actually prompted to imagine them. Jackson frequently overlays distinct sounds on top of one another, and takes pains to specify not just their volume but their rhythm and timbre as well. What is more, she heightens the impact of her most disturbing noises by contrasting them with moments of eerie silence: "The door was attacked without sound, seeming almost to be pulling away from its hinges, almost ready to buckle and go down, leaving them exposed... 'It knows we're here,' Eleanor whispered... She was aware, dully, the pounding had begun again, the metallic overwhelming sound of it washed over her like waves."

Wise's experience as an editor of both sound and pictures before he moved to the director's chair served him especially well when it came to *The Haunting*, and with help from Humphrey Searle's score he successfully presented what Jackson could only describe. The sheer density of the soundtrack was a technique Wise learned from his former mentor in atmospheric horror, Val Lewton.

5 STILL FROM "KILL, BABY... KILL!" (1966) A ghostly little girl (Valeria Valeri) frightens people to death in what many people consider to be Mario Bava's best horror movie.

6 STILL FROM "THE INNOCENTS" (1961) Peter Quint (Peter Wyngarde) and Miles (Martin Stephens). Is the haunting psychological or physical? A good ghost story, on the page or on the screen, always has elements of both.

7 STILL FROM "LADY IN WHITE" (1988) The Lady in White (Katherine Helmond) hovers nearby young Frankie Scarlatti (Lukas Haas) in a film that is much darker than it looks.

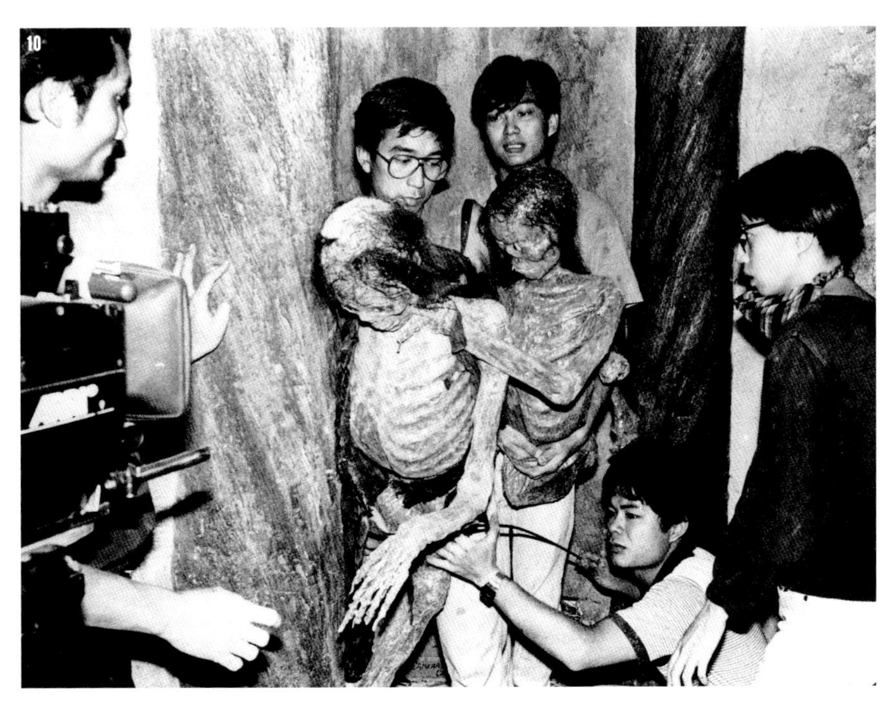

8 STILL FROM "THE HAUNTING" (1963) Dr. John Markway (Richard Johnson) and his psychic guinea pig Eleanor Vance (Julie Harris) ascend the rickety spiral staircase, which serves as an architectural manifestation of the female protagonist's unhinged mind.

9 STILL FROM "THE HAUNTING" (1963) Eleanor has never been kissed, never been cuddled. She finally finds her love in Hill House.

10 ON THE SET OF "A CHINESE GHOST STORY" (1987) Producer Tsui Hark oversees a special effects sequence for this hugely entertaining horror-comedy kung-fu ghost tale. Along with John Woo and Jackie Chan, Hark brought the kinetic style of Hong Kong cinema onto the world stage.

11 STILL FROM "KWAIDAN" (1964) Masaki Kobayashi directed a stunning quartet of ghost stories, with stylized design, color, and sound, to create a sustained atmosphere of unease.

"Horror is that which cannot be made safe—evolving, ever changing—because it is about relentless need to confront the unknown, the unknowable, and the emotion we experience when in its thrall."

Douglas Winters

12
13

14

One of the film's most chilling scenes is the famous "Whose hand was I holding?" set piece. Lying in bed, clutching what she mistakenly believes is her roommate's hand, an unhinged Eleanor hears a muffled male voice muttering insanely to itself. Added to this incomprehensible mumbling, on an entirely different register, is the sound of a child crying (or perhaps laughing, which is how Jackson describes it). A faint moaning can be detected as well. The overall effect is utterly, undeniably chilling. During other moments of chaos and terror, Wise and Searle pipe in an atonal fusion of blaring horns and shrieking strings, thereby increasing our sensory disorientation. And, proving once again how well he understood what Jackson was going for, Wise eliminates sound entirely during some of the movie's most frightening scenes—a lesson in haunted-house cinema that many contemporary horror directors would be wise (pun intended) to follow.

12 STILL FROM "DON'T LOOK NOW" (1973) Having pursued a red coat through the canals of Venice, believing it to be worn by the ghost of his daughter, John Baxter discovers the truth too late. Nicolas Roeg's visual style perfectly matched the Grand Guignol sexuality of Daphne Du Maurier's Venetian horror tale.

13 STILL FROM "DON'T LOOK NOW" (1973) Neither ghost nor child, Adelina Poerio as the blade-wielding killer in Roeg's haunting film.

14 STILL FROM "DON'T LOOK NOW" (1973) Blood on the lens. This image alerts John Baxter (Donald Sutherland) that something is wrong, but he is too late to save his daughter from drowning.

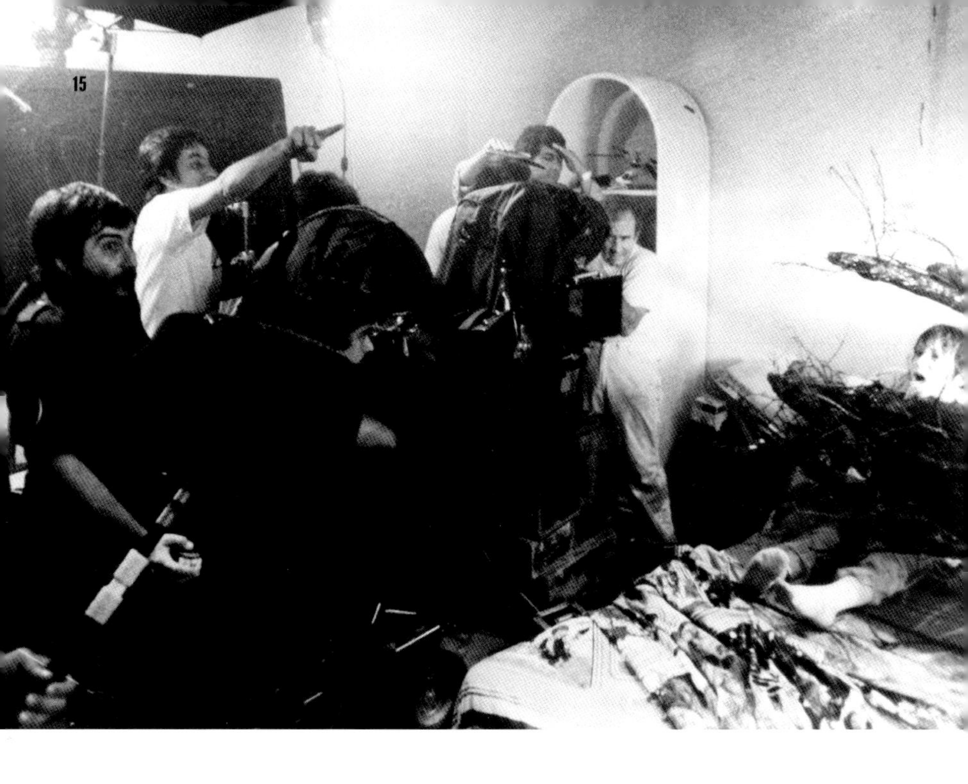

15 ON THE SET OF "POLTERGEIST" (1982) Tobe Hooper (left) directs a large-budget special effects extravaganza with a terrifying and all-too-real question at its heart: How do you cope when your child goes missing?

16 STILL FROM "POLTERGEIST" (1982) At first the ghosts are playful, but when youngest daughter Carol Anne (Heather O'Rourke) is pulled into a portal, mother Diane (JoBeth Williams) finds the courage to go after her.

17 STILL FROM "POLTERGEIST" (1982) Williams did not want to get into the pool with all the electrical equipment around, so producer Steven Spielberg got into the pool with her: "If a light falls in, we'll both fry."

16

17

POSSESSION, DEMONS & TRICKSTERS

1

PART SEVEN

Possession, Demons & Tricksters

The history of horror cinema is replete with all manner of monsters, from the supernatural to the scientific, from the alien to the avian, from the insectoid to the humanoid. But no monster species is quite as much fun as the demonic, or—to broaden this category so that we're not unnecessarily restricting ourselves to familiar religious myths and legends—what we might call the "evil trickster."

According to the influential psychoanalyst Carl Gustav Jung, since the beginning of recorded human history the archetypal evil (or, to use his term, *shadow*) trickster character has been raising the proverbial roof in legends, myths, and fairy tales all across the globe. Often depicted as a demon, he masks his true identity by adopting a charming, mesmerizing persona for the purpose of making friends and influencing people. And if the trickster is ever contained, it's only a temporary setback, since some unsuspecting fool will inevitably release him so that he can go back to tormenting poor schnooks far and wide.

"The devil's voice is sweet to hear." *Stephen King*

The cinematic evil trickster is easily identified by his cruel and sadistic sense of humor. While his victims are writhing around in agony, the trickster is usually cracking up or making lame jokes, clearly relishing in their pain. Some of the more popular evil tricksters in modern horror history are the eponymous *Dr. Phibes*, played by Vincent Price in 1971 and again in 1972, dream-stalker Freddy Krueger (Robert Englund) of the *A Nightmare on Elm Street* series (1984 and thereafter), devil doll Chucky of the *Child's Play* movies (1988 and thereafter), and Ghostface of the *Scream* franchise (1996, 1997, 2000, 2011). (Although slasher-film faves Michael Myers and Jason Voorhees seem to have a good ol' time dispatching of their victims in any number of creative ways, both these baddies are usually way too stoic to warrant true trickster status.)

The evil trickster has also been a central villain for legendary Italian horror director Mario Bava. Exerting control over his heroines' perceptions, the trickster makes it next to impossible for them to distinguish fantasy from reality. In his Gothic horror classic *Mask of the Demon* (aka *Black Sunday*, 1960), for example, the age-old trickster witch/bitch Princess Asa (Barbara Steele) seeks to rejuvenate herself by stealing the identity of her descendant Katia (also played by Steele). And two of Bava's lesser films, *Baron Blood* (1972) and *Lisa and the Devil* (1972), focus on the female lead's struggle with an evil trickster. (Coincidentally, the heroine in both of these movies is played by the lovely Elke Sommer.) The depiction of the trickster is left to the screen talents of American stars Joseph Cotten and Telly Savalas, respectively, who put on a show to convince us that beneath their everyday persona lurks a demonic presence just waiting to be unleashed on a naïve (and, of course, nubile) young woman… and, quite possibly, the world at large.

One of the evil trickster's most popular gambits is to make his, her, or its way inside the mind and/or body of a human being. What better way to practice malevolence than to possess a person, to corrupt and ultimately destroy an individual from the inside out, thereby causing maximum misery to the host, his or her loved ones, and strangers alike? But not all possession movies are the same; they can be broken down into various (not always mutually exclusive) subcategories. The familiar, but by no means outdated, demonic-possession film finds its paradigm and shining jewel in *The Exorcist* (1973). All others bow down and pay homage, consciously or not, to William Friedkin's masterpiece, in which the mystic side of Catholicism is foregrounded and put to the test against ancient evil.

The first horror blockbuster, *The Exorcist* has exerted a powerful influence on the subsequent development of the genre—and on public reception of it. Never before had a horror film been the subject of so much pre-release hype, so much gossip about post-production strife, so much speculation as to why people of all ages would stand in line for hours to watch something reputed to induce fits of vomiting, fainting, even temporary psychosis. The cultural impact of *The Exorcist* can hardly be overestimated: It challenged existing regulations specifying what was acceptable to show on the big screen, stole U.S. newspaper headlines away from the ongoing Watergate scandal (at least for a little while), led to a detectable increase in the number of "real life" possessions reported, and, in the words of gross-out film expert William Paul (in *Laughing Screaming: Modern Hollywood Horror and Comedy*), "established disgust as mass entertainment for a large audience."

In 1949, reports came out in the press of a 13-year-old Maryland boy whose body was said to have been taken over by demonic forces. After seeing household objects fly around his room, the boy's distraught parents called in a Jesuit priest, who conducted a 35-day exorcism with the help of numerous assistants. While the priests recited their holy incantations, the boy spit, cackled, urinated, writhed in his bed, and manifested bloody scratch marks on his body that spelled out words such as *Hell*, *Christ*, and the far more mysterious *Go to St. Louis*. Fortunately for everyone involved, the alleged demon departed shortly after Easter. Novelist William Peter Blatty, inspired by this tale, made the possessee a girl (supposedly to protect the boy's anonymity, though his readiness to disclose information in later media interviews suggests this was unnecessary), sensationalized many of the details, added heavy doses of philosophical-theological speculation on the nature of evil, and came out with *The Exorcist* in 1971. An instant sensation, Blatty's novel would remain on the *Publishers Weekly* best-seller list for almost an entire year.

Even before *The Exorcist* was published, Blatty signed a deal with Warner Bros. for the rights to make a film version of the novel. Warner agreed to Blatty's choice of director, William Friedkin, on the strength of his not-yet-released action movie, *The French Connection*, for which he would win an Academy Award in 1971. After numerous and painstaking rewrites of the original script, Blatty finally came up with a screenplay of *The Exorcist* that man-

1 STILL FROM "THE EXORCIST" (1973) Father Merrin (Max von Sydow) arrives for work. The light at the end of his tunnel.

2 STILL FROM "A NIGHTMARE ON ELM STREET" (1984) Robert Englund became world-famous for his role as the child murderer Freddy Krueger in Wes Craven's cult movie.

3 STILL FROM "FAUST" (1926) Mephisto (Emil Jannings) in F.W. Wilhelm Murnau's classic. Both star and director were titans of German cinema who, in the 1920s, moved to Hollywood and won Oscars at the very first Academy Awards in 1928.

4 STILL FROM "HÄXAN" (1922) The Devil accepts the sacrifice of dead children at a witches' coven.

3
4

aged to meet Friedkin's exacting demands for more mystery, more drama, and, above all, more direct confrontations between (good) priest and (evil) demon than were in the novel. For his own part—and with Warner Bros.' considerable financial backing—Friedkin employed a range of sophisticated cinematic techniques, along with state-of-the-art special-effects technology, to give the film's supernatural occurrences and gory physical details a degree of realism never before achieved.

The plot of *The Exorcist* is deceptively simple and has its roots in storytelling conventions well established in American cinema. After a lengthy, impressionistic prologue set around an archeological dig in Iraq, the first half of the film methodically develops the essential character relationships and establishes the crisis situation. Regan MacNeil (Linda Blair) is the adorable, almost-pubescent daughter of divorcée and well-known film star Chris MacNeil (Ellen Burstyn). After Regan prophesies the death of her mother's acquaintance and urinates (standing up, no less) in front of a roomful of shocked dinner guests, Chris starts to wonder what has "gotten into" her daughter. More odd behavior, and a wildly shaking bed, lands Regan in the hospital, where she is subjected to a battery of extremely invasive procedures best described as "medical pornography." A brain lesion is suspected, but the tests turn up nothing. When Regan, supposedly under hypnosis, responds to the smug questions of a hospital psychologist by grabbing his scrotum and rendering him immobile, it is recommended that Chris seek the Church's help. She does, pleading with doubt-ridden Jesuit priest Damien Karras (Jason Miller, Pulitzer Prize-winning playwright of *That Championship Season*) to perform an exorcism. The second half of the film culminates in an intense one-to-one fight to the finish between Karras and Regan's demonic possessor, after the more experienced exorcist on the scene, Father Merrin (Ingmar Bergman favorite Max von Sydow) dies in the struggle. Karras finally saves Regan by accepting the demon into his own body, only to throw himself—or, at least, allow himself to be thrown—out of a window to his death.

Although the Catholic Church originally supported Friedkin's efforts in the hopes that he would present Catholicism in a positive light, they ended up retracting that support after viewing the infamous scene in which Regan-demon violently masturbates with a crucifix in front of her powerless mother. For many audience members, the highly sexualized profanities spewing out of 12-year-old Regan's mouth (Mercedes McCambridge, who voiced the demon, had to sue for on-screen credit) were as offensive as the green bile she vomited on Karras's face. In an era of student protest, experimental drug use, and general questioning of authority, *The Exorcist* allowed viewers to take pleasure in the terrible punishments inflicted on the rebellious ("possessed") Regan. But by making Regan-demon so fascinating to watch, so filled with nasty surprises, *The Exorcist* also allowed viewers to take pleasure in that rebelliousness.

Besides the largely misguided *Exorcist* sequels and prequels that have followed in the wake of Friedkin's film, other demonic-possession movies include *Abby* (1974), William Girdler's blaxploitation take on the subject, with William Marshall of *Blacula* (1972) fame playing a reverend who accidentally (what else is new?) unleashes an

5 ON THE SET OF "DR. JEKYLL & MR. HYDE" (1931) Fredric March and Miriam Hopkins take tea with director Rouben Mamoulian.

6 STILL FROM "DR. JEKYLL & MR. HYDE" (1931) Fredric March received the Best Actor Oscar for his depiction of the sheer animal pleasure of the dark side.

7
8

7 STILL FROM "DR. JEKYLL & MR. HYDE" (1920) John Barrymore in the silent version. If March's Hyde was a sexual ape, Barrymore's was a scuttling bug.

8 STILL FROM "DR. JEKYLL & MR. HYDE" (1941) Spencer Tracy as Mr. Hyde with little makeup. Even the potent combination of Lana Turner and Ingrid Bergman couldn't turn up the heat on this big-budget but sanitized version.

9 STILL FROM "DR. JEKYLL & MR. HYDE" (1931) Ivy Pearson (Miriam Hopkins) and Mr. Hyde (Fredric March). The violence and sexuality of March's portrayal of Hyde has yet to be equaled.

10 STILL FROM "THE BAD SEED" (1956) Rhoda Penmark (Patty McCormack) assures her mother Christine (Nancy Kelly) it's all going to be alright. The film was so disturbing that after "The End" credit, Rhoda was spanked by her mother, and thus received the catharsis that the onlooker had already undergone.

evil African spirit that proceeds to possess his daughter-in-law, Abby (Carol Speed). Normally well behaved, Abby promptly starts freaking her family out: swearing like a sailor, removing her clothes in front of fellow church members, and picking up men in bars. The picture was so profitable a rip-off of *The Exorcist*, Warner Bros. sued to have it permanently pulled from theaters.

Horror icon Paul Naschy stars as a village priest trying to rid a young lady of her demons in the slow-burning Spanish *Exorcist* copy, *Exorcism* (1975). A more egregious rip-off is *Beyond the Door* (1974), an Italian/U.S. coproduction that became a surprise hit at the box office despite a lawsuit by Warner Bros. for plagiarism. In *Amityville II: The Possession* (1982)—a purported prequel to the 1979 horror hit, *The Amityville Horror*—not five minutes after a Catholic family moves into the Amityville house, eldest kid Sonny (Jack Magner) is possessed by a voice that talks to him out of his Walkman, compelling him to seduce his sister and murder the entire family with a shotgun. Good times. And in *Witchboard* (1987), a functional Ouija board is the lame device used to motivate (at least in theory) the full gamut of exorcism and possession clichés. (For all its flaws, the film did well enough to command a pair of sequels, in 1993 and 1995.) It wasn't until Scott Derrickson's 2005 sleeper hit, *The Exorcism of Emily Rose*, with its novel blend of courtroom drama and supernatural horror, that new life was breathed into the *Exorcist*-inspired demonic-possession film.

On the other end of the spectrum from "single possessee" movies like *The Exorcist* and *The Exorcism of Emily Rose*, with their inspired-by-a-true-story airs of authenticity and solemnity, are horror films in which a demonic horde basically goes apeshit and possesses anyone and everyone within reach. Sam Raimi set the standard here with *The Evil Dead* (1981), then re-set that standard on a bigger budget (and virtually the same story) with *Evil Dead II* five years later. Another notable entry in this group is Lamberto (son of Mario) Bava's Italian gorefest *Demons* (1985), in which Raimi's wicked cabin in the woods is replaced by an art deco movie theater in West Berlin.

Somewhere in the middle between these two extremes are what we might call body-hopping-demon movies. In Wes Craven's *Shocker* (1989), a convicted serial killer is sentenced to die in the electric chair. But instead of killing him outright, the chair somehow transforms him into a high-voltage electronic bogeyman capable of zapping from body to body, stealing souls along the way in a game of psychic tag. Weirdly, in *Jason Goes to Hell: The Final Friday* (1993), Jason conveniently develops the ability to transfer his "soul" from one body to another due to a parasite (!). And in Gregory Hoblit's *Fallen* (1998), cop protagonist John Hobbes (Denzel Washington) is induced to kill an innocent man who's been temporarily inhabited by the body-hopping demon Azazel precisely for the purpose of entrapping Hobbes. It is in fact Azazel's supernatural "invisibility"—his ability to hide behind a multiplicity of bodies used as masks—that exercises Hobbes's powers of detection in the film.

"And this is the forbidden truth, the unspeakable taboo—that evil is not always repellent but frequently attractive; that it has the power to make of us not simply victims, as nature and accident do, but active accomplices." *Joyce Carol Oates*

11 STILL FROM "THE MASQUE OF THE RED DEATH" (1964) Prince Prospero (Vincent Price) meets Death. Power corrupts, and absolute power corrupts absolutely… and we get to watch.

12 ON THE SET OF "THE MASQUE OF THE RED DEATH" (1964) Roger Corman (center) directs Hazel Court and Vincent Price. His literate and colorful series of Poe adaptations, classy tales of nobles behaving badly, were one of the most successful horror cycles of the 1960s.

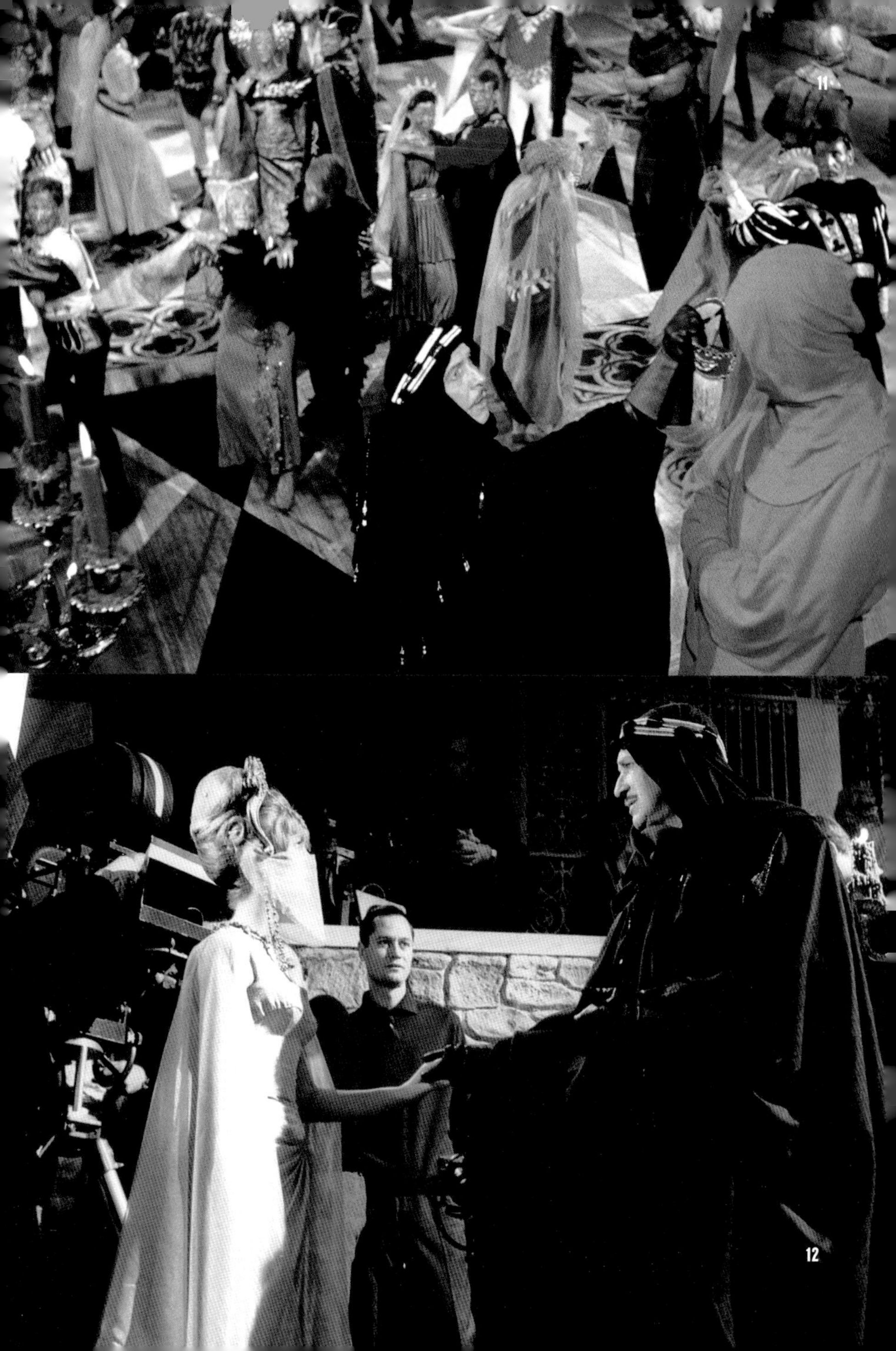

Predating *The Exorcist* by a dozen years is Jack Clayton's *non*-demonic possession movie, *The Innocents*, a brilliantly executed adaptation of Henry James's Freudian ghost story *The Turn of the Screw*. Here, a prim, repressed governess suspects that the kids in her charge are being inhabited by the spirits of the previous groundsman and governess. Other non-demonic possession films—none of them particularly inspired—include *The Reincarnation of Peter Proud* (1975), *J.D.'s Revenge* (1976), *Ruby* (1977), and *Audrey Rose* (1977). Maybe the most interesting—certainly the most fun—entry in this subgenre is Tom Holland's *Child's Play* (1988), in which the mind and soul of a just-departed serial murderer animates the plastic body of a two-foot-tall doll named Chucky. Four sequels later, Chucky's still killing with a smile in classic evil-trickster style.

One final possession subgenre warranting mention here is what we might call the extra-terrestrial-takeover film. Instead of a devil, demon, or malevolent human spirit seeking control of, or reincarnation in, some poor bastard's body, here an alien life-form invades and inhabits an unfortunate human host. Examples range from B movie *The Kiss* (1988) to studio picture *The Astronaut's Wife* (1999). There's also a body-hopping variation exemplified by John Carpenter's effects-laden sci-fi/horror masterpiece *The Thing* (1982)—a loose remake of the 1951 Cold War classic *The Thing from Another World*—and subsequent *Thing* rip-offs like *The Hidden* (1987) and *Proteus* (1995).

"What an excellent day for an exorcism." *Pazuzu, The Exorcist (1973)*

The most important lesson in all this? The evil trickster *always* has the last laugh...

13 STILL FROM "EXORCIST II: THE HERETIC" (1977) Regan MacNeil possessed anew in John Boorman's brave, if ill-fated, sequel. Makeup wizard Dick Smith again provided the look.

14 ON THE SET OF "THE EXORCIST" (1973) Linda Blair and director William Friedkin. Cast for her sweetness and nascent sexuality, Blair gave an extraordinary performance.

15 STILL FROM "WES CRAVEN'S NEW NIGHTMARE" (1994) Freddy Krueger (Robert Englund) opens wide in Wes Craven's postmodern horror film, which predated his own self-reflexive "Scream" by two years. In his new nightmare, Craven himself can't escape his most (in)famous creation. Sometimes movies, like monsters, take on lives of their own.

16 **STILL FROM "THE EXORCIST" (1973)** Regan MacNeil (Linda Blair), Father Merrin (Max von Sydow), and Father Damien Karras (Jason Miller) in the midst of the exorcism. Director William Friedkin maintained such a gritty sense of reality that the audience never questioned the fantastic events.

17 **STILL FROM "CANDYMAN" (1992)** The Candyman (Tony Todd) and Helen Lyle (Virginia Madsen). The black movie monster is still surprisingly rare, even when his motive is avenging racial injustice.

18 **STILL FROM "HELLBOUND: HELLRAISER II" (1988)** Dr. Philip Channard (Kenneth Cranham) and Julia Cotton (Claire Higgins) seal it with a kiss. Tony Randel's sequel to Clive Barker's wholly original splatterpunk hit delved further into Barker's mythos and continued to play on the extreme marriage of mortality, fear, and desire.

"Oh, no tears please.
It's a waste of good suffering."

Pinhead, Hellraiser (1987)

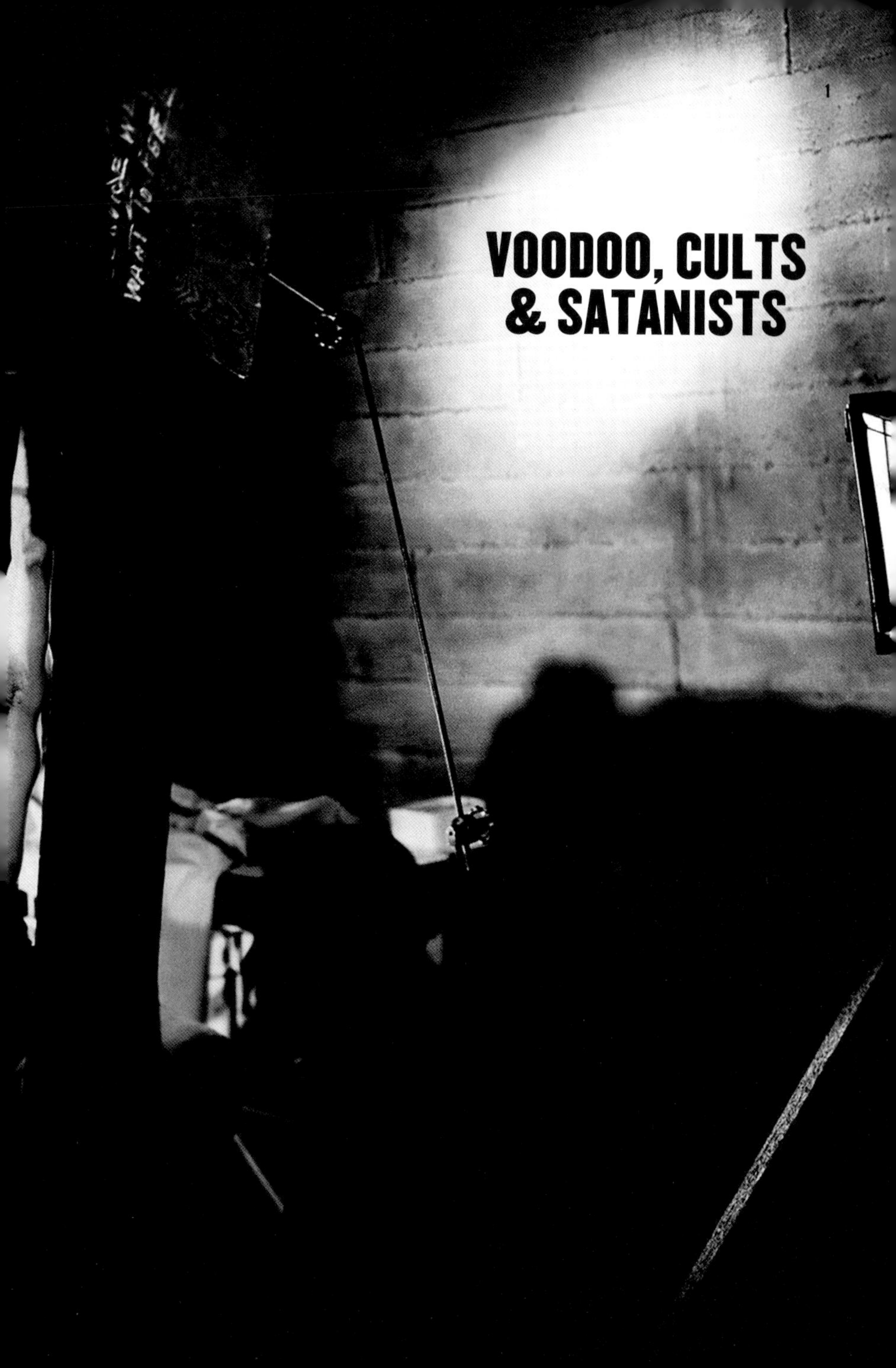

1

VOODOO, CULTS & SATANISTS

2

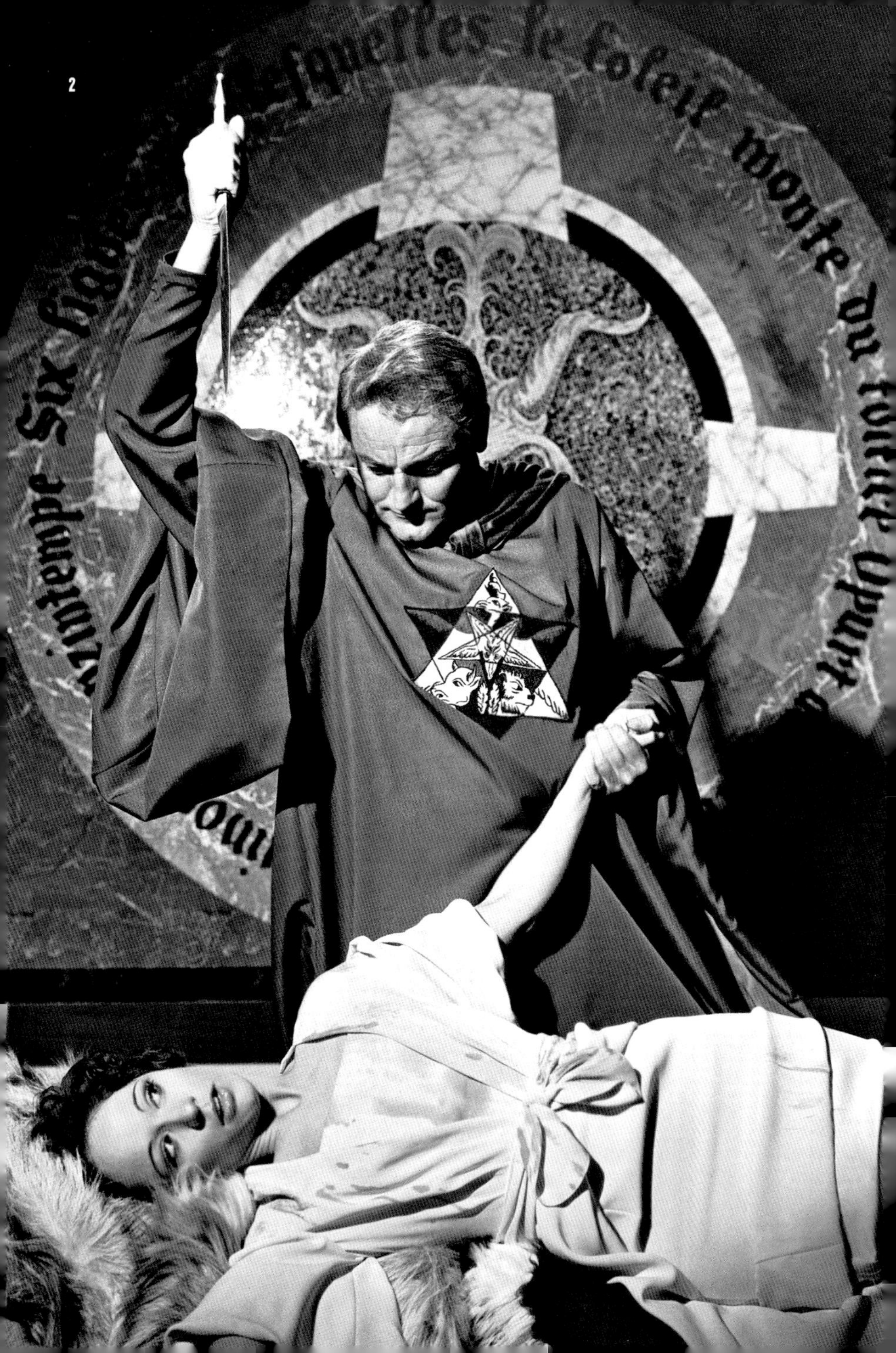

PART EIGHT

Voodoo, Cults & Satanists

Society, at its best, is a place of comfort and safety—a place of shared values. The society we keep puts us on the inside, snug in our shared beliefs, while the rest of the world remains shunned, forgotten, or ignored. Many great horror pictures are built on the fear generated when lead characters find themselves no longer in a majority, looking out at the kooks and the fringe dwellers. Instead, they're the ones who are isolated. Suddenly they become "the other," whose beliefs and values are all wrong. And it's the crazies, the lunatic fringe, who hold sway.

Though the seminal *Häxan: Witchcraft through the Ages* (1922) is a documentary-style overview, most of these films are contemporary stories, with modern, conscientious protagonists drawn into an alternative system that directly threatens both their beliefs and their bodies. Val Lewton and Mark Robson's *The Seventh Victim* (1943) sees sisters Jacqueline and Mary Gibson (Jean Brooks and Kim Hunter) tangle with a cult of Greenwich Village satanists; dare-devil auto enthusiasts are chased nearly to hell and back in *Race with the Devil* (1975); and cynical Dean Corso (Johnny Depp) thinks he's seen it all until he immerses himself in a mysterious book from the 17th century, from which Roman Polanski's movie *The Ninth Gate* (1989) lends its name. In two of the finest of these films, Polanski's *Rosemary's Baby* (1968) and Robin Hardy's *The Wicker Man* (1973; remade 2006), it is religious beliefs (and with them all of society's mores and norms) that come into opposition. In the better-known *Rosemary's Baby,* innocent young wife Mia Farrow is inexorably sucked into a coven, a group of satanists whose faith and efforts are seen in the end to be completely justified. These outsiders, it turns out, are really in the right. Such clear closure is denied in screenwriter Anthony Shaffer and director Robin Hardy's *The Wicker Man.*

This extraordinary film, as much a study of the structure of horror and detective stories as it is a horror-detective picture, pits a devout Catholic police sergeant—

"It has often been said, that it is not death, but dying, which is terrible." *Henry Fielding*

a modern man with ancient ideals—against the imagination and passion of an island society of pagans. Sergeant Howie (Edward Woodward) flies himself to remote Summerisle to investigate the possible disappearance and murder of a young schoolgirl. Before leaving the mainland, he is established as a chaste martinet, a stickler for the rules and regulations of the society he is sworn to police. A society still governed by the Catholic rule of law.

On the island everyone seems to lie and obfuscate to the officer. Even the girl's mother and sister seem prepared to tell him half truths regarding her whereabouts and even whether or not she is still alive. At the local inn where Howie must spend the night, Willow (Britt Ekland) and the rest of the island's young adults drink, sing, and engage in public and wonderfully shameless

displays of affection and procreation. She even tries her best to seduce Howie, but he passes the night with his morality intact. His investigation leads him to the missing girl's teacher, her classmates, her doctor, and Christopher Lee as the local noble... everyone here, it seems, is a happily practicing pagan, quite prepared to antagonize the sergeant and lead him astray. Finally, Howie determines that a virgin sacrifice is in the planning, and that the missing girl is not in fact dead yet, but will be used in the ceremony. The sergeant's ire rises with his sexual, intellectual, and spiritual frustration, and these aspects drive him forward blindly to save the girl and defeat the non-believers, but instead only wind up pushing him straight into the arms of his own demise. The ceremonial sacrifice will

1 ON THE SET OF "THE BLACK CAT" (1934) Satanist Boris Karloff is flayed. This wild, Nazi-tinged horror melodrama was directed by Murnau apprentice Edgar G. Ulmer. The picture welds a hypnotic visual power, combining Hollywood Art Nouveau with deep German Expressionism.

2 STILL FROM "THE DEVIL RIDES OUT" (1968) Mocata (Charles Gray) wants to sacrifice Tanith Carlisle (Nike Arrighi). What are we willing to do for power?

3 STILL FROM "WHITE ZOMBIE" (1932) Madeleine Short Parker (Madge Bellamy) under the power of "Murder" Legendre (Bela Lugosi). The film's title implies, of course, that zombies are *usually* black.

4 STILL FROM "I WALKED WITH A ZOMBIE" (1943) Jessica Holland (Christine Gordon) and Betsy Connell (Frances Dee) find Carrefour (Darby Jones) in Jacques Tourneur's atmospheric thriller from producer Val Lewton. Jessica is the zombie Betsy walked with.

5 STILL FROM "SUGAR HILL" (1974) Slaves dead for over a century rise up to kill white criminals. A missed opportunity from American International Pictures, whose other blaxploitation horrors included *Blacula* (1972), *Abby* (1974), and *J. D.'s Revenge* (1976).

1853
SLAVE

6 STILL FROM "THE 7TH VICTIM" (1943) Jacqueline Gibson (Jean Brooks) finds out the hard way that becoming involved with a satanist cult maybe isn't such a hot idea. Having discussed the cult with her therapist, she earns a death sentence and must hide out for fear of being killed.

7 STILL FROM "THE DEVIL RIDES OUT"(1968) Duc de Richleau (Christopher Lee, left) and guests summon God's Fallen Angel.

NOMINE PA + TRIS
ET FI + LII ET

7

RITUS + SANCTI +
EL + ELOHYM + SOTHER + EMMANUEL + SABAOTH
GLA + TETRAGRAMMAT

8

9

8 STILL FROM "THE WICKER MAN" (1973) Willow (Britt Ekland) dances and sings to the devout Sergeant Howie (Edward Woodward), who lies tormented on the other side of the wall. Nevertheless, her attempted seduction doesn't work.

9 STILL FROM "THE WICKER MAN" (1973) Sergeant Howie prays for both strength and answers. Like the heroes of so many horror films, his search for truth and his belief in right lead to his downfall. The bars of the bed echo the bars of the Wicker Man.

10 STILL FROM "THE WICKER MAN" (1973) Howie inside the Wicker Man. A fool brought to this place willingly, he becomes a sacrifice for the island's religion… and a martyr for his own.

11 STILL FROM "THE WICKER MAN" (1973) Howie makes a cross in the abandoned churchyard. He sees behind him not a beautiful Madonna and Child, but a filthy pagan desecrating once-hallowed ground.

be of him. His laws, his God, have no dominion on the island. And rather than returning to the mainland a righteous savior, he dies a martyred virgin, a man whose refusal to experience anything outside his own formal code stops him from seeing the truth right before his eyes.

Though the moment Howie realizes the depth of his deception is supremely horrific, *The Wicker Man* is neither gory nor even particularly frightening. It is instead an intellectually dazzling thriller, brilliantly structured by Anthony Shaffer, whose *Sleuth* had been such a hit the year before. And lending the picture a unique strangeness, Shaffer's scrupulous research and deft plotting are counterbalanced by Hardy's direction. Shooting on location and using an unusual amount of song, dance, and ritual, he evokes an extraordinary sense of time, place, and authenticity, creating a pagan society alive and well in the here and now, and a thriller of unusual look and dimension.

Along with religion, two other rich veins for cinematic horror to drink from are class and race in society. Voodoo pictures like Lewton and Jacques Tourneur's *I Walked with a Zombie* (1943) often detail the miseries conjured by "black" magic—powerful knowledge stored away in the hearts and minds of slaves brought over from Africa. Landed Europeans surrounded by acres of unhappy Africans makes for a pretty juicy setup, and when voodoo is used to flip the power structure, repressed sex and vio-

12 STILL FROM "THE WICKER MAN" (1973) "Reproduction without sexual union." These women do a fertility dance, much to Howie's consternation. Horror, like beauty, is in the eye of the beholder.

13 ON THE SET OF "THE WICKER MAN" (1973) Edward Woodward and Christopher Lee listen to director Robin Hardy explain a key scene that was cut from the film.

14 ON THE SET OF "THE WICKER MAN" (1973) The giant cue cards for everybody to sing when the Wicker Man and its contents burn.

EVERYONE
MIGHTY GOD OF THE SUN, ACCEPT
OUR SACRIFICE AND BE APPEASED.
BOUNTIFUL GODDESS OF
OUR ORCHARDS, ACCEPT OUR
ACRIFICE AND MAKE OUR BLOSSOMS
RUIT

14

lence walk the fields at night. The allure of the "forbidden" other race becomes literally magical and so blameless, and all sorts of violent urges become understandable and even permitted when caused by the dark arts rather than an oppressive and unjust society. These films, including *White Zombie* (1932), *Sugar Hill* (1974), and *The Believers* (1987), are some of cinema's most titillating and damning indictments of our colonial past.

Another film that takes on class as a fount for horror, Brian Yuzna's *Society* (1989), features a privileged young man who finds himself involved with an elite group that he is desperate to become a part of. Too late he learns that the rich truly are different, and that high society is a gooey species unto itself. *Society* says it is impossible to join them, and not surprisingly reveals that much of what is wrong with the world today derives from the fact that the inherently corrupt, disgusting, incestuous, and evil are lording it over the rest of us.

More literal wrangling between the believers in God and the Devil include *The Omen* (1976; sequelized 1978, 1981; remade 2006) and *The Devil Rides Out* (1968), both of which followed *Rosemary's Baby* and *The Exorcist* along the track of supporting the existence of the Horned One, while offering little or no evidence of the existence of God. This is, of course, what horror fans want—the fun stuff. Isn't it scarier to find out that "they" were right all along, and that everything you (and your society) hold dear is totally wrong?

"Taken in their original context—the Hollywood of the early forties—the movies of Val Lewton stand out as chamber music against the seedy bombast of the claw-and-fang epics of the day."

Carlos Clarens

15 STILL FROM "CHILDREN OF THE CORN" (1984) In Stephen King's H. P. Lovecraft-inspired tale, an underage cult sacrifices adults to an ancient evil.

16 STILL FROM "SUSPIRIA" (1977) The conclusion of another spectacular horror set piece in Dario Argento's terrifyingly surreal masterpiece.

17 STILL FROM "SUSPIRIA" (1977) American dance student Suzy Bannion (Jessica Harper) takes out a witch. Argento, along with sexualist Tinto Brass and others, created a new "cinema of stimulation" in the early 1970s. These "eurotrash" pictures, dedicated to design and sensuality but set among the ancient architectural splendors of Italy, physicalized the tension felt by so much of Europe's youth at the time—caught between the weight of history and the pull of "the now."

18–21 STILLS FROM "DARK SOCIETY" (1989) Makeup artist Screaming Mad George brought to life director Brian Yuzna's satiric view of the body politic—life really is different among the very rich.

16
17

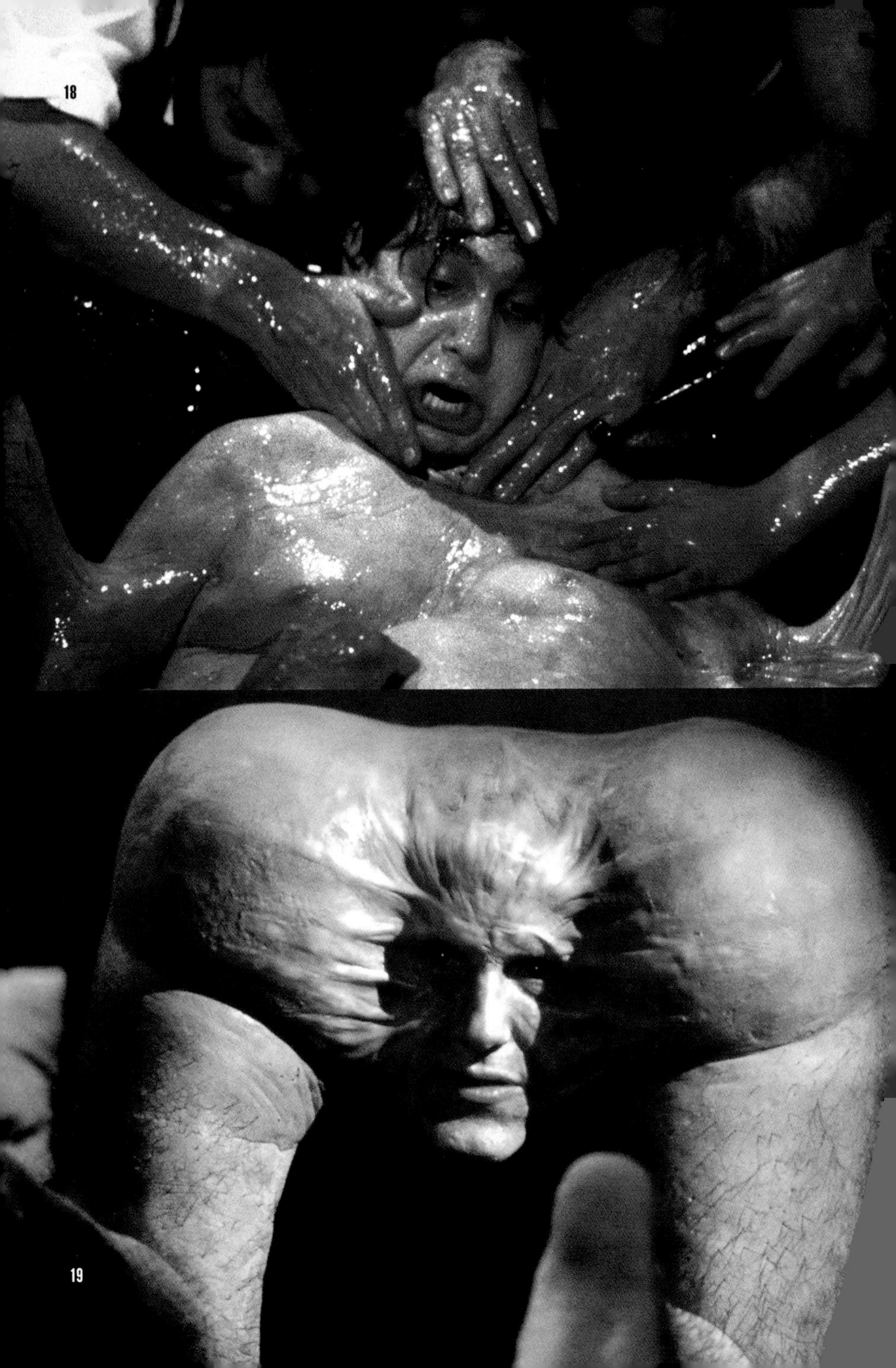
18
19

20

1

VAMPIRES & WEREWOLVES

2

PART NINE

Vampires & Werewolves

In Europe, the evil beasts of legend were the night dwellers of forest and mountain: the bats and rats and wolves. And from the many cautionary tales and myths surrounding them, two cinematic beasts have sprung: the vampire and the werewolf. Both appeal directly to our nocturnal urges for sexual power and physical dominance. Both frighten with their implications of our frailties. Anyone can become a vampire or a werewolf—it only takes one false move in the night for you to wind up on the dark side.

Born from the pen of Irish novelist Bram Stoker in 1897, only two years after movies themselves were introduced to the English isles, no other character, villainous or otherwise, has enjoyed such a long life on film as Dracula. And every subsequent vampire lives and dies in his shadow because Stoker, after years researching the folklore of Eastern Europe, created an extraordinary character and a sexy, exciting story that overflows with universal themes.

First produced on film as *Nosferatu* in 1922 by Germany's great F.W. Murnau, the count was renamed Orlok in a successful bid to avoid paying royalties to the Stoker estate. It was a huge hit and star Max Schreck's ratty/batty makeup has become almost as iconic as Bela Lugosi's widow's peak and cape. *Nosferatu* was a word Stoker himself had used to describe the undead, and Schreck and Murnau's collaboration—turning the count into a figure of pure evil and corruption—while poetic and stirring, was also actively horrific, pushing audiences harder than they had ever been pushed before.

Soon after *Nosferatu*, *Dracula* became a stage success, first in the West End and then on Broadway. Hamilton Dean and John Balderson's play streamlined and simplified the book's action, and Universal bought it as a Lon Chaney vehicle to be directed by Chaney's frequent collaborator, Tod Browning. But when "The Man of a Thousand Faces" died tragically of throat cancer in 1930 at the age of 47, the role was given to the relatively unknown Bela Lugosi—a star in his native Hungary who had played the count to great acclaim on Broadway. He was an overnight sensation. No actor has ever been so clearly associated with a role as Lugosi is with Dracula.

The picture itself is in the style of the day: whip-fast, barely pausing for motive or method. All the violence is offscreen, as are all of the count's transitions from man to bat and man to wolf, forcing the audience to fill in the blanks. And it is here that the picture holds much of its power, because so much is suggested that each audience member creates his or her own version of the film, with as much violence and eroticism as her or his imagination provides.

After 1931, Universal wasn't able to parlay its *Dracula* success into anything significant. Lugosi's career slid into a drug-addicted tailspin, and the world's most famous villain remained in the cinematic shadows for much of the 1930s, 1940s, and 1950s. Whether it was an overdose of Eastern European villains in the news, or the advent of nuclear weapons and fresher space-aged horrors, it took until 1958 for Dracula to get a full-blooded resurrection. England's Hammer Studios had enjoyed success with *The Curse of Frankenstein* in 1957, and the studio took that film's two stars and the next year delivered *Horror of Dracula* to the world. Christopher Lee kept the tragedy to a minimum as the count, but his fierce and desperate desire for blood made him a sexy, truly scary Prince of Darkness.

Of course, it's the various rich themes of the story that have sustained and nourished Dracula's long cinematic life. Some of them, like xenophobia, the inherent

3

1 STILL FROM "NOSFERATU, PHANTOM DER NACHT" (1979) Count Dracula (Klaus Kinski) and Lucy Harker (Isabelle Adjani) in Werner Herzog's atmospheric color remake.

2 STILL FROM "BRAM STOKER'S DRACULA" (1992) Dracula (Gary Oldman) and his brides (Michaela Bercu, Florina Kendrick, Monica Bellucci). Francis Ford Coppola's Gustav Klimt-inspired Gothic romance had Dracula as kind of rock star, liberating repressed London society. Coppola's only other horror film is the Roger Corman-produced *Dementia 13* (1963).

3 STILL FROM "NOSFERATU" (1922) Count Orlok (Max Schreck) looks like both rat and bat in F. W. Murnau's adaptation. A horror-comedy-biopic about the making of Nosferatu, E. Elias Merhige's *Shadow of the Vampire* (2000) posits that the unlikely named Schreck (German for "fright" or "terror") really was a vampire found by Murnau for his film.

corruption of the noble class, and the battles waged by science and Christianity against the darkness of superstition, are always accessible for audiences. So, too, the forbidden invasion of a lady's chamber and the bloody penetration of her virginal flesh always make for highly charged eroticism. And as times have changed, the relative importance of each of these themes and elements has shifted; as social mores relaxed, the sexual undertones became more overt, the bloody violence more horrific. In *Andy Warhol's Dracula* (1974), the poor count is constantly vomiting blood as the "virgins" he sucks off all turn out to be paying mere lip service to their chastity. And as Freud's theories have taken hold of popular consciousness, Dracula's condition has taken on tragic overtones: instead of a foreign evil come to plunder and desecrate Christian virgins and society, he's become a lonely man, consigned to an eternity of murder and moonlight.

"Listen to them—children of the night! What music they make!"

Count Dracula, Dracula (1931)

During the 1970s, Paul Morrissey directed the Andy Warhol version in 1974 and Werner Herzog beautifully remade *Nosferatu* in 1979, with the ravishing Isabelle Adjani and the nauseating and pathetic Klaus Kinski. Both these films come close to the transgressive extremes of the best in horror cinema. And, while Tony Scott's *The Hunger* (1983) is all surface and flesh, Kathryn Bigelow's *Near Dark* (1987) has became a cult favorite with its outlaw pack of night prowlers. A number of indie allegories made their marks, including George A. Romero's wonderful *Martin* (1977) and the heroin-chic trio *Nadja* (1994), *The Addiction* (1995), and *Habit* (1997). The long-delayed film version of Anne Rice's *Interview with the Vampire* (1994) finally arrived, playing like a Gothic-romance version of the Dracula story, renaming the character Lestat. Much more satisfying, though somewhat strained, is Francis Ford Coppola's painterly *Bram Stoker's Dracula* (1992), with Gary Oldman's count promising sex and drugs and the era's equivalent of rock 'n' roll. This sumptuous studio picture ambitiously ties vampirism to art and love, implying that these too are eternal elements that can liberate any human, once bitten.

Like all great horror characters, Dracula acts out our darkest desires, while (uniquely) also embodying so much that we actually do desire in a man. He is noble, exotic,

4 STILL FROM "VAMPYR" (1932) The most nightmarish sequence in a movie often compared to a nightmare: Carl Theodor Dreyer's camera gives us a disturbing, drawn-out point-of-view shot of Allan Grey (Julian West) inside a coffin being carried away and buried.

5 STILL FROM "VAMPYR" (1932) Skeletal remains. Though inescapably terrifying in its dreamlike aesthetics, the film is still pious in its reverent use of religious, symbolic, and literary imagery.

6 PUBLICITY STILL FROM "DRACULA" (1931) Count Dracula (Bela Lugosi) and Lucy Weston (Frances Dade) in the classic horror pose promising both sex and death.

6

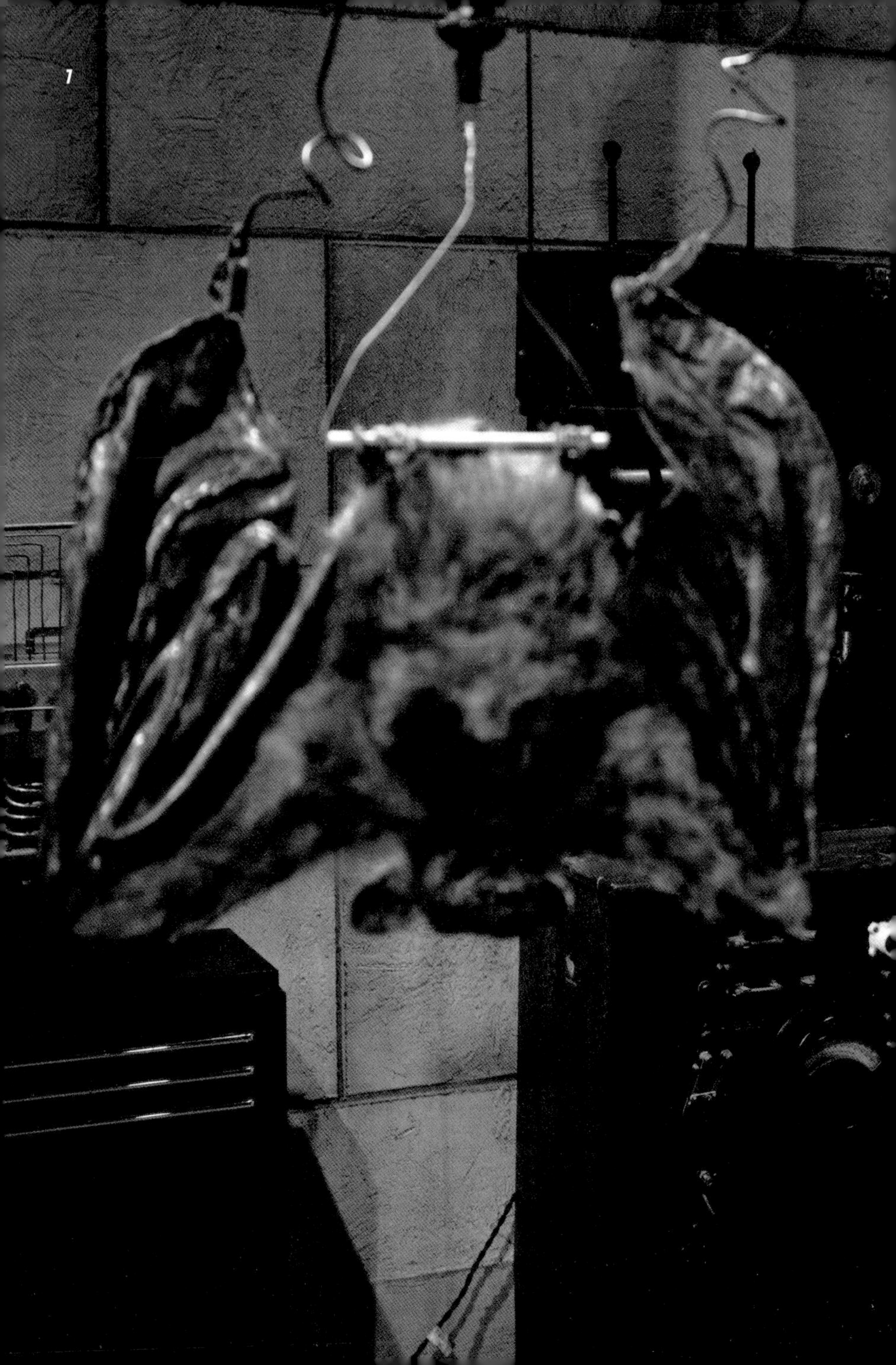
1

experienced, wealthy, and brilliant. Tortured, vulnerable, uncanny. Romantic. A character at once unnaturally base and exquisitely refined.

That refinement is exactly what is lacking from the werewolf, and that is why werewolf cinema is simpler, at once more literal and more visceral. Universal tried to tackle the beast first with the too-dry *Werewolf of London* (1935), staring Henry Hull as a Jekyll-like doctor with a Hydesque problem. Six years later, the studio created a more successful story line with *The Wolf Man*, putting Lon Chaney Jr. into six hours of yak-hair makeup and surrounding him with solid support from Bela Lugosi and Claude Rains. As with many of these stories, this is ultimately about the cycle of violence: An innocent is set upon by a "monster," and the attack transforms him into a monster himself. Chaney, as Lawrence Talbot, plays the part beautifully—as a big, hapless kid, ineffectual, almost effeminate, truly an innocent violated and taken forcibly to the dark side. We watch his genuine torment as he struggles to lift the burden of his trauma even as he feels the drawing power of the new beast inside him. One later picture, the Spanish *Legend of the Wolf Woman* (*La lupa mannara*, 1976), took this notion of rape as the genesis for monstrous transformation quite literally. Hammer also

7 STILL FROM "THE DEVIL BAT" (1940) Dr. Paul Carruthers (Bela Lugosi) enjoys Mary Heath's (Suzanne Kaaren) reaction to his beloved bloodsucker. His giant bats have been trained to attack people wearing a specific perfume!

8 STILL FROM "HORROR OF DRACULA" (1958) Count Dracula (Christopher Lee) and his prey in the first of the Hammer series, which provided audiences more heaving bosoms and red blood than Universal ever could.

9 STILL FROM "BRAM STOKER'S DRACULA" (1992) Lucy Westenra (Sadie Frost) encounters Dracula (Gary Oldman) in wolf/bat form—the animal drive toward sex and death.

based their film *The Curse of the Werewolf* (1961) on a rape, but here the cycle is passed from rapist to werewolf/bastard son—as if actualizing the sins of the father.

The year 1952 saw the extraordinary Finnish female lycanthrope tale *White Reindeer* (*Valkoinen peura*), and the 1970s saw Spanish writer-director-star Paul Naschy's cycle of Waldemar Daninsky movies—pictures whose sideburns and fuzzy flocked wallpaper made them period pieces within weeks of their completion. Other titles include *Werewolves on Wheels* (1971), *The Werewolf of Washington* (1973), and *The Beast Must Die* (1974), a whodunit notable for its black werewolf and an early appearance by Michael Gambon. Joe Dante's *The Howling* and John Landis's *An American Werewolf in London* (both 1981) each made loving references to werewolf pictures past, while utilizing the newest shock effects and liberal helpings of nudity and gore. *The Howling* referenced the "gift" that separates us from other animals—that is, our ability to embody *both* bestiality and civilization. And Landis, hot off the comedy *Animal House* (1978), made the "innocents abroad" picture he'd dreamt of since the late 1960s; *An American Werewolf in London* became

10 STILL FROM "THE VAMPIRE LOVERS" (1970) General von Spielsdorf (Peter Cushing) beheads Mircalla Karnstein (Ingrid Pitt) in Hammer's lesbian-themed thriller based on Sheridan Le Fanu's novella *Carmilla.* It was quickly followed by the even more explicit *Lust for a Vampire* (1971) and *Twins of Evil* (1972).

11 STILL FROM "NEAR DARK" (1987) Sunlight does the trick to combustible "vampire" patriarch Jesse Hooker (Lance Henriksen).

12 STILL FROM "LAKE OF DRACULA" (1971) A stake through the heart is enough to finish off this Japanese version of the Count.

13
14

13 STILL FROM "WEREWOLF OF LONDON" (1935) Dr. Yogami (Warner Oland) battles the lycanthrope Dr. Wilfred Glendon (Henry Hull) in Universal's first attempt at the werewolf myth. Jack Pierce, of course, did the makeup.

14 STILL FROM "WEREWOLF OF LONDON" (1935) Dr. Glendon tries to work out a solution to his problem in this Jekyll & Hyde-inspired take on the monster.

15 STILL FROM "THE WOLF MAN" (1941) Lawrence Talbot (Lon Chaney, here dropping the "Jr." for the first time) and Gwen Conliffe (Evelyn Ankers) on the moors in Universal's more successful lycanthrope tale. Jack Pierce perfected the look he started in the 1935 film. Although Chaney had a long career in film and television, he never fully emerged from his father's shadow.

16 STILL FROM "THE WOLF MAN" (1941) Talbot recovers from a bad night with the help of Gypsy fortuneteller Maleva (Maria Ouspenskaya), whose son Bela (Bela Lugosi) has turned him into a werewolf.

a surprise hit and, like *The Howling*, was lavished with humor, in-jokes, and amazing state-of-the-art makeup effects. *Wolfen* (1981) and *Wolf* (1994) both had big budgets but lacked bite, while *Ginger Snaps* (2000), *Dog Soldiers* (2002), *Underworld* (2003), and *Underworld: Evolution* (2006) were closer in spirit to B movies and gave audiences much more to sink their teeth into.

"Beware the moon, lads."

Chess Player, An American Werewolf in London (1981)

Werewolves and vampires will continue to haunt our theaters, taking us on the metaphoric journey from day to night, from innocence to experience. As long as there are parties and sex and drugs and bad men who smile with their teeth, these movies will continue to seduce us, terrify us, and mirror the tragic results of lives dissipated in darkness.

17 STILL FROM "THE CURSE OF THE WEREWOLF" (1961) Leon Corledo (the always-virile Oliver Reed) in a moment of transition. Rape and bastardy played significant roles in Hammer's more lurid take on the story.

18 STILL FROM "AN AMERICAN WEREWOLF IN LONDON" (1981) David Kessler (David Naughton) starts to change. John Landis's lycanthrope tale combined gore, comedy, suspense, and amazing makeup by Rick Baker.

19
20

21

19 ON THE SET OF "THE HOWLING" (1981) Working again with a John Sayles script, director Joe Dante (left) created another biting horror tale, this time skewering California self-help fads. Rob Bottin (right), who had studied under Rick Baker, helped revolutionize special effects makeup in the 1980s.

20 STILL FROM "THE HOWLING" (1981) Dante called on stop-motion artist Dave Allen to create these full-body werewolves for the long shots.

21 STILL FROM "LA LUPA MANNARA" (1976) Daniella Neseri (Annik Borel) was raped as a girl, but her anger helps her transform into an avenging werewolf. The Italian producers claimed it was based on a true story.

THE MONSTROUS-FEMININE

PART TEN

The Monstrous-Feminine

Men obsessed with sex and death are the primary makers of horror movies. So, the presence of women at the heroic center of so many of these films shouldn't surprise anyone; women seem more vulnerable and are better looking to the male audience. Having a young woman threatened and either saved by the hero (old-fashioned) or saved by her own resourcefulness (new-fashioned) makes a lot of sense. Men kill women, men watch women, men watch men try to kill women. But if women are the heroes—or, at least, the protagonists—of many of these movies, why are they so rarely flipped and portrayed as straight-up murder machines the way so many male characters are? Is it simply because (in reality) female killers are so rare? Aileen Wuornos was America's most famous modern murderess, and she was so unusual that her life was deemed worthy of a sympathetic (non-horror) film biography, *Monster* (2003), along with a pair of documentaries by Nick Broomfield (1992, 2003). Women are widely held to be more feeling, more expressive, and simply less violent than men. And so any story wherein a woman would be driven to murder becomes a story about justification, motivation, desperation, and fury unleashed. The roots of the horror are always explored, and the "why" of such anomalous behavior is always asked. Why is she killing? How does this happen?

These stories fall into three groups: the woman scorned, the witch, and, most unusually, the pure evil bitch.

"Hell hath no fury…" goes the saying, and in the movies women get scorned in all sorts of profound ways. Pictures like *What Ever Happened to Baby Jane?* (1962) and *Strait-Jacket* (1964), with their famous fallen stars Bette Davis and Joan Crawford, portray the scorn the world heaps on ladies of a certain age whom life and opportunity has passed by. Inspired by Billy Wilder's *Sunset Blvd.* (1950) with Gloria Swanson, this first real cycle of female-driven horror pictures, known as "Grand Dame Guignol," ran through the 1960s and includes *Hush… Hush, Sweet Charlotte* (1964), with Davis and Olivia de Havilland; *The Nanny* (1965), with Davis once again; *Whoever Slew Auntie Roo?* (1971), with Shelley Winters; and *What's the Matter with Helen?* (1971), with Winters and Debbie Reynolds. In them all, wonderful older actresses portray heroes and grotesques—not witches but hags, whose lost sexual appeal adds insult to the injury of their lost sexual lives. These are hurt and angry ladies who must dredge up their own sordid youths before they can move on to whatever futures await them. For the killers, the future is death—their pasts are finally catching up with them. For the older female heroes, there is redemption or catharsis. Just as these films gave the actresses in question a second chance in Hollywood, the surviving characters, having plumbed the past, earn a second chance at peaceful endings.

"One might say that the true subject of the horror genre is the struggle for recognition of all that our civilization represses and oppresses." *Robin Wood*

While the "Grand Dame Guignol" had one foot firmly planted in old Hollywood, another subgenre stands shakily on the bloodied fields of women's liberation and sexual revolution. *Play Misty for Me* (1971) and *Fatal Attraction* (1986) are both tales of women betrayed by the double standards of the times. In *Play Misty for Me*, Evelyn (Jessica Walter) sleeps with a disc jockey played by Clint Eastwood (making his directorial debut), while in *Fatal Attraction*, Alex Forrest (Glenn Close) has a one-night stand with married Dan Gallagher (Michael Douglas). The women are very much of their time, strong and independent, highly sexual beings free to do with and enjoy their bodies and their adulthoods as they please. But when the men they've chosen find these ladies too clingy, too needy, and essentially too traditional in their wants, they reject the women, who are way too emotionally involved to go gently into the night. But Evelyn and Alex don't go on rampages when they are wronged; they focus solely and (in their eyes) with great justification on the men who have scorned them. Yes, they're crazy, but they don't "start it." These are two of the rare but famous cautionary tales for men, so effective because the killer isn't wrong—she just sees and feels things in a way that might as well be alien. And the passion that's so exciting when expressed as love and desire is terrifying when it's turned against the man who would hurt her. They stab. They cry. They scream. They're monsters. Free love is a joke, these films say, since nothing is really free. Especially when a woman is involved, since society puts her in an impossible double bind. If she "gives it away," she's either mannish or a slut. But if she wants more than just casual sex, she's a psycho, a stalker. A venereal disease in heels.

"Words create lies. Pain can be trusted." *Asami Yamazaki, Audition (1999)*

Other films that could only exist thanks to the new permissiveness of the late 1960s and early 1970s explored the costs of the sexual revolution in far harsher and more exploitative terms. *Ms. 45* (1981), *I Spit on Your Grave* (1978), *Mother's Day* (1980), and *They Call Her One Eye* (1974) are among the more infamous of the pictures that graphically grapple with rape and revenge. In them, young beautiful women are horribly violated—literally filled with violence and desensitized with brutality. In *Ms. 45*, Thana (Zoë Tamerlis Lund) is struck dumb by the attacks. In *I Spit on Your Grave*, single writer Jennifer Hills (Camille Keaton) is brutalized by a gang rape. When she drags herself home to safety, the gang is waiting there to rape her again. The others follow the same basic story lines of rape and the revenge that "naturally" follows. But *Ms. 45*'s director, Abel Ferrara, intentionally removes his lead's "female" ability to communicate with words before letting her discover the satisfying joys of vigilantism and revenge. She, like all these blameless female characters, chooses to enter the cycle of violence. Instead of rejecting it—the classical feminine response—they embrace and accelerate it as the only viable course of action. They are allowed, even encouraged, to act as violently as those who have violated them. The playing field between the sexes

1 STILL FROM "THE WITCHES" (1990) From the book by Roald Dahl, Anjelica Huston is the Grand High Witch (aka Miss Eva Ernst) in Nicolas Roeg's wonderful and underrated horror flick for kids.

2 STILL FROM "STRAIT-JACKET" (1964) Lucy Harbin (Joan Crawford) spent 20 years in an asylum after axing her husband and his mistress to death in a crime of passion. She's out now, but will she revert to her old ways? William Castle gives tight direction from a script by the author of *Psycho*, Robert Bloch.

3 STILL FROM "ONIBABA" (1964) In the 16th century, a young widow and her mother-in-law must kill returning soldiers to survive, trading the armor for food. When the widow starts a relationship with a neighbor, the rejected mother-in-law dons a mask to frighten her off, setting in motion a horrific finale. Writer/director Kaneto Shindo deliniates how the sexuality of men and women can never be denied.

4 STILL FROM "MASK OF THE DEMON" (1960) In the opening scene, the witch Princess Asa Vajda (Barbara Steele) is put to death by her brother—a spiked mask is sledgehammered into her face. Two hundred years later, she is resurrected and wreaks revenge on her brother's descendents. This first credited feature by Mario Bava helped establish his international reputation, and made Steele into the horror queen of the 1960s.

3

4

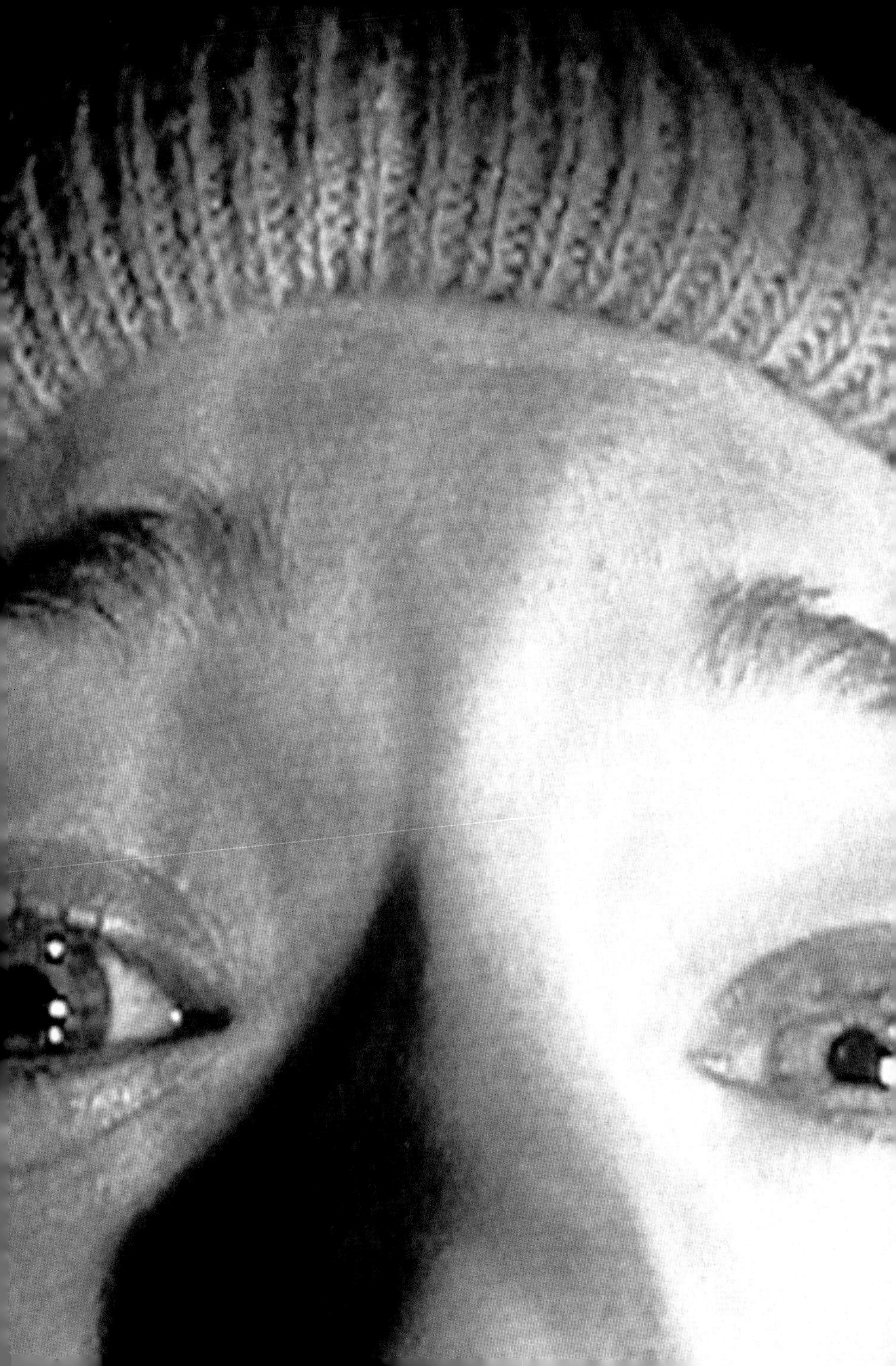

"You experience true horror in cinema when you sit in a dark room, eyes glued to the screen, and through a series of artful images have the bejesus scared out of you. When you're in that dark room it's what you don't see that truly terrifies you; it's what you imagine. The more you can connect the audience with their own dark demons, the better you've done your job." *Brian De Palma*

was getting leveled for worse as well as for better, and horror cinema has always wanted to show the dark side of such issues. But unlike many horror films, these are not "fun" pictures but grim reminders of both the permissiveness and the instability of a culture in flux. Clearly there was tremendous anger and confusion about gender roles. These films asked, "What kind of women demand to be treated like men?" and answered, "Women who get brutalized and then respond in kind."

Sisters (1973; remade 2006), Brian De Palma's breakthrough movie, was also released in the early 1970s and also falls squarely in the woman-scorned category, though its cinematic mastery and psychological complexity differentiate it from its more exploitative kin. In fact, with *Sisters*, horror cinema starts to see the changes that were overtaking American film in general at that time. De Palma's deliberate filmmaking virtuosity proved that he was at least as interested in the techniques of visual storytelling as he was in examining the mores and cultural land mines of the era. *Sisters* really was the first successful independent horror picture to presage the film-student-auteur movement that would hit Hollywood full force with *Jaws* just two years later.

One classic view of the slasher in horror is that this mute, masked murderer is simply the classic male "strong silent type" pushed to the nth degree. And in the same way, when women's uniquely "feminine" attributes are taken to imaginative extremes, here too horror happily ensues. The "seductive wiles," the "female intuition," and, most profoundly, the ability to create life within themselves all serve to make women nearly magical creatures to most men. Expand on this magical notion just a little bit further... and their powers can be truly frightening.

Witches are the most obvious magical she-monsters: shape-shifting seducers, love haters, the bane of little children and gormless woodcutters throughout history. At least one fascinating witch story takes a completely human tack. *Burn, Witch, Burn!* (aka *Night of the Eagle*, 1962), from the Fritz Leiber Jr. novel *Conjure Wife*, tells the story of Tansy Taylor (Janet Blair), a good woman who does what she can to protect her husband from the politics and maneuverings surrounding his position as a college professor. But it's the fact that she's a witch, and that the college (and presumably the world) is filled with magical wives all doing the same things everywhere, that makes the picture so fascinating. Her husband, typically capable, rational, and strong, denies the existence of magic and forbids her activities. Tragedy ensues, the message being that of course there is magic in the world—the existence of women themselves is the proof.

5 STILL FROM "THE BLAIR WITCH PROJECT" (1999) The witch was never seen, but Heather Donahue's terror was real. Using the "fact" that narrative cinema is never shot with consumer-grade digital handicams, directors Daniel Myrick and Eduardo Sánchez played on expectations and conventions to scare the shit out of audiences worldwide.

6 STILL FROM "BURN, WITCH, BURN!" (1962) Tansy Taylor (Janet Blair) performs her sorcery while husband Norman (Peter Wyngarde) sleeps. Tansy is a good witch protecting her man and his cushy university post, but when he finds out what she's up to, the ardent non-believer refuses her assistance, announcing there is no magic in the world.

7 STILL FROM "WHAT EVER HAPPENED TO BABY JANE?" (1962) Bette Davis as Joan Crawford's (justifiably) miserable sister.

6

Many movie witches are pure evil, creatures without soul or conscience. Anjelica Huston's Naziesque Grand High Witch in Nicolas Roeg's colorful adaptation of Roald Dahl's *The Witches* (1990) is actually a monster in human disguise. Barbara Steele's vampiric sorceress in Mario Bava's atmospheric *Mask of the Demon* seems to have no humanity in her at all—returning 200 years after her spectacular death to wreak havoc on the family of her accursed brother. And the groundbreaking *The Blair Witch Project* (1999) creates an unseen wraith named Elly Kedward whose only motive seems to be inflicting as much pain and terror as possible... even from beyond the grave.

A few other films feature women of pure evil who are not magical. *The Bad Seed* (1956) reveals that an obnoxiously "perfect" little suburban girl, bright as a button and impeccably turned out, is in fact a soulless sociopath, while both *Misery* (1990) and *Audition* (1999) feature quiet little ladies who are both so sick and sadistic they join the psychopathologic pantheon.

But the two greatest films of the monstrous feminine feature ladies who are magical indeed; not witches, but hardly "normal." In Brian De Palma's *Carrie* (1976), "woman's intuition" becomes telekinetic genius, and in David Cronenberg's *The Brood* (1979), the ability to procreate is taken to a bizarre and fantastic realm of horror.

De Palma's technical brilliance and sensitive direction of stars Margot Kidder and Jennifer Salt in *Sisters* helped earn him the job of bringing Stephen King's first novel, *Carrie*, to the screen. It's the story of a shy and sheltered high-school girl's painful coming of age. What sets Carrie White (played perfectly by Sissy Spacek in the film) apart from so many other awkward teens who finally reach puberty is that this milestone also brings on an amazing telekinetic ability—an ability that appears with her first menstrual blood. In the simplest, most graphic terms, King and De Palma empower her while taking her innocence away. And we watch her painful struggle, hoping she'll use her newly acquired gifts and break away from her mother and the victim role she's been carrying with her for her whole life. She's an outsider, an outcast, and it's the simple delineation of her hopes, fears, and finally crushing defeat and revenge that makes *Carrie* so memorable. It's everyone's high-school experience turned up to ten, emotional, thrilling, and filmed with startling ambition by a director known for his technical mastery but still underappreciated for his emotional empathy and understanding. It was a justifiable smash.

Made three years after *Carrie*, *The Brood* features a more mature, but no less troubled, lead character. Nola Carveth (Samantha Eggar) is a beautiful woman in the throes of a custody battle with her handsome husband, Frank (Art Hindle), over their young daughter, Candice (Cindy Hinds). But Nola is also in therapy with the brilliant Dr. Hal Raglan (Oliver Reed) at his Somafree Institute of Psychoplasmics, a medical campus where the good doctor keeps patients as they work with him using his landmark techniques. In Cronenberg's sly indictment of the

8–10 STILLS FROM "STRAIT-JACKET" (1964), "PLAY MISTY FOR ME" (1971), "MISERY" (1990)
Madwomen of American movies: Joan Crawford goes mad, Jessica Walter as Clint Eastwood's rejected lover, and Kathy Bates as James Caan's "number one fan."

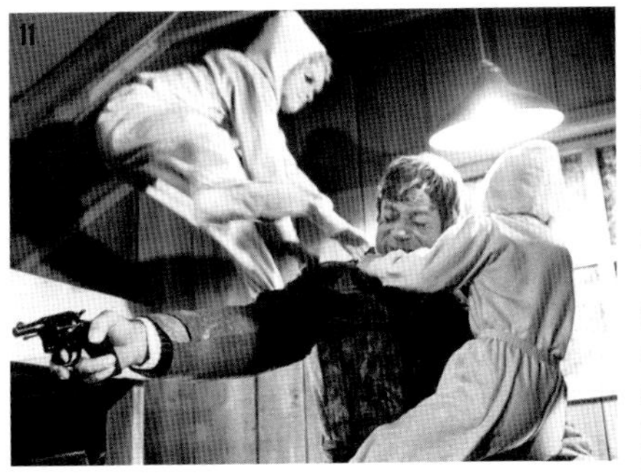

radical therapeutic systems of the day, psychoplasmics enables patients to role-play with the doctor and then physically manifest "the shape of rage" through their bodies. Bloody holes and cancerous growths are the norm, but Nola, it turns out, is special, and she is actually able to give birth to small creatures—not through uterine conception, but via a bizarre egg sac she keeps in her lap. These child-sized monsters, without speech or genitalia, are literally her anger personified, and when Nola is enraged they act out her feelings, lashing out with murderous results. Her own mother and father are killed, the young teacher of her daughter who she feels is a threat—even her daughter Candice is a possible victim.

Told from the perspective of Frank, desperate to understand what is happening to his wife and his daughter, *The Brood*'s amazing imagery and genuine pain create a truly horrific picture of a woman unable to come to terms with her wounded psyche or the roles she has assumed as an adult. Frank is unable to comprehend his wife's behavior and is justifiably terrified of the damage being done to his daughter. In the final confrontation, the pain is so great that Frank strangles Nola to death with his bare hands. It's a ferocious scene straight out of *Othello*—a man driven mad by the woman he once loved, but now hates. Only in this case, the evil Iago is Nola's own uncontrollable rage, her own female nature. And in the last shot of the picture, all of Frank's worst fears are confirmed—Candice is shown to possess the same cursed gift for manifesting the pain inside her... And we're left to wonder what will come when she hits puberty, or marries and has kids herself...

11 STILL FROM "THE BROOD" (1979)
Dr. Hal Raglan (Oliver Reed) encounters the brood. They are physical manifestations of Nola's fear and fury.

12 STILL FROM "THE BROOD" (1979)
Nola Carveth (Samantha Eggar) clutches tight her newest broodling. Cronenberg famously described the film, conceived during his divorce from his first wife, as his own version of *Kramer vs. Kramer*.

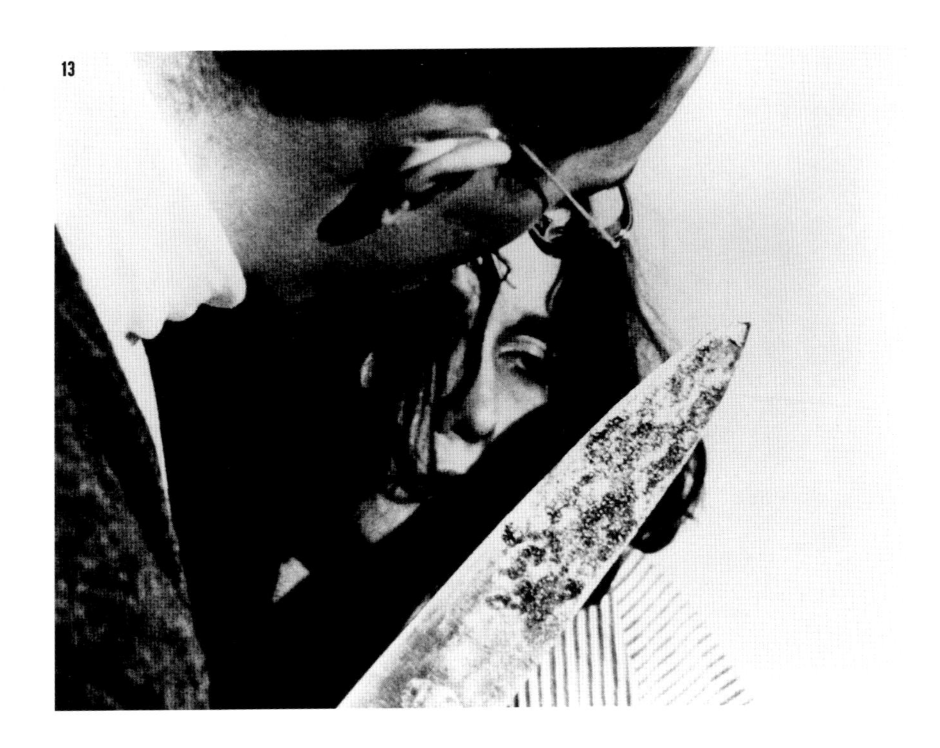

13 STILL FROM "SISTERS" (1973) Margot Kidder, as one of the sisters, undergoing a terrible abuse. Director and co-writer Brian De Palma took inspiration from both *Psycho* (1960) and *Rear Window* (1954), but wound up creating something wholly his own.

14 STILL FROM "CARRIE" (1976) After being humiliated by her classmates, Carrie uses her powers to punish them in a blood-splattered orgy of violence.

15 STILL FROM "MS. 45" (1981) The result of Thana's revenge. The extraordinary Zoë Tamerlis Lund, who also wrote 1992's *Bad Lieutenant* for director Ferrara, died at 37 after a long battle with cocaine and heroin addiction.

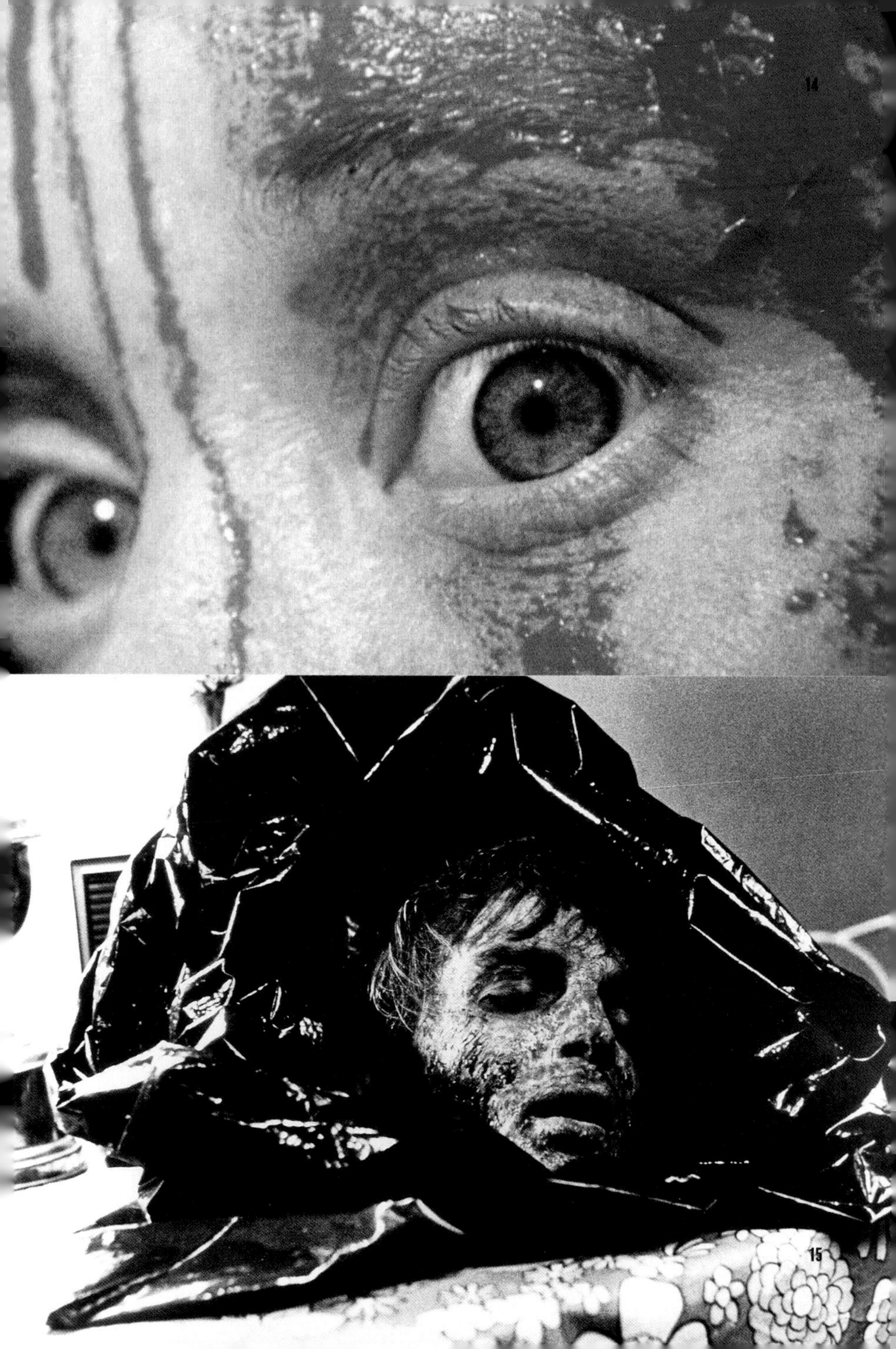
14
15

17

“*Carrie* was Steven King’s first novel —the Edgar Allan Poe of our era—and it was brilliant because it was that universal, high-school ‘I’m a freak’ experience and yet totally of its time. I mean, I don’t think there were too many menstruating-girl scenes in Gothic horror!” *Brian De Palma*

16 STILL FROM “MS. 45” (1981) Mute Thana (Zoë Tamerlis Lund) is raped twice in one night, then goes on a vengeful rampage in Abel Ferrara’s downtown exploitation twist on *Death Wish* (1974).

17 STILL FROM “CARRIE” (1976) Sensitive Carrie White (Sissy Spacek) at the prom—the calm before the storm.

18 STILL FROM “CARRIE” (1976) Director Brian De Palma, following Stephen King’s novel, forces us to both identify with Carrie’s plight and share responsibility for it.

18

TASCHEN'S TOP 50 HORROR MOVIES

THE GOLEM 1920

NOSFERATU – A SYMPHONY OF HORROR 1922

THE WITCHES / WITCHCRAFT THROUGH THE AGES 1922

THE PHANTOM OF THE OPERA 1925

FAUST 1925/26

DR. JEKYLL AND MR. HYDE 1931

DRACULA 1931

FREAKS 1932

KING KONG 1933

BRIDE OF FRANKENSTEIN 1935

THE HUNCHBACK OF NOTRE DAME 1939

THE WOLF MAN 1941

CAT PEOPLE 1942

I WALKED WITH A ZOMBIE 1943

THE THING FROM ANOTHER WORLD 1951

CREATURE FROM THE BLACK LAGOON 1954

GODZILLA 1954

INVASION OF THE BODY SNATCHERS 1956

THE INCREDIBLE SHRINKING MAN 1957

PEEPING TOM 1960

PSYCHO 1960

THE HORROR CHAMBER OF DR. FAUSTUS / EYES WITHOUT A FACE 1960

WHAT EVER HAPPENED TO BABY JANE? 1962

REPULSION 1965

NIGHT OF THE LIVING DEAD 1968

ROSEMARY'S BABY 1968

FLESH FOR FRANKENSTEIN 1973

DON'T LOOK NOW 1973

THE EXORCIST 1973

THE WICKER MAN 1973

THE TEXAS CHAIN SAW MASSACRE 1974

JAWS 1975

CARRIE 1976

SUSPIRIA 1977
DAWN OF THE DEAD 1978
HALLOWEEN 1978
ALIEN 1979
THE SHINING 1980
THE EVIL DEAD 1981
A NIGHTMARE ON ELM STREET 1984
THE COMPANY OF WOLVES 1984
THE FLY 1986
NEAR DARK 1987
MISERY 1990
DELICATESSEN 1991
THE SILENCE OF THE LAMBS 1991
SCREAM 1996
THE BLAIR WITCH PROJECT 1999
THE SIXTH SENSE 1999
THE OTHERS 2001

DER GOLEM, WIE ER IN DIE WELT KAM

THE GOLEM

1920 – GERMANY – 87 MIN.

DIRECTOR

PAUL WEGENER (1874–1948),
CARL BOESE (1887–1958)

SCREENPLAY

HENRIK GALEEN, PAUL WEGENER, based on themes taken from
GUSTAV MEYRINK'S novel of the same title

DIRECTOR OF PHOTOGRAPHY

KARL FREUND

EDITING

OSWALD HAFENRICHTER

MUSIC

HANS LANDSBERGER

PRODUCTION

PAUL DAVIDSON for PROJEKTIONS-AG UNION (PAGU)

STARRING

PAUL WEGENER (Golem), ALBERT STEINRÜCK (Rabbi Löw),
LYDA SALMONOVA (Miriam), ERNST DEUTSCH (Rabbi Famulus), HANS STURM (Rabbi Yehuda),
MAX KRONERT (Synagogue Sexton), OTTO GEBÜHR (Emperor),
DORE PAETZOLD (the Emperor's Concubine), LOTHAR MÜTHEL (Florian the Young Nobleman),
GRETA SCHRÖDER (Maid), LONI NEST (Girl), CARL EBERT (Synagogue Sexton),
FRITZ FELD (Court Jester)

DER GOLEM
WIE ER IN DIE WELT KAM
PAUL WEGENER–UFA UNION
UFA

1

"The art of bringing dead creatures back to life."

Rabbi Löw (Albert Steinrück) reads in the stars that disaster threatens his people. Indeed, his ominous presentiment is soon confirmed when the Emperor (Otto Gebühr) decrees that the Jews are to vacate their allocated district. Löw, however, remembers an ancient and powerful spell and in his laboratory he manages to bring to life a man made of clay (Paul Wegener). During the Christian Rose Festival the Rabbi begs the Emperor for mercy, presents his artificial man and also demonstrates more of his magical powers by summoning the presence of the Jews' oldest ancestors.

However, because a court jester (Fritz Feld) makes the audience laugh, the ghosts vow to take revenge and the great hall's ceiling begins to cave in ominously. Although the mute Golem and his supernatural powers save the entire court and the Jewish population are given a reprieve, new dangers threaten immediately. In defiance of the law, the Rabbi's daughter Miriam (Lyda Salmonova) has fallen in love with Florian (Lothar Müthel), a young nobleman, so the jealous apprentice Rabbi Famulus (Ernst Deutsch) sets the Golem onto his rival. In addition, a new constellation appearing in the stars affects the creature and causes it to become vicious. Florian is killed and the artificial man becomes unstoppable. Beside himself with rage the Golem sets fire to the ghetto, but as he looks through the ghetto's gate he sees an idyllic image of a little girl (Loni Nest). Filled with longing, he breaks down the wooden gate and carefully scoops her into his arms. The child, however, removes the star-shaped amulet containing a magic word from his clay body. As a result the Golem turns to stone and falls to the floor, after which he is carried back into the ghetto.

The myth of the Golem is based on Judeo-Cabbalist legend, and this particular story comes from a novel of the same name written by Gustav Meyrink in 1915. With its clay animation, it refers not only to divine creation but also to the myths of sculpture and art. When the illustration of the Golem from an ancient chronicle merges with the Rabbi's shadow, the film seems to suggest that Löw wished to create the Golem in his own image.

PAUL WEGENER Actor, screenwriter, and director Paul Wegener was born on December 11, 1874 in Jerrentowitz/Arnoldsdorf in what was then West Prussia. In 1906 Max Reinhardt hired him for the Deutsche Theater in Berlin. Wegener began to develop an interest in cinema in 1912. One of his starring roles was in *Der Student von Prag* (*The Student of Prague*, 1913) and only a year later he directed a first version of *Der Golem* (*The Golem*, 1914/15) in collaboration with Henrik Galeen. Later productions such as *Rübezahls Hochzeit* (*Old Nip's Wedding*, 1916) and *Der Golem und die Tänzerin* (*The Golem and the Dancing Girl*, 1917) are characterized by their fantastic, fairy-tale themes. In 1920 Wegener made a third film based on the Golem myth, which became a worldwide hit. In addition to directing he continued to act, as in *Alraune* (*A Daughter of Destiny*, 1927). In the 1930s Wegener supported Erwin Piscator's leftist agit-prop theatre, but it was not long afterwards that he lent his services to the National Socialist cinema production industry. Paul Wegener died on September 13, 1948 in Berlin.

2

3

“We have now experienced Wegener’s golem. For two hours the world around us sank away; for two hours our own selves were lost in a sphere that poured over us as from roaring rivers.” *Lichtbild-Bühne*

4

5

1 Director Paul Wegener often appeared in his own movies, such as *Old Nip's Wedding* (*Rübezahls Hochzeit*, 1916), in a dual role; here he is seen as the robot-like Golem.

2 *The Golem* was one of German cinema's first worldwide successes, paving the way for many variations on the same theme by different directors.

3 A gentle giant: the Golem has a way with children.

4 An early superhero: as long as the amulet still contains the secret cabalistic formula, the Golem remains immortal and has superhuman strength.

5 Other films of the period presented the same clichéd view of the Jewish scholar.

The character of the legendary Rabbi Löw represents an amalgamation of pure science, as represented by the telescope and the constellations, and the world of superstition and magic. From this point of view the magician and his creature can be understood as an allegory of the cinema. The studio sets, designed by the architect Hans Poelzig for this entirely studio-based film, clearly underline the fantastical aspects of the action. *The Golem* is considered to be one of the most important Expressionist films because the streets, façades, stairs, rooms, and pieces of furniture are crooked, without any right angles, while the sets and many dramatic lighting effects mirror the fear and psychological inner life of the characters. Despite the stylistic references to the art of its day, the action does not appear specific to time and place; the film seems to imply that the banishment of the Jewish population to a ghetto, the way they are forced to wear a circle on their clothes, the stereotyping and the hunting of the Golem, all belong exclusively to a period that lies way back in history. And yet, from today's vantage point it is difficult not to make a connection with the Germany of the 1920s, especially when Rabbi Famulus (of all people) tells Miriam that "the stranger" must be wiped out.

PLB

NOSFERATU – EINE SYMPHONIE DES GRAUENS

NOSFERATU – A SYMPHONY OF HORROR

1922 – GERMANY – 84 MIN.

DIRECTOR

F. W. MURNAU (1888–1931)

SCREENPLAY

HENRIK GALEEN, based on
the novel *Dracula* by BRAM STOKER

DIRECTOR OF PHOTOGRAPHY

FRITZ ARNO WAGNER

MUSIC

HANS ERDMANN

PRODUCTION

ALBIN GRAU,
ENRICO DIECKMANN for PRANA-FILM GMBH

STARRING

MAX SCHRECK (Count Orlok, Nosferatu), GUSTAV VON WANGENHEIM (Hutter),
GRETA SCHRÖDER (Ellen, his Wife), ALEXANDER GRANACH (Knock, a Real Estate Agent),
GEORG HEINRICH SCHNELL (Harding, a Shipowner), RUTH LANDSHOFF (Ruth, his Sister),
JOHN GOTTOWT (Professor Bulwer), GUSTAV BOTZ (Professor Sievers, a Doctor),
MAX NEMETZ (Captain), GUIDO HERZFELD (Innkeeper)

NOSFERATU

Der neue Großfilm

der PRANA-FILM G.m.b.H.

"Your wife has a lovely neck."

Knock (Alexander Granach), a shady real-estate agent in the town of Wisborg, dispatches his young assistant Hutter (Gustav von Wangenheim) to faraway Transylvania. There he is to meet with Count Orlok who wishes to buy a house in the North German seaport. The eager young man bids farewell to his wife Ellen (Greta Schröder) who stays at home, full of apprehension. Her feelings of terrible foreboding are confirmed when, after an arduous journey, Hutter arrives at Orlok's castle in the Carpathians. The mysterious Count (Max Schreck) proves to be a vampire who attacks his visitor during the night. When the bloodsucking fiend discovers a picture of Ellen among Hutter's things, his interest immediately switches to her. Without warning, he sets off by sea to Wisborg. Realizing the danger, Hutter pursues him overland, but to no avail. Nothing can prevent Orlok from reaching his new home. Soon after his arrival, plague breaks out and Ellen saves the city by sacrificing herself to the vampire.

Nosferatu was the first popular success for the still relatively inexperienced director, Friedrich Wilhelm Murnau. It was also the first-ever screen adaptation of Bram Stoker's 1897 novel *Dracula*, marking the debut appearance of what would become a remarkably popular film fantasy character—the vampire. Although screenplay writer Henrik Galeen changed names and places, removed some leading characters and rewrote the ending, the film

FRIEDRICH WILHELM MURNAU Born in 1888 into a wealthy middle-class family, Friedrich Wilhelm Murnau studied literature and art history at university. However, his academic career ended when the famous Berlin theater director Max Reinhardt saw him in a student production and invited him to join his company of actors. The First World War, in which he served as a fighter pilot, interrupted Murnau's acting career. When he returned to Berlin in 1919, like so many artists of his generation he was bitten by the movie bug. In partnership with the actor Ernst Hoffmann he set up a production company and made his first film *The Blue Boy / The Emerald of Death (Der Knabe in Blau / Der Todessmaragd)* in the same year. Like most of his early work, the film has not survived. In the space of only two years, Murnau made eight more movies and from surviving material there emerge the characteristics that would mark his later masterpieces. As well as a fascination with the unconscious and a tendency towards the melancholy and the romantic, Murnau's early movies have certain painterly qualities and a predilection for combining studio-based shots with location filming. *Nosferatu* (1922) established Murnau once and for all in the front rank of German directors. He became internationally known when he caused a sensation with the use of an "unchained" camera in the 1924 UFA production of *The Last Laugh (Der letzte Mann)*. Even more lavish was *Faust* (1925/26), whose rich visual imagery, including what the renowned German film critic Lotte Eisner described as some of "the most remarkable examples of German chiaroscuro," still fascinates modern audiences. Soon afterwards, studio mogul William Fox lured the young director to Hollywood with a sensational contract that allowed him to make his next movie with complete artistic freedom. Although, from an aesthetic point of view, *Sunrise—A Song of Two Humans* (1927) fulfilled all expectations, box-office takings came nowhere near to covering the cost of making the movie. In his next assignments for Fox, *Four Devils* (1928) and *City Girl*, a.k.a. *Our Daily Bread* (1929/30), Murnau was forced to make so many compromises that he finally terminated his contract and took off for Tahiti to shoot his next movie (1930/31). Murnau never lived to see this wonderful film set in the South Seas. He was killed in 1933 in an automobile accident a few days before the premiere.

“This is film: ghostly carriages flit through wooded gorges, nightmarish monsters hunt people down, pestilence breaks out, ships sail unmanned into harbors, coffins full of earth and mice are spirited out of cellars onto wagons, into ships and into moldering, dilapidated houses. This is film: a being creeps and clambers, half man, half ghost, over the screen—and meanwhile, as a concession to typical audiences, there is a love story with a tragic ending.”

Vossische Zeitung

1 The classic horror movie: Nosferatu (Max Schreck), however, has little in common with the gentleman bloodsuckers of later vampire films. Murnau portrays him as a monstrous, spider-like creature.

2 The start of a fatal passion: Count Orlok gazes at the photograph of Hutter's (Gustav von Wangenheim) wife Ellen.

3 Architecture made to measure: the ubiquitous pointed Gothic arches suggest Nosferatu's otherworldliness and at the same time create a visual link between the castle in the Carpathians and the port of Wisborg in the north of Germany.

recognizably follows the plot of the legendary Gothic novel. Even so, the bald, skeletal monster in the film has as little in common with his counterpart in the novel as he does with the debonair bloodsuckers of later vampire films. With his hooked nose, black-ringed eyes, rodent teeth and long claws, Orlok is both grotesque and frightening, a nightmare figure with the power to bring to life our most terrifying fantasies.

The vampire's bizarre appearance is certainly one of the main reasons for *Nosferatu's* enduring popularity. But most of all the film owes its classic status to its outstanding visual quality, due to Murnau's masterly handling of Expressionistic light and shade. It is clear, too, that the director was inspired by Scandinavian cinema and the 19th-century Romantic movement in painting. Unusually for the period, *Nosferatu* was largely filmed away from the studio, on location in northern Germany and Romania. And between them, Murnau and his director of photography Fritz Arno Wagner impressively succeeded in transforming real locations into fearful, eerie places. The film shows—a touch ironically—naïve young Hutter's adventures as a journey into darkness. Having left summery, carefree Wisborg, the villages and landscapes through which he passes become increasingly inhospitable until he is finally imprisoned in Orlok's shadowy realm. Similarly, as the vampire sets sail for Wisborg, this once tranquil town is slowly overwhelmed by shadows. Murnau vividly portrays encroaching horror as Orlok's black ship of death is steered by a ghostly hand into the harbor. Soon afterwards, a procession of black-clad men is seen moving through the street—pallbearers carrying the coffins of plague victims to a mass grave.

In the face of such spine-chilling imagery, it comes as no surprise that *Nosferatu* was often seen as a commentary on the contemporary political situation. Many interpreted the deaths of so many citizens of Wisborg as an allegory for the horror of the First World War. Others saw the scene where Knock, presumed to be a treacherous troublemaker, is hounded by a lynch mob, as a reminder of the hysterical social climate under the Weimar Republic. Admittedly, it makes more sense to see *Nosferatu* as an erotic fantasy, an evocative tale about the darkest depths of human desire. Since Murnau was gay, Orlok's nightly visits could be read as an "in joke." More disturbing is Ellen's relationship with the vampire. A mysterious telepathy links the melancholy young woman with the sinister Count Orlok, with whom she shares a fondness for nocturnal wanderings. Bizarrely, as she stands on the beach awaiting her beloved, she looks out to sea—in other words, in the direction from which not her husband but the vampire is approaching. It seems that, in her act of self-sacrifice, she is abandoning herself to masochistic sexual excitement, surrendering to a terrifying lover who makes her worthy spouse look like a passionless bourgeois, and the seemingly idyllic Wisborg like a dismal one-horse town of narrow-minded conformists. JH

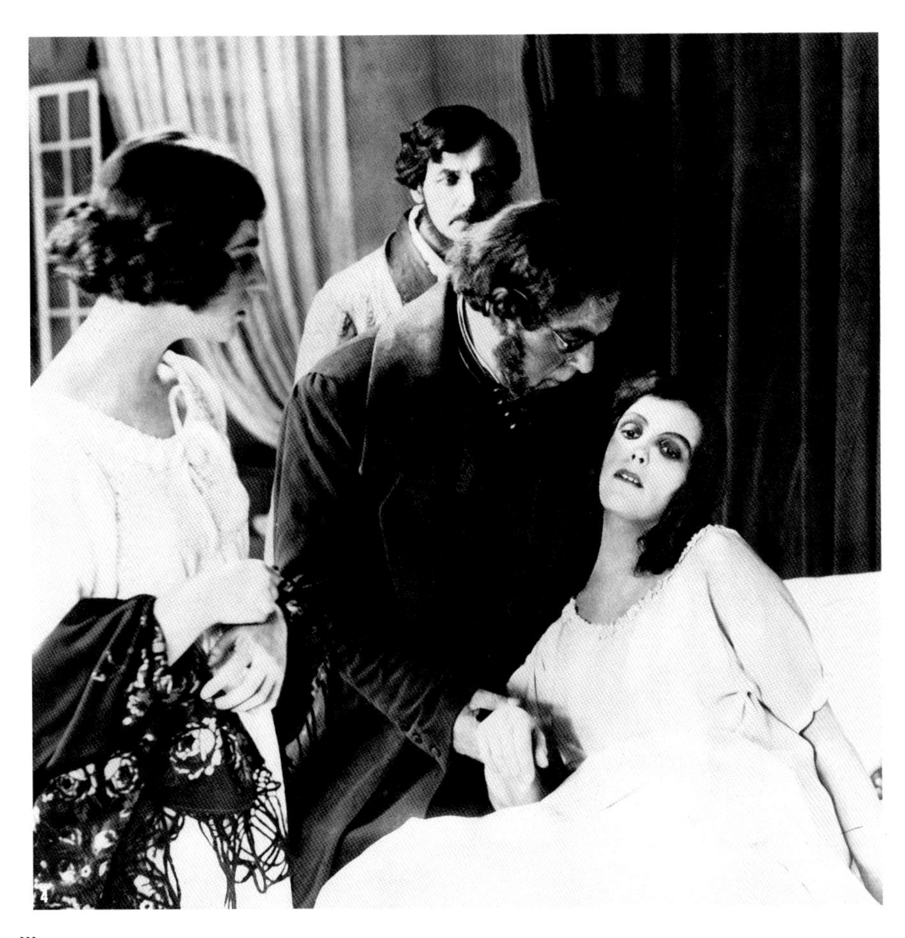

4

4 Strange fascination: there seems to be a mysterious attraction between Ellen (Greta Schröder) and the vampire, which neither her family nor the doctor suspect.

5 Threat to the small-town idyll: from the very beginning Ellen introduces a note of sinister melancholy to seemingly peaceful Wisborg. Her innocent husband notices nothing.

"Every gesture, every costume (from around 1840), every step and every movement must have been carefully calculated according to the laws of psychological effect on the viewer. In this, Grau and Murnau achieve a remarkably detailed work, without neglecting a wider, more majestic span." *Der Film*

HÄXAN

THE WITCHES / WITCHCRAFT THROUGH THE AGES

1922 – SWEDEN – 122 MIN. / 91 MIN. (original version)

DIRECTOR

BENJAMIN CHRISTENSEN (1879–1959)

SCREENPLAY

BENJAMIN CHRISTENSEN

DIRECTOR OF PHOTOGRAPHY

JOHAN ANKERSTJERNE

EDITING

EDLA HANSEN

PRODUCTION

SVENSK FILMINDUSTRI

STARRING

BENJAMIN CHRISTENSEN (Narrator / The Devil / Christ), ASTRID HOLM (Anna), KAREN WINTHER (Anna's Sister), MAREN PEDERSEN (Maria, the Weaver / the Witch), WILHELMINE HENRIKSEN (Apelone, a Poor Old Woman), KATE FABIAN (Old Maid), OSCAR STRIBOLT (Fat Monk), KNUD RASSOW (Anatomist), CLARA PONTOPPIDAN (Sister Cecilia, a Nun), ALICE O'FREDERICKS (Nun), JOHANNES ANDERSEN (Father Henrik, Inquisitor), ELITH PIO (Young Monk, Inquisitor), AAGE HERTEL (Inquisitor), IB SCHØNBERG (Inquisitor), TORA TEJE (Hysteric, Kleptomaniac), POUL REUMERT (Jeweler), ALBRECHT SCHMIDT (Neurologist)

HÄXAN
BENJAMIN CHRISTENSENS STORA FILM.
ENSAMRÄTT: A.B. SKANDIAS FILMBYRÅ, STOCKHOLM.

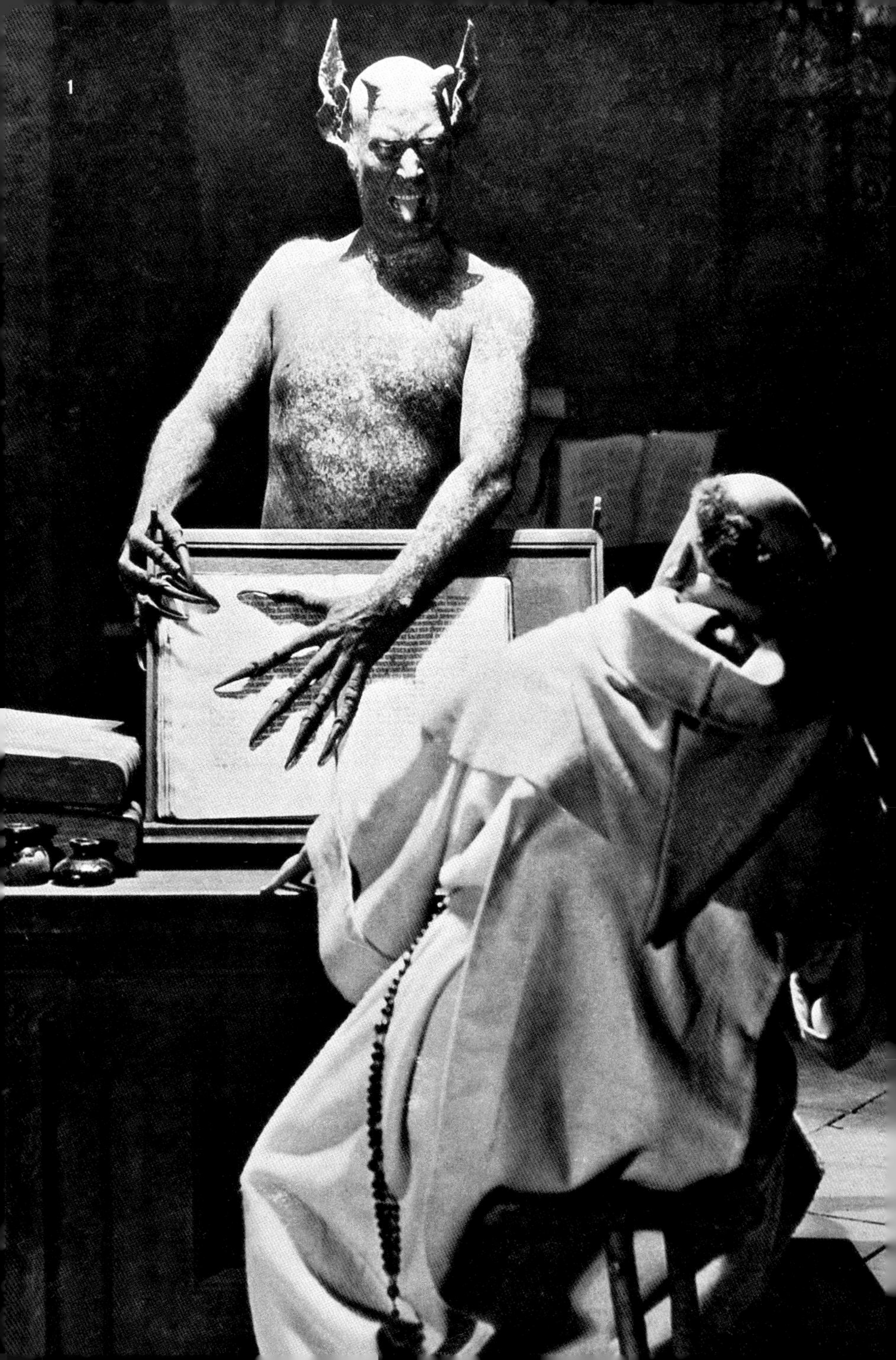
1

"A merry dance with the devils."

As its subtitle indicates, *The Witches (Häxan)* tells a tale of the cultural history of witchcraft. Benjamin Christensen, who appears at the very start of the movie as both the director and narrator, gives a presentation in seven chapters of facts that had been collected between 1919 and 1921. The movie seems to start off as a sort of slideshow in that it not only names numerous scientists, but it lists picture sources as well—such as the books that are quoted, or medieval manuscripts, paintings by Hieronymus Bosch, wood engravings from the notorious Witch's Hammer (Malleus Maleficarum) or by Albrecht Dürer, early modern age leaflets, prayer books, and an engraving by Francisco de Goya. What Christensen does is draw an arc from the early cultures of Persia and Ancient Egypt to the 18th century and in so doing he discloses the history of the motives of the devil, the demons, and the witches using this historical matrix and setting as a visual basis for the story that follows. Actors and fantastical backdrops lead us into the subterranean witches' kitchen; we see the dream of Apelone, the sorceress (Wilhelmine Henriksen) and her ride on a broomstick to the Blocksberg; or the Inquisition condemning Maria (Maren Pedersen), an innocent beggar woman, and torturing and burning her and others quite arbitrarily.

At the end of *Häxan* what we see is an image of the afterlife as though it is happening in the present, where the belief in demons and witchcraft is compared to what we call hysteria. The purpose of this sequence, however, is not one of scientific enlightenment; instead it shows that the hysterical woman (Tora Teje) seems to belong to the world of superstition as much as does the Witch. Finally one of the last sequences of the movie shows the comfortable shower room of a "modern clinic" fading into a scene of a burning pyre.

BENJAMIN CHRISTENSEN Benjamin Christensen was born on September 28, 1879 in Viborg in Denmark. After studying to be a doctor and then going into drama, he became an opera singer and from 1911 a movie actor. His first movie script was *The Mysterious X* (*Det hemmelighedsfulde X*, 1914), in which he not only took the starring role but was also the director. With an elaborate play of light and shade, the use of backlit shots, and mobile camera work, he created unusual visual forms for that era. His next movie, *Night of Revenge* (*Hævnens nat*, 1916), was equally successful. After making *The Witches* (*Häxan*, 1922), Christensen left Denmark and made six movies in the United States, following a short stay in Germany where he worked for Erich Pommer and took a part in Carl Theodor Dreyer's movie *Michael* (1923/24). The movies in the United States, included *Mockery* (1927) starring Lon Chaney. In 1934 Christensen returned to Denmark and after 1939 made three movies for the Nordisk Films Kompagni, dealing with children, divorce, and abortion. However, he was never able to repeat his success as a director and in 1944 he took on the management of a small suburban cinema theatre in Copenhagen. Christensen died on April 2, 1959 in Copenhagen.

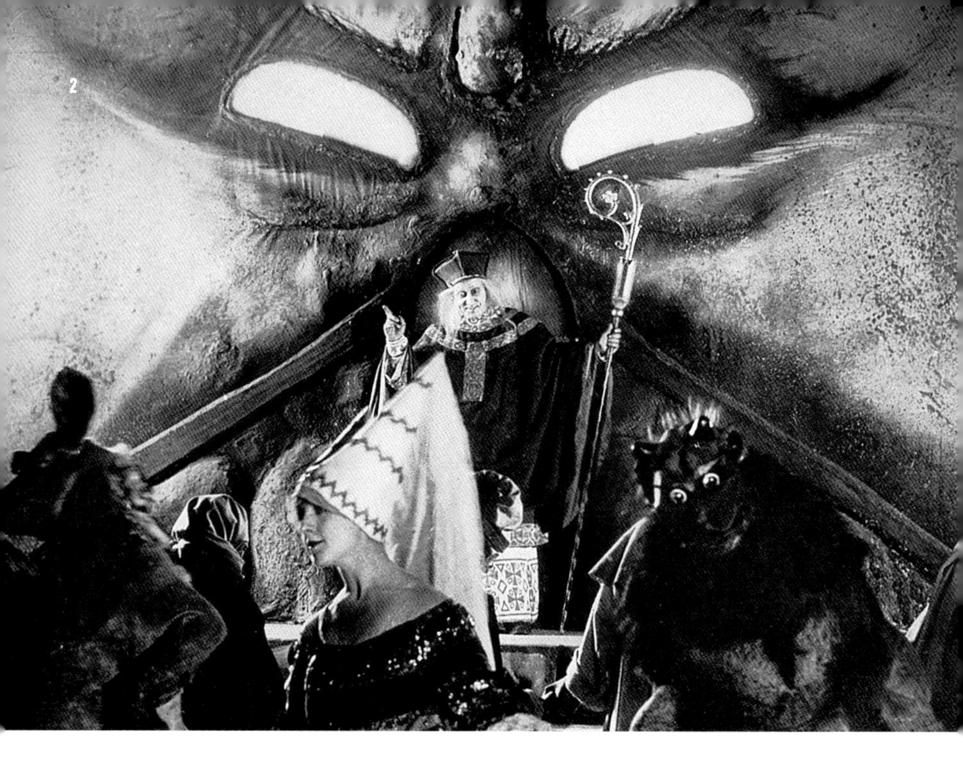

"Despite a certain underground reputation... Benjamin Christensen (1879–1959) has never really won the recognition he deserves as one of the cinema's earliest and greatest stylists." *Monthly Film Bulletin*

Häxan was one of the most extravagant and expensive movies to come out of Scandinavia at the time. Although the events are initially presented in a documentary style, the unusual ending clearly indicates that nothing is as it seems here. Christensen, who starts off in the role of a distant narrator, later takes on the part of the devil as well as making an appearance as the Christ figure. The pointer, which he continuously uses in the manner of a head teacher, time and again pointing out educational moments in the movie, is used in a later scene to carry out a satanic ritual. What the movie does is show how the moving picture can bring the subjects of past times up to date and by using Surrealist strategies *Häxan* combines scientific facts with hallucinatory pictorial worlds full of sexuality and violence. Reality and fantasy cannot be clearly distinguished from one another and even Christensen's role becomes more and more ambivalent in the course of the movie. In one scene he even combines his activity as the director with that of the inquisitors. One of his actresses, wearing contemporary dress, laughingly tries out the thumbscrews, one of the torture instruments.

The movie ends by touching on a point of social criticism. The question is raised as to whether the poor and the elderly are treated any better by contemporary society that they were in the past. And the reference to hysteria, a fashionable disease at the turn of the 20th century, does not explain the phenomenon of the exclusively female witches and of those suffering from obsessions. Instead, this anticlerical movie analogizes the institutions of medicine and the Church so that it can point to the First World War as the actual trigger for kleptomania, for example.

What *Häxan* wishes to suggest is this. Images from our cultural memory, settling in our consciousness over a long period of time, have created the belief in an irrational femininity, and in the existence of witches or female hysterics. PLB

1 The Devil and a vision of Christ are played by director Benjamin Christensen wearing elaborate masks.

2 Surreal dream sequences are seamlessly interwoven with documentary material.

3 Although the movie features real witches and sorcerers, most of those who appear are ordinary women caught up in the superstitious rituals of witchcraft.

4 The Witches' Sabbath in silhouette: the movie, which was reportedly filmed at night to capture the right atmosphere, uses wonderful visual solutions to create extraordinary scenes.

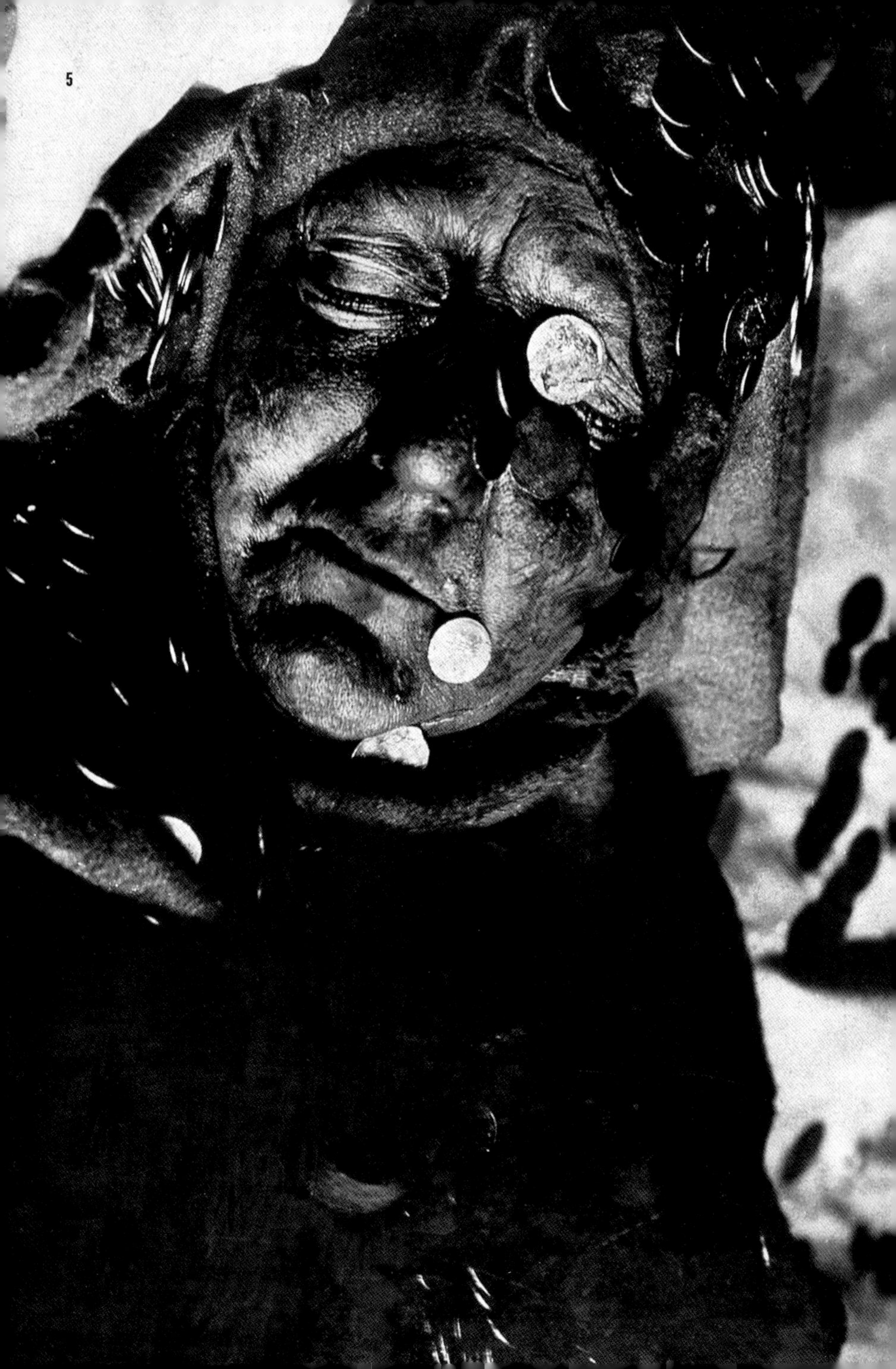

5

"If one remembers the date it was made, it is a remarkable piece of film history." *Monthly Film Bulletin*

5 Christensen stressed the documentary intention of his movie by recruiting amateur actors. He also spread the rumor that one of the women believed in the devil.

6 The Witches' Sabbath sequences feature imagined inhabitants of Hell and explicit scenes such as the notorious kiss on Satan's rear end.

7 A 1968 adaptation of *Witchcraft through the Ages* featured a narration by William S. Burroughs and a jazz soundtrack by Jean-Luc Ponty.

8 Luis Buñuel, who later offended religious sensibilities with movies such as *The Golden Age* (*L'Âge d'or*, 1930), would have loved the film's anticlerical stance.

THE PHANTOM OF THE OPERA

1925 – USA – 93 MIN.

DIRECTOR

RUPERT JULIAN (1879–1943)

SCREENPLAY

RAYMOND L. SCHROCK, ELLIOTT J. CLAWSON,
based on the novel *Le Fantôme de l'Opéra* by GASTON LEROUX

DIRECTOR OF PHOTOGRAPHY

VIRGIL MILLER, MILTON BRIDENBECKER,
CHARLES VAN ENGER

EDITING

MAURICE PIVAR

PRODUCTION

CARL LAEMMLE for UNIVERSAL PICTURES

STARRING

LON CHANEY (Erik, the Phantom), MARY PHILBIN (Christine Daaé),
NORMAN KERRY (Viscount Raoul de Chagny), SNITZ EDWARDS (Florine Papillon),
GIBSON GOWLAND (Simon Buquet), JOHN ST. POLIS (Philippe de Chagny),
VIRGINIA PEARSON (Carlotta), ARTHUR EDMUND CAREWE (Ledoux),
EDITH YORKE (Mama Valerius), ANTON VAVERKA (Prompter),
BERNARD SIEGEL (Joseph Buquet), OLIVE ANN ALCORN (La Sorelli),
GEORGE B. WILLIAMS (Ricard), WARD CRANE (Count Ruboff)

A UNIVERSAL
PRODUCTION
CARL LAEMMLE
PRESENTS
"THE PHANTOM
OF THE OPERA"
With LON CHANEY
NORMAN KERRY
MARY PHILBIN
AND A CAST OF 5000 OTHERS
STORY BY GASTON LEROUX
DIRECTED BY RUPERT JULIAN
Morgan

1

"Look not upon my mask."

The story begins in 1880, in the dark and long-forgotten dungeons and subterranean lakes deep beneath Paris's famous Opera House. In this sinister, claustrophobic parallel universe, so different from the light and airy world of ballet and opera, lives a nameless ghost. Every now and then artists and stagehands glimpse a mysterious figure in a cloak (Lon Chaney), his face hidden behind a mask. When the opera Faust is about to open, the Phantom sends the management a threatening letter demanding that the prima donna Carlotta (Virginia Pearson) step down to allow a new, as yet unknown, young singer named Christine Daaé (Mary Philbin) to play the starring role of Marguerite. In fact, the star is suddenly taken ill and Christine gradually falls under the spell of the enigmatic Phantom. As if mesmerized, Christine obeys a disembodied voice and steps through the secret door behind her dressing room mirror. The Phantom, a man once known as Erik whose face is concealed behind a mask, hopes that Christine's love can release him from his death-like state. But in the famous unmasking scene, as Erik feverishly plays the organ, Christine is horrified at the sight of the cadaverous face, colorless skin and sparse hair. Although the singer is allowed to return to her world, when Erik catches sight of her at a masked ball with her lover Raoul (Norman Kerry) he resolves to abduct her. Raoul and Ledoux (Arthur Edmund Carewe), a secret policeman, trail the supposed ghost but it soon becomes clear that this is no supernatural being but an insane criminal on the run. Erik flees yet again but Christine is able to escape. The Phantom is pursued through the night-time streets of Paris by angry stagehands, who beat him to death on the banks of the Seine as the young lovers are reunited.

The movie was based on Gaston Leroux's 1910 novel *Le Fantôme de l'Opéra*, but concentrated more on the fantasy aspects of the crime story. Shadows dancing on walls, waxen faces, visions of hell and Ancient Egyptian statues, on- and offstage—all serve to create a sinister, threatening atmosphere. Christine's dressing room separates the real world of the Opera House from the realm of the Phantom. Like Lewis Carroll's Alice, the young actress

GASTON LEROUX Gaston Leroux was born on May 6, 1868 in Paris, where he studied law, graduating in 1889. Soon afterwards he entered journalism, working as a theater critic and crime reporter. Between 1896 and 1906 he was a foreign correspondent, traveling widely throughout Europe, Africa and Asia, and rapidly became famous for his sensational reporting. From 1907 onwards he began writing full time. In the same year he published the novel *The Mystery of the Yellow Room (Le Mystère de la chambre jaune)*, which became a classic of French detective fiction. In this and six subsequent novels he created the young reporter and detective, Joseph Rouletabille, the French counterpart of Arthur Conan Doyle's Sherlock Holmes. But Leroux was best-known for *The Phantom of the Opera* (*Le Fantôme de l'Opéra*, 1910), a horror story inspired by a sightseeing tour of the Paris Opera House's underground vaults. Within the author's lifetime, the book was frequently adapted for stage and screen. As well as writing numerous plays, in 1916 Leroux turned his hand to screenplays and in 1919 he set up his own film company. A contemporary of Jules Verne, Leroux died in Nice on April 15, 1927.

“*The Phantom of the Opera* is an ultra fantastic melodrama, an ambitious production in which there is much to marvel at in the scenic effects.”

The New York Times

steps through the looking glass, not into Wonderland but into a catacomb-like underworld through which flows a river reminiscent of the Styx. This antechamber to Hell deep underground is full of memories of unrequited love, anguish, and torture. The shadowy figure of Erik can be seen as the embodiment of Christine's subconscious desires and fears and it is to his shadowy world that she flees when Raoul declares that he wishes to marry her. The scene in which Christine adopts the pose of the famous mechanical figure of the Sleeping Beauty in Madame Tussaud's waxworks, also suggested that, in this film, the boundaries between life and death are fluid.

However, the plot not only explores the nightmarish inner world of the psyche; it is also an allusion to the history of the Paris Opera. During the Paris Commune of 1871, the Opera House, which was reconstructed for the film, was actually used as an underground prison. As the Phantom declares when he appears at the masked ball clad as the “Red Death” from Edgar Allan's Poe's short story, this place is a reminder of those who have died in revolutions and war: “Beneath your dancing feet are the tombs of tortured men—thus does the Red Death rebuke your merriment.”

PLB

1 A ghostly being cloaked in scarlet: at the masked ball the Phantom cuts the same puzzling figure described by Edgar Allan Poe in his 1842 short story *The Mask of the Red Death.*

2 In the original version, the *Red Death* costume appeared in color. As was usual for the period, other scenes were tinted yellow, blue, brown, purple, and sickly green.

3 Lon Chaney, the early horror movie star, had already worked with Tod Browning in 1919 and in 1932 he went on to play the terribly misshapen Quasimodo in Wallace Worsley's *The Hunchback of Notre Dame.*

FAUST

1925/26 – GERMANY – 115 MIN.

DIRECTOR

F. W. MURNAU (1888–1931)

SCREENPLAY

HANS KYSER, based on scenes from the stage plays of the same name by JOHANN WOLFGANG VON GOETHE and CHRISTOPHER MARLOWE, as well as the manuscript *Das verlorene Paradies* (this translation by LUDWIG BERGER) and the Faust legend

DIRECTOR OF PHOTOGRAPHY

CARL HOFFMANN

MUSIC

WERNER RICHARD HEYMANN

PRODUCTION

ERICH POMMER for UFA

STARRING

GÖSTA EKMAN (Faust), EMIL JANNINGS (Mephisto), CAMILLA HORN (Gretchen), FRIDA RICHARD (Gretchen's Mother), WILHELM DIETERLE (Valentin), YVETTE GUILBERT (Marthe Schwerdtlein), WERNER FUETTERER (Archangel Gabriel), ERIC BARCLAY (Duke of Parma), HANNA RALPH (Duchess of Parma), HANS BRAUSEWETTER (Farmer's Boy)

IALTO
TUESDAY WEDNESDAY AND
TUESDAY
GOETHE'S
FAUST
Directed by F. W. Murnau
with EMIL JANNINGS
AN
UFA
PRODUCTION
Distributed by
Metro-
Goldwyn-
Mayer

1

"Mine is the earth!"

The plague is spreading through a medieval town. Faust (Gösta Ekman), a tireless scientist and alchemist, is helplessly staring death in the face. To put an end to the suffering, the old man sells his soul to the devil (Emil Jannings). Although the people recognize the evil in the scholar's sudden miracles and drive him away, Faust himself succumbs to the temptations of Mephisto, who grants him eternal youth and power, and a life of debauchery. That, however, is not enough to satisfy Faust. He falls in love with the virtuous Gretchen (Camilla Horn), and seduces her with Mephisto's help. Mephisto then causes the death of Gretchen's mother (Frida Richard) and her brother Valentin (Wilhelm Dieterle). Faust, suspected of murder, is obliged to flee once again. Ostracized and abandoned by her beloved, Gretchen gives birth to a child that, in her delirium, she allows to freeze to death during a snowstorm. Apprehended as an alleged child murderer, she is sentenced to death. Faust hears of her suffering and recognizes his own guilt. He rejects his youth and hurries to the place of execution, where he is finally united with Gretchen and they burn together at the stake. Since in this way pure, divine love triumphs over evil in death, Faust's soul is also saved.

There is no doubt that *Faust* counts as one of the most spectacular German film productions of the 1920s. It was a major film, with which Ufa hoped to gain international prestige, and which, as an example of cinematic art of national significance, was also expected to entice the conservative middle classes out of their homes and into the cinemas. It was the third and final film that celebrated director Friedrich Wilhelm Murnau and his leading actor Emil Jannings were to make together for the film studio. With *The Last Laugh* (*Der letzte Mann*, 1924), the two had created a worldwide sensation—and had also awakened

EMIL JANNINGS In Murnau's *Faust* (1925/26), he portrayed Mephisto as a jovial enticer to evil, a devil who takes visible pleasure in dissimulation and deceit. It was a showcase role for the arch performer Emil Jannings (1884–1950), the leading star of German cinema in the 1920s and 30s. Jannings was already acting in theater as a teenager, and arrived in Berlin via a succession of provincial and traveling theaters. There he worked sporadically in the Max Reinhardt ensemble and finally made his cinematic debut during the war. Jannings got his big film break in the role of Louis XV in Ernst Lubitsch's *Madame Dubarry* (1919). From then on, the heavyset actor was cast again and again in the role of vicious and brutal ruler—a type that he began to caricature. However, his most famous performance was probably that of a demoted hotel porter in Murnau's *The Last Laugh* (*Der letzte Mann*, 1924). This film brought Jannings to the attention of Hollywood and, after he had shone, once again under Murnau's direction, in *Tartuffe* (*Tartüff*, 1925) and *Faust*, and in E. A. Dupont's circus drama *Jealousy* (*Varieté,* 1925), he went in 1926 to the United States, where he was able to continue his previous successes seamlessly.

Victor Fleming's *The Way of all Flesh* (1927) and Josef von Sternberg's *The Last Command* (1927/28) once again showed Jannings in the role of the downtrodden man on the verge of destruction, and won him the Oscar for best actor in the very first Academy Awards Ceremony. With the arrival of the talkies, however, Jannings's Hollywood career soon came to a bitter end. He returned to Germany and renewed his popularity as Professor Rath in Sternberg's *The Blue Angel* (*Der blaue Engel*, 1930), in which, admittedly, Marlene Dietrich outshone him. After the Nazis came to power, Jannings willingly offered his services to Hitler's regime. In keeping with fascist ideology, he now embodied authoritative leadership figures and also played a significant part as a producer of various "politically valuable" films.

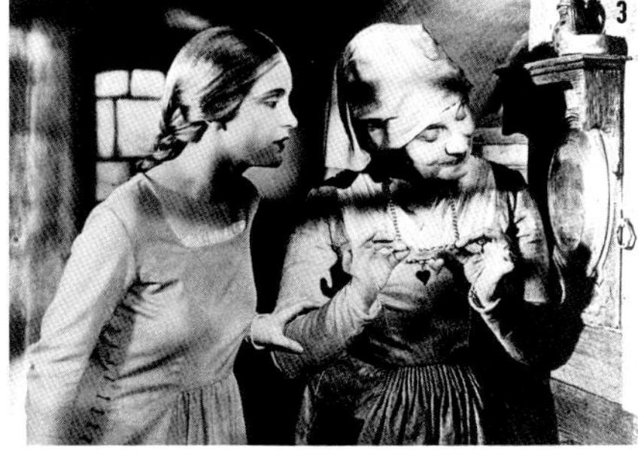

1 A vision of light and shade: Friedrich Wilhelm Murnau's *Faust* was one of the most spectacular works of German silent cinema (Emil Jannings, left; Gösta Ekman, right).

2 When Gretchen (Camilla Horn) falls in love with Faust, she leaves her idyllic childhood behind. The film graphically depicts the young woman's martyrdom.

3 A lovesick old lady: as Marthe Schwerdtlein, Yvette Guilbert (right) provides some of the few comic moments in this dark drama.

4 The Devil plays matchmaker: Gretchen's love for Faust will be her undoing.

5 Although *Faust* was UFA's most expensive movie ever, the sets are seldom as obtrusive as they are in the less convincing Italian episode.

5

"This film may be a disappointment—from the financial angle. From the artistic viewpoint there is some difference of opinion. Personally it is believed one of the best productions ever screened." *Variety*

interest in Hollywood. But, despite the two prominent artists and the enormous production costs, the response to *Faust* was not entirely positive. Some critics disapproved of the liberties that Murnau and his screenplay writer Hans Kyser had taken with the adaptation of the famous material. Some saw Mephisto's hypocritical wooing of Marthe Schwerdtlein (Yvette Guilbert) as an inappropriate foray into burlesque and Faust's courtship of Gretchen as pure kitsch. But even if the film occasionally places too much importance on the entertainment aspect, from a visual point of view *Faust* remains an overwhelming experience even today, giving a fascinating glimpse of the artistic originality and potential of German cinema at the time. For the film historian Lotte H. Eisner, *Faust* was nothing less than the "high point of chiaroscuro"—both masterpiece and essence of the "demonic" German silent film with its legendary use of light and shade.

Indeed, Murnau's cinematic vision of the Faust legend seems not least to be determined by the idea of translating the metaphysical battle between good and evil into a struggle between light and dark—in which, admittedly, in an evocation of Rembrandt's works, darkness prevails. In fact, according to the director of photography, Carl Hoffmann, Murnau apparently complained once that he could "see too much." But of course the film's visual magic does not depend entirely on the expert lighting

6 His most famous role: Emil Jannings clearly enjoyed playing Mephisto.

7 Tempted by the Devil: Murnau's *Faust* combined folk legend with the famous versions by Marlowe and Goethe—leading to accusations that it was insufficiently faithful to the original. (Ekman, left; Jannings, right).

8 In Offenbach's *Keller* Mephisto provokes Valentin with news of his sister Gretchen's love affair. Valentin was played by Wilhelm (William) Dieterle (second from left), who later became a Hollywood director.

9 Bye-bye Germany: when they finished filming *Faust*, Jannings and Murnau both tried their luck in Hollywood.

direction. In his analysis of the film, Eric Rohmer wrote that in *Faust*, "Murnau was able to mobilize all the resources that guaranteed him total control of the space." That includes camera movement and film composition just as much as ensemble choreography. It also includes the décor and trick photography, which Murnau uses with positively playful enthusiasm in order to create unreal picture worlds. When Faust, for instance, flies over the Alps on Mephisto's coat, the mountain range is manifestly a model; Murnau does not even try to show the fantastical as a concrete reality. He reveals the artifice, thereby demonstrating his close attachment to the Expressionist tradition. And, by flouting cinematic illusion, he infuses the film with the truthfulness of a dream.

This holds true for one breathtaking sequence in particular, which is enough on its own to establish Murnau as one of cinema's great visual geniuses. At the beginning of the film Mephisto stands over Faust's home town like an enormous angel of death and, as his black wings unfold, he plunges the peaceful little town into deepest darkness. Immediately a plague cloud appears, blowing its death-inducing breath through the winding lanes. Where the masses had just taken delight in the juggler's high-spirited performance, now panic and hopeless chaos reign. There can be no doubt that cinema has rarely illustrated the horror of the apocalypse more vividly than in this fantastical vision.

JH

"We look with awe at the grandiose imagery of Murnau... The amazing sight of the riders of the apocalypse, Plague, Hunger and War, striking out helplessly against the dazzling radiance of the heavenly powers, or when the mighty black wings of the devil overshadow the town beset by the demons... or when Faust and Mephisto glide on a flying cloak over towns and countryside, mountains and chasms, waterfalls and gorges." *Die Welt am Montag*

DR. JEKYLL AND MR. HYDE

1931 – USA – 98 MIN.

DIRECTOR

ROUBEN MAMOULIAN (1897–1987)

SCREENPLAY

SAMUEL HOFFENSTEIN, PERCY HEATH, based on the story
The Strange Case of Dr. Jekyll and Mr. Hyde by ROBERT LOUIS STEVENSON

DIRECTOR OF PHOTOGRAPHY

KARL STRUSS

EDITING

WILLIAM SHEA

MUSIC

HERMAN HAND, JOHANN SEBASTIAN BACH,
ROBERT SCHUMANN

PRODUCTION

ROUBEN MAMOULIAN for PARAMOUNT PICTURES

STARRING

FREDRIC MARCH (Doctor Henry L. Jekyll / Mr. Hyde), MIRIAM HOPKINS (Ivy Pearson),
ROSE HOBART (Muriel Carew), HOLMES HERBERT (Doctor Lanyon),
HALLIWELL HOBBES (General Danvers Carew), EDGAR NORTON (Poole, Jekyll's Butler),
TEMPE PIGOTT (Mrs. Hawkins), ARNOLD LUCY (Utterson, Carew's Butler),
DOUGLAS WALTON (Blond Student), ERIC WILTON (Briggs, Lanyon's Butler)

ACADEMY AWARDS 1932

OSCAR for BEST ACTOR (Fredric March)

Dr JEKYLL AND Mr HYDE

A ROUBEN MAMOULIAN PRODUCTION

WITH

FREDRIC MARCH

MIRIAM HOPKINS

AND

ROSE HOBART

"Isn't Hyde a lover after your own heart?"

Ambitious physician Dr. Jekyll (Fredric March) is a man with an obsession. He believes he can restore order to the human soul by using a synthetic substance to separate the two conflicting principles—the Apollonian and the Dionysian. The scientific community takes a skeptical view of his revolutionary research, and his prospective father-in-law, the conservative General Carew (Halliwell Hobbes), feels that Jekyll is too highly-strung for his own good. When Jekyll announces his desire to bring forward the date of his marriage to Muriel (Rose Hobart), the General refuses to give his consent. In his disappointment, Jekyll tests the new synthetic substance on himself. This daring, secret experiment has fatal consequences.

First published in 1886, Robert Louis Stevenson's famous story has inspired innumerable directors, cinematographers and actors. In 1920, John S. Robertson made a full-length silent version starring John Barrymore, and Victor Fleming's 1941 version featured Spencer Tracy in the title role. In both of these adaptations, the "transformation" of the protagonist was mainly the achievement of the lead actors.

Former theater director Rouben Mamoulian approached the story differently. He wanted to use innovative, visual, cinematic techniques, and the film is filled with surprising visual motifs and exquisite sound experiments. The unusual opening sequence demonstrates the director's talent, and his feeling for rhythmic narration. Mamoulian plays with our expectations by showing us everything through Jekyll's eyes—and immediately, our curiosity is awakened.

Slowly, the camera approaches a mirror in the hall. Sophisticated moviegoers would now expect to see the reflection of a camera appear in the mirror; instead, we see Fredric March as Dr. Jekyll. The trick is simple: instead of a mirror, the set designer had made a hole in the wall, and behind it, he had constructed a mirror image of the hall. March had to synchronize his movement with the camera's, so as to appear in the gap at just the right moment,

ROUBEN MAMOULIAN Rouben Mamoulian was born in Tbilisi, Georgia, in 1897. His father was an Armenian who served as a colonel in the Russian army. His mother shared her son's enthusiasm for the theater. After studying law in Paris and Moscow, where he made the acquaintance of Stanislavsky, Mamoulian moved to London and made his directing debut aged 25 at the well-known St James Theatre. A job on Broadway finally brought him to America, where he made his breakthrough in 1927: the play he directed, called "Porgy," would later form the basis for Gershwin's opera, "Porgy and Bess." By now, Paramount was interested in this successful stage director. They originally engaged him as a dialog coach, but Mamoulian quickly acquired the technical knowledge required of a film director. Shortly after the invention of the talkies, he was already making film history: his full-length film *Applause* (1929) was notable for its innovative experiments with sound, mobile camera, and surprisingly original narrative strategies. Again and again, Mamoulian astonished the studio bosses with his revolutionary visual ideas and his disregard for cinematic conventions. He used sound, image and editing to create rhythmical narrative units, always preferring a poetic reality to anything resembling naked naturalism. Film works with pictures, theater with words—this was his fundamental belief. With *Love Me Tonight* (1932), he created an early masterpiece of the musical genre. *City Streets* (1931) is said to be the only gangster film Al Capone really liked, and it demonstrates Mamoulian's genius in the deployment of light and shade. His mastery of narrated time is exemplified by the famous sequence in which a slowly burning cigarette creates the perfect alibi for a killer. The final scene of *Queen Christina* (1933) also made movie history: Mamoulian told Greta Garbo to think of nothing, and instead merely to stare into the distance, unmoved. The resulting sequence was so suspenseful that moviegoers were overwhelmed. Rouben Mamoulian died on December 12, 1987.

“Visual realism is not important. Psychological realism is. If you capture that, the scene will work, no matter what you do.” *Rouben Mamoulian*

1 Genius and madness: Man of science, Dr. Jekyll, is so smart it's frightening. Fredric March stars in an unforgettable dual role.

2 Painting the town dead: Dr. Jekyll gets spiffed up for a night out and shows Victorian London what he's really made of.

3 Antidote: Dr. Lanyon (Holmes Herbert) supplies Hyde with a shot of reality and reunites the two faces of insanity—if only temporarily.

as if he were his own reflection. This highly effective first appearance prepares us for the split in Jekyll's personality that forms the heart of the story.

His transformation into Mr. Hyde is achieved in an almost deliriously inventive piece of filmmaking, a scene achieved without cuts, blends or fade outs. Using only a clever system of filters in front of the lens, as well as some very effective make-up for the actor, Mamoulian creates an astonishingly convincing metamorphosis, as Jekyll swallows the steaming chemical cocktail, grasps his throat and begins to gurgle. Dark shadows form on his distorted face, emerging threateningly from his eyes, his nose and his mouth. Then the camera adopts Jekyll's perspective once more, and begins to turn on its own axis. The camera spins faster until we see nothing but a blur, accompanied by psychedelic sounds and visualized fragments of Jekyll's memory; then the transformation is complete. Jekyll walks towards the mirror… and, like us, he sets eyes for the first time on the grinning, ape-like face of Mr. Hyde.

Fredric March received an Oscar for his complex, multifaceted performance. His Mr. Hyde is a bestial, evil character, yet wittily played and positively funny at times. Miriam Hopkins is no less impressive as the good-time girl Ivy, whose sex appeal fires up Jekyll in the first place. The Doctor's hubris ends in death. After he finds himself turning into Hyde at the most inopportune moments, his friend Dr. Lanyon (Holmes Herbert) puts an end to his existence with a bullet. In the film's final frames, the director demonstrates his gift for the telling image once more: a bubbling cauldron on the fire boils over—a symbol of hell. Mamoulian's version is rightly regarded as the most impressive cinematic adaptation of the novel, not least because Hyde is less a monster than a man: an untamed, anarchistic character, crushed—no less than Jekyll—by the restrictions of the society he lives in. SR

4 Waving the white flag: A waiter learns the hard way that some patrons refuse to be ignored.

5 Poisoned Ivy (Miriam Hopkins): After hearing of his love interest's horrific encounter with Hyde, Dr. Jekyll realizes that there's no undoing the damage he's done.

6 Top hat and tails from the crypt: Mr. Hyde's will to survive threatens to crush Dr. Jekyll altogether. Director Rouben Mamoulian presents the alter-ego not as a monster but as a man driven by animal instinct.

"Fredric March is at the height of his powers in both roles. Although hidden behind ever-increasing layers of makeup, his Hyde is never reduced to a mere movie monster. Instead, his ghastly face always betrays Dr. Jekyll's inner struggles. As Jekyll, March embodies charm and grace as well as a relentless sense of pride, and the curiosity—or rather hybris—of Adam, which led to his expulsion from paradise."

Ivan Butler, in: The Horror Film

DRACULA

1931 – USA – 75 MIN.

DIRECTOR

TOD BROWNING (1882–1962)

SCREENPLAY

GARRETT FORT, based on the novel of the same name by BRAM STOKER
and the play of the same name by HAMILTON DEANE and JOHN L. BALDERSTON

DIRECTOR OF PHOTOGRAPHY

KARL FREUND

EDITING

MILTON CARRUTH, MAURICE PIVAR

MUSIC

PETER ILJITSCH TSCHAIKOWSKI,
RICHARD WAGNER, FRANZ SCHUBERT

PRODUCTION

CARL LAEMMLE JR., TOD BROWNING
for UNIVERSAL PICTURES

STARRING

BELA LUGOSI (Count Dracula), HELEN CHANDLER (Mina Seward),
DAVID MANNERS (John Harker), EDWARD VAN SLOAN (Prof. Abraham Van Helsing),
DWIGHT FRYE (Renfield), HERBERT BUNSTON (Dr. Jack Seward),
FRANCES DADE (Lucy Weston), JOAN STANDING (Briggs),
CHARLES K. GERRARD (Martin)

CARL LAEMMLE
presents
"DRACULA"
with
BELA LUGOSI
DAVID MANNERS
HELEN CHANDLER
DWIGHT FRYE and
EDWARD VAN SLOAN
A TOD BROWNING Production
FROM THE FAMOUS NOVEL AND PLAY BY BRAM STOKER
PRODUCED BY CARL LAEMMLE Jr.
UNIVERSAL PICTURES
UNIVERSAL
PICTURE
The story of the strangest Passion
the world has ever known!

"I never drink... wine."

When one thinks of the earliest vampire movies, two films immediately come to mind: Friedrich Wilhelm Murnau's *Nosferatu—eine Symphonie des Grauens* from 1922, and of course Dracula by Tod Browning, which was cobbled together ten years later in the workshops at Universal. Murnau's silent Expressionist masterpiece is a "classic text" that marked the birth of the genre yet produced no real successors (other than Werner Herzog's 1978 remake, *Nosferatu—Phantom der Nacht*). Dracula, on the other hand, launched an entire series including films like Lambert Hillyer's *Dracula's Daughter* (1936), in which a lady vampire struts her stuff, and Robert Siodmak's *Son of Dracula* (1943). Artistically, Tod Browning's vampire is a far less ambitious creation than Murnau's, yet he practically created the blueprint for the character of the Gentleman Vampire. In his performance as the Transylvanian aristocrat, Hungarian-born Bela Lugosi combined patrician charm with a diabolical aura. Count Dracula was *sexy*, and the peculiar fascination of the figure was fed by the audience's yearning for the exotic, and by the sexual repression of the times. The act of bloodsucking was a transparent metaphor.

The film portrays the upper-middle-class milieu of 1920s London as progressive and enlightened—in stark

BELA LUGOSI At the grave of Bela Lugosi, who had himself buried in his Dracula costume, Peter Lorre is alleged to have said: "Wouldn't it be better to put a stake through his heart—just to be on the safe side?" History books don't say whether Lugosi ever rose from the grave, yet he has achieved a kind of immortality. His embodiment of Count Dracula as an aristocratic gentleman-vampire made him world-famous, and the role was to haunt him all his life.

He was born in 1882, as Béla Ferenc Dezsö Blaskó, in Lugos/Lugoj, at that time Hungarian and now part of Romania. He later named himself after his home town. As a young theater actor, he spent years treading the boards in various parts of the Austro-Hungarian Empire. After the Empire collapsed, he moved to Berlin, where he appeared in Murnau's *Der Januskopf* (1920), among other films. In 1921, he continued his stage and film career in the United States, though he spoke little English at first. Six years later, the exotic Hungarian was given the role of his life: as Dracula in the Broadway play of the same name by Hamilton Deane and John L. Balderston. According to the actress Caroll Borland, he was "pure sex" on stage; for the film adaptation directed by Tod Browning (*Dracula*, 1931), however, he was not first choice. It was only the death of his rival for the role, Lon Chaney Sr., that cleared the path for his breathtaking international career. Until his star began to wane in the 1940s, Bela Lugosi had a string of successes, including *White Zombie* (1932) directed by Victor Halperin, and the Edgar Allan Poe adaptation *The Raven* (1935), directed by Lew Landers. In 1931, he had generously allowed his rival Boris Karloff to take over the role of the monster in *Frankenstein*, directed by James Whale; but in *Abbott & Costello Meet Frankenstein* (1948), he played Count Dracula one last time. From then on, he was ever more frequently unemployed, began to drink and developed a morphine addiction. In his penultimate film, Reginald Le Borg's *The Black Sleep* (1956), Lugosi's character was silent, because the actor was no longer capable of remembering his lines. His last appearance before a film camera was a few days' shooting for *Plan 9 from Outer Space* (1956/59), and the scenes featuring Lugosi were actually used. He died on August 16, 1956.

contrast to the benighted peasantry in the distant mountains of Romania. Renfield (Dwight Frye), an estate agent, has come to Transylvania to sell a house in London to a certain Count Dracula. When the "natives" tell him dark tales about vampires, he laughs them off as primitive superstition—and soon suffers the consequences. Turned into a vampire by Dracula, he returns to London as his slave, while the Count moves in to Carfax Abbey, opposite the sanatorium run by Dr. Seward (Herbert Bunston). The cultivated Count is very interested in Seward's daughter Mina (Helen Chandler) and her friend Lucy (Frances Dade). Lucy is his first victim, and from then on she glides through the night as one of the pallid undead. Mina, who is engaged to John Harker, also receives a nocturnal visit from Dracula, but she is not completely "vampirised." Physician and scientist Abraham Van Helsing (Edward Van Sloan) is a vampire specialist, and he reveals Dracula's true identity and attempts to protect Mina. Dracula takes Mina with him to Carfax Abbey, where Van Helsing manages to drive a stake through his heart. Mina is saved. The final scene shows her and her fiancé ascending a flight of stairs, arm in arm, with nothing standing in the way of their marriage.

Universal had bought the rights to Bram Stoker's novel from his widow, Florence. The Victorian sexual morality of the book is carried over into the film adaptation of 1931: the woman's desires are wakened by vampirism, and until these have been eradicated, she is not fit for

1 What a tangled web we weave: Bela Lugosi looks forward to a bite of dinner by candlelight as Tod Browning's *Dracula.*

2 Make a wish: Dracula always has his cake and eats it too.

3 Sweet dreams are made of these: Pine and oak and sycamore trees.

4 Stairwell to hell: John Harker (David Manners) will have to defeat the vampire king if he intends on saving his fiancée's soul.

"Certainly it is Lugosi's performance and the cinematography of Karl Freund that make Tod Browning's film such an influential Hollywood picture." *Chicago Sun-Times*

marriage. Men's fear of emancipated women seems to be very much part of the Dracula myth. As an aristocrat and an Eastern European, the bloodsucking Count is exotic in more ways than one; and as an object of female desire, he also constitutes a threat to bourgeois masculinity, here embodied by Mina's father and fiancé. Van Helsing appears as the savior, and as Dracula's counterpart and nemesis: "Perhaps I am in a position to prove that what was very recently called 'superstition' may today or tomorrow be shown to be scientific truth."

Thus, the real battle for the woman takes place between the vampire and the scientist. Although Mina's feelings appear moderate, she too has fallen under Dracula's spell, which has awakened her sexual desires. Admittedly, none of this is actually shown in this decidedly wordy film. Only in later films, beginning with the Hammer Horrors of the 1950s, was the actual act of vampirism salaciously depicted. Tod Browning's *Dracula* was the very first vampire film of the sound era, and though its horror elements may seem naïve or wooden today, they too must have touched a nerve in their time. In the end, traditional values triumph—but the movie's success had at least as much to do with the fact that audiences were as fascinated by illicit desire as were the Count's transported victims.

KK

FREAKS

1932 – USA – 64 MIN.

DIRECTOR

TOD BROWNING (1882–1962)

SCREENPLAY

WILLIS GOLDBECK, LEON GORDON,
EDGAR ALLAN WOOLF, AL BOASBERG,
based on the short story *Spurs* by TOD ROBBINS

DIRECTOR OF PHOTOGRAPHY

MERRITT B. GERSTAD

EDITING

BASIL WRANGELL

PRODUCTION

TOD BROWNING for MGM

STARRING

OLGA BACLANOVA (Cleopatra), WALLACE FORD (Phroso),
LEILA HYAMS (Venus), HARRY EARLES (Hans), DAISY EARLES (Frieda),
ROSCOE ATES (Roscoe), HENRY VICTOR (Hercules),
DAISY HILTON (Siamese Twin), VIOLET HILTON (Siamese Twin),
FRANCES O'CONNOR (Armless Girl),
JOSEPHINE JOSEPH (Half-Woman, Half-Man)

Do Siamese Twins make love?
What sex is the half-man, half-woman?
Can the Pinheads think?
Can a full-grown woman truly love a midget?
Such drama has never before been put on the screen! From the far corners of the world have been gathered the strangest of half-humans, who have been put into a thrilling and romantic story! Their loves and hates, their clashes with the world of normal men and women, make this a drama which must be seen to be believed!
TOD BROWNING'S production
FREAKS
makes these strange creatures as human as you! An unusual love drama with
WALLACE FORD, LEILA HYAMS, OLGA BACLANOVA, ROSCO ATES
Metro-Goldwyn-Mayer PICTURE

"Offend one and you offend them all."

Politically correct viewers be warned! The horrors of the traveling circus are about to come alive as a group of malformed entertainers put themselves on show to earn an honest buck. Moviegoers too shocked to turn away had better hold on to their hats—for *Freaks* ends with an image so frightening it burns indelibly into the mind.

The story is simple as a fairy tale. Hans (Harry Earles) is a dwarf in love with a stunning high-wire acrobat named Cleopatra (Olga Baclanova). Billed as the "Peacock of the Air," this queen of the trapeze makes eyes at the little guy, much to the chagrin of his fellow Lilliputian and fiancée, Frieda (Daisy Earles). One thing leads to another and soon jealousy prompts Frieda to have a word with her rival. Only, when she does, the tiny woman makes the mistake of informing Cleopatra that Hans is heir to a massive fortune. Every bit as evil as she is beautiful, Cleo works out a scheme with her strongman lover Hercules (Henry Victor) to marry Hans and then poison him on their wedding night. The "freaks," however, quickly wise up to her and devise a counterattack to give these "normal folk" a taste of their own medicine.

While *Freaks* does indeed expose how side-shows exploit handicapped performers, that isn't the point of the film. Instead, Tod Browning points the camera at Siamese twins, hermaphrodites, and pinheads because of their unique ability to entertain viewers while simultaneously creeping them out with acts like the torso man's cigarette lighting trick—performed using only his lips and teeth.

Despite the simplicity and predictability of the plot, Browning creates suspense with artistic precision. At the start of the film, the "Peacock of the Air" is introduced by the master of ceremonies as "the most amazing, most astounding living monstrosity of all time"; but only at the end of the picture do we glimpse her disfigurement. The framing story therefore puts the act of watching movies on a par with peering into a curiosities cabinet. Tod Browning, who had worked in a circus as a contortionist and clown in his youth, believed that a voyeuristic audience was as

TOD BROWNING Born with a silver spoon in his mouth, Tod Browning (1882–1962) said goodbye the good life at age sixteen to join the circus. It was there that he made the acquaintance of director D. W. Griffith and decided to pursue a career in film. *Intolerance* (1916) gave Browning the chance to assist Griffith and try his hand at screen acting. A year later he was directing silent movies of his own. Known as the Edgar Allen Poe of the cinema, Browning had an obsession with all things macabre and spooky, which always found a way into his art. For earlier works like MGM's *The Unholy Three* (1925), *London after Midnight* (1927) and *West of Zanzibar* (1928), the director teamed up with "man of a thousand faces" Lon Chaney to conjure up the dark side. This prosperous collaboration, which lasted ten pictures, came to an abrupt end when Chaney unexpectedly died during the pre-production stages of *Dracula* (1931). Browning chose the Hungarian Bela Lugosi, who had played the vampire on stage, to replace his favorite actor, and the rest—as they say—is history. Still, Dracula, was not to be the director's sole masterpiece: *Freaks* (1932), a film very much inspired by Browning's years at the circus, is every bit as poignant as his adaptation of Bram Stoker's tale. *Mark of the Vampire* (1935), *The Devil-Doll* (1936) and swan-song *Miracles for Sale* (1939) were the last three pictures completed in the Hollywood career of this erstwhile circus clown and leading pioneer of the thriller and horror genres.

essential to freak shows as it was to film. Even so the picture itself is substantially more complex than it may first appear. What starts out as a harsh examination of malformation subtly is made bearable by the film's element of black humor. For example, a stuttering circus member leaves the viewer in stitches by courting one of the Siamese twins (Daisy and Violet Hilton) to the dismay of the other. Another amusing encounter comes when the Half-Man Half-Woman (Josephine Joseph) flashes the strongman a toothy grin, and Phroso the clown (Wallace Ford) tells him, "I think she likes you, but he don't." And

"*Freaks* is filled with poignancy; it offers a premonition of eugenics, as well as a provocative comparison with the alienated condition of women and the freakish nature of all showbiz celebrity. It is a work of genius."

The Guardian

3

1 Give me your tired, your poor: The freaks look to each other for support and find a loving soul to lean on.

2 Love in a pinch: Cleopatra (Olga Baclanova) lowers her standards for a bit of hard cash. Harry Earles as Hans, the acrobat's pint-sized Romeo.

3 Fallen star: The former "Peacock of the Air" has to live off her looks after a freak accident leaves her permanently grounded.

4 Sex is her strong suit: But off stage, colleagues Hercules (Henry Victor, left) and Phroso (Wallace Ford) accept the gender-bending performer (Josephine Joseph) as one of the guys.

when little Hans is seen leaving Cleo's trailer, the performers nudge one another and remark that the trapeze star must have gone on a diet.

Beyond looking to humor for mere entertainment, Browning has the wisecracking Phroso demonstrate its powers as "the great equalizer." By laughing at the unwanted attention that "abnormalities" tend to attract, the clown is one of the few members of the circus who succeeds in meeting the freaks on equal footing. Conversely, the other "normal" circus performers only succeed in revealing their personal shortcomings every time they make fun of the outcasts. Such is the case when Cleopatra marries Hans and belittles the wedding party's gesture to accept her as "one of their own." This is the moment when she is confronted by her evil nature and made to see that a warped soul is a disfigurement all its own.

The scene implicitly shows us how the hostile outside world has forced these outcasts to form ties with each other. The resulting close-knit community, founded in humanity and solidarity, provides a welcome contrast to a "normal" world dominated by the vanity and malevolence. For, as Tod Browning teaches us in this extraordinary piece of cinema, it is the freaks' handicaps that shield them from the vanity of placing themselves above other people, and ultimately make them better people.

SH

KING KONG

1933 – USA – 100 MIN.

DIRECTORS

MERIAN C. COOPER (1893–1973),
ERNEST B. SCHOEDSACK (1893–1979)

SCREENPLAY

MERIAN C. COOPER, EDGAR WALLACE,
JAMES ASHMORE CREELMAN, RUTH ROSE

DIRECTOR OF PHOTOGRAPHY

EDWARD LINDEN, J. O. TAYLOR,
VERNON L. WALKER, KENNETH PEACH

EDITING

TED CHEESMAN

MUSIC

MAX STEINER

PRODUCTION

MERIAN C. COOPER, ERNEST B. SCHOEDSACK for RKO

STARRING

FAY WRAY (Ann Darrow), ROBERT ARMSTRONG (Carl Denham),
BRUCE CABOT (John “Jack” Driscoll), FRANK REICHER (Captain Englehorn),
SAM HARDY (Charles Weston), NOBLE JOHNSON (Native Chief),
STEVE CLEMENTE (Witch King), JAMES FLAVIN (Shipmate Briggs),
VICTOR WONG (Charlie), LYNTON BRENT (Reporter)

RKO
Radio
PICTURES
DAVID O. SELZNICK
Executive Producer
KING KONG
with
FAY WRAY ◆ ROBT. ARMSTRONG
BRUCE CABOT
A COOPER-SCHOEDSACK
PRODUCTION
FROM AN IDEA CONCEIVED BY
EDGAR WALLACE AND MERIAN C. COOPER

1

"Beauty killed the Beast."

King Kong reflects the artistic techniques established by its documentary filmmaker protagonist, Carl Denham (Robert Armstrong), as elements of scientific expedition meet the sensationalism of cinematic horror. It all starts when Denham embarks on the search for an actress willing to play vulnerable in his upcoming wildlife movie. A victim of the Great Depression, Ann Darrow (Fay Wray) is desperate enough to take on any job if it means getting out of New York. Six weeks later, she and an entire film team drop anchor on an East Indian island, where a skull-shaped mountain is the only thing more imposing than insurmountable cliffs. Those cliffs form a huge wall dividing the terrain, with humans inhabiting the one half and an untamable beast occupying the other. This creature is, of course, none other than the legendary King Kong, a 40-foot gorilla that can only be appeased with human female sacrifices. Needless to say, a love-struck Kong wants Ann from the moment he sees her, and the young woman is powerless to resist his advances.

In the rescue mission that follows, a spectacular prehistoric rainforest unfolds beyond the divisive wall. Dinosaurs claim a good portion of the ship's crew before Ann's love interest Jack Driscoll (Bruce Cabot) finally manages to free his dream girl from captivity. Carl Denham uses gas explosives to knock out King Kong and ship him back to the urban jungle of New York City.

On Broadway, billboards advertise the colossal ape as the wonder of the century. Then, at his stage debut, press photographers flashbulb him into a frenzy and he breaks free of his chains. Kong's next move is to reclaim Ann. This accomplished, he seeks seclusion at the top of the Empire State Building… only the National Guard has its own interpretation of his actions and sends in an airborne unit to shoot him down.

STOP MOTION PHOTOGRAPHY Used to animate three-dimensional models and machines, stop motion is one of the oldest techniques in cinematic trick photography. As early as 1910, Ladislas Starevich (1882–1965) was employing it in Russia and France to make entire movies. The principle was simple: stationary figures were placed on a set before a painted backdrop, where they were photographed and then minutely repositioned for the following shot. While the Starevich pieces demonstrate a degree of seamless perfection that would rarely be topped let alone matched by any other filmmaker, *King Kong* (1933) is considered to have made the most significant breakthrough in stop motion photography. Credited with this accomplishment is Willis O'Brien and his team of painters, miniaturists, and technicians.

Stop motion would continue to improve in the decades to come. In particular, Ray Harryhausen's special effects for films like *Jason and the Argonauts* (1963) were hailed by industry experts and audiences alike. Even recent movies like *Wallace & Gromit: A Grand Day Out* (1988/89) and *The Nightmare before Christmas* (1993) were filmed according to the principles of the age-old technique. Movies like *Toy Story* (1995) then brought the stop-motion look into the digital age.

2

“Imagine a 50-foot beast with a girl in one paw climbing up the outside of the Empire State Building... clutching at airplanes, the pilots of which are pouring bullets from machine guns into the monster’s body.” *The New York Times*

3

1 Hanging by a thread: not to worry, King Kong hasn't let Ann Darrow (Fay Wray) down yet.

2 Battle royal: King Kong knocks down opponent after opponent to save the woman he loves.

3 Scream queen: Robert Armstrong can't calm Fay Wray's nerves for the life of him.

King Kong tickets sold like hot cakes. The movie's many prehistoric animals appealed to an audience that had been won over by a silent era classic entitled *The Lost World* (1924/25, directed by Harry O. Hoyt). Indisputably, evolutionary theory was a popular topic in 1930s cinema. One could argue that bottle-blond Fay Wray a.k.a. Ann was the nexus between the "big black beast" from the virgin forest and the superior "civilized world" as presented by the film.

King Kong's main theme is views of other forms of society: Carl Denham comes across as a typically arrogant colonialist when he attempts to film the secret ritual of the island's inhabitants; conversely, the people he spies on look like something out of a spoof on voodoo tribal worship. It follows that heavy makeup, grass skirts, shell necklaces, and coconut bras are all the rage with these peculiarly black natives. India, it seems, looked a whole lot like Africa back in the 1930s, with Hollywood's confusion of the two at its most striking in the scenes of King Kong's slave-trade inspired journey from his homeland to America, followed by the caged scenes, which are reminiscent

4 Dinner at ape: tonight's entrée is sacrificial lamb.

5 New Yorkers won't allow King Kong to play with dolls.

6 Air show: the U.S. military disposes of Kong and reclaims its title as king of the skies.

of old New York freak shows and living village exhibits. There are no two ways about it: *King Kong* equates dark skin with savagery and worse. Its representation of the United States, on the other hand, is of a rational society rooted in order and progress. The overgrown baboon's fate is thus already sealed as he climbs to the then newly completed Empire State Building (1931); for the modern machinery of war must reign supreme in this piece of colonial propaganda. There is, however, more to the story than meets the eye. Having worked as ethnographic filmmakers in the 1920s, directors Merian C. Cooper and Ernest B. Schoedsack were quick to show how even a documentary examination of far-off worlds can be prone to the artificiality of media hype. The Denham character proves this by having his actress practice her big scene while still on board the ship. As the scene suggests, real documentary films did in fact rely on paid actors, or ape costumes if necessary, to make other cultures and wild animals behave according to viewer expectations. As with any other cinematic genre, much of what appears so strange on screen is nothing more than a construct of the filmmaker's mind. PLB

5

6

BRIDE OF FRANKENSTEIN

1935 – USA – 75 MIN.

DIRECTOR

JAMES WHALE (1889–1957)

SCREENPLAY

WILLIAM HURLBUT, JOHN L. BALDERSTON, based on themes and characters established in the novel *Frankenstein or The Modern Prometheus* by MARY WOLLSTONECRAFT SHELLEY

DIRECTOR OF PHOTOGRAPHY

JOHN J. MESCALL

EDITING

TED J. KENT

MUSIC

FRANZ WAXMAN

PRODUCTION

CARL LAEMMLE JR. for UNIVERSAL PICTURES

STARRING

BORIS KARLOFF (The Monster), COLIN CLIVE (Doctor Henry Frankenstein), ELSA LANCHESTER (The Monster's Mate / Mary Shelley), ERNEST THESIGER (Doctor Praetorius), VALERIE HOBSON (Elizabeth Frankenstein), GAVIN GORDON (Lord Byron), DOUGLAS WALTON (Percy Shelley), UNA O'CONNOR (Minnie), O. P. HEGGIE (Eremit), E. E. CLIVE (Burgomaster)

-more fearful than the monster himself!
CARL LAEMMLE presents
The BRIDE OF FRANKENSTEIN
starring KARLOFF
COLIN CLIVE
VALERIE HOBSON
ELSA LANCHESTER
ERNEST THESIGER AND E.E.CLIVE
SCREENPLAY BY WILLIAM HURLBUT & JOHN BALDERSTON
PRODUCED BY CARL LAEMMLE JR.
A UNIVERSAL PICTURE
Directed by JAMES WHALE

"Alone—bad. Friend—good!"

Dr. Frankenstein (Colin Clive) stands before the lab table of fellow scientist Dr. Pretorius (Ernest Thesiger) in utter disbelief. For arranged neatly atop it is a collection of bell jars, each with its own four-inch-tall "human" chattering away at mouse pitch. One such jar houses a dancing ballerina, while an archbishop prays away in another. A third is home to the world's littlest queen, who expects a visit from her debonair husband. He, in turn, has already slipped through his jar's paper lid and now makes a mad dash across the table to reach her. None of this, however, is lost to Dr. Pretorius who, using a pair of tweezers, snatches up the escape artist by his ermine collar and deposits him back where he belongs.

Dr. Frankenstein lowers himself into the lab armchair, captivated and repulsed by the grotesque display before him. "This isn't science," he protests. "It's more like black magic." Dr. Pretorius responds that his creatures are nothing of the sort. As a matter of fact, his homunculi were grown from an original human seed using natural cultures and are perfect in every regard except for size. Given Dr. Frankenstein's own success at animating larger beings, Pretorius sees potential for a collaboration. He sweetens the offer by suggesting that they start off by supplying Frankenstein's monster with a mate—an Eve who will mother a new and improved genetic race. After some hesitation, Dr. Frankenstein agrees to the plan. Then it's off to laboratory, where he and Dr. Pretorius start work on the so-called bride.

Bride of Frankenstein, the sequel to James Whale's *Frankenstein* (1931), picks up right where its predecessor left off. Whale thus introduces a prolog in which Mary Shelley (Elsa Lanchester) spends a stormy night telling her husband (Douglas Walton) and Lord Byron (Gavin Gordon) what happens to the monster (Boris Karloff) following the fire at the mill. It seems that after surviving the catastrophe by hiding in an underground niche of the mill, the stitched-up homunculus emerged determined to become human at all cost. Yet in the spirit of the story's first installment, basic misunderstandings and the callousness of his peers foil his attempts. Be that as it may, the monster does

JAMES WHALE Many might argue that bombastic staging remained James Whale's calling card until his dying day. His death was no exception. Found drowned in his own swimming pool in 1957, the general consensus is that the filmmaker committed suicide in the wake of a disabling stroke. Two decades prior to this tragedy, James Whale had been one of Hollywood's most prominent directors. His *Frankenstein* pictures (1931, 1935) were a complete success and Whale was given an artistic *carte blanche* at Universal. That all changed when the studio was sold and he directed box-office flop *The Road Back* (1937), a loose sequel to *All Quiet on the Western Front* (1930). The project's fate cost him his independence, and Whale retired from film-making a few years later.

Briton James Whale was 39 when he came to the United States in 1928. Before, he had worked as an actor, theatrical set designer and director for the London stage. In 1930, he transformed his previous work as a theater director into his first Hollywood production, making a screen adaptation of the successful wartime drama "Journey's End." *Frankenstein* (1931) was his third project as a filmmaker. Although the occasional comedy or musical were also a part of his repertoire, Whale built his reputation on sensational displays of horror like *The Old Dark House* (1932), *Bride of Frankenstein* (1935) and *Invisible Man* (1933), a film he regarded as his personal best. During his lifetime, Whale's openly gay lifestyle was a source of public scorn; today, it merely casts a different light on his work. Many people believe he drew on his own experiences of social ostracism for his direction of Frankenstein's monster. Throughout his lifetime, James Whale remained true to his British roots, as shown in Bill Condon's Oscar-winning *Gods and Monsters* (1997), a recent tribute to the early Hollywood filmmaker.

1 Here comes the bride: Dr. Frankenstein (Colin Clive) and Dr. Pretorius (Ernest Thesiger, right) declare mating season officially open.

2 Permanent fixture: Actress Elsa Lanchester gets kinky in a dual role as the monster's mate and Mary Shelley.

in fact get a true taste of friendship in what is perhaps the film's most endearing and comical episode. While hiding out in the German forest, he stumbles upon a secluded cottage inhabited by a pious and blind hermit (O. P. Heggie). The elderly man warmly invites the "mute traveler" into his home, cares for him and teaches him how to speak. Now fast friends, the men eat, drink and merrily while away the hours smoking and playing music. Unfortunately, their time together comes to an abrupt end when two hunters barge in on them and try to kill the monster. The cottage catches fire and the monster runs for his life, stopping only when he finds a new suitable hiding place—a cemetery crypt.

Following on from the original picture, director James Whale fills the synthetic man's tragic tale with distinctly Christian motifs. The fact that only a blind person is willing to befriend him is a clear comment on how the actions of ordinary mortals are dictated by surface appearances. Dr. Frankenstein, the man once bold enough to challenge the Creator, is coerced by the devilish Pretorius

3 Nip and tuck: The bride gets all dolled up for her wedding. Brigitte Helm, the machine man in *Metropolis* (1926), originally signed on to play the role, but she was just too rusty.

4 The monster mash: If he can't be the smash of society, he'll just smash society altogether.

5 Can't warm up to him: The very thought of locking lips with her future husband leaves the bride stone cold.

"Runner-up position from an acting standpoint goes to Ernest Thesiger as Dr. Praetorius, a diabolical characterization if ever there was one..." *Variety*

6 Tall, dark and back from the dead: Boris Karloff reprises his role as horror's prodigal son.

7 Gloom and doom in the bedroom: Elizabeth (Valerie Hobson) has good reason to worry. Within two years of his second stint as Dr. Frankenstein, 37-year-old actor Colin Clive died of pneumonia aggravated by severe alcoholism.

"Mr. Karloff is so splendid in the role that all one can say is 'he is the Monster'... James Whale, who directed the earlier picture, has done another excellent job; the settings, photography and the make-up... contribute their important elements to a first-rate horror film." *The New York Times*

"... one of the finest productions to come out of the Universal lot for many a day. Mounted extravagantly, gorgeously photographed, excellently cast..." *The Hollywood Reporter*

to do so again. Nevertheless, it is not these men of hubris who are ousted by society, but rather the product of their sins—a monster that makes mankind's innate imperfection painfully obvious. And the rejection this poor soul must endure is never-ending, for no sooner has the newly animated bride (Elsa Lanchester) felt the caress of his hand than she lets out a blood-curdling shriek. Tears stream down his cheeks as he realizes that even his own kind find him repulsive. In a fit of frustration, he grabs hold of a lever and blows the laboratory sky high, along with Dr. Pretorius and all his creatures.

Modern audiences tend to prefer *Bride of Frankenstein* to the original for its emphatically comic tone. There's no stopping Whale's love for the outrageous in the sequences staged in Pretorius's laboratory. It's not enough for the director to let his mad scientist have a miniature bishop keep a watchful eye over a potentially unchaste ballerina, king and queen; there simply has to be a bell jar with a lone mermaid twirling about a rock. Right next to her is the crowning achievement in this menagerie—a tiny devil complete with tail-coat and cape. Pretorius likes to be within close range of his favorite creation to provide him with a worthy example. After all, as the scientist goes to show, life might be a lot more interesting if the world were populated with little demons.

NM

THE HUNCHBACK OF NOTRE DAME

1939 – USA – 118 MIN.

DIRECTOR

WILLIAM (WILHELM) DIETERLE (1893–1972)

SCREENPLAY

SONYA LEVIEN, BRUNO FRANK, based on the novel
Notre-Dame de Paris by VICTOR HUGO

DIRECTOR OF PHOTOGRAPHY

JOSEPH H. AUGUST

EDITING

WILLIAM HAMILTON, ROBERT WISE

MUSIC

ALFRED NEWMAN

PRODUCTION

PANDRO S. BERMAN for RKO

STARRING

CHARLES LAUGHTON (Quasimodo), MAUREEN O'HARA (Esmeralda),
THOMAS MITCHELL (Clopin), CEDRIC HARDWICKE (Frollo),
EDMOND O'BRIEN (Gringoire), HARRY DAVENPORT (King Louis XI),
ALAN MARSHAL (Phoebus), KATHARINE ALEXANDER (Madame de Lys),
MINNA GOMBELL (Queen of Beggars), GEORGE ZUCCO (Procurator),
WALTER HAMPDEN (Archdeacon)

The HUNCHBACK OF NOTRE DAME

WITH

SIR CEDRIC HARDWICKE
THOMAS MITCHELL
MAUREEN O'HARA
EDMOND O'BRIEN
ALAN MARSHAL
WALTER HAMPDEN
KATHARINE ALEXANDER

PRODUCED BY PANDRO S. BERMAN
DIRECTED BY WILLIAM DIETERLE

SCREEN PLAY BY SONYA LEVIEN
ADAPTATION BY BRUNO FRANK

1

"Why was I not made of stone—like thee?"

Paris, at the end of the 15th century: the dawn of a new era. Gutenberg's printing press is a recent and dazzling technological innovation, and now rumors are circulating that the earth is not flat; a fellow called Columbus, it's said, is planning to reach India by sailing westwards. The world is ablaze with a new spirit of restless curiosity—but the common people are still mired in ignorance and superstition. As ever, they stream in their thousands to the square in front of Notre Dame cathedral, to enjoy the jesters, the jugglers, the floggings, and the executions. In the midst of this everyday pandemonium, one man is mocked and feared in equal measure: Quasimodo (Charles Laughton), the grotesquely deformed cathedral bellringer. Abandoned as a baby, he was adopted and brought up by the sinister Archdeacon Frollo (Cedric Hardwicke), to whom he is still cringingly devoted. Until, that is, the appearance of a stranger in the city rocks their relationship to the core: Esmeralda (Maureen O'Hara) is a dancer with a troupe of gypsies and Frollo is smitten by her charms. Possessed by desire for this dark and sensuous beauty, he murders a rival in a fit of jealousy. Worse: in order to cover up the deed and free himself from his obsession, he has Esmeralda hauled up in court for witchcraft and murder. She is sentenced to burn at the stake—but Quasimodo, who has also fallen for her hopelessly, frees the girl at the last moment and spirits her away to the belltower of Notre Dame.

Among the many film adaptations of Victor Hugo's *Notre-Dame de Paris* (1831), William Dieterle's version has probably most successfully captured the tension at the heart of the novel: the ideals of the Enlightenment in a gruesome mediaeval atmosphere.

Dieterle was an erstwhile apprentice of the legendary Berlin theater impresario Max Reinhardt, and his earliest experiences in cinema dated from the era of German Expressionist silent film. In *The Hunchback of Notre Dame*, Expressionist style is a means of rendering the gloomy atmosphere of the pre-war 1930s; see the dramatically

WILLIAM (WILHELM) DIETERLE In the 1930s, Warner Bros. saw the director William Dieterle as a specialist for film biographies of Great Men. Warner were best known for churning out reliably entertaining movies, and it was hoped that Dieterle's biopics would bring the studio a certain cachet—which they did. *The Story of Louis Pasteur* (1935) and *The Life of Emile Zola* (1937) each won three Oscars, and the latter even walked off with Best Film. It can fairly be said, then, that Dieterle was the only German director besides Ernst Lubitsch to gain a firm foothold in Hollywood. Yet his name is decidedly less familiar to film fans today, and this may be because Dieterle was never identified as an auteur. Instead, he is stuck with an unglamorous reputation as a solid craftsman with a penchant for pathos and a "message" laid on with a trowel. Perhaps, too, it has something to do with the fact that he always saw himself as essentially a man of the theater, despite having directed movies as impressive as *The Hunchback of Notre Dame* (1939).

Wilhelm Dieterle was born in Ludwigshafen, Germany, and spent nearly two decades working as a theater actor. One of the directors who most influenced him was the legendary Max Reinhardt. Dieterle also appeared in numerous silent movies and began directing films in 1923. Having enjoyed considerable success in Germany, he traveled to Hollywood in 1930 to direct German-language versions of sound films for Warner. Though aware of the importance of cinematography, Dieterle always regarded the actors as the heart of any movie. During his years in Hollywood, he also provided personal support to many refugees and distinguished himself as a committed anti-Nazi. In the 1950s, he returned to his native country.

"Look at those sets! Whole streets of 15th-century Paris, water-spouting gargoyles, mighty bells, and entire stories of Notre Dame Cathedral recreated with the most exacting precision!" *Der Spiegel*

effective treatment of light and shade, the creepy Gothic architecture and the carefully choreographed crowd scenes. The acting, too, is mercurial in a way that emphasizes the power of the irrational, and even the bizarre make-up (for certain characters) is less Hollywood Realist than German Expressionist.

The Hunchback of Notre Dame is a typical example of the allegorical costume dramas in which 1930s Hollywood encoded its response to contemporary events in Europe—and thereby maintained its neutrality, at least nominally, as the U. S. government (still) demanded. Though the film functions perfectly as a movie entertainment in its combination of horror and romance, Dieterle's political stance is unmistakable. His film quite clearly characterizes the advance of fascism as an atavistic return to the violent obscurantism of the Middle Ages; thus the brutal suppression of the gypsies inevitably reminds us of the Nazis' racial policies and the brutality of their uniformed hordes. When the Hunchback carries Esmeralda off to the cathedral, where she is safe from the clutches of the witch hunters, he triumphantly cries out to the crowd: "Sanctuary! Sanctuary!" We should remember that the film was made at a time when European refugees from fascism were not welcomed by everyone in the United States.

2

1 Just a hunch: Something tells gypsy beauty Esmeralda (Maureen O'Hara) that poet Gringoire (Edmond O'Brien) will only be writing love songs from now on.

2 Putting the cart before the horse: Believing her to have murdered one of their own, the Paris troops mount up in full regalia for Esmeralda's execution.

3 Testing the waters: When the rest of the land torments Quasimodo (Charles Laughton) for his hideousness, Esmeralda demonstrates a drop of compassion.

4 Belle tower: Quasimodo snatches Esmeralda out of death's hands and opens up his home to her.

5 Riding the Lord's coattails: No matter how much sympathy Frollo (Cedric Hardwicke) shows towards the hunchback, he never forgets that he is above him.

With his courageous action, Quasimodo demonstrates his full humanity. Until then, the Hunchback is merely a pitiable creature; but the deed transforms him into a tragic hero. Though Charles Laughton's face was almost immobilized by the heavy make-up, his performance is unforgettably moving.

Essentially, the poet Gringoire (Edmond O'Brien) fights a no less heroic battle. In a world ruled by torture, hysteria, and hatred of strangers, this character can be seen as the voice of the Enlightenment—and it's his untiring faith in the power of language and the triumph of

"We prefer to avert our eyes when a monstrosity appears, even when we know he's a synthetic monster, compounded of sponge rubber, greasepaint and artifice. Horror films have their following, but children should not be among them. The Music Hall is no place for the youngsters this week. Take heed!" *The New York Times*

6 Keeping the faith: All King Louis XI (Harry Davenport) and the Archdeacon (Walter Hampden) can do to stop Frollo from going too far is pray for a little divine intervention.

7 Festival of Fools: Too bad the aristocracy has no idea that they're the stars of the show.

8 You can ring my bell: Charles Laughton's portrayal of Quasimodo chimed perfectly with the way Victor Hugo had written the character. Actors Lon Chaney, Anthony Quinn and Anthony Hopkins are among the other great who have played the role.

justice that ultimately saves Esmeralda's life. (Here, the film diverged notably from the plot of Hugo's novel.)

Dieterle's film came at the end of a decade in which the horror-film genre had acquired an unprecedented popularity. It might be said that *The Hunchback of Notre Dame*, for all its Enlightenment impulses, is a little too interested in grabbing its audience with an opportunistic depiction of grotesque ugliness. At the very least, though, Dieterle does hint at the self-reflective attitude that distinguishes Victor Hugo's novel: when the King watches the antics of the populace at the annual Coronation of the Fool, he notes that such grotesque spectacles satisfy the people's hunger for sensation. His observation is undoubtedly directed at us, too—the moviegoers. UB

THE WOLF MAN

1941 – USA – 70 MIN.

DIRECTOR

GEORGE WAGGNER (1894–1984)

SCREENPLAY

CURT SIODMAK

DIRECTOR OF PHOTOGRAPHY

JOSEPH A. VALENTINE

EDITING

TED J. KENT

MUSIC

CHARLES PREVIN, HANS J. SALTER,
FRANK SKINNER

PRODUCTION

GEORGE WAGGNER for UNIVERSAL PICTURES

STARRING

LON CHANEY JR. (Larry Talbot / The Wolf Man), CLAUDE RAINS (Sir John Talbot),
WARREN WILLIAM (Doctor Lloyd), RALPH BELLAMY (Colonel Paul Montford, Chief Constable),
PATRIC KNOWLES (Frank Andrews), BELA LUGOSI (Bela, The Gypsy),
MARIA OUSPENSKAYA (Maleva, The Old Gypsy Woman), EVELYN ANKERS (Gwen Conliffe),
J. M. KERRIGAN (Charles Conliffe), FAY HELM (Jenny Williams),
HARRY STUBBS (Reverend Norman)

The
WOLF MAN
with
CLAUDE RAINS
WARREN WILLIAM
RALPH BELLAMY
PATRIC KNOWLES
BELA LUGOSI
MARIA OUSPENSKAYA
EVELYN ANKERS
and
LON CHANEY
as "The Wolf Man"

1

"There's something very tragic about that man."

After suffering the loss of his brother, Larry Talbot (Lon Chaney Jr.) rekindles family ties with his father (Claude Rains) and moves back to the country home he grew up in. In no time at all, Larry falls in love with the charming Gwen Conliffe (Evelyn Ankers) and discovers the wonders of life anew. Then, one evening, the young couple accompany Gwen's friend Jenny Williams (Fay Helm) to see a renowned gypsy and fortune-teller named Bela (Bela Lugosi). But instead of revealing the secrets of the stars to Jenny, the mysterious soothsayer sheds his human skin for that of a werewolf and attacks the defenseless girl. Larry takes on the beast without thinking twice, killing it with his bare hands.

The nightmare, however, has only just begun, for the werewolf manages to sink his teeth into the young man and pass his curse along before their battle ends. This means that if Larry can't find an antidote, he'll be doomed to wander the earth as a supernatural predator until the end of time, driven by instinct to hunt down the people he loves the most.

With *The Wolf Man* (1941), Universal Pictures carved itself a lucrative niche in the quick and easy B-movie market. As protagonist Larry Talbot, Lon Chaney Jr. wowed audiences with a grizzly combination of innocence and animalism he maintained for a total of five pictures (1941, 1943, 1944, 1945, and 1948). Each installment had him searching desperately for a way out of his nightmare and finding it in death by a silver bullet rather than in a restorative cure. But since mortality has never been an issue where horror movies are concerned,

CURT SIODMAK Born in Dresden, Germany, in 1902 Curt Siodmak was the younger brother of future director Robert Siodmak. Their careers got off to an impressive start when the Siodmaks collaborated with Eugen Schüfftan, Billy Wilder, and Fred Zinnemann for the impressive Berlin feature *People on Sunday* (*Menschen am Sonntag*, 1929). Curt Siodmak also wrote for periodicals, winning acclaim as an author. Trivia buffs will be also interested to know that he played a supporting role in Fritz Lang's *Metropolis* (1926).
Teaming up with Walter Reisch, Siodmak wrote the screenplay to his own successful sci-fi novel *F. P. 1 Doesn't Answer* (*F. P. 1 antwortet nicht*). Shortly afterwards, the Jewish brothers fled Nazi Germany to escape persecution. Once in the USA, Curt Siodmak got a job with the scriptwriting department at Universal Studios. Horror, gore, and mysteries became his areas of expertise. Unlike many of his contemporaries, Siodmak did not just see horror as a medium for blood, guts and shock value. In fact, his work was always rooted in reality and demonstrated an innate brilliance for drama. As he once said in an interview: "My films all have a scientific background—that's what gives them their authentic edge."
Besides penning the script for Jacques Tourneur's classic *I Walked with a Zombie* (1943), he was also responsible for the third of five Wolf Man installments to star Lon Chaney Jr.—the low-grade B-movie *House of Frankenstein* (1944) directed by Erle C. Kenton. Curt also joined forces with brother Robert to transform that self-same furry actor into the *Son of Dracula* (1943). His double-volume autobiography is entitled *Wolf Man's Maker: Memoir of a Hollywood Writer.* Curt Siodmak died in California on September 2, 2000.

the Larry Talbot character was happily returned as the protagonist of every sequel.

It is remarkable how well *The Wolf Man* fared with audiences, considering that the picture was shot in three short weeks. The subject matter clearly tapped into the zeitgeist of the era, and the German-born Curt Siodmak composed a script that was right on the mark. The Siodmak piece drew from a screenplay Robert Florey had written for Universal ten years earlier, which the studio would have produced much earlier had the censors not choked on a "blasphemous" metamorphosis scene Florey had set in a confessional. Werewolves themselves, on the other hand, were neither controversial nor revolutionary. Debuting in 1935, *The Werewolf of London*, who today is referred to the "Elvis werewolf" on account of an eye-catching bouffant, was the first of his celluloid breed. However, much like genre contemporary *The Invisible Man* (1933), based on the H. G. Wells novel of the same name, the picture's naturalistic horror sequences fell short of audience expectations.

The new and improved wolf man, Larry Talbot, would not make the same mistake as his predecessors. Trick photography was the name of the game, and also the reason Curt Siodmak had to scrap his original vision for the script which relied on subtle suggestion to evoke terror within the audience's imagination. Likewise, Siodmak's proposal of suspending the Larry Talbot character in a limbo between madness and sanity, only resolving the question at the plot's conclusion, was flatly rejected by the producers.

Entrusting himself to make-up artist Jack Pierce, Lon Chaney Jr. sat for hours on end to become the furry beast of Tinseltown. Basic cross-fades allowed for a cinematic man-to-monster transition that would give moviegoers their money's worth. The intellectual contours Siodmak had hoped to endow the film with were thus largely overshadowed by the cinematic shock-effect.

To the great joy of the studio, Lon Chaney Jr.'s portrayal of the character couldn't have been better. The special effects, too, sharpened over time, making the bloodcurdling metamorphosis increasingly realistic. Be that as it may, it was the tale's tragic subtext that made these pictures a major draw with audiences. Viewers felt for ill-fated hero Larry Talbot because, deep down, he wasn't a malicious monster at all. Much as in Greek tragedy, Larry was a man at the mercy of fate. In the first installment, it is the protagonist's father who frees his son from incurable agony, and in doing so, loses all hope of continuing the family line and his faith in the natural order of the universe.

Curt Siodmak's contemporary Val Lewton thought little of the picture, choosing instead to make films one could see as the flip-side of The Wolf Man saga. During the 1940s and 1950s, he and director Jacques Tourneur made numerous hits in the B-movie genre, starting with *Cat People* (1942). Lewton and Tourneur successfully pushed through a concept similar to the one Siodmak had originally tried to pitch to Waggner, and the result was astounding: by relocating horror to the viewer's imagination, the team evoked a sense of fear more potent than any image Hollywood could create for the screen.

SR

"Night monster... prowling... killing... terrifying the countryside... with the blood lust of a savage beast—*The Wolf Man*!"

Universal trailer for: The Wolf Man

1 Electrolysis anyone? Lon Chaney Jr. as wolf man Larry Talbot.

2 Beauty and the beast: Actress Evelyn Ankers actually passed out during rehearsal as soon as Lon Chaney Jr. got his paws on her.

3 Sins of the father: Sir John Talbot (Claude Rains) reckons that if he brought Larry into this world, he can just as well take him out of it.

4 Gone mental: Sir John believes his son to be psychologically disturbed, but fails to recognize the full extent of Larry's affliction.

CAT PEOPLE

1942 – USA – 73 MIN.

DIRECTOR

JACQUES TOURNEUR (1904–1977)

SCREENPLAY

DEWITT BODEEN

DIRECTOR OF PHOTOGRAPHY

NICHOLAS MUSURACA

EDITING

MARK ROBSON

MUSIC

ROY WEBB

PRODUCTION

VAL LEWTON for RKO

STARRING

SIMONE SIMON (Irena Dubrovna), KENT SMITH (Oliver Reed), JANE RANDOLPH (Alice Moore), TOM CONWAY (Doctor Louis Judd), ALAN NAPIER (Carver), JACK HOLT (Commodore), ELIZABETH RUSSELL (Cat Woman at the Restaurant), THERESA HARRIS (Minnie), ELIZABETH DUNN (Pet Store Employee), MARY HALSEY (Blondie), ALEC CRAIG (Zookeeper)

CAT PEOPLE

SHE WAS
MARKED WITH
THE CURSE
OF THOSE
WHO SLINK
AND COURT
AND KILL
BY
NIGHT!

with

SIMONE SIMON
KENT SMITH
TOM CONWAY
JANE RANDOLPH
JACK HOLT

Produced by
VAL LEWTON
Directed by
JACQUES TOURNEUR

WRITTEN BY
DeWITT BODEEN

1

"The darkness is lovely. It's where I feel most at home."

Oliver (Kent Smith) forgets that some creatures cannot be tamed when he spots the woman of his dreams at the zoo. A technical draftsman, he's mesmerized by the sleekly dressed, dark-haired beauty holding a sketchbook at the panther cage. Irena (Simone Simon) is a feline-obsessed fashion designer starved for inspiration. She has come here in the hope of seeing something that could link her incessant visions of wildcats to her profession, and to abate the nagging fears she has about being one of the "cat women" documented in old Serbian folklore. According to legend, when induced into a state of jealousy or covetousness, women of that kind shed their human skin and take on the form of a deadly panther. But Oliver is a pragmatic sort, and he dismisses these musings as folklore, and marries Irena, fully convinced that sooner or later she will recognize the superstitions for what they are. Needless to say, he's the one who refuses to recognize the truth.

In an effort to shield her husband from her animalistic nature, Irena soon starts to distance herself and lands on the therapist's couch for demonstrating signs of paranoia. However, the situation is far worse than anyone around her suspects, for Irena's affliction not only threatens to rock the foundations of her happy marriage, but might also end up claiming the life of Oliver's co-worker and secret admirer Alice (Jane Randolph).

Cat People was one of 1942's biggest sleepers. Conceived of and shot as a B-movie, the picture proved a massive hit and solidified the reputations of producer Val Lewton and director Jacques Tourneur as masters of the supernatural thriller. It was the first of three legendary films the RKO duo brought to the screen, the other two being *I Walked with a Zombie* (1943) and *The Leopard Man* (1943), a gruesome threesome that heralded the dawn of the modern horror era.

Lewton and Tourneur effectively broke with the "Gothic" tradition that had dominated the aesthetics of 1930s horror flicks. Rather than employing type-cast monster actors *à la* Bela Lugosi or Boris Karloff, and setting the story in some ancient ruins that scream "scary" in neon lights, *Cat People* relocates the bestial metamorphosis to the audience's imagination—i. e. from the visually explicit to the imagined. The most we ever see of Irena's transformation into her panther-self is shot in silhouette. The character's alter-ego and the other supernatural occurrences suggested in the film are thus never entirely corroborated. Likewise, the story's contemporary setting intensifies the terror felt by the audience in a way none of

VAL LEWTON He was born Vladimir Ivan Leventon in the Black Sea town of Yalta, but he emigrated to the United States with his mother and sister while still a young man and quickly shed his foreign-sounding name for the catchier Val Lewton. Although his aunt was the successful silent film actress Alla Nazimova, Lewton started off as a journalist and popular novelist before finding his way to the MGM public relations department. In 1933, he met David O. Selznick and became his assistant and right-hand man. Taken by Lewton's gift for storytelling, Selznick had him scripting dialog upon dialog for legendary Hollywood projects such as *Gone with the Wind* (1939). In 1942, Selznick secured Lewton a producing job with RKO, where his work on innovative and stylish B-horror movies would earn him a legendary reputation in the industry. His collaboration with director Jacques Tourneur gave rise to the three most significant films of his career: *Cat People* (1942), *I Walked with a Zombie* (1943) and *The Leopard Man* (1943). *Cat People's* astounding success inspired Lewton to pursue a sequel (*The Curse of the Cat People* (1943), and gave him a near monopoly in the production of low-budget horror flicks, which he held until heart failure ended his life prematurely in 1951. Vincente Minnelli paid homage to Lewton in his film *The Bad and the Beautiful* (1952) by including a producer character assigned by the studio to create a horror movie about cat people; rather than having the actors dressing up as gigantic kitty-cats, the executive deems it more effective to suggest a sense of menace via shadow.

2

1 Cat got your tongue? Ravishing French beauty Simone Simon as the screen's first *feline fatale.*

2 The cat's meow: Typical American Oliver (Kent Smith) hopes Irena will turn out to be a sex kitten; little does he realize that he's come face to face with a Serbian lioness.

3 Scaredy cats: The maxims of science are about to come crashing down on Oliver and co-worker Alice (Jane Randolph).

its genre predecessors could. Nothing attests to this better than *Cat People's* much-cited swimming pool scene.

One evening, Irena secretly follows Alice, the woman competing for her husband's affections, to the swimming pool at her apartment complex. A hissing sound emanates from the shadows, sending Alice into a panic as she jumps into the unlit pool. Fearing for her life, she wades into the center, scanning the premises for potential danger. But, given the irregular motion of the water against the tiles, it is impossible for her to assess what might be lurking in the shadows. The suspense lifts only after Alice has burst into screams. We see Irena flip the light switch and normalize the situation by claiming to have just wanted to have a word with her. But the instant Irena disappears from the scene Alice discovers that her robe has been torn to shreds.

The venue of this scene, a place where people are permitted to dress scantily, layers the underlying horror with sexual overtones. In addition, Tourneur utilizes the swimming pool's ordered architecture as a means of visually communicating the conflict at the heart of the genre—the intrusion of the supernatural on a world built on reason. The intangible threat is heightened by the swimming facility's uncompromising geometry, the slippery stage of a perpetual play of light and dark. This isn't the sole instance where *Cat People* proves to be a reflection on cinema as

a medium of concealment. Nicholas Musaraca's cinematography, which pioneered the low-key lighting style that would later emerge as the hallmark of film noir, keeps the action submersed in a realm of impenetrable shadow. The structure supplied by the screen's physical borders ceases to exist and the film's inherent darkness spills into the viewing space. Projected images no longer provide the security of visual recognition. The film's supernatural potential is unleashed, like the cat out of the bag, leaving us at a loss to predict where terror will strike next.

UB

"The story is one of those 'it-might-happen' dramas, if an old Serbian legend be true." *Variety*

4 Scratching post: Even though Irena's deadly mystique drives their marriage into the ground, the fatalistic Oliver still loves it when she digs her claws into him.

5 Speak now or forever hold your peace: The highpoint of Oliver and Irena's wedding reception at a Serbian restaurant comes when another cat woman asserts that the bride is one of her kind.

6 There's more than one way to skin a cat: But rather than allowing therapy to dissect Irena, Tourneur shuns a rational explanation of her affliction.

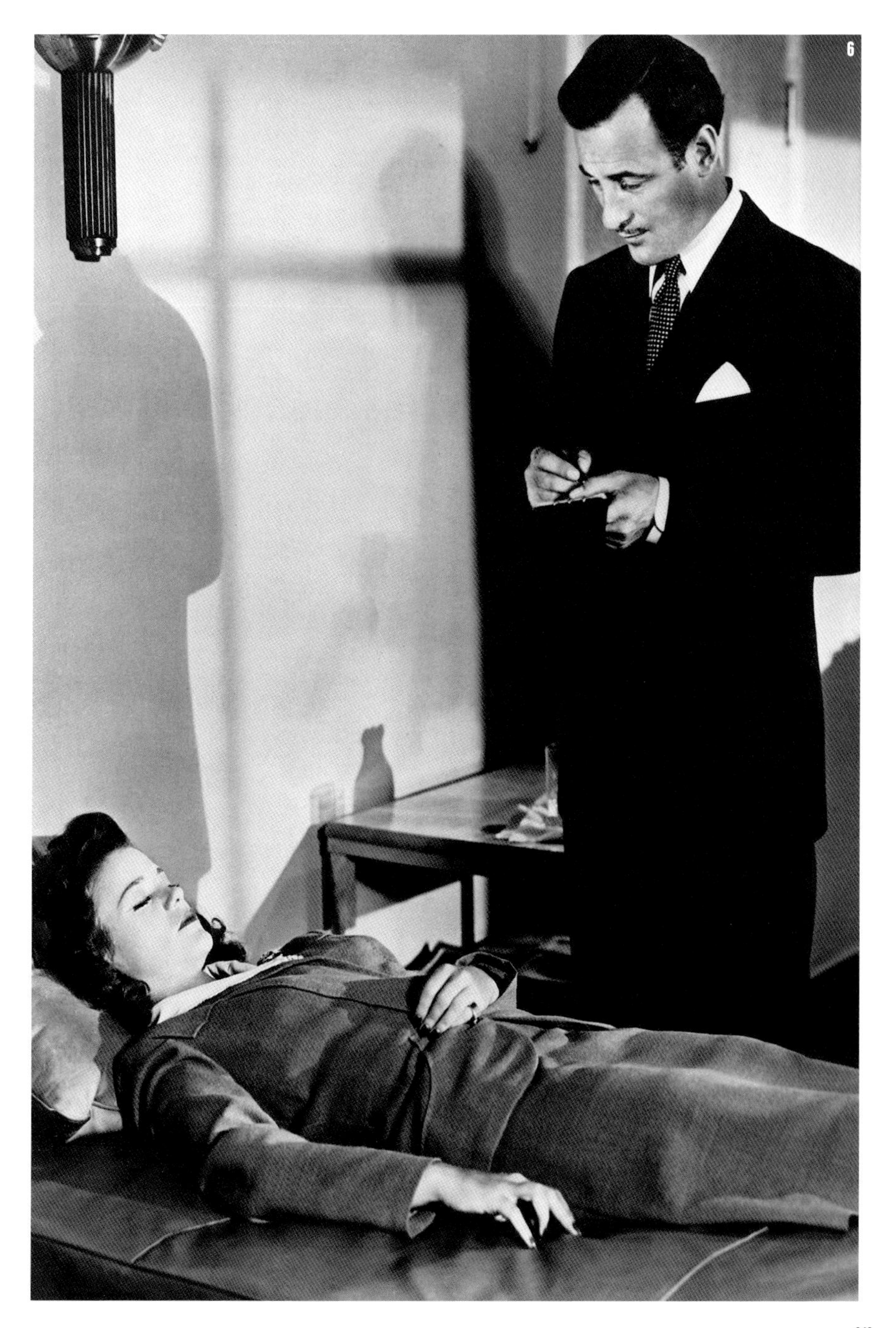

I WALKED WITH A ZOMBIE

1943 – USA – 69 MIN.

DIRECTOR

JACQUES TOURNEUR (1904–1977)

SCREENPLAY

CURT SIODMAK, ARDEL WRAY,
based on characters created by INEZ WALLACE

DIRECTOR OF PHOTOGRAPHY

J. ROY HUNT

EDITING

MARK ROBSON

MUSIC

ROY WEBB

PRODUCTION

VAL LEWTON for RKO

STARRING

FRANCES DEE (Betsy), TOM CONWAY (Paul Holland),
JAMES ELLISON (Wesley Rand), CHRISTINE GORDON (Jessica Holland),
EDITH BARRETT (Mrs. Rand), JAMES BELL (Doctor Maxwell),
THERESA HARRIS (Alma, Maid), SIR LANCELOT (Calypso Singer),
DARBY JONES (Carrefour), JENI LE GON (Dancer)

I WALKED WITH A ZOMBIE

with

JAMES **ELLISON** · FRANCES **DEE** · TOM **CONWAY**

RKO RADIO PICTURES

Produced by
VAL LEWTON

Directed by
JACQUES TOURNEUR

SCREEN PLAY BY CURT SIODMAK & ARDEL WRAY
BASED ON AN ORIGINAL STORY BY INEZ WALLACE

"Everything good dies here— even the stars."

When Western medicine turns its back on Betsy (Frances Dee), the young nurse crosses over to voodoo. Somewhere in the sugarcane of her employer's plantation, a witchdoctor is expecting her. Armed with a piece of cloth the guardian of the temple is to identify her by, Betsy can't make out any path at all—even with her flashlight. Jessica (Christine Gordon), her patient, doesn't have much time left. A tropical illness has trapped her in a trance, leaving her a mindless shell of flesh and blood. Like the blind leading the blind, Betsy persists with their haphazard search; for at this point it seems that if the witchdoctor can't cure Jessica of her soul-robbing affliction, no one can.

Most locals already believe "the zombie woman" to be beyond help. But they keep their opinions to themselves, as Jessica's husband, wealthy plantation owner Paul Holland (Tom Conway), is the head of the small West Indian island's first colonial family. The fact that Holland is willing to go all the way to Canada to find his wife a nurse tells Betsy all she needs to know. The situation, however, is even graver than she suspects. On their seaward journey to his island home, Holland warns her that the tropical waters are nothing but a cesspool of death and decay. Then, as they sail by a school of flying fish, he suggests that it is fear which prompts them to perpetually break the surface. And before dropping anchor, Holland purports that the reason the waters themselves shimmer so brilliantly at night is because countless tiny cadavers reflect the moonlight.

David Lynch may have made a name for himself in 1990s postmodern film by examining "things that are not always as they seem," but Jacques Tourneur practically invented the concept for the cinema. Suddenly, viewers were left to imagine unspeakable things that were poten-

RKO What do masterpieces like *Citizen Kane* (1941), *King Kong* (1933), Howard Hawks's absurd *Bringing Up Baby* (1938) and Alfred Hitchcock's thrilling *Notorious* (1946) all have in common? Three little letters: RKO. It was a time when people still thought of filmmaking in terms of studios and Radio-Keith-Orpheum (RKO) was one of the so-called Big Five, holding its own against giants like Metro-Goldwyn-Mayer (MGM), Paramount Pictures, 20th Century Fox, and Warner Bros. In addition to producing pictures, each of these studios ran its own distribution and owned a chain of movie houses where its productions were screened.

The RKO story dates back to 1928. To profit from its self-developed sound film processing format, The Radio Corporation of America merged with several movie industry power players, the most prominent of which was Keith-Albee-Orpheum, a cinema chain that controlled approximately 200 units on the eastern seaboard. One of the first RKO studio bosses was none other than David O. Selznick, who went on to become one of the most legendary producers in Hollywood history. The horror classic *The Most Dangerous Game* (1932) was one of the greatest hits born under his reign at the company. Indeed, the studio mainly focused its creative efforts on making B-horror flicks like Val Lewton and Jacques Tourneur's *I Walked with a Zombie* (1943), Fred Astaire musicals, and formulaic mainstream fare. Nonetheless, RKO wasn't really able to develop a style of filmmaking that might have set it apart from other studios.

In 1948, the book closed on Classic Hollywood when an antitrust verdict forbade any single company from unilaterally producing movies, distributing them, and running its own cinemas. That same year, billionaire Howard Hughes bought RKO, but only held onto it for a relatively short time. In its final years, the studio exclusively produced television programming until it finally closed its doors for good in 1957. Today, RKO is the most readily overlooked member of the former Big Five. The studio itself lives on primarily through its beloved logo—a radio tower atop a globe that can still be seen at the opening of the classic films it produced.

2

1 That old black magic: Nurse Betsy (Frances Dee) and sugar farmer Paul Holland (Tom Conway) find out that life in the West Indies is anything but sweet.

2 The voodoo that you do: A trance party where the only music to be heard is the steady beat of bongo drums.

3 Wheel of fortune: Although RKO only supplied Val Lewton with a 150,000 dollar budget and a four-week shoot, the producer had no difficulty spinning straw into cinematic gold.

4 Science fiction or science fact? Screenwriters Curt Siodmak and Ardel Wray claimed their script was based on research about voodoo rituals and possession. Siodmak the horror expert was also responsible for penning *The Wolf Man* (1941). Need we say more?

"In a realm located on the edge of reason, what is reality, what is hocus-pocus, what is dream? Just as in *Cat People*, Lewton and Tourneur never find their way back to the banal world of the fully explicable; instead, their film's final images symbolize the fatal attraction of evil and the stubborn robustness of love. *I Walked with a Zombie* is an exceptional Hollywood product, and it needn't fear comparison with the classic works of cinematic history."

Der Tagesspiegel

"The blackest magic of voodoo keeps this beautiful woman alive... yet dead!"

Movie poster

tially lurking behind every façade. And when it comes to the films of producer/director team Val Lewton and Jacques Tourneur, imagination is everything. More than anyone else, the pair of them knew how to generate fear through innuendo. Their collaborative efforts, which in addition to *I Walked with a Zombie* include *Cat People* (1942) and *The Leopard Man* (1943), made the best of B-movie budget constraints, and minimalism was their lifeblood. In situations where other studios would go all out with bloodcurdling monsters, Tourneur and Lewton simply dimmed the lights. Where others would resort to shock effect, the RKO team would turn the camera away from the action and let it grab audiences from behind.

These ambivalent images that played havoc with the audience's imagination made *I Walked with a Zombie* the classic it is today. The two interceding love-triangles that make up the meat of the plot, on the other hand, are a far cry from spectacular: no sooner has Betsy set foot on the island than she falls in love with Holland and is compelled by her affections to cure his wife—who, incidentally, Holland's half-brother is in love with. Just as the melodrama peaks, a family tragedy surfaces involving the

5 Gated community: Paul Holland has fenced himself off from his impulsive and alcoholic brother Wesley (James Ellison). Not that he cares—he's only interested in Paul's wife Jessica.

6 In your head, in your head: Dream team Val Lewton and Jacques Tourneur make the implicit more horrifying than the explicit with their masterful interplay of shadow and light.

brothers' mother, which readily explains why Jessica has fallen under a spell only death can break.

Until then, Betsy is willing to brave it in the grass to restore Jessica to her former state of health. The night of their sugarcane expedition is marked by owl hoots, snapping twigs and rhythmic percussion—all the makings of a voodoo symphony. The flashlight uncovers a skull, and then we see a dead animal hanging from a tree. From out of nowhere, a foot comes into view. Gradually looking upward, Betsy scans a tall, gaunt black figure. When she reaches the head, a pair of gigantic eyes stare back at her that seem to be on the verge of popping out of their sockets. And then the most shocking thing of all: Betsy has lost the tattered bit of fabric she was supposed to show this man, who is clearly the witchdoctor's guardian. Although she cannot identify herself, he lets her pass anyway—never uttering a single word.

Effortlessly and stylishly, Jacques Tourneur defies our expectations many times over throughout the film. First, he creates suspense, showing us the piece of fabric caught on a tree branch, and then he expertly diffuses it with the wave of a hand. Potentially meaningful images pop up all over the place, leaving us uncertain as to what we should pay attention to and what to ignore. Not only does Tourneur play his red herrings for all they're worth, but he also does his best to leave things unexplained whenever possible—like why zombie Jessica is capable of obeying voodoo commands. And yet this intentional lack of answers points to the director's belief in the inexplicable and supernatural. Indeed, whenever Tourneur is at the helm, the otherworldly, in this case voodoo culture, is less a potential danger than a gateway to an intriguing world at the outer reaches of our perception.

NM

6

THE THING FROM ANOTHER WORLD

1951 – USA – 87 MIN.

DIRECTOR

CHRISTIAN NYBY (1913–1993)

SCREENPLAY

CHARLES LEDERER, based on the short story
Who Goes There? by JOHN W. CAMPBELL JR.

DIRECTOR OF PHOTOGRAPHY

RUSSELL HARLAN

EDITING

ROLAND GROSS

MUSIC

DIMITRI TIOMKIN

PRODUCTION

HOWARD HAWKS for RKO RADIO PICTURES INC.,
WINCHESTER PICTURES CORPORATION

STARRING

KENNETH TOBEY (Captain Patrick Hendry), MARGARET SHERIDAN (Nikki),
JAMES ARNESS (The Thing), DOUGLAS SPENCER (Ned Scott),
JAMES R. YOUNG (Eddie Dykes), ROBERT CORNTHWAITE (Doctor Carrington),
DEWEY MARTIN (Bob), EDUARD FRANZ (Doctor Stern),
JOHN DIERKES (Doctor Chapman), SALLY CREIGHTON (Mrs. Chapman),
EVERETT GLASS (Professor Wilson), WILLIAM SELF (Corporal Barnes)

HOW DID IT GET HERE?
WINCHESTER PICTURES CORPORATION Presents
HOWARD HAWKS'
Astounding MOVIE
THE THING
from another world!
Distributed by RKO RADIO
Directed by CHRISTIAN NYBY
Producer– HOWARD HAWKS • Associate Producer– EDWARD LASKER
Screen Play by CHARLES LEDERER

1

"No pleasure, no pain... no emotion, no heart. Our superior in every way."

The Thing from Another World tells the story of a crashed UFO and its surviving pilot—a blood-guzzling Martian who threatens a U. S. research base at the North Pole. It could have been a typical trashy and forgettable run-of-the-mill B-movie, if it hadn't been for two things: the political climate of the United States in the early 1950s and Howard Hawks's involvement as a producer.

The film is directed by Christian Nyby, who had worked with Hawks as an editor for many years. Yet although the old master took a back seat to his protégé, Hawks's influence on the movie is quite unmistakable. The dialog, often fiery and sometimes witty, reminds us of his screwball comedies such as *Bringing Up Baby* (1938). The fast-paced, frequently overlapping verbal exchanges are so engrossing that the near-total absence of special effects is easily forgotten. Only occasionally is the war of the words interrupted by the grotesquely inarticulate grunting of the "creature" in its rubber suit. Much of the film's humor comes from the contrast between the wisecracking soldiers' bawdy talk and the anemic language of the scientists. Typically for Hawks, there's also a woman in the midst of it all, adding endless complications because she refuses to behave like a lady. And here's another very Hawksian irony: ordered by their superiors in Washington to spare the alien's life, the two "camps" react quite unexpectedly. The scientists, normally interested only in the future, turn out to be compliant conservatives, ready to follow the government line and do their appointed duty. The soldiers, by contrast, throw all military discipline overboard, defying their commander-in-chief and doing their damnedest to settle the monster's hash. This movie is one more proof that a limited budget and a sparing use of the means available can result in highly creative solutions. The claustrophobically narrow environment of the

CUTTER / EDITOR In the early days of the cinema, the editor's tasks were relatively simple: to cut the exposed film mechanically, and to piece it together according to the wishes of those in charge. The finished version was expected to provide an elementary continuity of time, place, and narrative—no more and no less. Very quickly, however, film editing became an art form with its own expressive possibilities.

"Cutters" began to acquire respect as artists, and were increasingly expected to play a creative role in the filmmaking enterprise. By analogy to the profession of journalism, the lowly cutter-and-paster was transformed into an editor. And far from simply sticking the stuff together, artists such as Edwin S. Porter (*The Great Train Robbery*, 1903), David W. Griffith (*The Birth of a Nation*, 1915) and Sergei Eisenstein (*Battleship Potemkin*, 1925) developed highly expressive new techniques, from continuous montage to parallel, rhythmic, tonal, metric, and "associative" montage. Though they tend to be less conspicuous than directors and cameramen, film editors have a very significant influence on the final form of the movies we see on the screen.

2

3

1 Hawks and predators: With a gun in one hand and a woman in the other, Captain Patrick Hendry (Kenneth Tobey) investigates all things alien. Margaret Sheridan as Nikki.

2 The scientists and soldiers spread out on the ice to trace the shape of the object trapped underneath.

3 Technical difficulties: State-of-the-art gizmos can't give the research team the upper hand against the cosmic being.

4 The trap is set: But they've got their picks, axes, and cleavers ready to go just in case something goes wrong.

"Chris Nyby had done an awfully good job as the cutter on *Red River* and he'd been a big help to us too, so I let him do it. He wanted to be a director and I had a deal with RKO that allowed me to do that. I was at rehearsals and helped them with the overlapping dialog—but I thought Chris did a good job." *Howard Hawks*

research station is a case in point: there's no way out of there, except to certain death in the eternal Arctic ice.

The powerful effect of *The Thing from Another World* also has a lot to do with the period in which it was made. With its numerous allusions to the political zeitgeist, this sci-fi spectacle is actually a parable on the vicissitudes of contemporary history. From the frozen wastes of the Cold War, an unknown creature emerges, and it's nothing like you or me: it has the physiology of a plant and the skin of an insect, it's asexual and unfeeling, it's more than two meters tall, it can't speak, it's bloodthirsty and it has the strength of a bear. Though vaguely humanoid in

appearance, The Thing is clearly very far from human; we are faced, of course, with a creature from another planet. And though its intentions are unclear, one fact is obvious: The Thing wants into that research station double quick, because it can only survive by drinking human blood. We hear about atmospheric disturbances, an explosion in the East, radioactive contamination… and without a doubt, we're deliberately being served up stereotypes of the communist enemy. This is disarming. Unlike many sci-fi B-movies, *The Thing from Another World* never becomes ridiculous, simply because it never takes itself too seriously. If sci-fi movies are often artless to the point of fatuity, then this movie makes a virtue of the genre's vices. It takes a clichéd situation seriously—a dumb monster threatening a bunch of frightened humans—and goes on to make a highly ironic statement about a country driven half-crazy by fear of Red infiltration.

Thank you, Howard Hawks, for a minor masterpiece of subversive Hollywood filmmaking!

BR

8

5 Little shop of horrors? The scientists try to cultivate an alien offspring as a means of studying the species.

6 She blinded them with science: But is Nikki's intellectual prowess enough to knock the monster back into deep space?

7 The iceman cometh: The Martian awakes from within a block of solid ice and heats up the scene.

8 Taking on the unknown: There's no telling what horrors lie in store for the romantic leads—apart from a happy ending.

"*The Thing* has turned out to be the best thriller... since *King Kong*." *Films in Review*

CREATURE FROM THE BLACK LAGOON

1954 – USA – 79 MIN.

DIRECTOR

JACK ARNOLD (1916–1992)

SCREENPLAY

HARRY ESSEX, ARTHUR A. ROSS, MAURICE ZIMM

DIRECTOR OF PHOTOGRAPHY

WILLIAM E. SNYDER

EDITING

TED J. KENT

MUSIC

HENRY MANCINI, ROBERT EMMETT DOLAN,
MILTON ROSEN, HANS J. SALTER, HERMAN STEIN

PRODUCTION

WILLIAM ALLAND for UNIVERSAL INTERNATIONAL PICTURES

STARRING

RICHARD CARLSON (David Reed), JULIE ADAMS (Kay),
RICHARD DENNING (Mark Williams),
ANTONIO MORENO (Carl Maia), NESTOR PAIVA (Lucas),
WHIT BISSELL (Thompson), BERNIE GOZIER (Zee),
HENRY A. ESCALANTE (Chico), RICOU BROWNING (Creature in the water),
BEN CHAPMAN (Creature on land)

with RICHARD DENNING · ANTONIO MORENO · NESTOR PAIVA · WHIT BISSELL

DIRECTED BY JACK ARNOLD · SCREENPLAY BY HARRY ESSEX AND ARTHUR ROSS · PRODUCED BY WILLIAM ALLAND · A UNIVERSAL-INTERNATIONAL PICTURE

1

"It sounds incredible, but it appeared to be human!"

In the uncharted regions of the Amazon, a research team makes a startling discovery. For millions of years, an anomaly—part man, part sea creature—has been nesting in the tropic waters. Now, at long last, scientists have stumbled upon what they believe to be the missing link between humanity and fish-kind! Efforts to trap it are foiled, not by the beast, but by conflicting human interests. David (Richard Carlson) is concerned about the ramifications of removing the amphibian from its natural habitat. But recognition-hungry Mark (Richard Denning) wants to unveil it—dead or alive—for all mankind to behold. Oblivious to the internal squabbles, the creature from the black lagoon has taken a fancy to David's fiancée, Kay (Julie Adams). It climbs aboard the research boat every chance it gets in the hopes of sweeping the beautiful woman off her feet with its slippery fins. Each time, it leaves the vessel empty-handed, but not before killing a member of the crew out of sexual frustration.

Creature from the Black Lagoon has all the ideal B-movie ingredients: barely passable acting, wooden dialog about human nature, and, above all else, a factory-assembled icky goon. Teenagers everywhere raced to the drive-in to see Universal's latest contribution to the hall of monster classics. The star, a top-heavy oaf with lobster claws on land, yet a regular ballerina underwater, proved immensely popular with audiences, supplying the studio with a generation successor to hits like *Frankenstein* (1931) and *The Mummy* (1933). The stuntman in the ever-so-imaginative black rubber and latex wetsuit saved the company a bundle on special effects expenditures. After all, who needs stop-motion photography when you can see scaly flippers flopping through the Amazon? And who needs the Amazon when you can shoot the picture in a Florida swamp for less than half the price?

A cut and paste plot ensured that the film wouldn't create any other sort of industry upsets. There isn't a trace

RICOU BROWNING Will the real creature from the black lagoon please stand up? Difficult, as horror fans all over the world continue to argue over who holds the title. Ben Chapman wore the scaled rubber-suit on land, and Ricou Browning sported it in the water. The creature itself remains one of the cinema's all-time most popular monsters. The role demanded that Browning hold his breath for up to four minutes at a time. In 2003, the two men saw each other again for the first time since the shoot at the Creaturefest in Wakulla Springs, Florida: Chapman resurfaced a party animal, whereas Browning had clearly devoted his life to other interests. Born in Florida in 1930, Browning entered the work force as a rescue diver and aquatic show producer. His film career began with *Creature from the Black Lagoon* (1954) and continued to flourish well after the picture's spawn had come and gone. Browning is the creator of the hit TV series *Flipper* (1964–68), for which he also served as director, writer, and producer. He tried his hand at children's films time and again, active on projects like *Salty* (1975)—the tale of a sea lion. Browning kept to the water throughout his professional life in Hollywood, whether as a stuntman, stunt coordinator or, most often, as an underwater cameraman. He showed his gusto in the field as the director of the underwater sequences in the James Bond film *Thunderball* (1965), and recreated the magic 20 years later for the remake *Never Say Never Again* (1982/83). In recent years, Browning has also been active as „marine coordinator" in numerous U. S. TV series such as, for instance, *Graceland* (2013–15) and *Bloodline* (2015–16). He also held this function for Bill Purple's drama about an Atlantic crossing on a raft entitled *The Devil and the Deep Blue Sea*, which is coming to the movies in 2017.

"The underwater scraps between skin divers and the pre-historic thing are sure to pop goose pimples on the susceptible fan, as will the close-up scenes of the scaly, gilled creature." *Variety*

of any globally dire issue akin to a nuclear threat, something that later inspired numerous other works of B-movie movie aficionado Jack Arnold, such as *Tarantula* (1955) and *The Incredible Shrinking Man* (1957). Instead, the picture follows in the formulaic footsteps of great horror flicks like *King Kong*, and is nothing more than a rehashed telling of "Beauty and the Beast." The scantily clad Kay plays the pivotal role of flaunting her figure and screaming at the top of her lungs whenever the creature surfaces—and rest assured she's always the first to spot him. Meanwhile, the men are busy at work, trying to one up each other as hunters: Mark develops a newfangled water harpoon, and David, in a stroke of genius, comes up with a method of anesthetizing all the river's plant life (whatever that's supposed to accomplish). Four indigenous men lose their lives helping them, and the fifth, a Caucasian, finally moves the research team to emotion.

This enduring vision of all things trashy exhibits an ounce of taste in the staging of a few select scenes. Kay's bathing excursions, accompanied by the occasional crocodile and lovesick monstrosity, are filmed from below with an underwater lens. It makes for the same winning

1 Leapin' latex: No-one can make the crowd go wild like this granddaddy of horror.

2 Missing link or science project gone awry? And why do its fingers seem to twitch whenever the lovely Kay (Julie Adams) is around?

3 Satan's cesspool: Behold an ecologically sound being, who's not about to let mankind muck up his lagoon. Lady-kind is another matter altogether…

suspense that *Jaws* (1975) would capitalize on twenty years later. Taken by her swimming technique, the creature shadows Kay in what looks like an erotically charged, synchronized Olympic routine. But minutes later, it is disgusted after she shamelessly contaminates its beautiful abode with a cigarette butt.

Like some sixty-odd movies filmed in 1953 and 1954, including Jack Arnold's debut feature *It Came from Outer Space* (1953), *Creature from the Black Lagoon* was shot in 3-D, a nifty trend that ended with the advent of the CinemaScope format. Here, however, it proves especially impressive during the graceful underwater sequences. Furthermore, it stunningly enhances the faux Amazon jungle as it brings the viewer into close contact with the gruesome beast lurking in these shimmering black streams. What Arnold can really take pride in is that despite being hokier than hokey this classic B-movie is expertly edited to a suspense-packed seventy-nine minutes, entirely free of drag time. The much beloved badman of the Southern swamplands resurfaced in two sequel projects, *Revenge of the Creature* (1955) and *The Creature Walks among Us* (1956). PB

GOJIRA

GODZILLA

1954 – JAPAN – 98 MIN.

DIRECTOR

ISHIRÔ HONDA (1911–1993)

SCREENPLAY

ISHIRÔ HONDA, SHIGERU KAYAMA,
TAKEO MURATA

DIRECTOR OF PHOTOGRAPHY

MASAO TAMAI

EDITING

KAZUJI TAIRA

MUSIC

AKIRA IFUKUBE

PRODUCTION

TOMOYUKI TANAKA for TOHO FILM

STARRING

AKIRA TAKARADA (Hideto Ogata), MOMOKO KŌCHI (Emiko Yamane),
AKIHIKO HIRATA (Dr. Daisuke Serizawa), TAKASHI SHIMURA (Prof. Kyohei Yamane),
FUYUKI MURAKAMI (Tabata), SACHIO SAKAI (Reporter Hagiwara),
REN YAMAMOTO (Masaji the Fisherman), KATSUMI TEZUKA (Reporter / Godzilla),
RYOSAKU TAKASUGI (Godzilla), HARUO NAKAJIMA (Godzilla)

水爆大怪獣映画
ゴジラ
ゴジラか科学兵器か驚異と戦慄の一大攻防戦!
放射能を吐く大怪獣の暴威は日本全土を恐怖のドン底に叩き込んだ!
原作・香山滋
宝田明
河内桃子
平田昭彦
志村喬
製作 田中友幸
脚本 村田武雄 本多猪四郎
撮影 玉井正夫
美術監督 北猛夫
美術 中古智
照明 石井長四郎
音楽 伊福部昭
特殊技術 円谷英二 渡辺明 向山宏 岸田九一郎
東宝
東宝株式会社 製作・配給

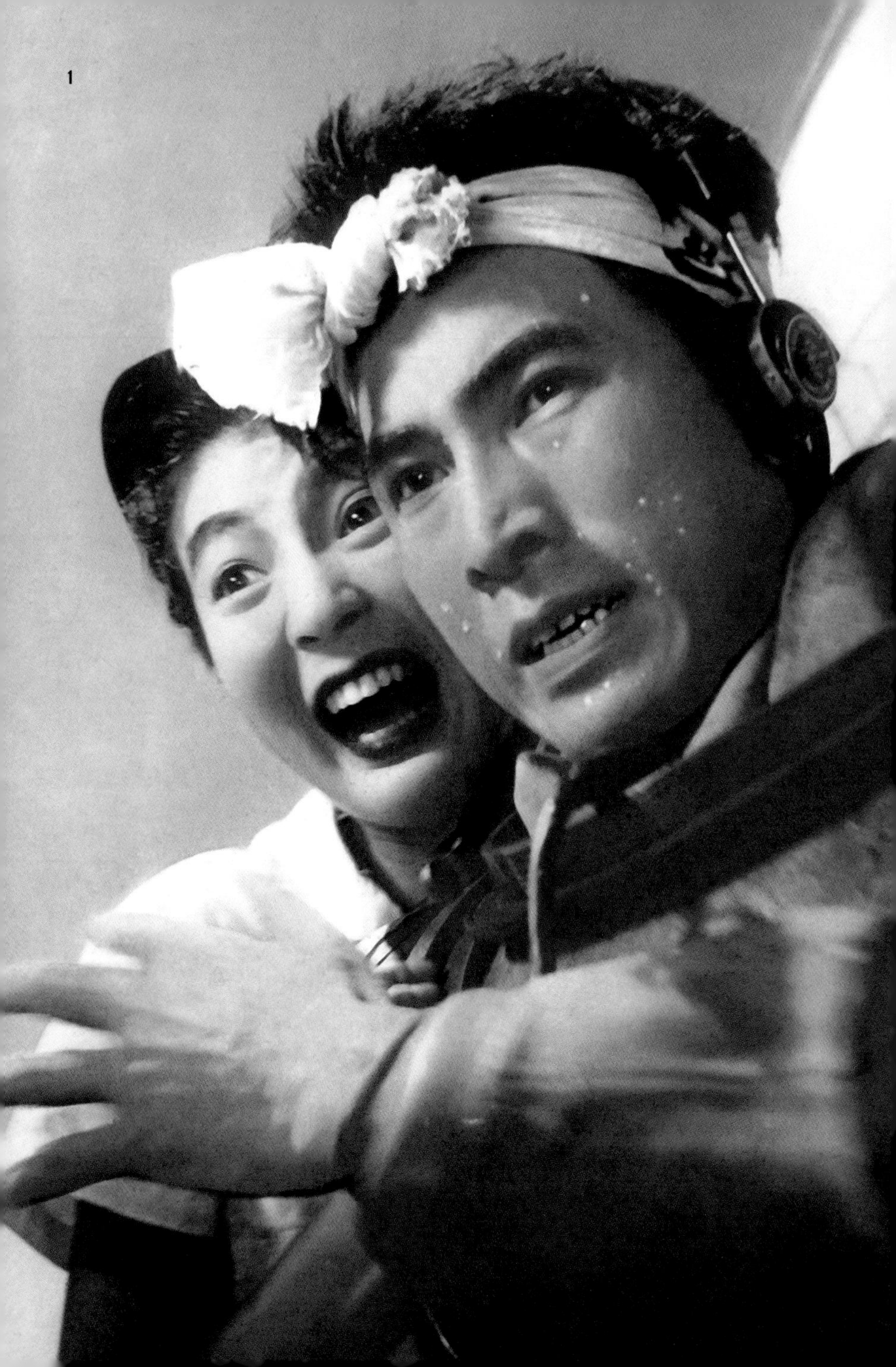

1

"The century's most frightening monstrosity."

Crushing the maxims of 1950s science fiction, *Godzilla's* horrors are firmly rooted in contemporary historical and scientific fact. Underwater volcanic eruptions or mines are thought to be steadily sinking fishing boats off the Japanese coast. Then a prehistoric monster sighting on the island of Odo gets paleontologist Kyohei Yamane (Takashi Shimura) and his daughter Emiko (Momoko Kōchi) wondering whether something else could lie at the heart of the mystery. Their suspicions are confirmed when they arrive on Odo and are confronted by a one-hundred-foot tall radioactive reptile known as Godzilla (Katsumi Tezuka, Ryosaku Takasugi, Haruo Nakajima).

It seems that nuclear testing in the Pacific has coaxed the beast out of its submarine cavern and into the world of man, leaving Japan at its mercy. Electric fences, bombs, machine guns and all other forms of defense are no match for Godzilla, and the island nation suddenly becomes a war zone. Those who can flee the cities in a panic, others pray they'll be evacuated. But nuclear spitfire Godzilla can tear through even the heftiest of barriers. Tokyo is burned to a crisp, and the monster threatens to vent its fury on the rest of the world.

Volunteering at a hospital, Emiko comes face to face with Godzilla's path of mass destruction. Unable to bear the plight of her people any longer, she entrusts her lover, a member of the coastguard, with top secret information: her fiancé Dr. Daisuke Serizawa (Akihiko Hirata) has developed a deadly oxygen blaster, capable of wiping out any conceivable living organism. Despite feeling torn by the great moral obligation of implementing such a weapon,

GODZILLA MOVIES Movie monsters, along with mythological creatures and dinosaurs, enjoyed overwhelming popularity in the 1950s. Combining animation with live action, filmmakers like Ray Harryhausen shot their larger-than-life beings, which were actually model miniatures, with stop-motion photography, painstakingly integrating the beasts into the story one frame at a time. Not so *Godzilla* (*Gojira*, 1954), where an actor squeezed himself into a 100 lb. rubber monster suit. The film was such an astounding success that, to date, 24 further installments have made it to the screen. Highlights include: *King Kong vs. Godzilla (Kingukongu tai Gojira*, 1962), *Son of Godzilla* (*Kaijûtô no kessen: Gojira no musuko*, 1967), *All Monsters Attack / Destroy All Monsters* (*Kaijû sôshingeki*, 1968), *King Kong vs. The Bionic Monster* (*Gojira tai Mekagojira*, 1974), *GK2: Godzilla 2000* (*Gojira ni-sen mireniamu*, 1999), *Godzilla vs. Megaguirus* (*Gojira tai Megagirasu: Jii Shômetsu Sakusen*, 2000), and most recently Gareth Edward's *Godzilla* (2014). In contrast to the original picture, subsequent adaptations were made as tongue-in-cheek B-movies. Unlike in Western monster flicks, where beasts like King Kong are meant to represent subconscious desires, the Japanese angle on the genre often depicts them as caricatures of current politicians. In later installments, Godzilla, assisted by other imaginary creatures, not only defends Japan against the sea monster Ebirah, but also against alien invaders.

1 Hold on to your headbands, here comes Godzilla!

2 Lunch.

3 Kamikaze pilots: War planes are like wind-up toys in the claws of the monster.

"*Godzilla* is a collective metaphor and a collective nightmare, a message film that says more than its message, that captures, with a horrified poetry, the terrors that stomped through the minds of people 50 years ago." *San Francisco Chronicle*

Serizawa is prepared to construct a single bomb to save the planet. He ends up sacrificing himself to kill the monster, annihilating all but a mammoth skeletal silhouette that sinks to the bottom of the ocean.

Unlike the numerous follow-ons it inspired, the original *Godzilla* has a documentary feel to it. By 1954, the United States, Great Britain, and France had all been testing newly developed atomic weapons in the Pacific. One such American test exposed the entire crew of a Japanese fishing vessel to nuclear radiation. It is therefore no surprise that Godzilla does not stem from mythological tradition as such, but is to be seen as the embodiment of a ubiquitous, post-war atomic threat. Initially, the catastrophe is treated as environmentally related; something faceless that wreaks havoc on marine life and the water supply. Soon, however, the crisis is pegged to something more immediate; for *Godzilla* is actually a Japanese reflection on the outcome of the Second World War, and the cataclysmic violence experienced on the home front. We are shown images reminiscent of the nightly bomb raids, the flight for shelter, and the storms of poisonous black rain and nuclear fallout. A state of panic floods the streets. Crying children are stranded, forlorn families search frantically for missing loved ones. The battle against the unthinkable not only requires the most advanced technology and the solidarity of the Japanese people, but also a full demon-

4

4 Death star: Hideto Ogata (Akira Takarada) and Dr. Serizawa (Akihiko Hirata) try to score a hole-in-one with an atomic golf ball.

5 Fishing for compliments: Doctor Serizawa's secret weapon turns his aquarium into dust.

6 Oh, the grass is always greener on Godzilla's lawn. Paleontologist (Takashi Shimura) is sick of models and longs for a close-up view of a real-life dinosaur.

"This is a bad movie, but it has earned its place in history, and the enduring popularity of Godzilla and other monsters shows that it struck a chord." *Chicago Sun-Times*

stration of the nation's military muscle as tanks, aircraft, bombs and even documentary footage of Japanese soldiers practicing maneuvers. Only when Serizawa hears a song that reminds him of the victims at Hiroshima and Nagasaki does he feel compelled to build the bomb that will end the suffering. Yet the picture clearly states that only humanity is to blame for Godzilla's visit and his devastating rampage. We are left with the echo of Professor Yamane's chilling reminder that while Godzilla may be gone for now, the atomic forces that awakened him are far from being in check. PLB

INVASION OF THE BODY SNATCHERS

1956 – USA – 80 MIN.

DIRECTOR

DON SIEGEL (1912–1991)

SCREENPLAY

DANIEL MAINWARING,
based on the novel *The Body Snatchers* by JACK FINNEY

DIRECTOR OF PHOTOGRAPHY

ELLSWORTH FREDERICKS

EDITING

ROBERT S. EISEN

MUSIC

CARMEN DRAGON

PRODUCTION

WALTER WANGER for ALLIED ARTISTS PICTURES CORPORATION,
WALTER WANGER PRODUCTIONS INC.

STARRING

KEVIN MCCARTHY (Doctor Miles Bennell), DANA WYNTER (Becky Driscoll),
LARRY GATES (Doctor Dan Kauffman), KING DONOVAN (Jack Bellicec),
CAROLYN JONES (Theodora), JEAN WILLES (Nurse Sally Withers),
RALPH DUMKE (Chief of Police, Nick Grivett), VIRGINIA CHRISTINE (Wilma),
TOM FADDEN (Uncle Ira), KENNETH PATTERSON (Stanley Driscoll)

WALTER WANGER CREATES THE ULTIMATE IN SCIENCE-FICTION!

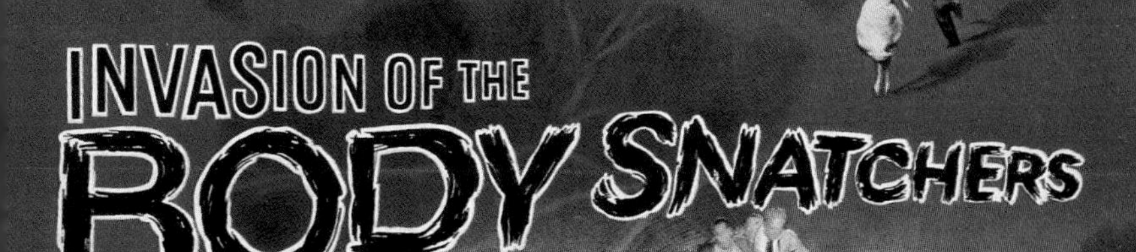

COLLIER'S MAGAZINE
called it
"THE NIGHTMARE THAT
THREATENS THE WORLD"

AN
ALLIED ARTISTS
PICTURE

starring

KEVIN McCARTHY · DANA WYNTER

with LARRY GATES · KING DONOVAN · CAROLYN JONES · JEAN WILLES · RALPH DUMKE

Directed by DON SIEGEL · Screenplay by DANIEL MAINWARING · Based on the COLLIER'S MAGAZINE Serial by JACK FINNEY

FILMED IN
SUPERSCOPE

1

"Tomorrow you'll be one of us!"

After a two-week absence, Dr. Miles Bennell (Kevin McCarthy) returns home to sleepy Santa Mira, his piece of Californian utopia to find the community stricken by a bizarre outbreak of mass hysteria. A young boy insists that his mother just isn't his mother anymore. An agitated woman doesn't recognize her uncle. And during a visit to the home of his horror novelist friend, Bennell spots a gigantic embryo the size of a full-grown man.

The next morning, both the grotesque fetus and the psychological afflictions of his patients have vanished. Still, Dr. Bennell can't shake the feeling that an unseen force is closing in on his world, and his worst fears are confirmed when he stumbles upon enormous peapods containing spitting-image replicas of Santa Mira inhabitants. An alien life form, growing in his own backyard, is conspiring to take over the town. Soon Miles is the last human being alive, and must run for his life in a desperate attempt to escape the mind-controlled masses better known as "pod people."

Now one of the great classics of science-fiction cinema, Don Siegel's *Invasion of the Body Snatchers* took years to catch on with audiences and critics. Compared to the standards of the time, it was a study in understatement (look closely and you'll even get a glimpse of uncredited co-writer Sam Peckinpah as a gas station attendant). Special effects were kept to a minimum, and horror was evoked without a monstrous face. Here, paranoia is not a symptom of xenophobia, but rather the fear of a sinister force at the heart of normality. The pod people are humanoid doppelgangers, incapable of emotion or individuality. In a chilling scene, Miles observes how nondescript passers-by respond to orders from an unseen commander and cluster together into a workers battalion to receive a new shipment of pods from a delivery truck.

WALTER WANGER Although by no means a household name, Walter Wanger had a career that spanned almost 50 years and is among Hollywood's most intriguing personalities. In 1919, he signed with the legendary Paramount Pictures forerunner Famous Players-Lasky Corporation. Later on, he became a freelance producer working with almost all the major studios. As one of the few intellectuals holding such a position, he spoke out for the cinema's social responsibilities, a stance which was, however, only reflected in a handful of his 65 projects. His best-known work includes *Queen Christina* (1933) with Greta Garbo, *Stagecoach* (1939) and the Hitchcock thriller *Foreign Correspondent* (1940). At one point, he came close to a professional crash, although not as a result of his box-office flop *Joan of Arc* (1948), but because of a personal tragedy in 1951. Having discovered that his wife, actress Joan Bennett, was two-timing him with her agent, Wanger shot him in the groin, and spent four months behind bars as a result. Wanger rebuilt his reputation with the independent films *Riot in Cell Block 11* (1953/54) and *Invasion of the Body Snatchers* (1956). In 1958, he produced *I Want to Live!*, directed by Robert Wise, for which Susan Hayward won an Oscar as death row's Barbara Graham. In the early 1960s, 20th Century Fox got him to climb aboard *Cleopatra* (1963), the 44-million-dollar bomb that nearly bankrupted the studio. This was to be his last picture. In 1968, Walter Wanger died in New York.

1 Split pea soup: What Miles (Kevin McCarthy) and Becky (Dana Wynter) will become, if they don't find another hiding place pronto.

2 Taking a stab at genetic engineering: Cold War hysteria lets off steam in horror novelist Jack's (King Donovan) hot house.

"Well, I think there's a strong case for being a pod. These pods, who get rid of pain, ill health, and mental disturbance are, in a sense, doing good. It happens to leave you with a very dull world. But that, my dear friend, is the world that most of us live in." *Don Siegel*

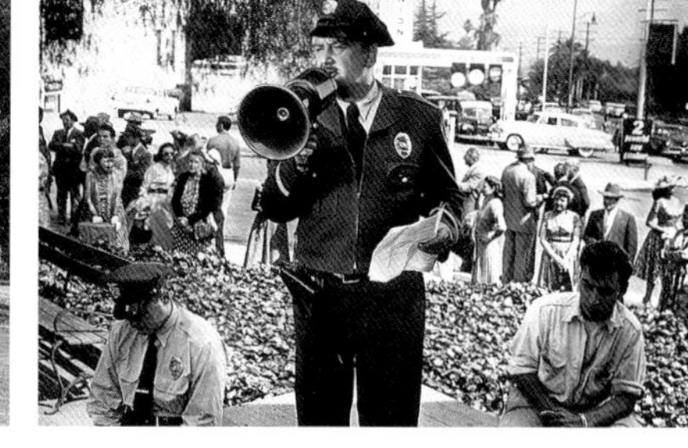

3 Utopian lynch mob or weeding out individuality: Miles and Becky decide it's time to check out of suburbia.

4 Obedient, organized, and orderly: Pod people or neo-conservatives? You decide.

5 Home grown: By equating Americans with vegetables, Don Siegel puts film noir and horror in one neat husk.

But only much later, after kissing his beloved Becky (Dana Wynter), does he feel the full horror of the mindlessness and blind obedience that has the town in its grip; for Becky's cold lips reveal that she too has become one of them, having surrendered her humanity in exchange for sleep.

As with so many science fiction films of the decade that depicted an invasion from outer space, the mind-stealing element of the Body Snatchers facilitated an anti-communist reading of the picture. Other interpretations saw it as a reflection on the wave of fascism inspired by McCarthyism or on Middle America's consumer conformity.

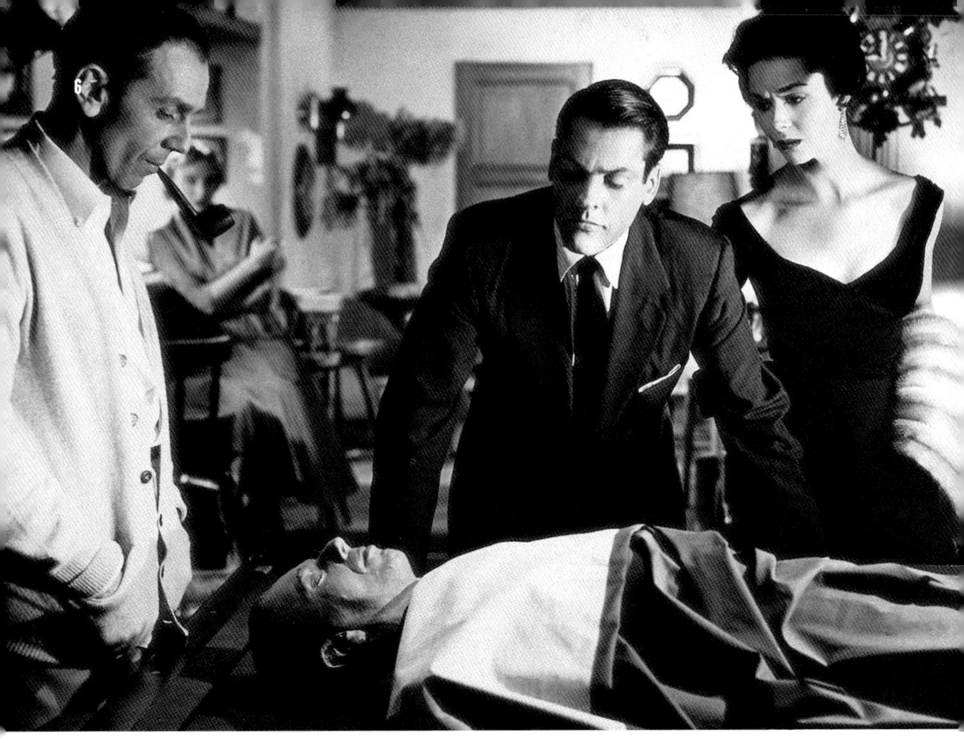

6 Cool as a cucumber: Jack doesn't seem the least bit disturbed to see his spitting image gestating in his living room—an almost inhuman reaction.

7 Car hop: In an effort to alert the authorities about the space invaders, Miles tries to keep his wits about him while grabbing a lift.

8 Break it up, you guys: Miles kills alien impostors before they kill his neighbors.

"In a California town not too far away practically the entire population turned into a vegetable salad of sorts and the results—well, see this picture, Invasion of the Body Snatchers, this almost terrifying science-fiction yarn." *Los Angeles Examiner*

Don Siegel's ingeniously subversive tactic was, of course, to question the state of so-called normality rather than any particular political ideologies. As the director said in an interview: "People are pods. Many of my associates are certainly pods. They have no feelings. They exist, breathe, sleep. To be a pod means that you have no passion, no anger; the spark has left you." And a population of drones is naturally the ideal basis for all forms of state control.

Sadly, Siegel himself also conceded to conformist pressures within the industry. The studio forced him and producer Walter Wanger to embed the main plot within a framing story that showed Miles raving about his run-ins with the pod people to a psychologist. Finally, they buy his story and the FBI intervenes. Don Siegel took pride in the fact that for years many underground movie houses would stop the film prematurely at its originally foreseen endpoint: the viewer is left with an extreme close-up of Miles, almost out of his mind, as he fervently preaches his warning into the camera, "They're here already! You're next, You're next…"

Because of its short length and spartan budget of 417,000 dollars, *Invasion of the Body Snatchers* is categorized as a B-movie. But what really makes the film stand head and shoulders above the crowd of cheaper flicks is its clever integration of elements from other genres. The stark black-and-white contrasts, the motifs of sleep and underlying social instability are straight out of film noir; the same applies to Siegel's original title "Sleep no more," which was most likely rejected by the studio because of its cross-genre implications. Two successful remakes attest to the universal appeal of the story: Philip Kaufman's *Invasion of the Body Snatchers* (1978) reworks the piece as a look at modern urban isolation, and Abel Ferrara's *Body Snatchers* (1993) relocated the action to an army base.

PB

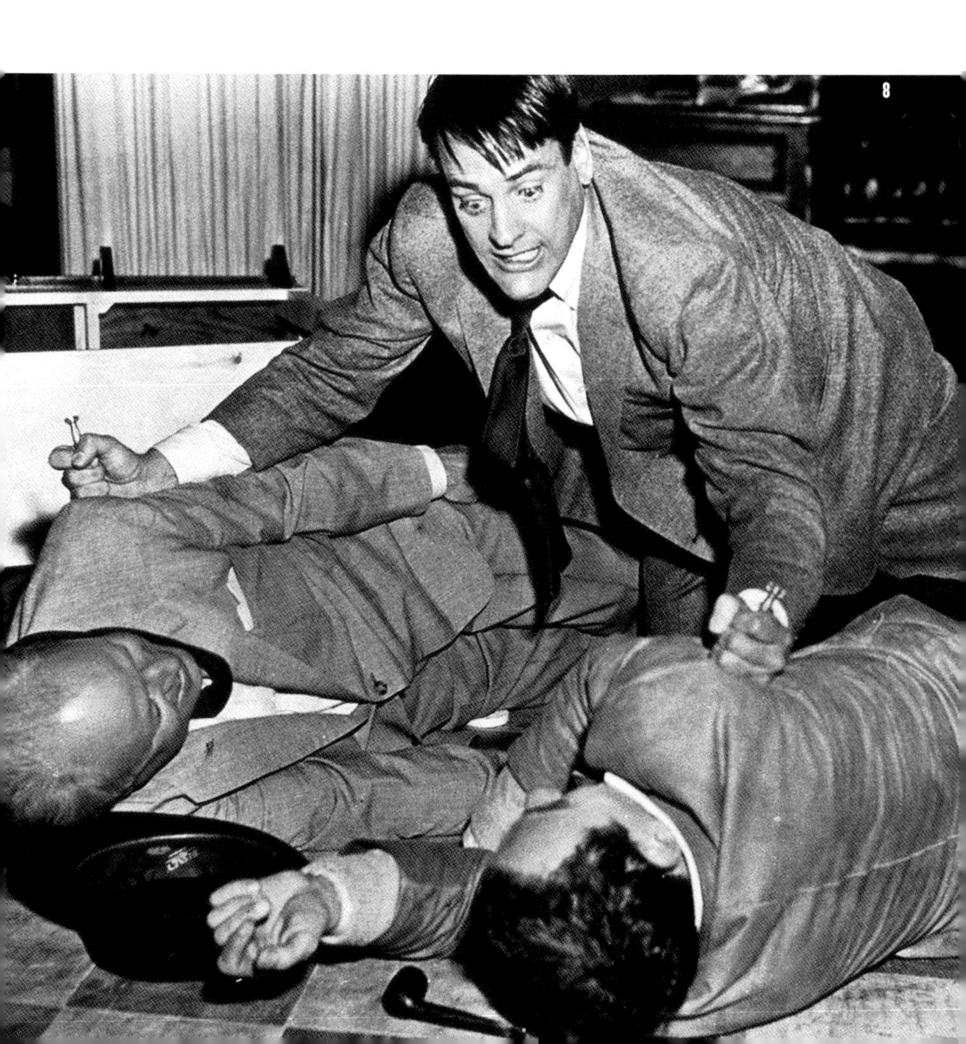

THE INCREDIBLE SHRINKING MAN

1957 – USA – 81 MIN.

DIRECTOR

JACK ARNOLD (1916–1992)

SCREENPLAY

RICHARD MATHESON, based on his novel *The Shrinking Man*

DIRECTOR OF PHOTOGRAPHY

ELLIS W. CARTER

EDITING

ALBRECHT JOSEPH

MUSIC

FOSTER CARLING, EARL E. LAWRENCE

PRODUCTION

ALBERT ZUGSMITH for UNIVERSAL INTERNATIONAL PICTURES

STARRING

GRANT WILLIAMS (Scott Carey), RANDY STUART (Louise Carey),
RAYMOND BAILEY (Doctor Thomas Silver),
PAUL LANGTON (Charlie Carey), APRIL KENT (Clarice),
WILLIAM SCHALLERT (Doctor Arthur Bramson),
FRANK J. SCANNELL (Barker), HELENE MARSHALL (Nurse),
DIANA DARRIN (Nurse), BILLY CURTIS (Midget)

A FASCINATING ADVENTURE INTO THE UNKNOWN!

THE INCREDIBLE

SHRINKING MAN

A UNIVERSAL-INTERNATIONAL PICTURE STARRING

GRANT WILLIAMS · RANDY STUART

with APRIL KENT · PAUL LANGTON · RAYMOND BAILEY

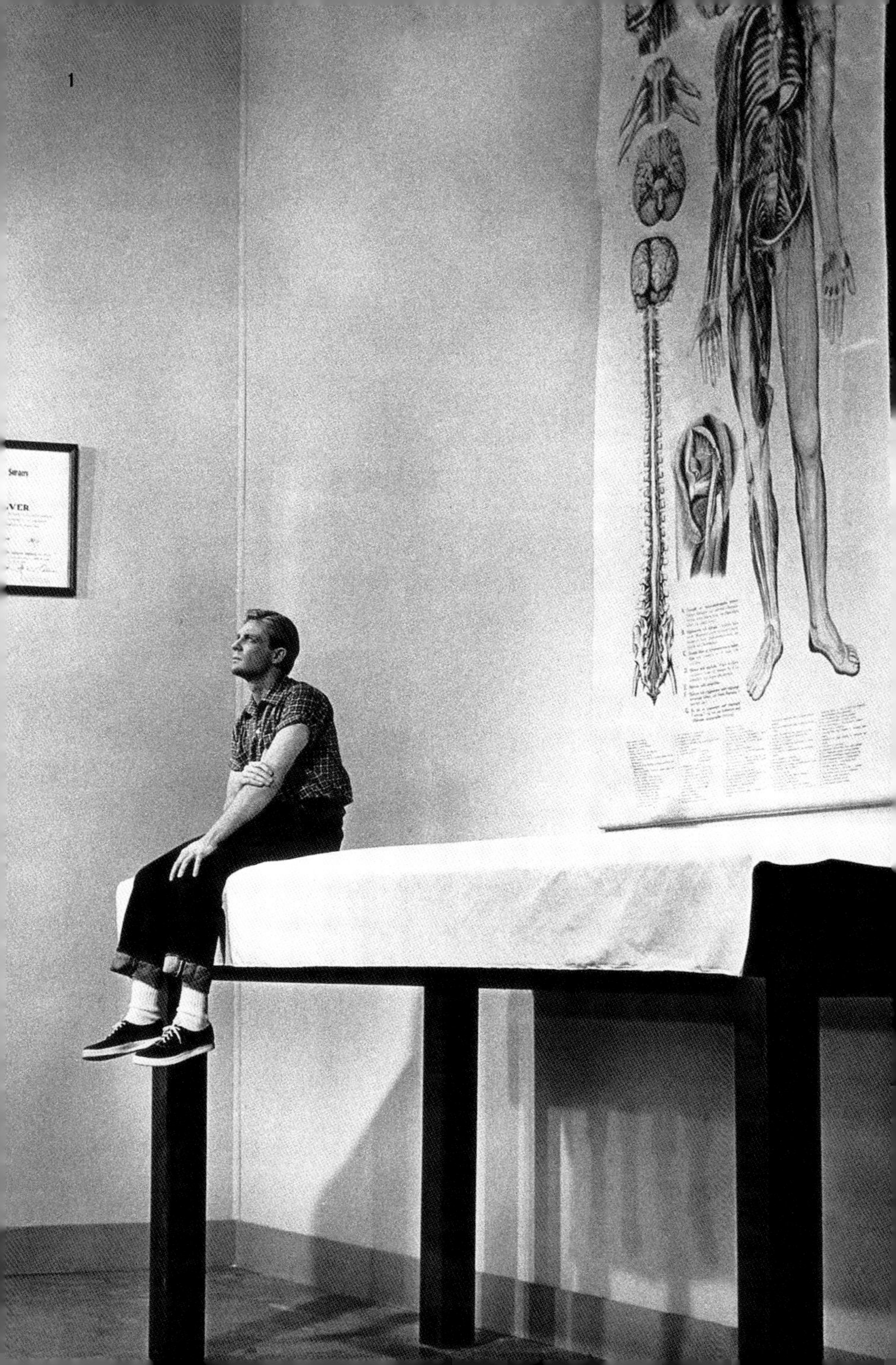

1

"To God there is no zero. I still exist."

Those of you who wish that the inches would just melt away, take heed. Imagine you woke up one morning to find that—joy of joys—your wardrobe fit is a bit looser. Five minutes later you discover that the arms and legs of all your clothes are noticeably longer than they should be. Has panic already wiped the smile off your face? Whatever for? It's not as if people can inexplicably start shrinking. At least that's what the physician attending Scott Carey (Grant Williams) says. But expert opinion can't deny what's plain as day: Scott is getting slightly smaller with each passing minute.

As nothing was beyond the comprehension of science in the rational 1950s, medical experts eventually pinpoint the cause of the bizarre phenomenon: an unfortunate combination of toxins, brought on by contact with an insecticide and a radioactive cloud, has activated a steady shrinking process within Scott's body. An antidote is found shortly after diagnosis, but it only temporarily curbs the effects. In the meantime, Scott has no choice but to adjust his lifestyle, first relocating to his children's playhouse and then to the dollhouse in the family room as he proceeds to "out-shrink" his residences.

One day, while wife Louise (Randy Stuart) is off running errands, an unexpected turn of events sends Scott's life completely out of orbit. Trying to escape the clutches of his cat, teeny tiny Scott just manages to squeeze through a crack in the door, only to plummet into the basement. A tattered bit of bloodstained fabric convinces his loved ones that daddy's fallen victim to the family pet. Trapped in his new environs—which to him resemble an insurmountable, monster-laden war zone—Scott prepares to play the hand fate has dealt him...

While at first glance a sci-fi adventure, *The Incredible Shrinking Man* is actually an allegory about the alienation of modern man. Here, chance incidents effortlessly send ivory-tower concepts like private property and financial security tumbling down, leaving the cornerstones of society in ruins. Although he is otherwise physically and

JACK ARNOLD Born in New Haven, Connecticut, the so-called "neorealist of science fiction directors" got his start in the business as an actor. While in military service, Arnold tried his hand at documentary filmmaking and was promptly nominated for his first directing Oscar in 1950. Working for Universal Pictures from 1953–59 he shot many an off-beat B-movie, whose fantastic subject matter was far removed from his former achievements. Nonetheless, Arnold films like *It Came from Outer Space* (1953), *Creature from the Black Lagoon* (1954), *Tarantula* (1955), and *The Incredible Shrinking Man* (1957) are today considered masterpieces in their respective genres. He made use of simple, yet highly effective trick photography in pictures that primarily dealt with external threats to well-ordered lives. These ominous clouds would often manifest themselves as a foreign power or—as was more frequently the case—a nasty side effect of human hubris and ignorance. Yet Arnold's work is not concerned with tackling issues like good and evil. His characters always act according to their nature, be it human, alien or that of an overgrown spider, making it almost impossible to apply a moral yardstick to their conduct. In addition to the impressive range of technical innovations, Arnold's films stand out from countless others of the genre precisely because of their refusal to adhere to sci-fi and horror movie conventions. He is less known for his numerous Westerns, including *Man in the Shadow / Seeds of Wrath* (1957) with Orson Welles, and comedies. His over-the-top satire *The Mouse that Roared* (1959) starred legendary funnyman Peter Sellers as three characters at war with the United States. Throughout the 1960s and 1970s, Jack Arnold devoted his professional life to projects for television. He died of arteriosclerosis in Woodland Hills, California, in March 1982.

mentally healthy, Scott's diminishing stature is enough to ostracize him from his family, peers, and society at large. Regarded by the outside world as nothing more than a freak show curiosity, he quickly loses all footing in his trusted world. Estranged from his wife and emasculated, his dollhouse abode supplies him with a pathetic shell to crawl back into. His fall into the basement abyss, i. e. into oblivion, is the logical conclusion of his unfaltering degeneration.

Director Jack Arnold stages the film as a semi-documentary portrait of a middle-class married couple—

"I am convinced that a film should also have a social meaning. And if it has a social meaning, then it also has a political meaning. These two things go hand in hand. But I think they both have to be approached with great care and sensitivity."

Jack Arnold

4

1 Minor afflictions: After getting zapped by a mean dosage of radiation, Scott Carey (Grant Williams) is through complaining that nothing ever happens to little old him. And if his wife has anything to say about it, this will be Scott's last look at any sort of foreign anatomy.

2 The hypocrite's oath: When modern science provides no explanation, the doctors leave Scott to shrivel up and die.

3 Moving house: After it becomes clear that her husband has lost all hope of the presidency, Mrs. Carey (Randy Stuart) enforces her prenuptial agreement and claims their stately residence for herself. She does, however, still treat hubby like a regular doll.

4 The cat's meow: When a feline from across the way makes a beeline toward Scott, he opts for self-imprisonment in the basement.

a tactic that readily wins the audience's sympathies. The Careys live in a safe, pristine world. Even as Scott learns of his extraordinary affliction, we are reassured by a sober-minded, paternal doctor that science will succeed in remedying the matter. What makes *The Incredible Shrinking Man* so unnerving is that the trajectory of Scott's destiny cannot be averted, despite the supposedly ironclad safety of the world he lives in.

We watch as Arnold inconspicuously and masterfully introduces melodramatic elements into the plot: when Scott's wedding band, the symbol of marital cohesion, proves too big for his finger, it simply slips off; it's no

"I was continuing to shrink, to become... what? The infinitesimal? What was I? Still a human being? Or was I the man of the future?" *Film quote: Grant Williams as Scott*

5 Sparks fly in the matchbox: Scott regrets not ever lugging that old TV down to the basement. Now that he's stuck there, he has a burning desire to live out his Shirley Temple and Snow White fantasies. How's that for trick photography?

6 The pencil is mightier than the sword: The question is whether it is weapon enough to help him avoid the veritable Charybdis that lies ahead—namely, the drain.

7 Lion tamer: Despite what this image suggests, no tarantula was hurt or injured during the shoot. Much like the larger-than-life household objects—in truth gigantic set pieces—the entire shot is a brilliant trompe l'œil.

8 Ain't nothing like a little ingenuity: Careful now, Scott. You don't want to cut the cheese.

accident that this is also the first moment in which Scott is shown to be shorter than his wife, even if only by a drop. An eerier albeit subtler scene occurs immediately thereafter. A friend of the family is seen standing in front of an easy chair with its back to the camera. As the camera rotates 180° we lay eyes on Scott seated in the chair, now no bigger than a small child, and bear witness to what has become a shocking transformation.

Bit by bit, all the comforts of home start to present a serious threat. What was once a trusted living space mutates into an alien planet, on which a new power struggle between man and beast takes shape and life's essentials are redefined. This becomes especially clear when Scott uses a sewing needle as a lance to ward off a proportionately enormous garden spider, or nearly loses his life to a clogged drain. It is thanks to a superior intellect that mankind manages to triumph even in such perilous realms. But this is cold comfort in a world where individuality has lost its intrinsic value, where your own cat thirsts for your life, and you've been abandoned by mankind to rot in the cellar. Jack Arnold's film accounts for the fragility and constant uncertainty of the human condition while managing to leave us with a grain of hope in the end, as if to say: as long as we continue to reflect upon ourselves and our actions, and refuse to blindly follow destiny, we can preserve our human integrity—no matter what the obstacle. SH

PEEPING TOM

1960 – GREAT BRITAIN – 101 MIN.

DIRECTOR

MICHAEL POWELL (1905–1990)

SCREENPLAY

LEO MARKS

DIRECTOR OF PHOTOGRAPHY

OTTO HELLER

EDITING

NOREEN ACKLAND

MUSIC

BRIAN EASDALE, ANGELA MORLEY,
FREDDIE PHILLIPS

PRODUCTION

MICHAEL POWELL for ANGLO-AMALGAMATED PRODUCTIONS

STARRING

KARLHEINZ BÖHM (Mark Lewis), MOIRA SHEARER (Vivian),
ANNA MASSEY (Helen Stephens), MAXINE AUDLEY (Mrs. Stephens),
BRENDA BRUCE (Dora), ESMOND KNIGHT (Arthur Baden),
PAMELA GREEN (Milly, the Model), MARTIN MILLER (Doctor Rosan),
BARTLETT MULLINS (Mr. Peters), JACK WATSON (Chief Inspector Gregg)

"Do you know what the most FRIGHTENING thing in the world is...?"

PEEPING TOM

IN EASTMAN COLOUR

CARL BOEHM
MOIRA SHEARER
ANNA MASSEY
MAXINE AUDLEY

An Original Story and Screenplay by LEO MARKS
Produced and Directed by MICHAEL POWELL

Distribution by ANGLO AMALGAMATED FILM DISTRIBUTORS LIMITED

1
2

"Whatever I photograph— I always lose!"

Whenever the movies show us eyes in close-up, we're confronted with questions about the nature of visual perception and filmic representation. When the open razor sliced through the eye in Luis Buñuel and Salvador Dalí's *An Andalusian Dog* (*Un Chien andalou*, 1929), it also cut through the audience's habits of perception, which had been formed in the theater at a safe distance from the stage. Many spectators found the notorious sliced-eyeball scene literally impossible to watch, for what they were seeing was their own still-innocent moviegoer's eye, attacked as they wallowed in the cinematic illusion. *Peeping Tom* operates in the same field of visual trespass, although it intrudes on the spectator's senses less harshly than the Surrealist shocker.

The film begins with a close-up of a human eye—closed, as if the person it belongs to were dreaming. Then it snaps opens like a camera shutter and stares horror-struck from the screen. This eye is a filmic emblem. It introduces a complex constellation of perceptions, in which the spectator will participate in a highly unusual manner. The eye that fills the screen also stares at the spectator like a camera lens, returning his interested gaze. The watcher is being watched: the spectator—a voyeur, a Peeping Tom—is himself under observation.

In a separate introductory section before the titles sequence, a slow zoom draws the spectator into the lens of a 16mm amateur film camera, half-hidden under a young man's coat. Then the point of view changes: we're now walking towards a prostitute; the camera's crosshairs disfigure the frame. The streetwalker takes us with her to her room. We have become the eye of the camera. And as the woman undresses, the camera moves slowly towards her. Terrified, she raises her hands to her face, and screams. And the camera keeps rolling.

For almost 20 years, critics either ignored *Peeping Tom* or vilified it. From a contemporary perspective, it's

KARLHEINZ BÖHM Karlheinz Böhm was an exceptionally versatile and multifaceted actor, and his finest performances were all distinguished by a certain quality of alertness and powerful concentration. The son of the famous conductor Karl Böhm, he was born in Darmstadt, Germany, in 1928. He was much loved for his performance as the Emperor Franz Joseph in the three notoriously kitschy "Sissi" films of the 1950s. His partner in these movies was the young Romy Schneider as the Empress Sissi herself. She and Böhm spent their lives trying to escape the image they had acquired in the process: "the pink marzipan piglet image," as Böhm memorably put it. Both of them wanted to be seen as the excellent character actors they were, and Böhm believed he had achieved this goal in Michael Powell's *Peeping Tom* (1960). However, the film was torn to pieces by shortsighted critics. Böhm went to Hollywood and signed a three-year contract. He didn't like it there; after only four films, he returned to Germany, where the social upheaval of 1968 left its mark on him politically. He worked a lot in the theater before he landed up with Rainer Werner Fassbinder. His roles in *Martha* (1973) and *Faustrecht der Freiheit* (1975) finally brought him the change of image he had been seeking for so long. In 1981, his life and career took another surprising turn, when he appeared on the German TV show "Wetten dass..." ("Wanna bet, that..."). Seven million people were watching as he wagered that not even half of them would contribute a single Deutsche Mark to an emergency charity project for starving people in the Sahel-Sahara zone. Böhm won his bet; and with the 1.7 million Marks sent in by viewers, he went to Ethiopia and founded the aid organization "Menschen für Menschen" (People for People), for which he collected money year after year and which he headed until 2011. Karlheinz Böhm died on May 29, 2014.

1 Make love to the camera: It's about the only thing Mark Lewis (Karlheinz Böhm) shares a tender moment with.

2 Smile for the birdie: Helen Stephens (Anna Massey) is horrified to discover what lies beyond Mark's bashful veneer. Her disgust, however, is tempered by concern.

3 Self-inflicted punishment or just posing? Mark serves as his own stand-in to calculate the perfect angle for photographing mortal fear.

4 Neatly partitioned lifestyle: Mark's darkroom and archives are set off from the rest of his apartment. Even though she hasn't seen them yet, Helen senses that Mark's artsier shots might not exactly suit her taste.

5 Jack the rip-roaring photographer: Like most men in his field, Mark only selects a certain type of individual to partake in his art projects—namely, prostitutes, cover girls, and actresses.

hard to understand why. Not until 1979 was the film rehabilitated, when Martin Scorsese and Paul Schrader presented it at the New York Film Festival and placed it on a list of their "guilty pleasures." Better late than never, one might say; but for Michael Powell, it was definitely too late. Since the London premiere of *Peeping Tom* in 1960, his reputation had been ruined. The critics had simply been unable or unwilling to understand the film, ignoring the clear thematic parallels between the eye (of the camera) and the "I" of the killer, the director, and the spectator. "I, the eye:" it's this that provides the key to the conflict-ridden personality of Mark Lewis (Karlheinz Böhm), the shy, film-obsessed assistant cameraman whose traumatic childhood made him a voyeur and a murderer.

The little 16mm film camera that accompanies Mark everywhere he goes is literally a deadly weapon. When he has found a victim, he moves towards her, filming all the while; then he flips up a leg of the tripod, which he has converted into a deadly stiletto, and stabs. And it's not enough for him to see and film the death struggle of his petrified victims: he also confronts them with their fear by holding up a parabolic mirror, so that the victims can see themselves dying. As he says to Helen (Anna Massey) at one point: "Do you know what the most frightening thing in the world is?" The answer, we learn, is fear itself.

Helen, a novice author of children's books, is the only human being he can trust. The pathologically shy son of a renowned psychologist, Mark had himself been the victim of an inhuman form of voyeurism, for his father's lust for knowledge had known few limits: in a long series of experiments on fear, he had placed the boy in nightmarish situations and filmed his reactions.

Night after night, Mark watches his own homemade snuff movies, but they cannot solve his conflicts or straighten his twisted soul. The victims' final terror is finally just a sequence of film in a rattling projector. It's never enough. In order to free himself from his trauma and lend some meaning to his life through the medium of his "art," Mark ultimately chooses to kill himself—and to leave a photographic record of his own extinction. He attaches his murderous apparatus to a cupboard and walks towards it. On the short path to his death, he captures the story of his own life in a series of photos shot with a self-timer: from the abused boy he has always remained to the now-dying adult. And perversely, he's keeping a kind of promise: for Helen had wanted such a series of "magic photos" to illustrate her first children's book to be accepted for publication. No doubt she had had something rather different in mind.

Peeping Tom is a film that does what it sets out to do, staring unflinchingly into the abyss of the soul and the cinema, and reflecting upon what it sees there. It is neither self-consciously avant-garde nor timidly subject to the dictates of taste, following only its own dramaturgical laws. And as a study of filmmaking itself, *Peeping Tom* has a positively timeless quality. SR

PSYCHO

1960 – USA – 109 MIN.

DIRECTOR

ALFRED HITCHCOCK (1899–1980)

SCREENPLAY

JOSEPH STEFANO,
based on the novel of the same name by ROBERT BLOCH

DIRECTOR OF PHOTOGRAPHY

JOHN L. RUSSELL

EDITING

GEORGE TOMASINI

MUSIC

BERNARD HERRMANN

PRODUCTION

ALFRED HITCHCOCK for SHAMLEY PRODUCTIONS INC.

STARRING

ANTHONY PERKINS (Norman Bates), JANET LEIGH (Marion Crane),
VERA MILES (Lila Crane), JOHN GAVIN (Sam Loomis),
JOHN MCINTIRE (Al Chambers), MARTIN BALSAM (Milton Arbogast),
LURENE TUTTLE (Mrs. Chambers), SIMON OAKLAND (Doctor Richmond),
PATRICIA HITCHCOCK (Caroline), MORT MILLS (Policeman)

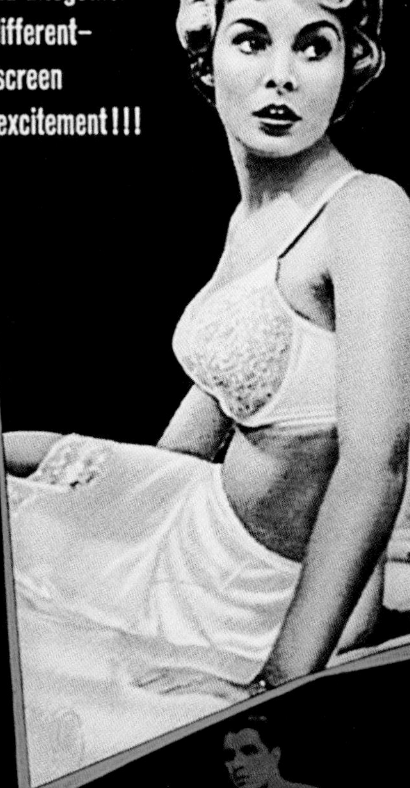
A new—
and altogether
different—
screen
excitement!!!
starring
ANTHONY
PERKINS
VERA
MILES
JOHN
GAVIN
co-starring
MARTIN
BALSAM
JOHN
McINTIRE
and
JANET
LEIGH
as
MARION
CRANE
Directed by
ALFRED
HITCHCOCK
Screenplay by
JOSEPH
STEFANO
A PARAMOUNT
Release
ALFRED
HITCHCOCK'S
PSYCHO

1

"Mother, she's just a stranger!"

It's what you might call a *twisted* fate. Marion Crane's (Janet Leigh) illicit affair with the married Sam Loomis (John Gavin) awakens deviant impulses within her. Entrusted with 40,000 dollars in company funds, she promptly invests in the future, making off with a sum that will allow her to start a new life with Joe. But the cops are on to her, and Marion thinks twice about executing her plan. The choice, however, isn't hers: a storm forces Marion to seek sanctuary at a remote motel, where a relaxing shower ends as a bloodbath. The murderess, it seems, suspected the overnight guest of making advances toward her son, the motel's introverted manager Norman Bates (Anthony Perkins), and decided to nip danger in the bud. Attempting to cover up his mother's regrettable actions, Bates wipes the scene clean, stuffs Marion's corpse into her car, and sinks the vehicle in a swamp—40 grand and all.

Then the real investigation begins. Despite all their hard work, the gruesome twosome don't get to close shop just yet. Sam, Marion's sister Lila (Vera Miles), and a private detective named Arbogast (Martin Balsam) come in search of the missing woman and the stolen funds. Sticking his nose in the wrong place, Arbogast is also disposed of by the deranged old lady, who apparently resides in the seclusion of the familial estate overlooking the motel. After Sam and Lila wise up to the horrors of the Bates mansion, they are dumbfounded to learn from the authorities that Mrs. Bates has been dead for a good ten years…

JANET LEIGH Jeanette Helen Morrison (1927–2004), born in Merced, California, was just 15 years old when she finished high school and began her studies in music and psychology. Her rise to fame is something of a Hollywood fairy tale: actress Norma Shearer apparently saw her while vacationing at a ski resort where Janet's father was working. Soon the young woman was cast in films opposite some of the industry's biggest names, including Robert Mitchum in *Holiday Affair* (1949), James Stewart in *The Naked Spur* (1953), John Wayne in *Jet Pilot* (1957), and both Charlton Heston and Orson Welles in *Touch of Evil* (1958). With *Psycho* (1960), Alfred Hitchcock supplied her with her most memorable role: Marion Crane, a heroine who is murdered before the first half of the picture is over. The part earned Leigh an Oscar nomination. John Frankenheimer's classic political drama *The Manchurian Candidate* (1962) proved to be one of the last high-caliber Hollywood films she would appear in; playing the girlfriend of the brainwashed Bennett Marco (Frank Sinatra), Leigh relies on her particular brand of aloof understatement to help him get his life back on track. From 1951 to 1962, the actress was married to favorite co-star Tony Curtis. They had two daughters, Kelly and Jamie Lee Curtis, both of whom followed in their parents' professional footsteps. Janet made an appearance in front of the camera at the side of daughter Jamie Lee in *Halloween H20—20 Years Later* (1998), the eighth installment in the horror film series made popular by Janet Leigh's world-famous child.

2

1 Who? *Moi?* Mama's boy Norman Bates (Anthony Perkins) fears the gaze of stranger's eyes—especially when they belong to his attractive hotel guests.

2 Lila Crane (Vera Miles) searches for her missing sister Marion, and discovers the horrific truth of her demise at the Bates Motel.

3 Behind bars and closed doors: all the conniving Marion Crane (Janet Leigh) ever wanted in life was to elope with lover Sam Loomis (John Gavis). And she would have, had it not been for one little, but fatal, mistake. But then you only get to make one now darling, don't you?

Psycho is undoubtedly Hitchcock's boldest film—although the critical uproar of the time, fixated on a close-up of a toilet bowl, seemed to miss the point. Tauntingly, the master of suspense plays with the viewer's expectations time and again: mercilessly killing off his leading lady in the first third of the picture, and introducing plot elements like the suitcase of money that amount to nothing more than red herrings. Arguably, the entire plot is a network of set-ups and visual suggestions meant to keep the audience unnerved until the curtain falls. And the seamless manner in which these subversive images undermine the story and suck it into the background makes *Psycho* more reminiscent of an experimental arthouse piece than a Hollywood blockbuster. The most striking example of this is the

“After Hitchcock’s suspense pictures and romantic adventure stories could he come up with a shocker, acceptable to mainstream American audiences, which still carried the spine-tingling voltage of foreign presentations such as *Diaboliques*? The answer is an enthusiastic yes. He blended the real and the unreal in fascinating proportions and punctuated his film with several quick, grisly and unnerving surprises.” *San Francisco Chronicle*

shower scene, where a total of 70 camera shots fill 45 seconds of scream time—the hard cuts between shots and Bernard Herrmann’s screeching score viscerally tuning us to each stab of the killer’s knife. The scene was so shocking Hitchcock abstained from the further inclusion of similarly violent displays in the rest of the film for he clearly already had the audience just where he wanted them.

Equally remarkable is how ingeniously the film-maker and cinematographer John L. Russell come up with excuses not to reveal the face of Norman’s mother until just before the end. We never suspect that Arbogast’s stairwell death is shot from a bird’s eye for anything other than artistic reasons. *Psycho*’s narrative takes just as many experimental liberties. Much like in a television

“What makes *Psycho* immortal, when so many films are already half-forgotten as we leave the theater, is that it connects directly with our fears: Our fears that we might impulsively commit a crime, our fears of the police, our fears of becoming the victim of a madman, and of course our fears of disappointing our mothers.” *Chicago Sun-Times*

4 Drowned out screams: how many cuts does it take to kill Marion Crane? Hitchcock used approximately 70. Urban legend would have you believe that renowned cinema graphic artist, Saul Bass, staged *Psycho*'s shower scene. But it's a bloody lie!

5 Don't tell mama: Mother will be livid if she finds out who's been sleeping in one of Norman's beds.

drama, lengthy dialogue clarifies plot and subtext. Of prime importance is Norman and Marion's conversation at the motel, in which a bond is established between the killer and his victim. It is here that the viewer learns of Norman's interest in taxidermy, with the stuffed birds themselves acting as an eerie congress of witnesses: no amount of money can make them divulge the grizzly acts they've seen. These petrified beasts, and the peephole that Norman uses to spy on Marion as she undresses, are reminders of the camera's voyeuristic nature.

Everywhere we turn, *Psycho* confronts us with visual analogies of watching and being watched: from the eyelike shower drain into which Marion's blood disappears, to the smirking toilet seat that stares us down in one of the final shots. And there is no misunderstanding the accompanying dialogue: “They're probably watching me. Well, let them. Let them see what kind of person I am. I hope they are watching. They'll see. They'll see and they'll know.”

It's more than just a coincidental choice of words Hitchcock placed in Bates's mouth. In truth, the soliloquy is as much a personal confession on the part of the director as of its speaker. At the peak of his career, Hitch couldn't have picked a more poignant moment to make it. For beyond the façade of terror, what is *Psycho* if not a great master's artistic manifesto? SH

LES YEUX SANS VISAGE

THE HORROR CHAMBER OF DR. FAUSTUS / EYES WITHOUT A FACE

1960 – FRANCE / ITALY – 88 MIN.

DIRECTOR

GEORGES FRANJU (1912–1987)

SCREENPLAY

PIERRE BOILEAU, PIERRE GASCAR, THOMAS NARCEJAC, CLAUDE SAUTET, based on the novel of the same name by JEAN REDON

DIRECTOR OF PHOTOGRAPHY

EUGEN SCHÜFFTAN

EDITING

GILBERT NATOT

MUSIC

MAURICE JARRE

PRODUCTION

JULES BORKON for CHAMPS-ÉLYSÉES PRODUCTIONS, LUX FILM

STARRING

PIERRE BRASSEUR (Doctor Génessier), EDITH SCOB (Christiane), ALIDA VALLI (Louise), FRANÇOIS GUÉRIN (Jacques), ALEXANDRE RIGNAULT (Inspector Parot), BÉATRICE ALTARIBA (Paulette), JULIETTE MAYNIEL (Edna), CLAUDE BRASSEUR (Inspector), MICHEL ETCHEVERRY (Forensic surgeon)

une production JULES BORKON

PIERRE BRASSEUR
ALIDA VALLI
dans

LES YEUX SANS VISAGE

UN FILM DE
GEORGES FRANJU
D'après le roman de JEAN REDON
ÉDITIONS DU FLEUVE NOIR
Adaptation de BOILEAU - NARCEJAC
JEAN REDON · CLAUDE SAUTET
Dialogue de PIERRE GASCAR
avec
JULIETTE MAYNIEL
ALEXANDRE RIGNAULT
BEATRICE ALTARIBA
et
FRANÇOIS GUERIN
EDITH SCOB
CO-PRODUCTION FRANCO-ITALIENNE
CHAMPS-ELYSEES PRODUCTIONS / LUX FILM
PARIS ROMA

1

"You shall have a proper face."

The clinic of Dr. Génessier (Pierre Brasseur) is only a short distance from Paris. He's an ambitious surgeon, famed as a specialist in skin transplants, but no-one realizes his terrible secret: since his daughter Christiane (Edith Scob) was disfigured in an accident, Génessier has sworn to do everything he can to restore her beauty. With the help of his assistant Louise (Alida Valli), he lures young women to his remote villa, where he anesthetizes them and sets to work. In an operating theater concealed in the basement of his house, he removes their facial skin and transplants it onto his daughter. To no avail.

When this film was released, almost everyone disliked it. Many critics accused Georges Franju of a severe lapse of taste, while others missed the aggressive social criticism of his previous films and lamented that he had wasted his talent on a mannered horror movie. Nonetheless, *Eyes without a Face* was soon hailed as a classic of the genre. With this fascinating film, Franju, the former co-founder of the legendary Cinémathèque Française, succeeded in making film history a source of inspiration for his own unique cinematic vision. It's still an extremely disturbing film, not least thanks to Eugen Schüfftan's camerawork. His brilliant black-and-white photography is worthy of comparison with the great works of German Expressionism. It lends Génessier's villa an eerie life of its own, transforming it into a weird labyrinth from which there is apparently no escape. The stair-rails cast their barred shadow on everyone who enters this house; they are the

EUGEN SCHÜFFTAN Eugen Schüfftan, born in Wrocław in 1893, studied art and architecture before turning to the cinema. He began as a special-effects specialist, inventing the famous Schüfftan technique, which made it possible to reflect models or painted backdrops into real scenes. This was method used, for example, by Fritz Lang for his impressive futuristic visions in *Metropolis* (1926). Soon after this, however, the technique was replaced by simpler methods.
Today, Schüfftan's work as a cinematographer seems more important. For Robert Siodmak and Edgar G. Ulmer, he made the legendary Berlin film *People on Sunday* (*Menschen am Sonntag*, 1929), before emigrating to France. There, he changed his name to Eugène Shuftan and made a name for himself as a master of light, with his work on movies such as Marcel Carné's *Port of Shadows* (*Quai des brumes*, 1938). He went on to consolidate this reputation with Georges Franju's *Head Against the Wall / The Keepers* (*La Tête contre les murs*, 1959) and *The Horror Chamber of Dr. Faustus / Eyes without a Face* (*Les Yeux sans visage*, 1960). Towards the end of his career, he worked mainly in the United States, where he changed his name yet again to Gene Shufton. In the States, he was able to capitalize on the reputation he had built up in Europe. Robert Rossen's study of a pool-shark (*The Hustler*, 1961, starring Paul Newman) won him an Oscar for Best Cinematography (Black-and-White). His monochrome photography for Rossen's *Lilith* (1964) was no less impressive. Eugen Schüfftan died in New York in 1977.

"One of the greatest horror films ever made, and one of the most bizarre." *Edinburgh University Film Society*

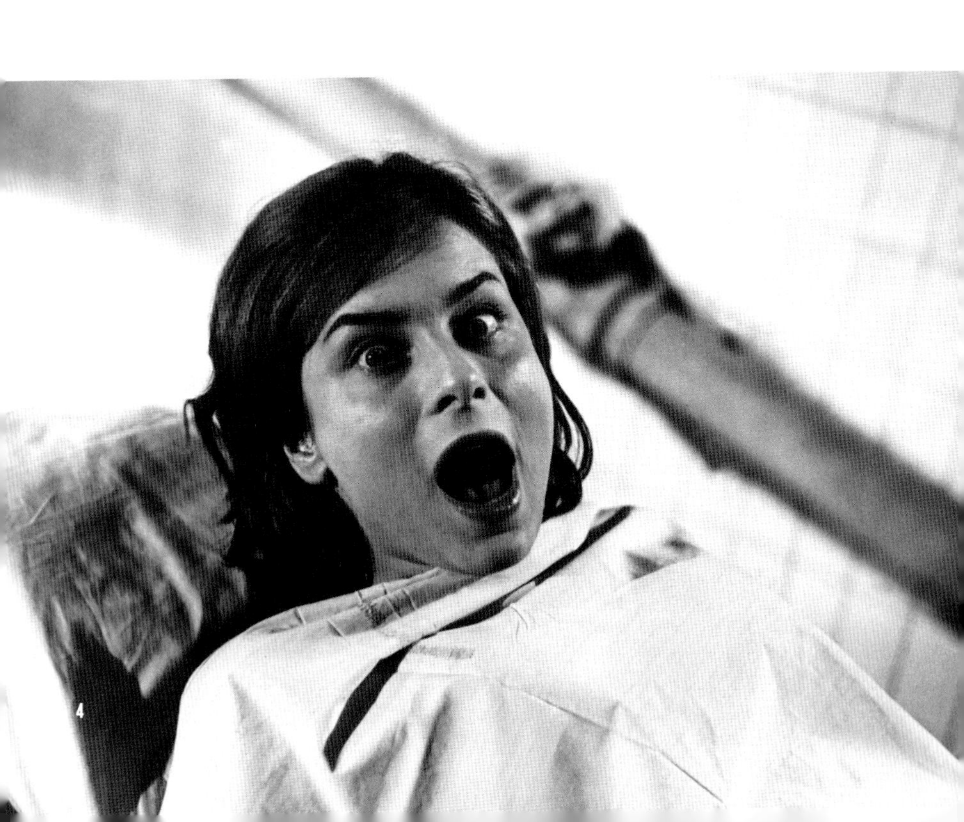

1 Nip and tuck: Everything about Christiane (Edith Scob) is smooth as porcelain—even though she's 100% plastic.

2 Medicine man or witch doctor? Workaholic, Dr. Génessier (Pierre Brasseur) cleanses his conscience by restoring his daughter to her former state of glory. The task, however, has him washing his hands in blood.

3 Need a lift? Christiane still harbors hopes of reuniting with her fiancé, but he wrote her off for dead long ago.

4 Silence, lamb! A routine checkup with Dr. Génessier leaves young ladies with more than they bargained for.

5 Face pokers: Dr. Génessier and his assistant Louise (Alida Valli) wear expressions as enigmatic as the human masks they create.

prisoners of Génessier's madness. As is his daughter, who floats through her father's house like a ghost, her ravaged face hidden behind a white porcelain mask. Its permanently sad expression seems to foretell her fate.

Christiane's mask is also one manifestation of the film's central formal characteristic: much of its tension arises from the interplay between the visible and invisible, the exposed and the hidden. Franju skilfully evokes a nightmarish atmosphere without explicitly showing what Génessier does—until some time into the film… When the surgeon does suddenly insert his scalpel into the face of one young girl, it has the shocking intensity of the sliced eye in Salvador Dalí and Luis Buñuel's Surrealist classic *An Andalusian Dog* (*Un Chien andalou*, 1929). Franju, like his famous predecessors, is gleefully provocative. A sober series of close-up photos shows Christiane's perfectly-restored face; and then we see how the grafted skin grows mottled, starts to peel, and eventually—after two weeks—drops off.

The horror of these two sequences unmasks Génessier: not only is he a murderous physician who has betrayed his Hippocratic oath, but his fatherly love is

6 A plea against plastic surgery: The more artificially beautiful Christiane becomes the more fragile she seems. Eat your heart out, Michael Jackson!

7 The children's hour: Although Christiane longs to be a „good girl," there's just no way she'll ever be good enough.

"A horrifying brew of terror and allegorical poetry... The author's most impressive work to date."

Le Monde

shown to be a brutal obsession. In attempting to equip his daughter with a new face, he is also erasing her identity. Frankenstein-like, he wishes to recreate her as an ideal woman—and in the end, he suffers a terrible punishment for his hubris. Tellingly, though, it's not the police who finally bring Génessier to his knees. Deceived by his respectable façade, they withdraw after making enquiries. So it's left to Christiane to put a stop to her father's crimes and to free herself from her prison. She stabs Génessier's assistant with the scalpel and helps the last victim to flee. Her final act is to free the dogs Génessier has been using in his skin-grafting experiments. Let loose from their cages, they attack their tormentor and tear him to pieces. Christiane walks free into the night. JH

"Narrow and haunted, *Eyes without a Face* is a truly French-style film fantasy, and will forever inhabit one of those dark recesses of the realm of the imaginary." *Le Monde*

WHAT EVER HAPPENED TO BABY JANE?

1962 – USA – 132 MIN.

DIRECTOR

ROBERT ALDRICH (1918–1983)

SCREENPLAY

LUKAS HELLER, based on the novel of the same name by HENRY FARRELL

DIRECTOR OF PHOTOGRAPHY

ERNEST HALLER

EDITING

MICHAEL LUCIANO

MUSIC

FRANK DE VOL

PRODUCTION

ROBERT ALDRICH for ALDRICH ASSOCIATES,
SEVEN ARTS, WARNER BROS.

STARRING

BETTE DAVIS ("Baby" Jane Hudson), JOAN CRAWFORD (Blanche Hudson),
VICTOR BUONO (Edwin Flagg), WESLEY ADDY (Marty),
JULIE ALLRED ("Baby" Jane Hudson in 1917), ANNA LEE (Mrs. Bates),
MAIDIE NORMAN (Elvira Stitt), MARJORIE BENNETT (Mrs. Dehlia Flagg),
DAVE WILLOCK (Ray Hudson), ANNE BARTON (Cora Hudson)

ACADEMY AWARDS 1962

OSCAR for BEST COSTUMES (Norma Koch)

Bette Davis and Joan Crawford

SEVEN ARTS PRESENTS AN ASSOCIATES AND ALDRICH PRODUCTION

"WHAT EVER HAPPENED TO BABY JANE?"

Things you should know about this motion picture before buying a ticket:

❶ If you're long-standing fans of Miss Davis and Miss Crawford, we warn you this is quite unlike anything they've ever done. ❷ You are urged to see it from the beginning. ❸ Be prepared for the macabre and the terrifying. ❹ We ask your pledge to keep the shocking climax a secret. ❺ When the tension begins to build, try to remember it's just a movie.

VICTOR BUONO ROBERT ALDRICH LUKAS HELLER FRANK DeVOL HENRY FARRELL WARNER BROS.

1

"You wouldn't be able to do these awful things to me if I weren't still in this chair."

Some people take their secrets to the grave. Others take their sisters. As Blanche (Joan Crawford) steers her wheelchair toward the table where dinner is being kept warm, images of her sister Jane's (Betty Davis) torturous machinations race through her mind. She comes to a halt, seized by the sight of the silver service lid lying before her. It was only recently that she discovered her pet parakeet dead underneath, allegedly having flown out of the cage while Jane was cleaning it. And now, Blanche has been left to contemplate the words Jane sneered on her way out the door, announcing that rats have infested the cellar. She reaches for the lid, and her worst fears are confirmed as she discovers the roasted rodent that adorns her plate. Echoes of maniacal laughter fill the hallway. We understand that Blanche is caught in a mousetrap, and all she can do is spin round and round in circles. And the front door, her only exit to freedom, is an insurmountable flight of stairs away…

There was a time when Blanche was a big Hollywood star. That was before a car accident left her a paraplegic. Jane too was a starlet—a child actress whose career fell victim to alcohol and the hysteria of fame. This is a classic case of sibling rivalry: Blanche only remembers a blonde curly Sue who got all the attention by lighting up the stage with songs from Tin Pan Alley; whereas Jane despises a wall-flower who grew up to steal the show.

Though they resent each other, they are completely co-dependent. Today, not a penny is left of a fortune amassed in baby booties, and Jane relies on her sister's film royalties for survival. Good thing that Blanche can't

BETTE DAVIS Did those famous eyes of hers really make all the boys think she was a spy? Let's just say Kim Carnes believed it enough to sing about their secret magnetism and the star was wildly flattered. Not a surprise, as Carnes's 1980 hit won Davis points with her granddaughter. One of the immortal legends of classic Hollywood cinema, Bette Davis was indeed the highest paid actress at the Hollywood dream factory during the 1940s. Showered with Oscars for her work in Alfred E. Green's *Dangerous* (1935) and William Wyler's *Jezebel* (1938), her performances continued to win nominations each year from 1939 to 1942, and then again in 1944. Her final Oscar nod came in 1962 for *What Ever Happened to Baby Jane?* The accolades aside, Davis never thought that success had come easy to her, and her engraving on her tombstone bears testament to this: Bette Davis—She did it the hard way.

Born Ruth Elizabeth Davis in Lowell, Massachusetts, she trained as an actress in New York and took to the stage. Even before being contracted by Universal pictures in 1930, Bette Davis had already dazzled Broadway. At the time of her rise to fame, Hollywood needed actors like her, whose voices would add sizzle to the talkies. As such, her stage experience made her a great asset to the movie studios. Universal, however, had a funny way of showing their appreciation, handing Davis slim pickings rather than choice parts. It wasn't long before she switched over to Warner Brothers, where Darryl Zanuck, head of production, turned her into a star. The first great highlight of her career came with John Cromwell's *Of Human Bondage* (1934) in which she played a sultry waitress. Despite her Oscar wins, Davis always had to fight for good roles and didn't always win. Over the course of her career, she appeared in over 100 motion pictures. Her work in the TV show *Hotel* (1983–88) was to be some of her last. In 1989, the woman who had lived so fast and furiously retired from the earthly stars she had known so well to claim her place in heaven.

2

“As an ugly hag, Bette Davis, with her ghastly layers of make-up and her shuffly-clumb walk, is rather appealing. And Joan Crawford is—oh, just Joan Crawford. She is in a wheelchair, and she is starving to death..., but her eyes blaze out soulfulness.” *Newsweek*

get by physically without a nurse and that Jane feels so guilty about her crippling accident…

What Ever Happened to Baby Jane? is a psycho-thriller about two middle-aged women bent on ripping each other to shreds. Robert Aldrich, known primarily for his Westerns and war pictures like *Vera Cruz* (1954) and *Attack!* (1956), earned his reputation as a master of chilling suspense thanks to the invisible camera and no frills direction. Unfortunately, the critics tended to compare Aldrich's piece to Hitchcock's *Psycho* (1960) and then slated it for a lack of originality, dramatic arcs, and interesting visuals. Still, there were those who viewed it as a fascinating, self-reflective study on Hollywood taboos, which walked the fine line between cinematic reality and fiction. In the words of *Movie* magazine's Andrew Sarris: "The thought of taking on Bette Davis and Joan Crawford at the same time is formidable enough, but here the plot itself is immersed in the presences and pasts of these two ageless stars. In fact, if *Baby Jane* is about anything at all, it is about *Bette Davis* and *Joan Crawford.*"

Sarris was dead right. The on-screen personas weren't an act. Their mutual animosity is said to have begun when Davis purported that Crawford had "slept with every male star at MGM except Lassie." The slighted Crawford responded by saying that Davis made up for a lack of talent with bloodshot glances, nicotine, and three-cent comments. Ironically, the two women's physique and temperaments were as different as their careers were similar. Both had acted in dozens of pictures and received Oscars by the time *Baby Jane* was made, and both were

1 Divas behind bars: All Blanche's (Joan Crawford, right) pleading won't get her sister Jane (Bette Davis, left) to free her from their cage. To this day, *What Ever Happened to Baby Jane* remains one of the most intense displays of Hollywood hatred.

2 Truth serum: "Why am I so good at playing bitches? I think it's because I'm not one. Maybe that's why Miss Crawford always plays ladies." Bette Davis on Joan Crawford.

3 Down for the count: Blanche tries to phone for help, but the Baby tampers with the line before she has the chance.

3

considered has-beens. Starving for roles by the time the 1960s rolled around, this was to be the last great hurrah of their careers.

Indeed, it is a film that is fueled by the terrorizing intensity of its leading ladies. On the surface, Bette Davis a.k.a. Baby Jane plays the wicked sister, who torments meek sister Joan Crawford a. k. a. Blanche with her diabolical whims. In truth, Blanche has been harboring a sinister secret about the actual cause of her dependency. Maybe if she'd been more forthcoming, Jane wouldn't have hit the bottle or spiraled into psychosis. Too late now. So when she finds out that Blanche wants to lock her up in an insane asylum, Jane starves her of food and contact with the outside world, deciding it's time for the Baby to plan her big comeback.

Watching a film this well cast and this telling is a rare pleasure. Davis is mesmerizing as she waddles through the house, caked in makeup with a cigarette dangling from her lips. Equally exceptional is Crawford, whose eyes betray all the horror and disgust she has for her sister. These two bitter biddies of Hollywood pulled out all the stops to show us their true selves—and that, ladies and gentlemen, is how they prove their real grandeur.

NM

4 True Hollywood stories: "They were all terrible, even the few I thought might be good. I made them because I needed the money or because I was bored or both. I hope they have been exhibited and withdrawn and are never heard from again." Joan Crawford on the downfall of her career

5 Hello, Dolly! Jane meets accompanist Edwin Flagg (Victor Buono) through a newspaper advertisement. Rumor has it that, on account of her professional dry spell, Davis actually did place a "job wanted" ad in the paper just before landing this role.

6 A career stretch: Baby Jane plans a comeback with the same Tin Pan Alley standards that once made her a star.

7 No din-din, Blanche? Rest assured, these two actresses tortured each other even when the cameras weren't rolling.

REPULSION

1965 – GREAT BRITAIN – 105 MIN.

DIRECTOR

ROMAN POLANSKI (b. 1933)

SCREENPLAY

ROMAN POLANSKI, GÉRARD BRACH

DIRECTOR OF PHOTOGRAPHY

GILBERT TAYLOR

EDITING

ALASTAIR MCINTYRE

MUSIC

CHICO HAMILTON

PRODUCTION

GENE GUTOWSKI for COMPTON, TEKLI

STARRING

CATHERINE DENEUVE (Carole Ledoux), IAN HENDRY (Michael),
JOHN FRASER (Colin), PATRICK WYMARK (Landlord),
YVONNE FURNEAUX (Hélène Ledoux), RENEE HOUSTON (Miss Balch),
VALERIE TAYLOR (Madame Denise), JAMES VILLIERS (John),
HELEN FRASER (Bridget), HUGH FUTCHER (Reggie)

IFF BERLIN 1965

SILVER BEAR (Roman Polanski)

The nightmare world of a Virgin's dreams becomes the screen's shocking reality!!

A Michael Klinger-Tony Tenser Production

ROMAN POLANSKI'S

REPULSION

From The Award-Winning Director
of "Knife In The Water"

STARRING

CATHERINE DENEUVE

Screenplay by ROMAN POLANSKI and GERARD BRACH

Produced by EUGENE GUTOWSKI · Directed by ROMAN POLANSKI A ROYAL FILMS INTERNATIONAL PRESENTATION

1

"I don't think Cinderella likes me."

Carole (Catherine Deneuve), a manicurist in a London beauty salon, lives in a world that seems dominated by women. She shares a flat with her sister Hélène (Yvonne Furneaux), and her only other human contact is with her colleagues in the salon, and the elderly customers, whose faces seem mummified under mudpacks and moisturizers. Yet men are everywhere: at work, in the anecdotes of her workmates, who complain that theirs are only interested in one thing, and at home, in the form of Michael (Ian Hendry), her sister's married lover. When Hélène sleeps with Michael in the neighboring room, Carole twists and turns sleeplessly in her bed, and when morning comes, she's disgusted to find his toothbrush in her glass.

Men... for Carole, they're a permanent threat. Unable to reveal her fears to anyone else, she withdraws further and further into the world of her daydreams. And then there is Colin (John Fraser), who makes persistent but clumsy advances towards this quiet and seemingly fragile young woman.

Gradually, the world around Carole begins to change. Reflected in a coffee pot, her face is monstrously distorted; a skinned rabbit on a plate looks like a human foetus; cracks in the tarmac conjure up a woman's wide-open legs. The external world reflects the horrors that haunt her mind. Though we can't say exactly why, it's clear that this woman is in hell. From her living-room

GILBERT TAYLOR British cinematographer Gilbert Taylor is regarded as a master of the black-and-white film. Born in 1914, he was already working as an assistant cameraman by the age of 15. In Stanley Kubrick's *Dr. Strangelove, or: How I Learned to Stop Worrying and Love the Bomb* (1963) and Richard Lester's *A Hard Day's Night* (1964), he exploited the visual potential of the black-and-white medium with an imaginative force that still impresses today. Wowed by Taylor's pleasure in experimentation, Polanski hired him for *Repulsion* in 1965—and Taylor is said to have protested vehemently when asked to use a wide-angle lens for the close-ups of Catherine Deneuve's face. Nonetheless, they went on to make two further films together: *Cul-De-Sac* (1965) and *The Tragedy of Macbeth* (1971). In *Macbeth*, Taylor demonstrated that he could also create morbid and menacing atmospheres when filming in color.

In 1972, Hitchcock came knocking at his door, and Taylor became the cameraman for his blackly humorous *Frenzy*. Since creating the hauntingly claustrophobic images of *Repulsion*, Taylor had become pigeonholed as a specialist for thrillers and horror films. Yet his filmography, which comprises more than 70 works, doesn't only include such classics of the genre as *The Omen* (1976) and *Dracula* (1979); we also find movies such as *Star Wars* (1977) and *Flash Gordon* (1980)—further proof of the surprising versatility of this workaholic perfectionist. The last film he worked on, Curtis Hanson's *The Bedroom Window* (1986), demonstrated once more that he was a true master of visual suspense. In 2013 Gilbert Taylor died at the age of 99.

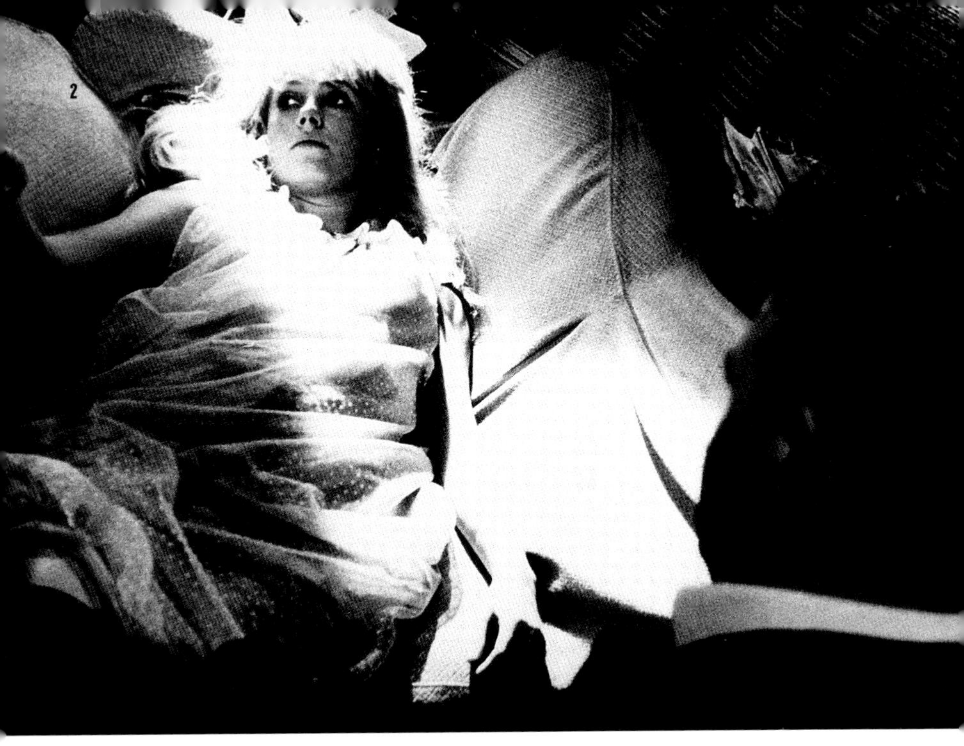

1 That girl: Carole (Catherine Deneuve) is convinced she has everything a girl could ask for—until she takes a good look at herself.

2 Afraid of the bogeyman: Unshakable visions of sinister men plague Carole's slumber.

3 Virgin suicides: As Carole's paranoia comes to a head, every aspect of her life becomes a matter of disclosure and exposure.

"The nightmare world of a virgin's dreams becomes the screen's shocking reality!" *Advert for Repulsion*

window, she observes and admires a community of nuns, who seem to represent another life—a "purer" existence, free of men. But it's a world that Carole has no prospect of joining.

For men have taken possession of Carole's soul. After an almost painfully uneventful start, Roman Polanski shocks the audience with a sudden apparition: the reflection of a stranger in the mirror on a door—the door of Carole's wardrobe. This is the straw that breaks Carole's back, the shock that throws her completely out of orbit. She stops going to work; and as her sister is gone for a few days, she's now all alone in the apartment. There is now nothing to stop her slipping ever deeper into the abyss of her own mind. At night, she is raped by strange, demonic creatures, and the façade of her middle-class normality falls apart, as the walls of the flat crack open and Carole herself cracks up. And when, one after the other, Colin and the landlord turn up, she no longer knows what's real and what's not. All she can do is defend herself...

4 Lending a helping hand: This manicurist brings her clients back to life at the price of her own.

5 He can cut you like a knife: Her sister's married lover, the edgy Michael (Ian Hendry), confirms Carole's repulsion and fear of the opposite sex.

Polanski and Gérard Brach wrote the screenplay to *Repulsion* in a single 17-day session. It had been commissioned by a firm that was best known for soft porn productions. Despite the success of *Knife in the Water* (*Nóz w wodzie*, 1962), which had even been nominated for an Oscar, Polanski had to wait a long time for the chance to make his second movie. Now he was expected to put together a horror film for 45,000 pounds sterling. The film he really wanted to make was *Cul-de-Sac*, but he had been obliged to place the project indefinitely on hold. So Polanski simply realized his artistic ambitions in a film he hadn't really chosen to make—and to the producers' dismay, he overshot his budget by more than 100%.

The director described what he had tried to do in this, the first film he had made outside Poland: "It was my intention to show Carole's hallucinations through the eye of the camera, and to use more and more extreme wide-angle lenses to intensify their menacing effect." Later, in

“A wicked tale of madness and female paranoia.”

San Francisco Chronicle

fact, Polanski judged the film to be technically inadequate; but despite this harsh self-criticism, *Repulsion* is a terrifying portrait of a lost soul.

Together with his cameraman Gilbert Taylor—whom the producers had felt to be far too expensive—Polanski created a disturbing black-and- white masterpiece that can easily bear comparison with the works of Buñuel and Hitchcock, two of the directors the Pole most admired. (In the opening titles, the eye sliced through by lettering is a tribute to one of the Spanish master's most famous shots.) In any case, Polanski had already reached his actual goal: *Repulsion* was such a success that he was given the green light for *Cul-de-Sac*, and he began filming it before the year was out. SH

NIGHT OF THE LIVING DEAD

1968 – USA – 96 MIN.

DIRECTOR

GEORGE A. ROMERO (b. 1940)

SCREENPLAY

GEORGE A. ROMERO, JOHN A. RUSSO

DIRECTOR OF PHOTOGRAPHY

GEORGE A. ROMERO

EDITING

GEORGE A. ROMERO, JOHN A. RUSSO

MUSIC

SCOTT VLADIMIR LICINA

PRODUCTION

KARL HARDMAN, RUSSEL STREINER for IMAGE TEN

STARRING

DUANE JONES (Ben), JUDITH O'DEA (Barbra), KARL HARDMAN (Harry Cooper), MARILYN EASTMAN (Helen Cooper / Bug-eating Zombie), KEITH WAYNE (Tom), JUDITH RIDLEY (Judy), KYRA SCHON (Karen Cooper/Upstairs Body), RUSSELL STREINER (Johnny), CHARLES CRAIG (Newscaster/Ghoul), WILLIAM HINZMAN (Cemetery Ghoul) GEORGE KOSANA (Sheriff McClelland)

THEY WON'T STAY DEAD!

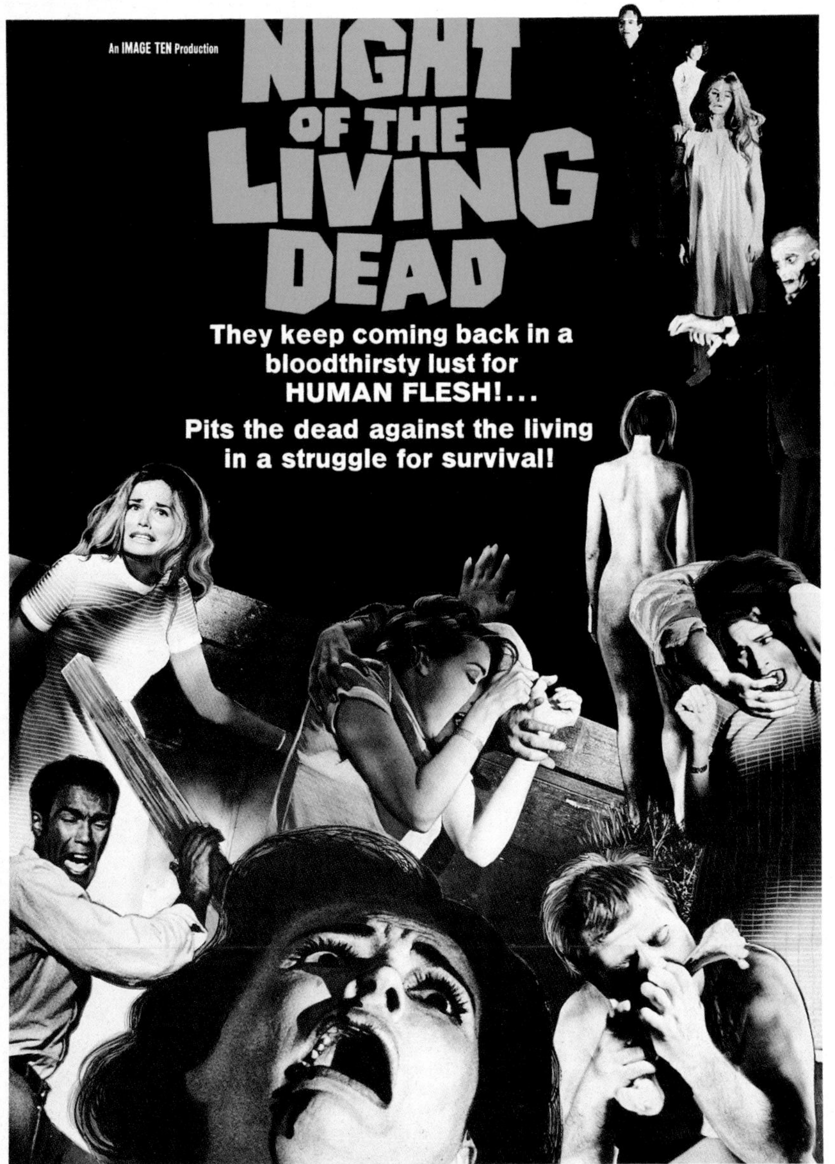

Starring JUDITH O'DEA · DUANE JONES · MARILYN EASTMAN · KARL HARDMAN · JUDITH RIDLEY · KEITH WAYNE

Produced by Russel W. Streiner and Karl Hardman · Directed by George A. Romero · Screenplay by John A. Russo · A Walter Reade Organization Presentation — Released by Continental

1

2

"Shoot 'em in the head."

It could just as well have been the opening to a touching family melodrama. Barbra (Judith O'Dea) and her brother Johnny (Russell Streiner) head to the countryside on the outskirts of Pittsburgh, where their deceased father has been put to rest in their family plot. But even before the audience has a chance to warm up to what seem to be the movie's protagonists, Johnny is abruptly struck dead by a mysterious man. Barbra manages to flee to the safety of a nearby farmhouse. An African American named Ben (Duane Jones) spots her and follows suit. They soon discover a couple, Tom (Keith Wayne) and Judy (Judith Ridley), hiding out in the cellar with a small family who are Harry and Helen Cooper (Karl Hardman and Marilyn Eastman) and their young daughter Karen (Kyra Schon). The main action remains confined to these tight quarters for the duration of the film. The only reminders of a "civilized" outside world streaming into the house are the round-the-clock radio and television broadcasts about further cases of the deadly epidemic terrorizing the nation. Allegedly the crash of a NASA spacecraft has emitted toxic radiation into the air that causes people to die and rise again as flesh-eating zombies. When Barbra lapses into a state of shock, Ben takes charge of the situation and defends the group from the advancing battalions of the undead. He rounds up a rifle, ammunition, and an American flag from one of the house closets. But despite Ben's valiant efforts, a great number of their party die. Meanwhile, a civilian army has formed and joined forces with the police, systematically shooting zombies after daybreak. The army, however, is exclusively white and hardly the bearer of the salvation that Ben, the farmhouse group's final living member, had hoped for. With the words "Good shot, another one for the fire!" the movie's hero is executed and set aflame as the troops march onward on their rampage for justice.

George A. Romero's claustrophobic cult hit is poignantly shot in black and white. The flickering shadows

THE ZOMBIE FILM In Victor Halperin's *White Zombie* (1932) and Jacques Tourneur's *I Walked with a Zombie* (1943), which take place in the Caribbean, voodoo and black magic are responsible for the reanimation of the undead. As early as 1966, the Hammer Production *Plague of the Zombies* relocated the ghouls to England. George A. Romero's *Night of the Living Dead* (1968) was the first picture to radically break with the zombie's traditional background story and depict them as a mindless army on the offensive. The director's work eventually evolved into a zombie trilogy, which includes the further installments *Dawn of the Dead* (1978) and *Day of the Dead* (1985).

By the 1980s it became clear that an excess of revolting, decaying human tissue as a subversive—and often censored—motif was incompatible with mainstream cinema. Nonetheless, a slew of films were produced in which corpses rise again as a result of atomic radiation, scientific experiments or viral epidemics. The subject matter was particularly popular in Italy, where Lucio Fulci's *Zombie* (*Gli ultimie zombi*, 1979) quickly became a classic. After the initial resurgence of the genre in the 1960s and 70s, zombies soon became a favorite spoof target as seen in Sam Raimi's masterpiece *The Evil Dead* (1981) or the stomach-turning *Braindead* (1992) by *Lord of the Rings* director Peter Jackson. In 2002, zombie films experienced an unexpected revival thanks to Paul W. S. Anderson's film adaptation of the videogame *Resident Evil* and Uwe Boll's *House of the Dead*. In Danny Boyle's *28 Days Later*, the undead were finally liberated from their trademark somnambulism and began chasing living human beings at full speed. The most successful zombie movie to date is Marc Forster's *World War Z*, an action movie starring Brad Pitt and based on Max Brook's novel *World War Z: An Oral History of the Zombie War*. In 2017 a sequel will be released in the theaters.

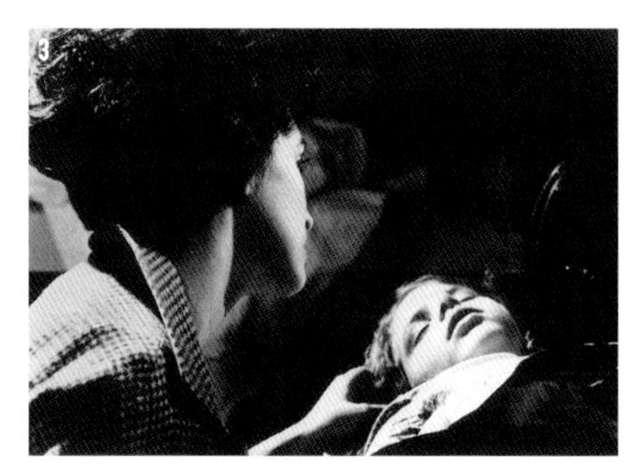

1 A flesheater's fantasy: Botticelli as edible art erotica.

2 Death comes knocking at the door: Zombies start rehearsals for Michael Jackson's legendary Thriller video. They've got all the right moves and are headed for a common goal—to reach the hearts of their undying fans.

3 Picking her mother's brain: After being infected by the zombie plague, young Karen (Kyra Schon) takes a jab at family values when she chews out her mummy.

"The coarse sheriff survives; the unfeeling television people survive; the Washington bureaucrats survive; and the family, the hero, and traditional American values of individualism are destroyed." *Stuart M. Kaminsky, in: Cinefantastique*

4 Bibbidi bobbidi boo: A little flame and few sparks are enough to get the zombies to retreat. Why is it that all movie monsters seem to be afraid of fire?

5 Rest in peace: The last survivors head for the claustrophobic nuclear fallout shelter. However, even Ben (Duane Jones), the sanest among them, will not live to see the dawn.

6 Black Power: In principle, Ben is a Rambo forerunner who burns countless living dead to ash in the name of humanity and the American way.

instill the picture with a dreamlike and even delusional quality. Nonetheless, the horrific events depicted in *Night of the Living Dead* hint at the possibility of an imagined reality. The audiovisual assault on the senses includes shattering window panes, blinding headlights, and principally, the mutilated cadavers, bowels, and body parts feasted upon by the zombies provide cinema's darkest chambers with a new degree of visceral intensity. This unadulterated display of violence struck a chord with audiences. In 1968, the year the film was in production, the Vietnam War had encroached upon the lives of every American via the non-stop media war bulletins. Law enforcement and opponents of war were pitted against each other in full-blown street fights. Bloodshed swept across inner cities nationwide. Two beloved public figures, Robert F. Kennedy and Martin Luther King, were also both assassinated that year.

It would be overly simplistic to see the movie's undead as an allegory for the Red Scare, and neither can the events of the story be explained away by the spacecraft's mysterious emission of radiation, which is of course a reference to the ever-present nuclear threat of the Cold War era. George A. Romero did more than this: he updated the classic horror zombie for a 1960s audience. In his apocalyptic vision, the national crisis—as evidenced in the zombies' fashionable clothing—originated from within America itself, and racial discrimination is one of the piece's prominent issues. For its final sequences, the film takes on the quality of a documentary newsreel. After Ben's death, as Armageddon breaks up the structure of the earth, the visuals denature into static, grainy stills. These frozen images draw attention to the meat hooks used to lay the zombies corpses—as well as Ben's—on the funeral pyre. The sight makes the police force and people's army seem like the real monsters. As one movie reviewer put it, "Those who survive the film are a kind of *dead living.*"

PLB

ROSEMARY'S BABY

1968 – USA – 137 MIN.

DIRECTOR

ROMAN POLANSKI (b. 1933)

SCREENPLAY

ROMAN POLANSKI, based on the novel of the same name by IRA LEVIN

DIRECTOR OF PHOTOGRAPHY

WILLIAM A. FRAKER

EDITING

SAM O'STEEN

MUSIC

JKRZYSZTOF KOMEDA

PRODUCTION

WILLIAM CASTLE for PARAMOUNT PICTURES

STARRING

MIA FARROW (Rosemary Woodhouse), JOHN CASSAVETES (Guy Woodhouse),
RUTH GORDON (Minnie Castevet), SIDNEY BLACKMER (Roman Castevet),
MAURICE EVANS (Hutch), RALPH BELLAMY (Dr. Sapirstein),
ANGELA DORIAN (Terry Fionoffrio), PATSY KELLY (Laura-Louise),
ELISHA COOK, JR. (Mr. Nicklas), CHARLES GRODIN (Dr. Hill),
EMMALINE HENRY (Elise Dunstan), WILLIAM CASTLE (Man in the Phone Booth)

ACADEMY AWARDS 1968

OSCAR for BEST SUPPORTING ACTRESS (Ruth Gordon)

Paramount Pictures Presents

Mia Farrow

In a William Castle Production

Rosemary's
Baby

co-starring

John Cassavetes

Ruth Gordon / Sidney Blackmer / Maurice Evans / and Ralph Bellamy

Produced by William Castle / Written for the Screen and Directed by Roman Polanski / From the novel by Ira Levin

Technicolor® / Production Designer - Richard Sylbert / A Paramount Picture / Suggested for Mature Audiences

1

"He has his father's eyes."

Neighbors, begone! I will have no more of thee… Rosemary Woodhouse (Mia Farrow) discovers that hellish neighbors can be included in the cost of rent shortly after she and her husband Guy (John Cassavetes) happen upon the Bramford (a building ill-fated in real life and better known as the Dakota, where John Lennon was shot in 1980). The newly-weds, an actor and his homemaker wife, are intrigued by the lovely brownstone, even before their friend Hutch (Maurice Evans) charms them with tales of its illustrious former occupants. Intending to provide the couple with cautionary fatherly counsel, Hutch fills them in on the practices of the eccentric Trent sisters, who are rumored to feast on human children, and Adrian Marcato, America's most prominent Satanist. Concluding that devil worshipers and a coven of witches can't be nearly as frightening as the real estate market in 1960s New York, the Woodhouses decide to move in anyway.

Folklore intrudes on reality when death visits the building. A young woman, who had been living with the Woodhouse's new neighbors, Minnie and Roman Castevet (Ruth Gordon and Sidney Blackmer), inexplicably commits suicide. The incident leaves the elderly couple at a loss for words and without youthful companionship. Despite initial reservations, Guy befriends the charismatic Roman. Soon foreboding shadows are replaced with cheer. Guy's floundering acting career suddenly takes off and Rosemary learns that she is pregnant. Yet the couple's joy is lined with ill fortune. Not only does a freak accident leave Guy's professional rival blind, but Rosemary learns that she conceived while unconscious. In the first weeks of pregnancy she comes down with what is clearly more than just a case of morning sickness. Dr. Sapirstein (Ralph Bellamy), a renowned gynecologist referred to her by the Castevets, assures her that what she's experiencing isn't out of the ordinary, and that the excruciating cramps will subside in a matter of days—but they don't.

Rosemary's world spirals into a living nightmare. Hutch, who had some pressing news to share with her, unexpectedly falls into a coma and dies. However, he manages to bequeath a book to her that reveals the name

IRA LEVIN A New York City native (b. 1929), author, playwright and lyricist Ira Levin is best known in the world of theater. Nonetheless, as the majority of his novels have been adapted for the silver screen (not to mention the several Broadway shows adapted for American television), his work is equally revered by moviegoers. His film career began with *A Kiss Before Dying* (1956, remade in 1991), long before *Rosemary's Baby* saw the light of day. Yet it goes without saying that Roman Polanski's 1967 critical and box-office sensation provided Levin with his Hollywood breakthrough. The 1997-published sequel *Son of Rosemary*, on the other hand, has failed to spark interest in Hollywood.
Film adaptations of Levin's other work have also met with acclaim—albeit from a primarily artistic standpoint. In 1975, *The Stepford Wives* were fully automated for the screen in an electrifying low-budget sci-fi thriller. *The Boys from Brazil* (1978), a spoof on Nazi war movies, wooed audiences with an all-star cast featuring Gregory Peck, Laurence Olivier, and James Mason. Phillip Noyce's 1993 film thriller *Sliver* (written for the screen by Joe Eszterhas) met with limited enthusiasm. Nonetheless, the biggest mystery of this acclaimed writer's career is that the novel many consider his masterpiece, an Orwellian vision of the future entitled *The Perfect Day*, has yet to be filmed, while *The Stepford Wives* starring Nicole Kidman was remade in 2004. Ira Levin died in 2007 in New York.

2

1 Breaking and entering: Rosemary's neighbors have invaded her most personal space—her body (Mia Farrow as Rosemary Woodhouse).

2 A sign of the times: It's no wonder so many people are thinking twice about bringing children into this world.

3 Her little bundle of joy: Rosemary discovers that baby Andy takes after his father.

4 How to succeed in business without really trying: Hubby Guy Woodhouse (John Cassavetes) suddenly hears music in the sound of Rosemary's name.

"It may not be for the very young, and perhaps pregnant women should see it at their own risk."

Motion Picture Herald

5

Roman Castevet to be an anagram of Steven Marcato, the son of the Bramford's aforementioned Satanist. Rosemary is positive that a conspiracy has been plotted against her and her baby, never suspecting that the baby growing inside her could in fact be the Antichrist himself.

Contrary to Ira Levin's surreal novel, Polanski is intentionally ambiguous about informing the audience as to whether the events are actually taking place or simply the product of a woman's progressively absorbing paranoia. Characteristic of the film's underlying ambivalence is the dream sequence in which Rosemary cries out, "This is no dream! This is really happening!" For in dreams, there is no certainty; and without certainty there can be no indisputable truth.

It was to be the only liberty Polanski took in his adaptation of Levin's novel, given that the director wanted to remain as true as possible to the written original for his first Hollywood production. Even the symbolic dream sequences are employed as a means of setting up counterpoints between the realistic manner in which the story is presented and its incredible content.

Like the manuscript it is based on, a seemingly self-perpetuating chain of events lures the viewer into the picture and refuses to loosen its grip even after the story's outcome has been made clear. Every sentence, every shot, and every last detail all contribute to the development of the characters and plot. For instance, when Guy and Rosemary play scrabble early on in the picture,

5 Nowhere to run to, Baby. Nowhere to hide: Even a secluded phone booth provides no vestige of hope.

6 Beast feeding: Rosemary and Guy contemplate the mysteries of life over a game of scrabble and some take out.

"Tension is sustained to a degree surpassing Alfred Hitchcock at his best." *Daily Telegraph*

Polanski supplies Rosemary with the device she eventually uses to decipher the Marcato anagram.

Ironically, this perfectly streamlined cinematic narrative was the product of a grossly impractical and uneconomical approach to filmmaking. The first edit of the movie was a five-hour monster, containing numerous scenes that, at the time of filming, Polanski was uncertain would make it into the final cut. If the conception was immaculate, then that's just one more miracle to emerge from the mysteries of the editing suite. SH

FLESH FOR FRANKENSTEIN

1973 – USA / ITALY / FRANCE – 95 MIN.

DIRECTORS

PAUL MORRISSEY (b. 1938),
ANTONIO MARGHERITI (1930–2002)

SCREENPLAY

TONINO GUERRA, PAUL MORRISSEY

DIRECTOR OF PHOTOGRAPHY

LUIGI KUVEILLER

EDITING

JED JOHNSON, FRANCA SILVI

MUSIC

CLAUDIO GIZZI

PRODUCTION

ANDREW BRAUNSBERG, CARLO PONTI,
ANDY WARHOL for BRAUNSBERG PRODUCTIONS,
CARLO PONTI CINEMATOGRAFICA
RASSAM PRODUCTIONS, YANNE ET RASSAM

STARRING

JOE DALLESANDRO (Nicholas), MONIQUE VAN VOOREN (Baroness Katrin Frankenstein),
UDO KIER (Baron Frankenstein), ARNO JUERGING (Otto), DALILA DI LAZZARO (Female Monster),
SRDJAN ZELENOVIC (Sasha / Male Monster), NICOLETTA ELMI (Monica),
MARCO LIOFREDI (Erik), LIU BOSISIO (Olga), CRISTINA GAIONI (Nicholas' Girlfriend)

Andy Warhol's

FRANKENSTEIN

A Film by

Paul Morrissey

ANDY WARHOL'S "FRANKENSTEIN" • A Film by PAUL MORRISSEY • Starring Joe Dallesandro
Monique Van Vooren • Udo Kier • Introducing Arno Juerging • Dalila Di Lazzaro • Srdjan Zelenovic
A CARLO PONTI – BRAUNSBERG – RASSAM PRODUCTION • COLOR • A BRYANSTON PICTURES RELEASE

1

"Otto, look at this! Finally we find the right head with the perfect nasum! For my male zombie..."

The opening credits to *Andy Warhol's Frankenstein* might have been made by Charles Addams: two children, a boy and a girl, dissect a doll before beheading it with a miniature guillotine.

Baron Frankenstein (Udo Kier with a strong German accent) wants to create not just one human being but a couple, who will conceive and bear the representatives of a new race. In this he is assisted by his henchman Otto (Arno Juerging). Only one body part is lacking, for the male half of the couple: not the brain, as we might expect, but the perfect "Serbian" nose; for the Baron's racist ideology will accept nothing less. In order to secure the propagation of the race, Frankenstein and Otto head off to the village brothel in search of a suitable victim. This turns out to be Sasha (Srdjan Zelenovic), whom they promptly kill, not realizing that he is in fact homosexual. His friend Nicholas (Joe Dallesandro), a farm laborer and servant to the Baroness, rushes to Sasha's aid, but too late: Sasha's head already adorns another man's body. In a bloody showdown, almost everyone ends up dead: Sasha murders both the Baroness and his creator Frankenstein, before killing himself. The only survivors are the Frankenstein children, who have witnessed everything, and who now calmly step up to accept their inheritance—much to the horror of the bound and helpless Nicholas.

Flesh for Frankenstein and the project that followed on its heels, *Andy Warhol's Dracula* (*Blood for Dracula*, 1973) were low-budget projects, filmed entirely in the Factory in a single seven-week period. Both were produced by Warhol himself. According to the director Paul

ANDY WARHOL'S FACTORY From 1963 onwards, the Pop artist Andy Warhol (1928–1987) produced hundreds of films in his Factory, a meeting place for artists, writers, dancers, transvestites, musicians, exhibition-makers, and exhibitionists. These movies were often collective efforts, made in collaboration with avant-garde filmmakers such as Jonas Mekas and Jack Smith. In the initial phase, Warhol was clearly influenced by experimental films of the time: *Empire* (1964), for example, is an eight-hour shot of the Empire State Building, filmed with a static camera and without a single cut. Other works, such as *Chelsea Girls* (1966), were provocative in different ways, featuring endless improvisations, a gritty documentary feel, or pornographic scenes, often explicitly homoerotic. Most of Warhol's actors were amateurs, but he called them "superstars" in line with his credo that in the age of the mass media anyone can be a star. In 1968, he began to produce more commercially oriented films, directed by Paul Morrissey. Although smartened up in appearance by conventional post-production, the imagery, sound, and narrative structure of these films are still a very long way from Hollywood. Besides *Andy Warhol's Frankenstein* (*Flesh for Frankenstein*, 1973) and *Andy Warhol's Dracula* (*Blood for Dracula*, 1973), his best-known films are: *Flesh* (1968), in which Morrissey's protagonist-of-choice Joe Dallesandro played a male prostitute, *Trash* (1970), and *Andy Warhol's Women* (*Women in Revolt*, 1971).

1 Modern day Salomé? Baron Frankenstein (Udo Kier) with his heart's desire—the head of a young man with the perfect nose.

2 Lo and behold! Henchman Otto (Arno Juerging) presents the female prototype (Dalila Di Lazzaro).

3 A new man: Frankenstein's guest Sasha (Srdjan Zelenovic) after his successful head transplant.

4 Doctor Frankenstein's anatomy lesson.

Morrissey, the actors were given their lines on a daily basis. Viewers of this spectacle are disappointed all along the line, and this is by no means unintentional: if the title misleads anyone into expecting some creepy entertainment or even a faithful adaptation of Mary Wollstonecraft Shelley's novel, what they're given instead is a set of protagonists who are thoroughly bored, blasé or just plain beat. Not that the film isn't pretty much "in your face"; indeed, thanks to the film version's 3-D effects, it's quite often all over your clothes. Lopped limbs and entrails are sometimes close enough to taste.

Flesh for Frankenstein owes much to two genres: splatter and soft porn. Other versions of the story have seen Frankenstein's bodybuilding as a subtle compensation for his repressed sexual needs, and Warhol's Baron is certainly no high-minded Prometheus, no genius of the arts or sciences. He awakens his creatures to life by means of bloody penetration and a variety of necrophiliac activities. While the late 1960s had hailed the coming of the sexual revolution, sexuality in this film offers no liberation from the constraints of society. On the contrary, desire is either unfulfilled or can only find expression through exploitation and rape. The plot is dominated by the protagonists' decadence and narcissism; little is to be seen, for example, of the normally obligatory villagers, often portrayed as a revolutionary counterforce to the French aristocracy. Nor is it the holy family of bourgeois mythology that triumphs over the Baron and his monster, revealing the hubris of those who would dare emulate God. Nicholas does manage to expose Frankenstein's doings; but he ends up helpless in the hands of the children—incestuous siblings like their parents before them—who will simply

“*Flesh for Frankenstein* is no biting satire, but a gruesome burlesque. One only hopes that anyone who sees it will have enjoyed a vegetarian meal beforehand.” *Frankfurter Rundschau*

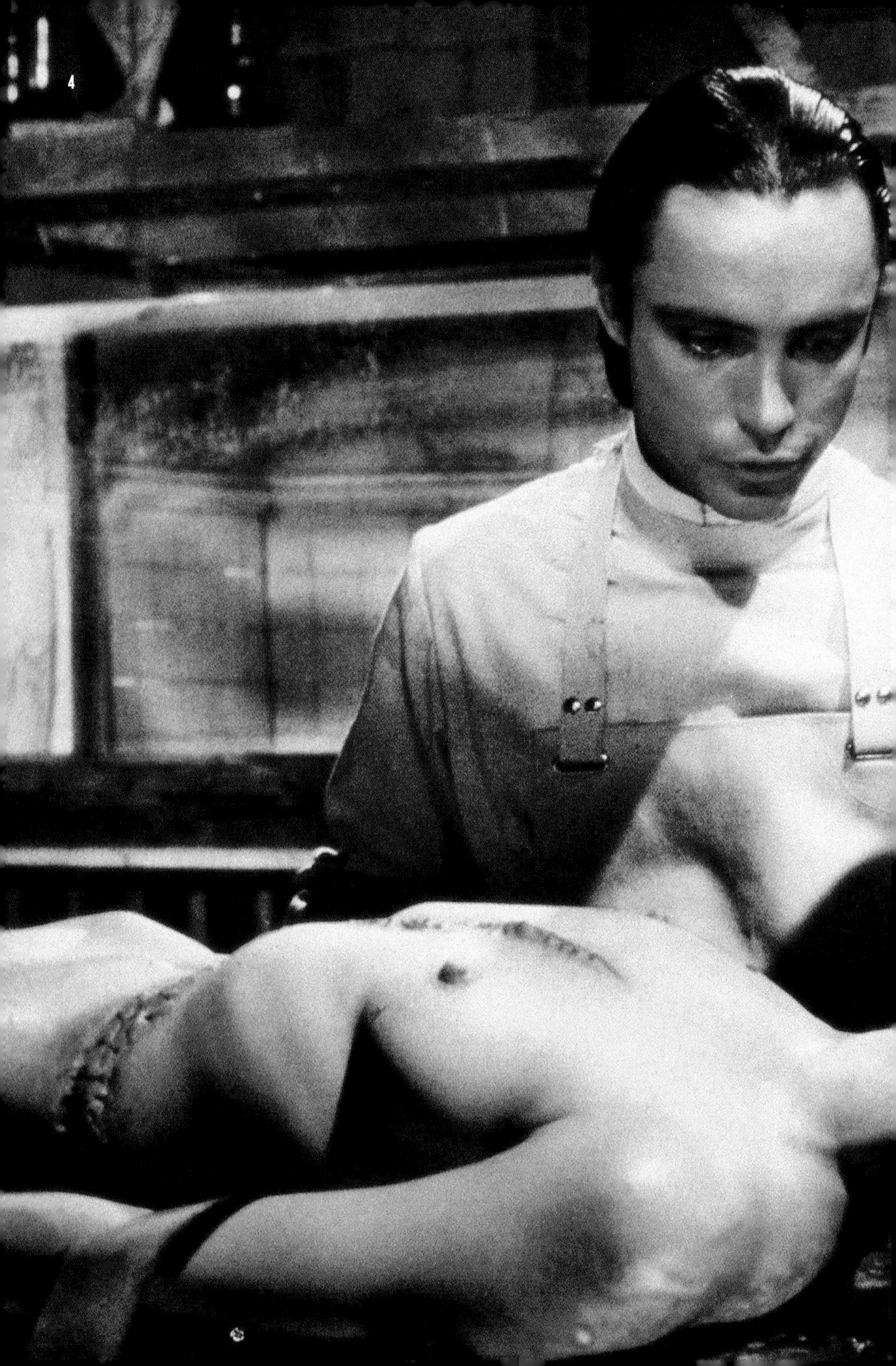

4

5 No cliché too cheap: The insatiable Baroness Katrin Frankenstein (Monique Van Vooren) seduces her willing servants.

6 Bottoms up: Sasha remains indifferent to the charms of the fairer sex.

7 Walking the straight and narrow: Warhol cast Joe Dallesandro, gay underground star, as Nicholas. Here, he takes a trip to the village brothel.

"Each night I'd think of what further absurdity might logically follow from where I began."

Paul Morrissey, in: Maurice Yacowar, The Films of Paul Morrissey

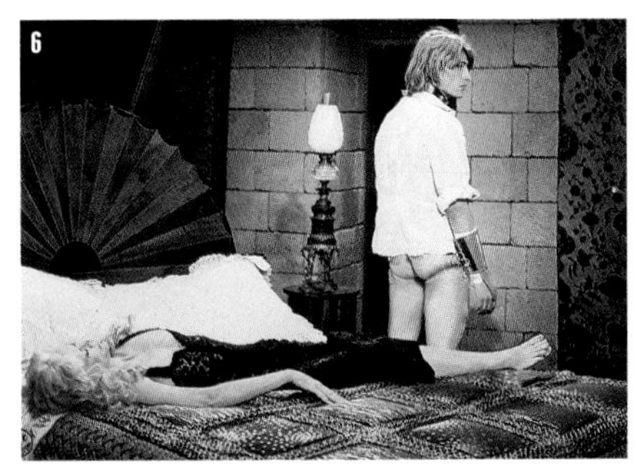

carry on where the older generation left off. The monstrous Frankenstein family structure remains unscathed, an artificial and hermetically closed system.

Frankenstein is no mere parody: Morrissey dwells exclusively on the negative aspects of the tale, like the misogynistic episodes, Frankenstein's fascist ideas and the children's icy lack of feeling. And faced with this grim lack of alternatives, we soon find the laughter sticking in our throats.

PLB

DON'T LOOK NOW

1973 – GREAT BRITAIN – 109 MIN.

DIRECTOR

NICOLAS ROEG (b. 1928)

SCREENPLAY

CHRIS BRYANT, ALLAN SCOTT
based on the story of the same name by DAPHNE DU MAURIER

DIRECTOR OF PHOTOGRAPHY

ANTHONY B. RICHMOND, NICOLAS ROEG

EDITING

GRAEME CLIFFORD

MUSIC

PINO DONAGGIO

PRODUCTION

PETER KATZ, FREDERICK MULLER,
STEVE PREVIN for CASEY, ELDORADO FILMS

STARRING

JULIE CHRISTIE (Laura Baxter), DONALD SUTHERLAND (John Baxter),
HILARY MASON (Heather), CLELIA MATANIA (Wendy),
MASSIMO SERATO (Bishop Barbarrigo), RENATO SCARPA (Inspector Longhi),
ANN RYE (Mandy Babbage), NICHOLAS SALTER (Johnny Baxter),
SHARON WILLIAMS (Christine Baxter), BRUNO CATTANEO (Detective Sabbione),
ADELINA POERIO (Dwarf)

Pass the warning.

Paramount Pictures presents
A Peter Katz-Anthony B. Unger Production

JULIE CHRISTIE

DONALD SUTHERLAND

"DON'T LOOK NOW"

A psychic thriller.

Based on a story by DAPHNE DU MAURIER · Produced by PETER KATZ · Directed by NICOLAS ROEG · Screenplay by ALLAN SCOTT and CHRIS BRYANT

R RESTRICTED Under 17 requires accompanying Parent or Adult Guardian

Executive Producer ANTHONY B. UNGER · in Color · Prints by Movielab · A Paramount Picture

1

"I have seen her... and she wants you to know that she is happy."

Two children frolic through the autumnal garden of a house in the English countryside. The children's parents, Laura and John Baxter (Julie Christie and Donald Sutherland), sit comfortably inside the house. While John looks over slides, Laura rests on the couch and reads. It is an idyll that is soon brutally shattered. Stirred by a dark premonition, John runs outside. But he is too late. His daughter Christine is already dead—drowned in the garden pond. To gain some distance from the horrible event, the couple travel to Venice, where John begins directing the restoration of a church. But when they meet two odd Scottish sisters (Hilary Mason and Clelia Matania) in a restaurant, their daughter's death catches up with them: one of the two old women is blind and presumably gifted with a supernatural talent. With a friendly laugh, she tells Laura that she has been in contact with Christine. Laura breaks down upon hearing this, but she then gains a new confidence from the stranger's vision and tries to convince John, who considers the entire story absurd, that their daughter is not yet lost.

Briton Nicolas Roeg began his career toward the end of the 1950s as a cameraman. He quickly became one of the most sought-after men in his field. In the 1960s, he worked as director of photography for directorial icons such as Roger Corman, Richard Lester, John Schlesinger, and David Lean, before making his long-overdue directorial debut alongside Donald Cammel with *Performance* (1969), an extravagant gangster film that offered a reflection on the popular culture of the 1960s. Roeg worked as director of photography on *Performance*,

JULIE CHRISTIE British actress Julie Christie was born on April 14, 1941 in the Indian province of Chukua, where her father ran a tea plantation. Early on, she traveled to Europe, studied art history in Paris, and collected theater experience before she debuted in the television series *A for Andromeda* in 1961. Without a hitch she made the jump into film and, as the ideal embodiment of the new independent woman of the "swinging sixties," soon became a star.

In 1965 she won an Oscar for her depiction of an immoral "Jetset" girl in John Schlesinger's *Darling*. In the same year, she brought tender sensuality to David Lean's sweet and opulent Pasternak adaptation, *Doctor Zhivago*. Despite her distinctive beauty, combining boldness, coolness, and sensitivity, she escaped being typecast and was able to develop as an actress. François Truffaut cast her in a double role in *Fahrenheit 451* (1966). Later she portrayed the title character in Richard Lester's *Petulia* (1968) and played alongside Warren Beatty in Robert Altman's *McCabe & Mrs. Miller* (1971), a role that earned her another Oscar nomination. Christie also worked with further directorial stars of the time, like Joseph Losey in *The Go-Between* (1970), Nicolas Roeg in *Don't Look Now* (1973), and Hal Ashby in *Shampoo* (1974). Toward the end of the 1970s things grew quiet around Christie, who, like Jane Fonda, was politically active and apparently lost interest in acting. She once again confirms her acting class in Alan Rudolph's *Afterglow* (1997) as well as the film version of Alice Munro's story *Away from Her* in which she plays a woman fallen ill with Alzheimers disease.

2

“*Don't Look Now* is such a rich, complex and subtle experience that it demands more than one viewing. Roeg's insistence on the power of the image, his reliance on techniques of narrative that are peculiarly cinematic, remind us how undemanding and perfunctory so many movies still are. Roeg's is one of those rare talents that can effect a new way of seeing.” *Time Magazine*

and again on his second film, *Walkabout* (1971). In *Don't Look Now*, he is also credited alongside Anthony B. Richmond as director of photography, unmistakable evidence that indicates just how important the visual aspect of filmmaking is for Roeg. Accordingly, *Don't Look Now*, which like several Alfred Hitchcock films is based upon a Daphne du Maurier story, is a masterpiece of timeless beauty thanks to its visual qualities.

It's often the case in cinema that an unspecified, implicit threat produces a more lasting scare than any terror explicitly depicted on the screen. This is especially true for movies that convert human fears into a system of symbols, like horror films or thrillers. *Don't Look Now*, which effectively straddles these two genres, is a prime example. Even today, the film derives most of its extraordinarily disturbing effect and subtle horror from the tense atmosphere that Roeg evokes with his powerfully suggestive images, accentuated by a seemingly avant-garde montage technique, which almost anticipates the refined editing of Steven Soderbergh. From the very beginning, the film's time and reality planes are constantly interrupted by unsettlingly stark cuts, abrupt segues, and enigmatic associations. A second, hidden meaning seems to lurk behind each image and the constant threat of something unexpected and inexplicable questions what has just been seen. As with the mosaics John Baxter reconstructs in the church, the truth is hidden behind a

"A modern Hitchcock. His film shows that he has already absorbed and reflected upon the turmoil of the 70s." *Kölner Stadt-Anzeiger*

1 The end of innocence: In just minutes, the child in the red raincoat will drown in the garden pond. In Nicolas Roeg's film, each image holds multiple meanings.

2 After the death of his daughter, John Baxter (Donald Sutherland) experiences things in Venice that threaten his rational worldview.

3 Dialing up the dead: Laura (Julie Christie) is hoping two mysterious women will help her contact her deceased child.

"... a haunting, beautiful labyrinth that gets inside your bones and stays there. *Don't Look Now* still has the power to frighten and disorient—to suggest a world that's perilous, cruel and out of control."

San Francisco Chronicle

4 Indecent exposure: Tiny red details in gray, wintry Venice recall the drowned girl at the start of the film—Laura's shoulder bag, for example...

5 ... and her boots.

6 The labyrinthine alleys of Venice reflect John's inner chaos.

number of broken pieces in small symbols that seem to defy rational association, for which normal explanations simply do not suffice.

Roeg's suggestive coloration hugely intensifies the surreal, threatening atmosphere. The color red is given an especially significant meaning. At the beginning, little Christine runs around the garden in a radiant red raincoat. The premonition that the girl is in danger comes to John as he discovers a figure clad in a red hooded jacket on the slide of a Venetian church and a red fluid—it is not clear if it's John's blood—subsequently spreads out on the screen. When later in Venice, Laura wears red boots or carries a red bag, it suggests that the Baxters are oppressed by thoughts of their daughter. It seems as if John is even visited by visions, as he repeatedly sees a mysterious small figure in a red raincoat scurrying away. The film appears to slowly but surely take over John's perspective, who in contrast to Laura is a committed rationalist and fights against his delusional visions, growing more and more bewildered as a result. Far from romantic glamour, wintry gray Venice, with its labyrinthine streets, becomes a mirror image of his inner chaos. In the end, the city exudes an almost Gothic horror. It shockingly reveals itself to John as a kingdom of the dead.

The directorial projects of former cameramen are often plagued by a technical brilliance that renders films cold and sterile. The natural interaction between the leading actors, Julie Christie and Donald Sutherland, ensures that this is not case here. Their wonderfully long love scene has passed into legend, its discrete sensuality all the more evident today, long after the scent of scandal has faded. JH

6

THE EXORCIST

1973 – USA – 122 MIN.

DIRECTOR

WILLIAM FRIEDKIN (b. 1935)

SCREENPLAY

WILLIAM PETER BLATTY based on his novel of the same name

DIRECTOR OF PHOTOGRAPHY

OWEN ROIZMAN, BILLY WILLIAMS

EDITING

NORMAN GAY, EVAN LOTTMAN, BUD SMITH

MUSIC

JACK NITZSCHE, KRZYSZTOF PENDERECKI

PRODUCTION

WILLIAM PETER BLATTY for WARNER BROS., HOYA PRODUCTIONS

STARRING

ELLEN BURSTYN (Chris MacNeil), MAX VON SYDOW (Father Merrin),
LEE J. COBB (Lieutenant Kinderman), LINDA BLAIR (Regan MacNeil),
KITTY WINN (Sharon Spencer), JASON MILLER (Father Damien Karras),
JACK MACGOWRAN (Burke Dennings), REVEREND WILLIAM O'MALLEY (Father Dyer),
BARTON HEYMAN (Dr. Klein), PETER MASTERSON (Barringer)

ACADEMY AWARDS 1973

OSCARS for BEST ADAPTED SCREENPLAY (William Peter Blatty),
and BEST SOUND (Robert Knudson, Christopher Newman)

WILLIAM PETER BLATTY'S

THE EXORCIST

Directed by WILLIAM FRIEDKIN

Something almost beyond comprehension is happening to a girl on this street, in this house ...and a man has been sent for as a last resort. This man is The Exorcist.

ELLEN BURSTYN · MAX VON SYDOW · LEE J. COBB
KITTY WINN · JACK MacGOWRAN JASON MILLER as Father Karras
LINDA BLAIR as Regan · Produced by WILLIAM PETER BLATTY
Executive Producer NOEL MARSHALL · Screenplay by WILLIAM PETER BLATTY based on his novel
From Warner Bros. A Warner Communications Company R RESTRICTED Under 17 requires accompanying Parent or Adult Guardian

1

2

"What an excellent day for an exorcism."

Evil neither stems from a dark abyss nor from a cosmic realm. It neither limits its dominion to dark shadows and blind alleys, nor does it attack in the form of a werewolf that can be slain with a silver bullet. When we are struck by the fear that without warning, something horrific could infiltrate our lives and turn our precious little worlds on their heads, perhaps we are tuning into something very real and tangible. Maybe evil has already made a nest for itself, where we'd least expect it. Namely, in our most intimate surroundings.

Although this is the central topic of the story involving American actress Chris MacNeil (Ellen Burstyn), whose twelve-year-old daughter Regan (Linda Blair) is transformed into the Antichrist before her very eyes, *The Exorcist* director William Friedkin opens his film with far off images of the Middle East. It is on an archaeological dig in Iraq that Father Merrin (Max von Sydow) unearths several ancient artifacts that send him into a state of panic, including decapitated statue heads and a most unnerving amulet.

The ensuing scenes, in which pure evil appears to take possession of Merrin's entire environment, are among the picture's most powerful. The vacant and yet piercing stares of the locals, the hammering of the blacksmiths that Merrin confuses with the sound of his own racing heart and a clock that stops cold are just a few of the images that contribute to the audience's visceral incorporation of the imminent danger.

When, at the end of this sequence, Merrin sits directly across from a statue of an ominous demon with rabid dogs running rampant at its feet, the essence of the story becomes clear. According to the director, the film is "a Christian parable about the eternal struggle between good and evil."

Cut to "Georgetown." The on-screen caption and the bird's eye view of the city evoke a deceptive picture of order and distanced safety. Friedkin referred to the fade-in technique he often used as the "Means of luring the audience onto the wrong track." Nonetheless, the peace of

SUBLIMINAL MESSAGES At the speed of 24 frames per second in film and 30 NTSC frames per second in television, subliminal messages are usually only visible for less than the blink of an eye, and certainly not long enough to leave an imprint on the human retina. The term itself comes from the Latin *sub limen* (below the threshold).
The theory that even an image which people are not capable of consciously perceiving can still impact their minds is an age-old concept. In particular, the advertising industry has tried countless times to make use of scientifically and ethically disputed techniques of visual manipulation. "Invisible advertising" was tested in New Jersey in 1957 during the screening of *Picnic* (1955). The results, which contended that the several spliced in, split-second-long frames showing popcorn and Coca Cola caused sales to sky rocket, turned out to be falsified. Be that as it may, as recently as the U. S. presidential race in 2000, President George W. Bush ran a smear ad in which the word "rats" appeared in conjunction with a prescription drug proposal put together by his opponent, Al Gore. Strictly speaking, subliminal messages have only had a limited impact on the cinema directly. Filmmakers who experiment with them, like David Lynch, tend to implement montage sequences of image snippets. These, however, can be perceived by the naked eye of an alert viewer. In *The Exorcist: The Version You Haven't Seen Yet* (1973/2000) such a device was used briefly to show Satan's face—yet another attempt on the part of the director to petrify his audience.

3

1 That little devil: Regan (Linda Blair) is about to have a religious experience.

2 Satanic verses: The Prince of Darkness moves in mysterious ways.

3 Who's been sleeping in my bed? Father Damien Karras (Jason Miller) suppresses his doubts and aids Father Merrin (Max von Sydow) in the ancient exorcism.

4 That thing upstairs is not my daughter: Actress Chris MacNeil (Ellen Burstyn) wants to be a good mother to Regan, but Dr. Spock never said anything about spitting up pea soup.

Georgetown's idyllic autumn and the illusion of the stable family unit fall like a house of cards after one of the Jesuit priests from the university, Father Karras (Jason Miller) breaks down and admits that he has "lost faith." With these words, something wicked this way comes.

It comes in the form of an appalling, disfigured little girl spewing out profanities and blaspheming uncontrollably. Wretched displays of gasping, choking, and shrieking are let loose on the audio track, accompanied by a visual deluge of regurgitated green mucus. Never before and never since for that matter, has a director been so intent on terrorizing his audience. At the time of its release, screenings often had spectators vomiting in the aisles, fainting and breaking into hysterics. This highly provocative work even made movie critic Roger Ebert question his faith in humanity, asking whether "people (are) so numb that they need movies of this intensity in order to feel anything at all?"

The intoxicating shock value of the gore can make one overlook the masterful web of allusions, contrasts, analogies, and sociopolitical arguments Friedkin has woven here. One example of this intricate layering can be witnessed when Regan forms a clay model of a bird with wings that recall those of the demonic statue in the Iraq

4

“*The Exorcist* makes no sense, but if you want to be shaken, it will scare the hell out of you.”

The New Republic

sequence. Later on, Lieutenant Kinderman (Lee J. Cobb), assigned to investigate the mysterious death of Chris's close friend, finds yet another clay object at the scene of the crime. It is the pagan counterpart to the crucifix, which Chris recently discovered in her daughter's bed.

The way in which the film attempts to diagnose the cause of Regan's possession is also worthy of close examination. The arrogance of the doctors, Chris's outbursts of rage, her friend Burke's alcoholism, the burden of guilt Father Karras feels towards his dead mother are all signs that the source of evil could be human. Karras's work as a psychologist for the university's Jesuit community makes him doubt God's existence, providing the audience with another possible clue to the origin of Regan's infection. Other events, including the Jesuit priest who comes across a defiled statue in the chapel, but doesn't acknowledge the Madonna as he enters, also point to lack of faith as a contributory.

All these factors are devices Friedkin uses to vary the film's underlying principle mentioned in the opening paragraph. Namely, that evil lurks in everyday life and even in our very hearts. In this respect, it is not a battle with the devil that Father Karras ends up winning. It's a battle with his own self. SH

THE WICKER MAN

1973 – GREAT BRITAIN – 84 MIN.

DIRECTOR

ROBIN HARDY (1929–2016)

SCREENPLAY

ANTHONY SHAFFER

DIRECTOR OF PHOTOGRAPHY

HARRY WAXMAN

EDITING

ERIC BOYD-PERKINS

MUSIC

PAUL GIOVANNI

PRODUCTION

PETER SNELL for BRITISH LION FILMS

STARRING

EDWARD WOODWARD (Sergeant Howie), CHRISTOPHER LEE (Lord Summerisle), DIANE CILENTO (Miss Rose), BRITT EKLAND (Willow), INGRID PITT (Librarian/Registrar), LINDSAY KEMP (Alder MacGreagor), RUSSELL WATERS (Harbor Master), AUBREY MORRIS (Old Gardener/Gravedigger), IRENE SUNTERS (May Morrison), WALTER CARR (Schoolmaster), IAN CAMPBELL (Oak)

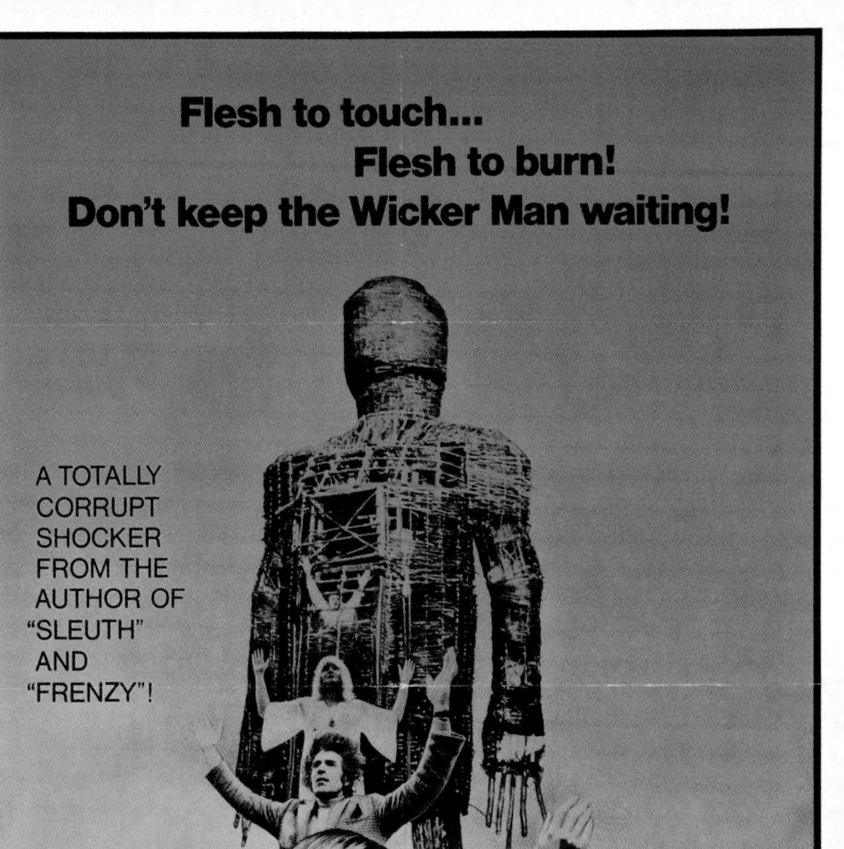

Starring
"THE WICKER MAN" · EDWARD WOODWARD · BRITT EKLAND · DIANE CILENTO · INGRID PITT
and CHRISTOPHER LEE as Lord Summerisle Produced by PETER SNELL · Directed by ROBIN HARDY · Screenplay by ANTHONY SHAFFER
From Warner Bros. A Warner Communications Company R RESTRICTED

1

"You'll simply never understand the true nature of sacrifice."

Since 1958, Christopher Lee had appeared in seven Hammer films as Dracula. He wrote in his autobiography, "At the age of 50, I took the firm decision to Draculate no more." With playwright and screenwriter Anthony Shaffer (*Sleuth*, 1972; *Frenzy*, 1972) and Canadian producer Peter Snell, he bought the film rights to David Pinner's novel *Ritual*, which was about a police detective investigating the death of a young girl in a Cornish village.

Shaffer's interest had been piqued by the idea of ritual sacrifice, and by the qualities that a person must possess to make them suitable for sacrifice. Both Shaffer and his friend Robin Hardy—in the 1960s Shaffer had written and Hardy had directed television ads as Hardy Shaffer Associates—discussed a possible scenario and researched texts, especially James George Frazer's *The Golden Bough*, a 12-volume study of magic and religion. Frazer claimed that the legend of the king dying at the harvest festival and being reincarnated in the spring is central to almost all of the world's mythologies. Peter Snell became the managing director of British Lion Films, so when he received Shaffer's script of *The Wicker Man*, he gave it the green light, and filming began on October 9, 1972, in Dumfries and Galloway in Scotland.

The Wicker Man begins with Sergeant Neil Howie (Edward Woodward) flying out to a remote island, Summerisle, off the west coast of Scotland. After landing his seaplane in the harbor, Howie commences his investigation into the mysterious disappearance of schoolgirl Rowan Morrison, which has been prompted by a letter and photo sent to him on the mainland. The locals deny that Rowan is known to them, or is even from the island. May Morrison (Irene Sunters), the postmistress, says that she does not have a child named Rowan.

The bullheaded sergeant is determined to solve the mystery and stays overnight at the Green Man Inn. The townspeople regale him with bawdy songs about the landlord's daughter, Willow (Britt Ekland), and that night Willow invites him into her room, but Howie fights temptation and remains true to his Christian faith and the belief that he should remain celibate before marriage.

The following morning, Howie is outraged by the teachings at the school—the students are told that the Maypole is a phallic symbol, representative of the generative powers of the penis—and then finds out that Rowan Morrison's name is on the class register. The schoolmistress Miss Rose (Diane Cilento) tells Howie that they do not believe that Rowan is dead: "Here, we believe that when human life is over the soul returns to trees, to air, to fire, to water, to animals. Rowan Morrison has simply returned to the life forces in another form. The children find it far easier to picture reincarnation than resurrection."

Howie finds Rowan's grave, but the registrar (Ingrid Pitt) has no record of her death, so Howie visits Lord Summerisle (Christopher Lee) to ask permission to exhume the body. Lord Summerisle explains the history of the island, how his grandfather came, found it barren, and encouraged the disheartened islanders to embrace their joyous old Gods in return for a fruitful harvest. What he did, of course, was develop and introduce hardy fruits that would thrive in the harsh environs. The practice continues, and the current Lord Summerisle enjoys "the reverence, the music, the drama, and the rituals of the old Gods. To love nature, and to fear it, and to rely on it, and to appease it when necessary."

Howie exhumes Rowan's grave and finds nothing but a hare in the coffin. He breaks into a photo laboratory to find

"Sergeant Howie: I believe in the life eternal, as promised to us by our Lord, Jesus Christ. Lord Summerisle: That is good. For believing what you do, we confer upon you a rare gift, these days—a martyr's death." *Film quote*

a picture of the previous year's harvest festival; he sees that Rowan is in the picture and that the crops failed. Fearing that Rowan is to be sacrificed during the May Day Festival, Howie searches every house in the village for her, but to no avail. After he hears the landlord (Lindsay Kemp) whisper in conspiratorial tones about the festivities, Howie knocks him out and dons his costume, that of Punch, the Fool.

Howie joins the May Day parade in the masked costume. At the beach he sees Rowan, rescues her, escapes through the caves, and emerges at the cliff top. There the whole community is waiting for them. Howie is to be burned alive inside the wicker man, as a sacrifice to Nuada, the sun god. As Lord Summerisle explains, "Animals are fine, but their acceptability is limited. A little child is even better, but not nearly as effective as the right kind of adult." It is clear now that Rowan's mysterious disappearance, the sexual temptations, and the interactions with the islanders had all been one long May Day parade, with Howie as the Fool, being led to this place at this time.

1 The wicker man accepts the human sacrifice.

2 Willow (Britt Ekland) and Alder MacGreagor (Lindsay Kemp) welcome Sergeant Howie to the Green Man Inn.

3 As part of the May Day festivities, the islanders are masked appropriately to their professions.

4 Devout Christian Sergeant Howie (Edward Woodward) makes a cross in the abandoned church.

5 Sergeant Howie searches for the missing schoolgirl Rowan Morrison, believing her to be in mortal danger.

6 Lord Summerisle (Christopher Lee) leads the islanders in celebratory song as Sergeant Howie burns.

7 Sergeant Howie arrives willingly, dressed as the Fool, as a representative of the crown, and as a virgin, thus fulfilling all the criteria for a human sacrifice.

8 Willow invites Howie into her bed, but he resists the temptation.

"We don't commit murder here. We're a deeply religious people." *Film quote: Lord Summerisle*

Upon completion, Robin Hardy edited together a 99-minute version, which the new owners of British Lion cut down to 84 minutes. The film was not supported upon release in the UK or America and soon disappeared from cinemas. However, in 1977, the American magazine *Cinefantastique* devoted an issue to the film, calling it "The Citizen Kane of horror films." Since then the film has been established as one of the finest British horror films ever made, and a number of restored versions have been released as "The Final Cut" and "The Director's Cut."

PD

THE TEXAS CHAIN SAW MASSACRE

1974 – USA – 84 MIN.

DIRECTOR

TOBE HOOPER (b. 1943)

SCREENPLAY

KIM HENKEL, TOBE HOOPER

DIRECTOR OF PHOTOGRAPHY

DANIEL PEARL

EDITING

LARRY CARROLL, SALLYE RICHARDSON

MUSIC

TOBE HOOPER, WAYNE BELL

PRODUCTION

LOU PERAINO, TOBE HOOPER for VORTEX

STARRING

MARILYN BURNS (Sally Hardesty), ALLEN DANZIGER (Jerry),
PAUL A. PARTAIN (Franklin Hardesty), WILLIAM VAIL (Kirk),
TERI MCMINN (Pamela), EDWIN NEAL (Hitchhiker), JIM SIEDOW (Old Man),
GUNNAR HANSEN (Leatherface), JOHN DUGAN (Grandfather),
JOHN HENRY FAULK (Narrator), JOHN LARROQUETTE (Voice of Narrator)

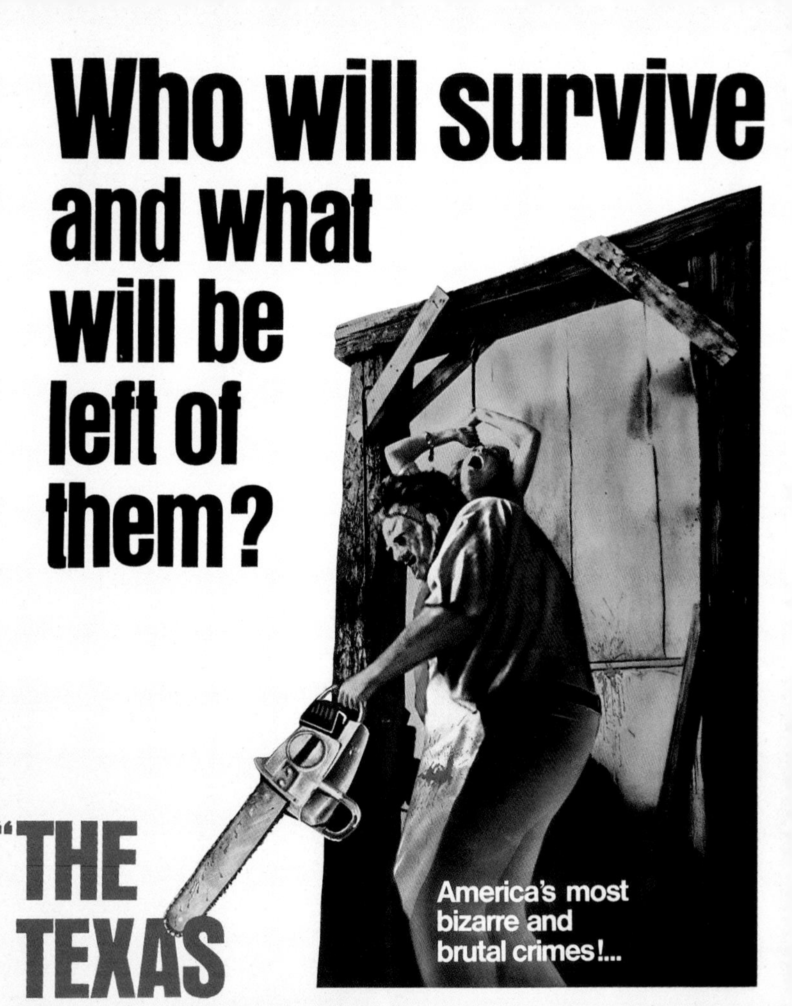
Who will survive
and what
will be
left of
them?
America's most
bizarre and
brutal crimes!...
"THE
TEXAS
CHAINSAW MASSACRE"
What happened is true. Now the motion picture that's just as real.
THE TEXAS CHAIN SAW MASSACRE · A Film by TOBE HOOPER · Starring MARILYN BURNS, PAUL A. PARTAIN, EDWIN NEAL, JIM SIEDOW and GUNNAR HANSEN as "Leatherface"
Production Manager, RONALD BOZMAN · Music Score by TOBE HOOPER and WAYNE BELL · Music Performed by ARKEY BLUE, ROGER BARTLETT & FRIENDS, TIMBERLINE ROSE,
LOS CYCLONES · Story & Screenplay by KIM HENKEL and TOBE HOOPER · Producer/Director, TOBE HOOPER · COLOR · A BRYANSTON PICTURES RELEASE.
R RESTRICTED

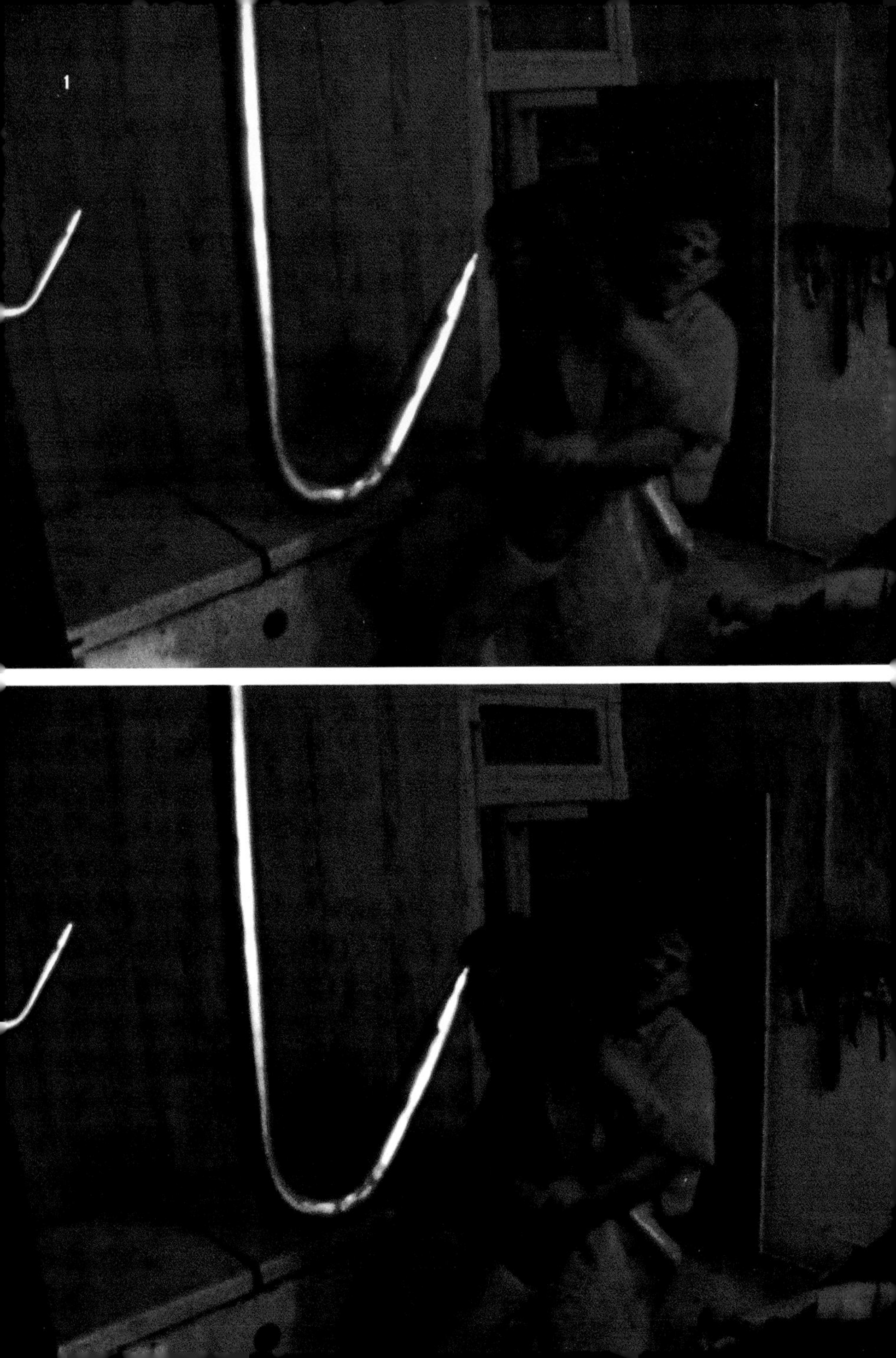

1

"My old grandpa is the best killer there ever was."

The Texas Chain Saw Massacre begins like a documentary, creating a dense, claustrophobic atmosphere. A blend-in promises the disclosure of one of the most unbelievable crimes in American history and the ensuing sequence leaves no doubt. Darkness, a sinister electronic sound with intermittent hacking and panting sounds, illuminated by flashing images of decaying body parts—followed by a radio report on the desecration of a Texan cemetery. We know that the idyll that follows will end in disaster. Pamela (Teri McMinn), Kirk (William Vail), Sally (Marilyn Burns), and her wheelchair-bound brother Franklin (Paul A. Partain) drive through this area. Short on gas, the friends decide to spend the night in the old house of Sally's grandparents.

But next to the partially dilapidated building live multiple generations of an unemployed butcher family who have developed into cannibals to survive. The youths fall victim to "Leatherface" (Gunnar Hansen) and his chainsaw, and in the end it is only the heroine Sally Hardesty, who in a breathtaking showdown fights for her life and—covered in blood—is ultimately able to escape.

Despite New York's renowned Museum of Modern Art purchase of *The Texas Chain Saw Massacre*, the film still repeatedly falls victim to censors. Watch it for a second time, and it becomes surprisingly apparent that in contrast to other works of the genre, dismembered body parts and organs or mutilations are often not seen directly, but rather disappear behind doors or out of the camera's sight. Nonetheless, Tobe Hooper was still able to depict violence and make it absolutely palpable. There is no psychological or sociological commentary to create distance from what is portrayed or offer an explanation for the overwhelming brutality. The last half hour is particularly stark in its transgression of the boundaries of reason,

LEATHERFACE—SERIAL KILLERS IN FILM Fritz Lang hunted a serial killer in *M* (1931), but it wasn't until the 1970s that this theme gained an immense popularity. One of the most notorious characters is Leatherface, who hunts his victims wearing a roughly sewn mask of tanned human skin and a butcher's apron. In fact, he wears three different masks. Aside from the killing mask, one is of an old woman, and the other is of a made-up woman, worn when he cooks for the family in his mother role.

Whereas in *The Silence of the Lambs* (1991), Jame Gumb also wanted to slip into another skin, patching together a female shell out of the remains of his victims, Leatherface's disguise indicates neither sexual fantasies nor the motive behind his murders. His identity remains a riddle and consequently "the evil" behind this spooky masquerade—as was the case of Michael Myers in *Halloween* (1978)—is not given a true face. Leatherface, who has long since advanced to an international cult figure, is on the one hand a projection surface for subconscious fears and—on the other hand—perfect for identification: in the film, parallels are suggested between the outsider of the group, Franklin, and Leatherface. Alexandre Bustillo and Julien Maudry's *Leatherface*, which came to the movies in 2016, is about the character's teenage years.

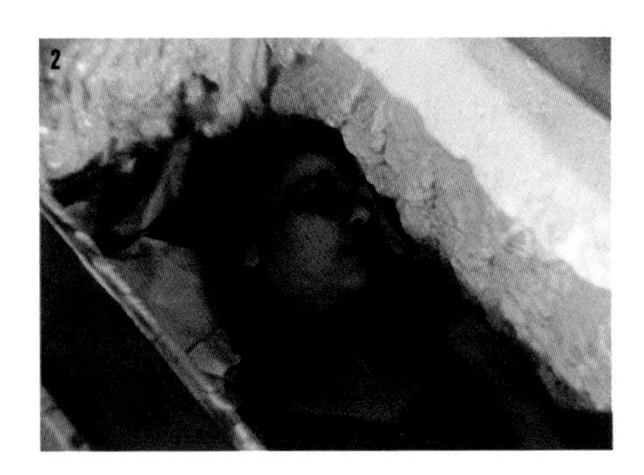

"Rather than choosing violence as its theme, *The Texas Chain Saw Massacre* makes violence tangible. Tobe Hooper doesn't analyze the causes of violence. He shows us what it feels like to run right into it." *Ulrich von Berg*

1 Cannibals' kitchen: The home as abattoir.

2 Colder than the grave. Take a look in the freezer.

3 Family Values in the American South.

4 Conflict management, country style.

5 When the chainsaw shrieks… be very afraid.

as the violence is not, as is more usual, diluted with entertaining or aesthetic components. Instead, the audience is increasingly forced to identify with the victim.

When the film was released in America, it was immediately associated with the atrocities of the Vietnam War. Indeed, Tobe Hooper drastically deals with the collective trauma in America—touching on true events like the crimes of the serial killer Ed Gein or the "Manson Family." As in Wes Craven's *Last House on the Left* (1972), it is not monsters or supernatural beings, but rather humans who become cold-blooded murderers. Though Leatherface is surely one of the most famous screen killers, the real monster on a metaphorical level is the American family.

Sally's grandparents' house, and that of their neighbors, is a haunted house with forbidden rooms that are not to be entered. As in a fairy tale, unintentionally breaking a rule results in death or sadistic tortures—tortures that often evoke memories of helplessness or nerve-wracking pranks from childhood or adolescence. Several surreal sequences have the structure of nightmares, for example when Sally flees from Leatherface into a large forest and, although she is much faster, she is unable to escape her pursuer. Though the Sally Hardesty character is a female long at the mercy of her sadistic tormentor, Hooper's dramatization avoids making her an object of sexual desire. When she tearfully offers to do anything the family ask of her, they respond with sinister cackling. Later, Sally displays an extraordinary strength. Twice she jumps through windowpanes Western-style, and ultimately succeeds in escaping the clutches of this most monstrous of families.

PLB

JAWS

1975 – USA – 124 MIN.

DIRECTOR

STEVEN SPIELBERG (b. 1946)

SCREENPLAY

CARL GOTTLIEB, PETER BENCHLEY
based on the novel of the same name by PETER BENCHLEY

DIRECTOR OF PHOTOGRAPHY

BILL BUTLER

EDITING

VERNA FIELDS

MUSIC

JOHN WILLIAMS

PRODUCTION

RICHARD D. ZANUCK, DAVID BROWN for
ZANUCK/BROWN PRODUCTIONS, UNIVERSAL PICTURES

STARRING

ROY SCHEIDER (Police Chief Martin Brody), ROBERT SHAW (Quint),
RICHARD DREYFUSS (Matt Hooper), MURRAY HAMILTON (Mayor Larry Vaughn),
LORRAINE GARY (Ellen Brody), CARL GOTTLIEB (Ben Meadows),
JEFFREY KRAMER (Lenny Hendricks), SUSAN BACKLINIE (Chrissie),
CHRIS REBELLO (Mike Brody), JAY MELLO (Sean Brody)

ACADEMY AWARDS 1975

OSCARS for BEST FILM EDITING (Verna Fields), BEST MUSIC (John Williams),
and BEST SOUND (Robert L. Hoyt, Roger Herman Jr., Earl Mabery, John R. Carter)

The terrifying motion picture
from the terrifying No.1 best seller.

ROY SCHEIDER

ROBERT SHAW

RICHARD DREYFUSS

JAWS

Co-starring LORRAINE GARY · MURRAY HAMILTON · A ZANUCK/BROWN PRODUCTION
Screenplay by PETER BENCHLEY and CARL GOTTLIEB · Based on the novel by PETER BENCHLEY · Music by JOHN WILLIAMS
Directed by STEVEN SPIELBERG · Produced by RICHARD D. ZANUCK and DAVID BROWN · A UNIVERSAL PICTURE ·
TECHNICOLOR® PANAVISION®

ORIGINAL SOUNDTRACK AVAILABLE ON MCA RECORDS & TAPES

1

"You're gonna need a bigger boat."

A hot summer night, a beach party, a little too much red wine, and some teenage sex is just the stuff Hollywood horror films are made of. While her drunken companion sleeps off his hangover on the beach, young Chrissie (Susan Backlinie) takes a midnight dip in the water and is torn to pieces by a shark. The fact that the monster with the dead eyes cynically emerges in innocent white from the depths of the water makes it all the more threatening. The shark—the fear and guilt in all of us—awakens our prehistoric terror of the incomprehensible, the truly wild. It is evil incarnate.

But in the small American beach town ironically named Amity, nobody wants to hear about the threat to a safe world and free-market economy, least of all from the mouth of visiting New York cop Martin Brody (Roy Scheider) who, to cap it all, is afraid of the water.

Accordingly, the authorities, in the form of the mayor Larry Vaughn (Murray Hamilton), and the profit- and pleasure-seeking public win out over Brody, who wants to close the beaches in light of the menacing danger. It comes as no surprise that the town has a new victim the very next day. A reward of $3,000 for the capture of the shark incites hunting fever in Amity, and the gawking mob on the pier is duly presented with a dead shark. But it is quickly determined that the captured shark can't possibly be the feared killer: upon cutting open its stomach they find a few small fish, a tin can, and a license plate from Louisiana.

It is a motley trio that sets out to capture the beast—a water-shy policeman, a "rich college boy" named Matt Hooper (Richard Dreyfuss), and shark-hunting Vietnam veteran Quint (Robert Shaw), a modern Captain Ahab who unsuccessfully attempts to disguise a

THE END OF ARTIFICIAL CREATURES "Compressors, tanks, winches, pneumatic hoses, welding torches, blow lamps, rigging, generators, copper, iron, and steel wire, plastic material, electric motors, crammers, hydraulic presses"—just some of the trappings required to make "Bruce," as the film team christened the model of the white shark, come alive. In his book, *The Jaws Log*, co-screenwriter Carl Gottlieb tells of the immense problems encountered trying to simulate real-life shark attacks with a life-sized model (because actually Bruce was made of three different models). Shooting was repeatedly interrupted by technical problems, most memorably when they first put Bruce in the water, only to see him sink like a stone. The hiring of long-retired Hollywood veteran Robert A. Mattey, creator of the special effects for Disney's *Mary Poppins* (1964) and countless other films, makes it clear that the mid-1970s marked the end of conventionally created film monsters. "Bruce" was one of the last of his kind and craftsmen like Bob Mattey were increasingly replaced by computer programmers. Steven Spielberg proved his ability to incorporate their work into his projects in 1981 with *Raiders of the Lost Ark*, in which entire sequences were created with the help of computer animation.

2

“If *Jaws* was a kind of skeleton key to the angst of the ’70s, from the puritanical fear of sex to the war in Vietnam, then its heroes were models of America’s wounded masculinity, who meet and join to face a test of character.”

Georg Seeßlen: Steven Spielberg und seine Filme

1 Baywatch: Police Chief Martin Brody (Roy Scheider) is fighting nature, the ignorance of those he's trying to protect, and his own fears.

2 Beach, blanket, bloodbath: beautiful Chrissie (Susan Backlinie) is the shark's first victim.

3 Smile for the camera: three separate models, each seven yards long and weighing over a ton, brought the monster to life. The film crew dubbed the shark "Bruce"—after Steven Spielberg's lawyer.

wounded psyche with a façade of disgust for everything around him. For each of the three men, the shark hunt also turns into a search for their true selves.

The unmistakably sexual aspect of the story of the unnamed monster—a terrifying mixture of phallus and vagina—which afflicts the home and the family has often been pointed out. But *Jaws* is also a film about human fears and character flaws, the overcoming of which gives birth to heroes. That the story also tells of the capitalistic, self-endangering society, of patriotic America, of mass hysteria, guilt, atonement, and the sacrifice of the individual for the good of the whole is proof of Spielberg's ability to give a simple story plausible readings on multiple levels.

But let's not forget that *Jaws* is one of the most nervewracking thrillers of all time. When Spielberg explains that during the filming he felt as if he could direct

4 Brody's scared of water, but he's about to undergo some shock therapy…

5 Rub a dub dub, three men in a tub: *Jaws* is also a parable about social conflicts in the United States.

6 Shark fin soup: evil feeds on ignorance and Americans.

the audience with an electric cattle prod, it speaks volumes about the cold precision with which, supported by an exceptionally suggestive soundtrack, he was able to raise the tension and lower it again, all in preparation for the next dramatic highlight.

Just one example of Spielberg's virtuoso storytelling technique is the scene in which the men show one another their scars below deck. In the middle of the scene, the audience is told the story of the *USS Indianapolis*, the boat with which the Hiroshima bomb was transported to the Pacific. Under fire from Japanese submarines, the crew threw themselves into the ocean and the majority of them were eaten by sharks.

During this sequence, which is actually quite humorous, Spielberg and his writers succeed in setting a counterpoint even before the appearance of the shark illustrates the terror of the story. Quint's tale contains a political dimension. Ultimately, this scene also reveals something about storytelling itself—reality catches you up in a flash. Right when Quint and Hooper attempt to stem their apprehension with loud song, Mr. Spielberg is right there with his electric shocker.

SH

“If Spielberg’s favorite location is the suburbs, *Jaws* shows suburbanites on vacation.”

Chicago Sun-Times

CARRIE

1976 – USA – 98 MIN.

DIRECTOR

BRIAN DE PALMA (b. 1940)

SCREENPLAY

LAWRENCE D. COHEN based on the novel
of the same name by STEPHEN KING

DIRECTOR OF PHOTOGRAPHY

MARIO TOSI

EDITING

PAUL HIRSCH

MUSIC

PINO DONAGGIO

PRODUCTION

PAUL MONASH, BRIAN DE PALMA for REDBANK FILMS

STARRING

SISSY SPACEK (Carrie White), JOHN TRAVOLTA (Billy Nolan),
PIPER LAURIE (Margaret White), AMY IRVING (Sue Snell),
WILLIAM KATT (Tommy Ross), NANCY ALLEN (Chris Hargenson),
BETTY BUCKLEY (Miss Collins), P. J. SOLES (Norma Watson),
PRISCILLA POINTER (Mrs. Snell), SYDNEY LASSICK (Mr. Fromm)

IF YOU'VE GOT
A TASTE FOR TERROR...
TAKE CARRIE TO THE PROM.

If only they knew she had the power.

A PAUL MONASH Production A BRIAN DePALMA Film "CARRIE"
starring SISSY SPACEK
JOHN TRAVOLTA and PIPER LAURIE · Screenplay by LAWRENCE D. COHEN
Based on the novel by STEPHEN KING · Produced by PAUL MONASH · Directed by BRIAN DePALMA

R RESTRICTED

United Artists

1

"They're all gonna laugh at you!"

High school can be quite a blood bath. It's a world dominated by vanity, envy, and petty fears. For those who don't fit the mold, teasing, sneering, and even total ostracism can lie in store. But can't this clichéd view of the growing years be partly attributed to countless soap operas and teen flicks? Maybe so. Nevertheless, real reports of rampant violence repeatedly hit the headlines, a testament to the fact that the social microcosms within schools are no place for kids who journey the path less traveled.

Carrie (Sissy Spacek) is one such person. She is the daughter of the mentally ill Margaret (Piper Laurie), who became a religious fanatic after Carrie's father left them. In her relentless crusade to protect Carrie from earthly sins, Margaret beats the word of God into her daughter. Thus, while showering in the girls' locker room, the innocent Carrie is horrified when she menstruates for the first time.

Only gym teacher Miss Collins (Betty Buckley) extends Carrie her support. Still, her efforts to discipline the malevolent, traumatizing girls present for the event only adds fuel to their sadistic fire. When one of the girls, Chris (Nancy Allen), is prohibited from attending the prom as a result of the embarrassing incident, she swears revenge on Carrie, which meets with disastrous consequences... For meanwhile Carrie has discovered that she possesses an extraordinary gift. She is a telepathic medium. When faced with the eternal callousness of her immediate environment, this seemingly mousy homebody turns into a ticking time bomb.

Even though the image forever engrained in the memories of world audiences is that of the young Sissy Spacek drenched in pig's blood, *Carrie* cannot be deemed a horror film in the classic sense. It is at its most gruesome when it shakes the audience with images of the true-to-life, spiteful machinations of the snide cliques led by John Travolta and De Palma's later wife Nancy Allen. *Carrie* is not, however, a scathing critique of American high schools. Above all else, the film is a heart-pounding thriller that keeps you on the edge of your seat even though the story's ending is clear from the start.

De Palma takes great pleasure in torturing his audience to the bitter end, manipulating its voyeuristic expectations and then tweaking the plot in such a way as to leave everyone hung out to dry. Which, according to Brian De Palma, is giving the audience their just desserts. For when it comes down to it, moviegoers are not that different from the on-screen juvenile brat pack, eager to put a rise in Carrie's sails on prom night. With diabolic precision, he

SISSY SPACEK The German newspaper *Die Zeit* once described Sissy Spacek, an actress born in Quitman, Texas in 1949, as "the phenomenology of backroads America captured in a single face." Spacek's America is one filled with characters from the nooks and crannies of small towns, like the awkward, intimidated schoolgirl, Carrie, and the birdhouse-building handicapped daughter in David Lynch's *The Straight Story* (1999). It is the America associated with romanticized hospitality that Spacek is most familiar with. At one time, this seemingly meek, homely-looking woman toured the nation's foothills as a country music singer, performing under the name "Rainbow" and relying on her fire and brimstone constitution to forge her way. After completing her acting studies with Lee Strasberg and winning critical acclaim for Terrence Malick's *Badlands* (1973), she cemented her career with her performance as *Carrie* (1976). Shortly thereafter, she was cast as country singer Loretta Lynn in *Coal Miner's Daughter* (1980), a role that must have fit like a glove, and was awarded the Best Actress Academy Award for her outstanding performance. The following year, Spacek received another Oscar nomination for her work opposite Jack Lemmon in *Missing* (1981). Oscar nodded twice more in her direction, for her portrayal of a farmer's wife in *The River* (1984) and for her artistry *In the Bedroom* (2001), for which she won a Golden Globe. In 2005 she performed alongside Glenn Close, Jason Isaacs, and Holly Hunter in Rodrigo Garcia's *Nine Lives* as well as in Niki Caro's *North Country* with Charlize Theron and Frances McDormand. In 2008 she played alongside Vince Vaughn and Reese Witherspoon in the Christmas comedy *Four Christmases*. Since March 2015 Sissy Spacek can be seen on Netflix as matriarch Sally Rayburn in the series *Bloodline*.

2

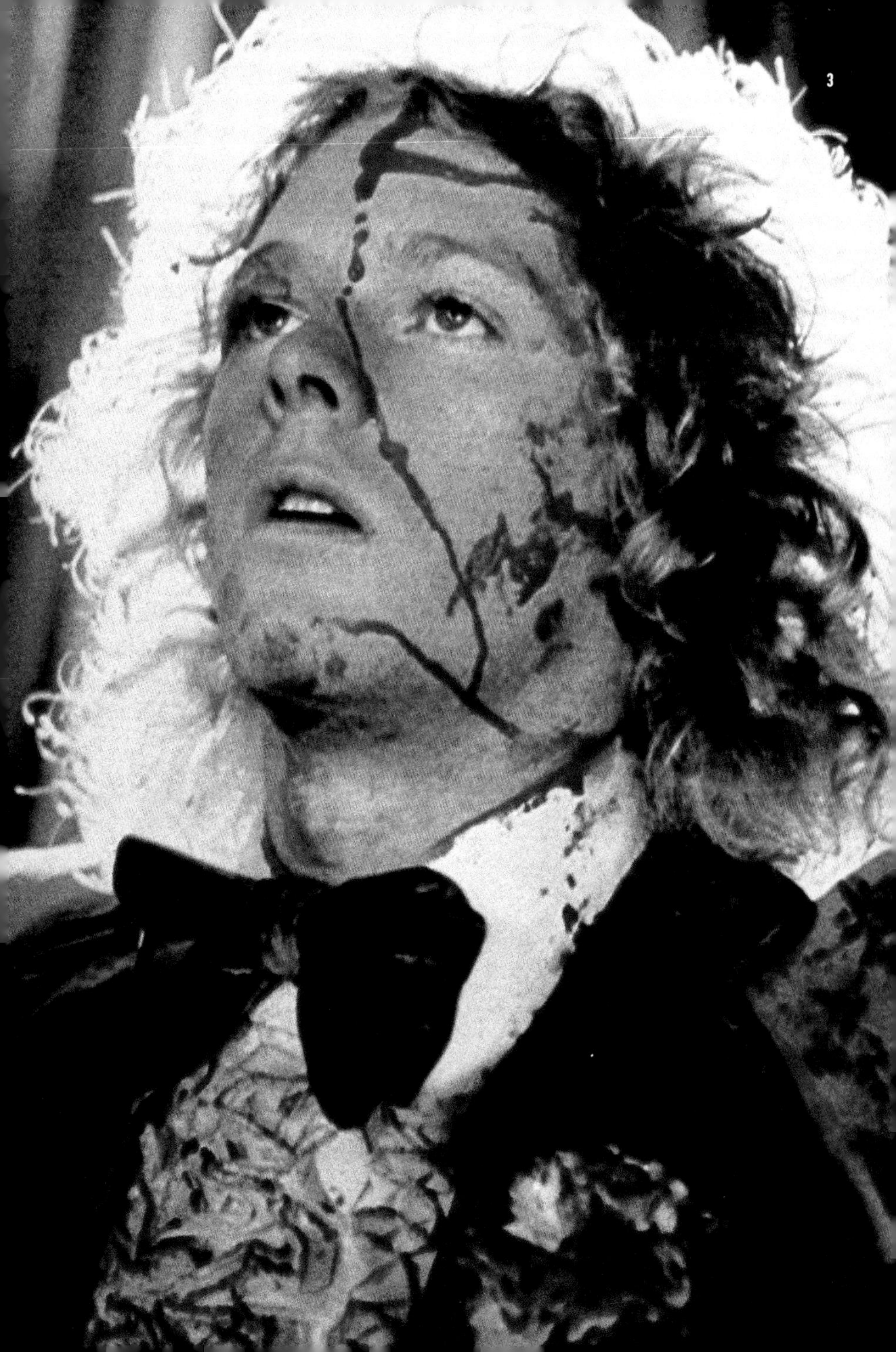

3

4

5

1 Baptized in blood: The poster image of Carrie White (Sissy Spacek) remains engrained in the minds of audiences to this very day.

2, 3 Splitting images: Brian De Palma's infernal ending was Mannerist to say the least.

4 Just your average, ordinary schoolgirl: Carrie becomes a woman in the girl's locker room.

5 Instilling the fear of God: Margaret White (Piper Laurie) raises a hand to her heretic daughter.

6 Coal Miner's Slaughter: The former country singer Sissy Spacek made her breakthrough in the role of poor, monstrous Carrie White.

"Combining Gothic Horror, offhand misogyny and an air of studied triviality, *Carrie* is De Palma's most enjoyable movie in a long while, and also his silliest." *Newsweek*

intensifies the audience's basic desire to put an end to the heroine's perpetual ridicule, by pairing it up with the growing anticipation of the most climactic event of every high school girl's life—the prom. The dance's culmination is accompanied by the unleashing of an unstoppable act of apocalyptic wrath.

You could describe the last third of the film as pure mannerism. It's a fireworks display, including the slow motion camera, split-screen action, extreme close-ups and pointedly dramatic lighting. Though many a director would have shied away from a finale that could be branded as a cavalcade of cheap effects, De Palma implemented it flawlessly and turned its elements into his signature style.

What's more astonishing is that *Carrie* was shot on a spartan budget of just under two million dollars. The financial limitations forced De Palma to abstain from filming the total destruction of the town that takes place in the novel. Nevertheless, *Carrie* proved to be a milestone in the career of the then unknown director. The picture's popularity also most likely contributed to the acclaim of the story's author, Stephen King, who is considered today to be the most successful writer of all time. SH

SUSPIRIA

1977 – ITALY – 98 MIN.

DIRECTOR

DARIO ARGENTO (b. 1940)

SCREENPLAY

DARIO ARGENTO, DARIA NICOLODI, based on the novel
Suspiria de Profundis by THOMAS DE QUINCEY

DIRECTOR OF PHOTOGRAPHY

LUCIANO TOVO

EDITING

FRANCO FRATICELLI

MUSIC

GOBLIN, DARIO ARGENTO

PRODUCTION

CLAUDIO ARGENTO, SALVATORE ARGENTO for SEDA SPETTACOLI, P.A.C.

STARRING

JESSICA HARPER (Suzy Benner), STEFANIA CASINI (Sara), FLAVIO BUCCI (Daniel),
MIGUEL BOSÉ (Mark), BARBARA MAGNOLFI (Olga), SUSANNA JAVICOLI (Sonia),
EVA AXÉN (Pat Hingle), RUDOLF SCHÜNDLER (Professor Milius),
UDO KIER (Dr. Frank Mandel), ALIDA VALLI (Miss Tanner), JOAN BENNETT (Madame Blanc)

The Only Thing More Terrifying
Than The Last 12 Minutes Of This Film
Are The First 92.

Once You've Seen It
You Will Never Again Feel Safe In The Dark

R RESTRICTED Under 17 requires accompanying Parent or Adult Guardian

RELEASED BY INTERNATIONAL CLASSICS INC.

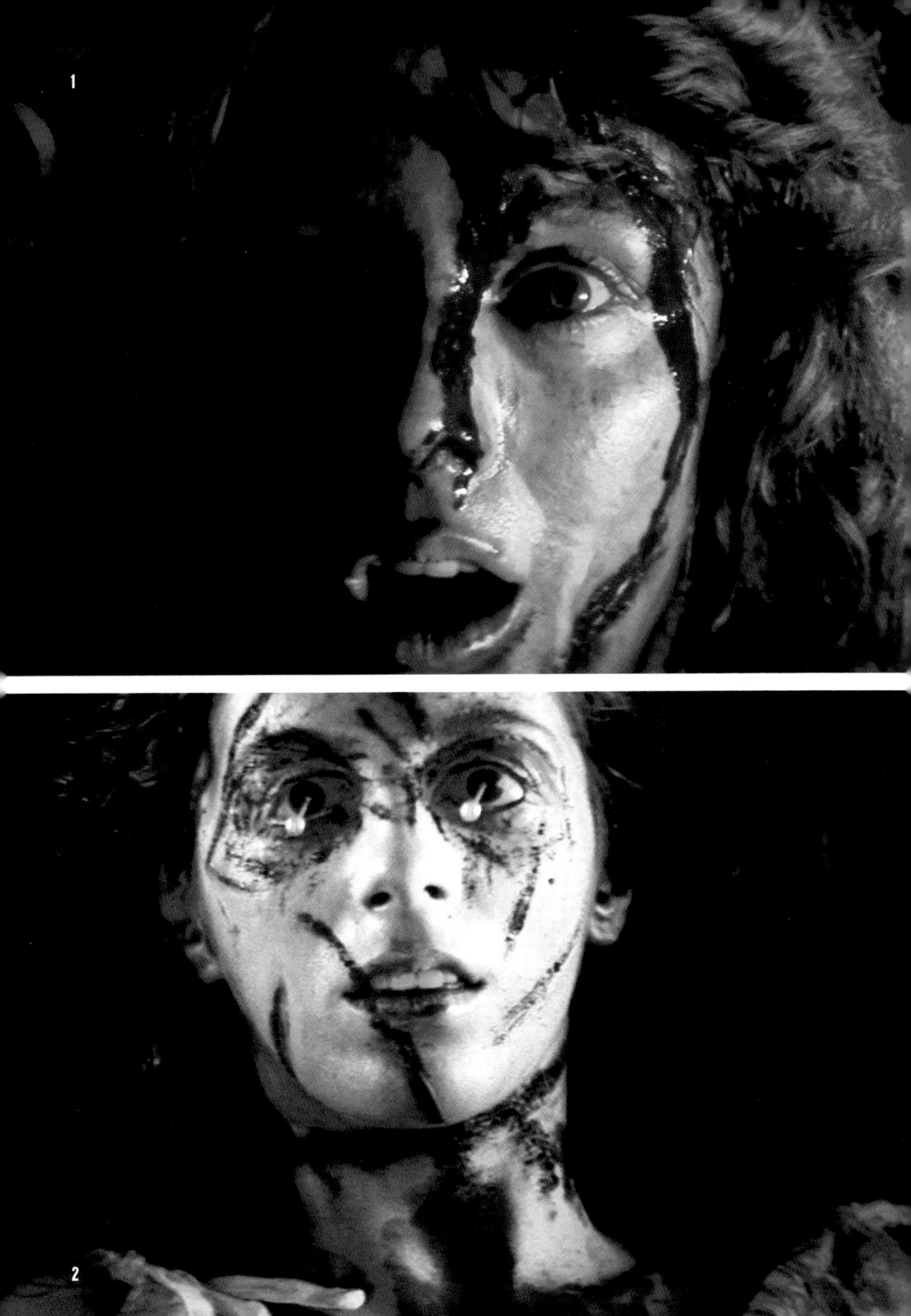
1
2

"Hell is behind that door! You're going to meet death now..."

"I was six years old," director Dario Argento remembered. "Every night after supper, I would say goodnight to my parents and go to bed. My room was at the other end of the house. I had to go all the way along a dark corridor lined with doors on either side. I used to be terrified. Every half-open door I passed was a threat, concealing obscure dangers. That's probably where my nightmares were born." Thirty years later, Argento constructed his sixth film as director, *Suspiria*, as an unending series of doors that American Suzy Bannion (Jessica Harper) seems compelled to walk through despite the darkness and apparent danger that may lurk behind them.

The very first door that Suzy encounters is the automatic, hissing glass door at the airport when she arrives in Munich, Germany. This simple scene tells us everything we need to know about how Argento is going to tell the story.

As Suzy begins walking towards us in the airport, she is bathed in red light. The colors are deeply saturated. Argento worked with cinematographer Luciano Tovoli to manipulate the colors using the Technicolor process. The colors seem to almost pulsate. Argento commented, "We were trying to reproduce the color of Walt Disney's Snow White."

Suzy walks towards us, and then we see the automatic doors from her point of view as the camera moves towards them. "Subjectiveness is very important in my films," Argento said. "The camera becomes the eye of the person. It walks, moves, and approaches things from the person's point of view. I want the spectator sucked into the scene. In the end, it is you, the spectator, who kills, or who is murdered." When we see Suzy, we hear the ambient sounds of the airport, yet when we see the doors from Suzy's point of view, we hear the lyrical electronic musical motif that will recur throughout the movie. The music is courtesy of Goblin, an Italian progressive rock band, who had worked successfully with Argento on his giallo thriller *Profondo Rosso* (*Deep Red*, 1975)—the soundtrack album sold over a million copies. The group recorded the music for *Suspiria* before filming began. Keyboard player Claudio Simonetti remembered, "Dario called us (in 1976) and said, 'I would like to have music that lets people feel that the witches are there, in the air, everywhere, even when (they're not).' We recorded in two and a half months, experimenting with ethnic instruments. We used the Indian tabla, the Greek bouzouki... and I used the big Moog (and) the Mellotron. We didn't have libraries (of sounds/samples) so we had to create our own sound. We started using plastic cups in front of the microphones and to scream and carry on. Every day we tried something new. It was very creative."

As Suzy walks through the opening automatic doors, suddenly we have a close-up of the mechanism, accompanied by the sharp pneumatic hiss. The sudden cuts and noise after the smooth camerawork and lilting music are shocking. Suzy is also assaulted, by the driving rain and howling wind. This remains the editing template for the story—sounds and images luring the viewer into a false trancelike state of serenity, then quick slashes of movement and noise that shock and awe.

Suzy makes her way via taxi to the prestigious Tanz Dance Academy in Freiburg, where she hopes to improve her ballet technique. When she arrives at the imposing red and gold façade of this Gothic monstrosity, the door opens and a student, Pat Hingle (Eva Axén), speaks to an unseen person and then runs off, through the forest, into the night. We follow Pat back to her apartment in a building that is a kaleidoscopic assembly of Escher-like patterns. Pat is killed by an unseen assailant: her face smashed through a window, stabbed seven times, and her neck snapped by a cord as she is hung after falling through a colorful glass skylight. Her mother is also killed by slabs of falling glass.

1 When ballet student Sara (Stefania Casini) investigates where the teachers go each night, she is attacked and killed.

2 Sara becomes one of the living dead, a puppet of the witches.

3 Suzy Benner (Jessica Harper) confronts the head witch, Helena Markos.

4 When the head witch is killed, the rest of the coven, including Miss Tanner (Alida Valli) and Madame Blanc (Joan Bennett), lose their powers.

5 Helena Markos (Lela Svasta) is Mother Suspiriorum ("Our Lady of Sighs"). Argento went on to make the *Three Mothers* trilogy with *Inferno* (1980) and *Mother of Tears* (2007).

6 Pat Hingle (Eva Axén) is stabbed and hung by an unknown hand. Argento wrote homages to M.C. Escher and Oskar Kokoschka, who inspired him, into the script.

According to Argento, "Murder is very important in my films. It is also very beautiful. Do you think it is scandalous to say it is beautiful? Why? Everybody knows that movie murders are not real, that the blood is a chemical preparation. That's why I say it is beautiful. It is like a celebration for me in which I concentrate totally on the technical point of view, the camera's view, in minute details. It is in these moments that my creativity explodes."

The plot is simple. Suzy joins the academy and meets teacher Miss Tanner (Alida Valli) and the vice-directress Madame Blanc (Joan Bennett). Between them, Valli and Bennett had appeared in the film noirs of Alfred Hitchcock, Fritz Lang, and Carol Reed, among others. Further murders follow—the blind piano player Daniel (Flavio Bucci), and fellow student Sara (Stefania Casini)—while Suzy is secretly drugged at night.

The film is almost without plot and character, and the dialogue is banal, yet it is a symphony of color, movement, sounds, and music that give it the texture of a waking nightmare. In the final 20 minutes, Suzy walks through seven foreboding doors to uncover the mystery of the academy: it is a witches' coven. Dario Argento: " Pasolini said that film was divided in two—the cinema of prose and the cinema of poetry. The cinema of prose, you never see the camera move. But the cinema of poetry, the camera is important. I (subscribe to) the cinema of poetry, of course." PD

4

5

"I'm interested in aggressiveness, violence, and the color of blood. I'm fascinated by the aesthetic of it, and through style it's possible to represent and translate these passions, because in the end, horror is a passion."

Dario Argento

6

7

8

"Bad luck isn't brought by broken mirrors, but by broken minds."

Dr. Frank Mandel

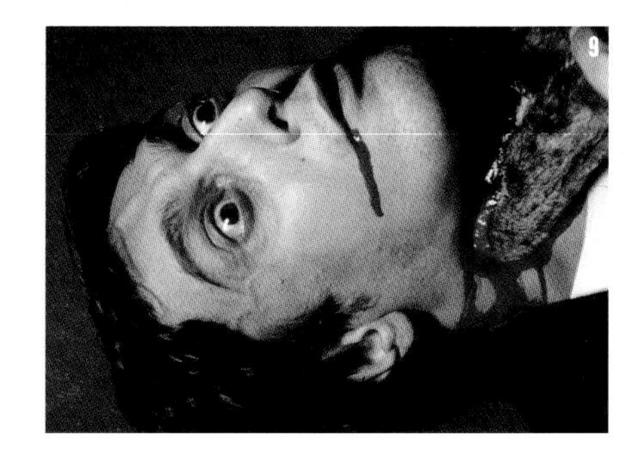

7 Pat Hingle is stabbed repeatedly. Argento: "When a gloved hand or shadow appears in one of my films, it usually belongs to me. I don't do it to show off. I do it because I am in fact quite an expert in this field. After all the years I have been making these films, I would probably make a pretty good murderer."

8 Argento: "In such an intense physical act like murder, between the victim and murderer there is something sensual, something erotic deep down. There is a link between the death orgasm and the sexual one."

9 The blind pianist Daniel (Flavio Bucci) is killed by his dog in a deserted plaza.

10 Argento: "Making movies is my job. For me it is a complete dream world. I think that a filmmaker is more or less interesting depending on whether his dreams, his nightmares, and even his illusions, are interesting or not."

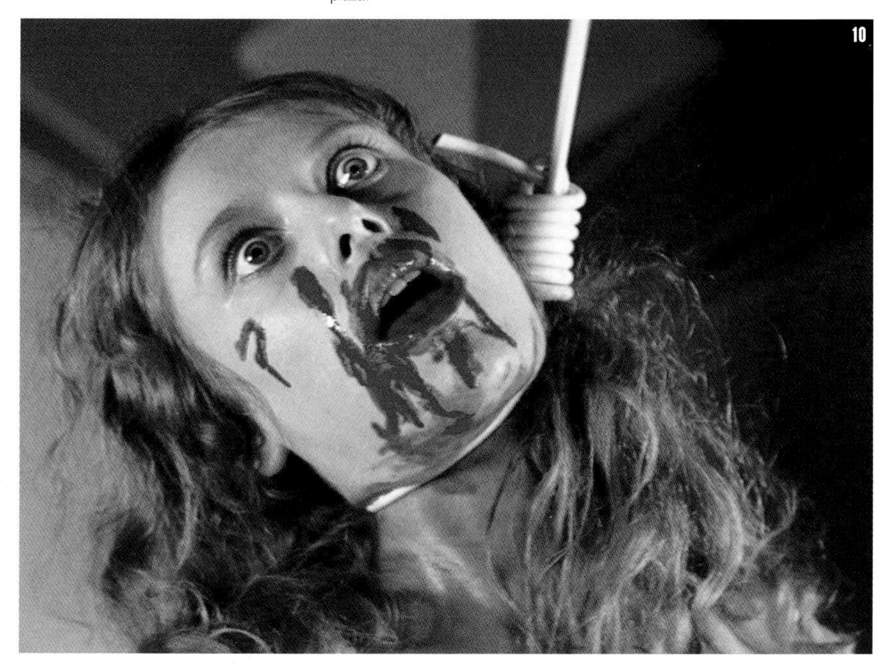

DAWN OF THE DEAD

1978 – USA / ITALY – 126 MIN. / 137 MIN. (Director's Cut)

DIRECTOR

GEORGE A. ROMERO (b. 1940)

SCREENPLAY

GEORGE A. ROMERO, DARIO ARGENTO

DIRECTOR OF PHOTOGRAPHY

MICHAEL GORNICK

EDITING

GEORGE A. ROMERO

MUSIC

DARIO ARGENTO, THE GOBLINS, AGOSTINO MARANGOLO,
MASSIMO MORANTE, FABIO PIGNATELLI,
GEORGE A. ROMERO (Director's Cut), CLAUDIO SIMONETTI

PRODUCTION

DARIO ARGENTO, RICHARD P. RUBINSTEIN for LAUREL GROUP

STARRING

DAVID EMGE (Stephen Andrews), KEN FOREE (Peter Washington),
SCOTT H. REINIGER (Roger DeMarco), GAYLEN ROSS (Francine Parker),
DAVID CRAWFORD (Doktor Foster), DAVID EARLY (Mr. Berman),
RICHARD FRANCE (Doctor Milliard Rausch), HOWARD SMITH (TV Commentator),
JESSE DEL GRE (Priest), FRED BAKER (Police Commander)

When there's
no more room in HELL
the dead will walk the EARTH

First there was
'NIGHT OF THE LIVING DEAD'
Now
GEORGE A. ROMERO'S

DAWN OF THE DEAD

HERBERT R. STEINMANN & BILLY BAXTER PRESENT A LAUREL GROUP PRODUCTION in Association with CLAUDIO ARGENTO & ALFREDO CUOMO

Starring: DAVID EMGE KEN FOREE SCOTT H. REINIGER GAYLEN ROSS

Director of Photography: MICHAEL GORNICK Music By: THE GOBLINS with DARIO ARGENTO

Produced By: RICHARD P. RUBINSTEIN Written and Directed by: GEORGE A. ROMERO

READ THE ST. MARTIN'S BOOK TECHNICOLOR® ©DAWN ASSOCIATES MCMLXXVIII Released by UNITED FILM DISTRIBUTION CO.

There is no explicit sex in this picture.
However, there are scenes of violence which may be considered shocking.
No one under 17 will be admitted.

1

"Who the hell cares. Let's go shopping first."

Dawn of the Dead doesn't exactly go easy on its viewers. Terror immediately lunges into the opening shot, dominated by an unsteady camera and distorted voices. It is a portrait of disorientation, clearly indicating that a state of emergency has broken out in the USA. An epidemic is spreading like wildfire that turns humans into the living dead. When police squadrons storm a house in Puerto Rico, annihilating not only zombies but also massacring a large number of healthy humans in cold blood, there is no more denying it: America is at war.

Stephen (David Emge) and his girlfriend Francine (Gaylen Ross), both television station employees, have lost all faith in social cohesion and in the government's ability to uphold law and order. Along with SWAT team sharp shooter Peter (Ken Foree) and his friend Roger (Scott H. Reiniger), they make up their minds to flee the chaos of the city by helicopter, leaving their fellow citizens to fend for themselves. The zombies, however, are everywhere. The four take flight from this perished civilization not to hit ground in undiscovered country, but rather on the roof of a surrounded Pennsylvania shopping center. They quickly barricade themselves inside the mall and even succeed in shutting out the entire contingency of living dead. The plentiful supply of goods within their citadel allows the human crusaders to maintain the illusions of the life they left behind them. That is, until Stephen and Roger fall prey to the undead, making antiheroes of the pregnant Francine and the African American Peter who quickly abort "Consumer Island" and head off in their helicopter towards an uncertain future.

Dawn of the Dead's gratuitous violence, something the critics couldn't stop talking about at the time of the movie's original release, is an unmistakable sign that the Age of Aquarius and its Utopian dreams were suddenly a thing of the past. In its place we find the jarring pessimism of the late 1970s, brought on to a great extent as a response to U.S. involvement in the Vietnam War. Romero's film expands on this American trauma of the last 15 years. Tom Savini, who created the movie's special effects, worked as a battlefield photographer in Vietnam and drew from his endless experience with manifestations of violence. Nonetheless, the actual source of this piece's

GEORGE A. ROMERO American director and screenwriter George A. Romero was born in the New York Bronx in 1940. He studied art, design, and theater at Carnegie Mellon University in Pittsburgh. His *Zombie Trilogy* (1968, 1978, 1985) turned him into a household name and sparked an onset of offspring by other filmmakers. Romero's directorial debut, *Night of the Living Dead* (1968), was a radical departure from many of the established conventions of Hollywood movies. In addition to its staunch critique on American politics, the film's underlying tone is one of pessimism and despair. This was also the case for the sequels *Dawn of the Dead* (1978) and *Day of the Dead* (1985). More sequels followed in 2005 and 2007. Romero's last zombie movie to date is *Survival of the Dead*, which was nominated for the Golden Lion in Venice in 2009. In 2015 it became known that Romero's comic series "Empire of the Dead" would be filmed as a TV series. Romero's later works included less remarkable stints in television, although he did collaborate with Stephen King in the 1980s on two projects. The first, *Creepshow* (1982), was a horror movie anthology that lacked the sizzle of his earlier works, and the second was a rather high-profile production entitled *The Dark Half* (1992/93). George A. Romero works from time to time as an actor and, despite breaking all the rules, follows in Hitchcock's tradition of making cameo appearances in his own movies. In his zombie trilogy he played a reporter, the C. E. O. of a television station, and a member of the living dead, respectively.

"When the world is falling apart there are no heroes, only the need for self-preservation." *Films in Review*

1 In your head: Stephen (David Emge) and Francine (Gaylen Ross) wonder where the zombies will turn up next…

2 Open for business: It's unclear whether the zombies are hungry for human flesh or mall merchandise.

3 Shop till you drop: Chain store bargains can't buy me love.

4 Nowhere to run to: You can flee to the sales all you want—there's still nowhere to hide.

5 Breeding on a jet plane: As humanity's last remnants, Francine, Stephen, and Roger (Scott H. Reiniger) escape on a helicopter in search of the undiscovered country.

"horror" is the emotional numbness and egotism of its main characters.

Stephen, Francine, Peter, and Roger block out all traces of the looming apocalypse upon them and help themselves to the shopping center's commodities. In doing so, they forge a pristine world, a veritable hedonistic wonderland, which they are willing to defend at all costs. Unlike many other works born out of this genre, the supernatural beings do not manifest themselves as the terrifying pawns of some greater power. Instead, they are intended to function primarily as an out-and-out critique on capitalism. The scenes in which the zombies mindlessly wander about the mall, as if commanded by remote control, hold up a mirror to the face of Middle America. Despite their insatiable hunger, the undead, who nourish themselves exclusively on human flesh, are remarkably passive and often do not appear to pose any physical danger. Additionally, these ungodly creatures represent the army of the impoverished, who have not only been shut off from consumerism, but have also been declared as inhuman so that they may be justifiably eliminated. Even Romero's first zombie movie, *Night of the Living Dead* (1968), voiced strong social criticism against issues like racism in American society. In that earlier picture, Ben, an African American serving as the group's human leader, was the only one to survive the plague of the undead, only to be murdered by the white civilian army. *Dawn of the Dead* expands on this aspect and explores how readily people throw morality to the wind when self-interest is at stake. The film is, therefore, significantly more powerful than its predecessor in the assertion that "we must stop the killing or lose the war." PLB

HALLOWEEN

1978 – USA – 91 MIN.

DIRECTOR

JOHN CARPENTER (b. 1948)

SCREENPLAY

JOHN CARPENTER, DEBRA HILL

DIRECTOR OF PHOTOGRAPHY

DEAN CUNDEY

EDITING

TOMMY LEE WALLACE, CHARLES BORNSTEIN

MUSIC

JOHN CARPENTER

PRODUCTION

JOHN CARPENTER, DEBRA HILL for
COMPASS INTERNATIONAL PICTURES, FALCON FILMS

STARRING

DONALD PLEASENCE (Doctor Samuel Loomis), JAMIE LEE CURTIS (Laurie Strode),
NANCY LOOMIS (Annie Brackett), P. J. SOLES (Lynda van der Klok),
CHARLES CYPHERS (Sheriff Brackett), KYLE RICHARDS (Lindsey Wallace),
BRIAN ANDREWS (Tommy Doyle), JOHN MICHAEL GRAHAM (Bob Simms),
NANCY STEPHENS (Marion Chambers), TONY MORAN (Michael Myers, 21 years old),
WILL SANDIN (Michael Myers, 6 years old)

HALLOWEEN

R

The trick
is to
stay alive.

Everyone is
entitled to
one good scare.

MOUSTAPHA AKKAD PRESENTS DONALD PLEASENCE IN JOHN CARPENTER'S "HALLOWEEN"
WITH JAMIE LEE CURTIS, P. J. SOLES, NANCY LOOMIS • WRITTEN BY JOHN CARPENTER AND DEBRA HILL
EXECUTIVE PRODUCER IRWIN YABLANS • DIRECTED BY JOHN CARPENTER • PRODUCED BY DEBRA HILL
PANAVISION TECHNICOLOR
A COMPASS INTERNATIONAL PICTURE HOYTS DISTRIBUTION

"Was that the bogeyman?"— "As a matter of fact—it was!"

His eyes are the eyes of a devil. For 15 years, says psychiatrist Sam Loomis (Donald Pleasence), he has been trying to get a glimpse of what goes on behind those evil eyes, to make sense of what is going on inside that head. But all his efforts have been in vain. The boy seems to be driven by a single instinct: to kill. It was this heinous thirst for blood that propelled him back then, when he brutally stabbed his sister to death at the age of six. Ever since that fateful day, Michael Myers has been under lock and key in an asylum. But now he's escaped. This dangerous beast is on the loose again and he begins stalking teenagers, returning to Haddonfield, the scene of his last homicidal rampage. And the timing of his escape couldn't be more threatening. It's Halloween, the most terrifying day of the year.

Halloween is a horror classic. Few films have made such a lasting mark on the genre. And this despite the fact that director John Carpenter did nothing to reinvent the art of filmmaking. The critics compared *Halloween* to Hitchcock's *Psycho* (1960), but felt that Hitch composed his murder scenes much more deftly than the young Carpenter. Though they gave him credit for mastering his craft, it was generally agreed that the film was shot far too conventionally.

Nevertheless, *Halloween* became one of the most successful independent films of all time. It cost $325,000 to make and grossed $100 million, perhaps because its strength lies in its supposed weakness: the simplicity of the dramatization. With simple means he made no attempt to camouflage, Carpenter aptly struck the public nerve. The eerie soundtrack hammers away with its few incessantly repetitive notes. The vague images of the subjective camera conjure up an overwhelming insecurity, and excessively protracted tension slowly but surely escalates into naked fear. This suspense-building quality is palpable when Laurie (Jamie Lee Curtis) ventures across the empty, dark, small town street to visit her school friends. She lives in a house across the way, and although the course of her path is filmed in standard time, the distance seems endless, because the audience knows something Laurie doesn't: Michael Myers (Tony Moran) is waiting for her on the other side of the street. A few minutes before,

SUBJECTIVE CAMERA An arm reaches into the screen—our arm. A hand grabs a knife—our hand. The knife plunges into living flesh—we did it. The beginning of *Halloween* (1978) depicts the young Mike Myers as he butchers his sister. But the boy himself is not shown; we only see his action. The subjective camera assumes his perspective, through which the audience slips into the role of the protagonist and leaves its function as the omniscient and unnoticed observer. The subjective camera is able to create an atmosphere of insecurity or menacing danger because it gives the audience nothing more than the information that the film character also has.
The technique, however, seems to work best if used sparingly. Robert Montgomery failed with his Marlowe thriller *Lady in the Lake* (1947), which he filmed from the protagonist's point of view from beginning to end. Delmer Daves used the subjective camera much more adeptly in *Dark Passage* (1947): the audience only sees Humphrey Bogart's face a half an hour into the film after he undergoes a surgical operation—beforehand the action was filmed entirely from Bogart's perspective. Stanley Kubrick masterfully used the subjective perspective in his horror film *The Shining* (1980), continually leaving the audience in doubt as to whether the images are a part of the plot or just the fantasies of the characters.

“Replete with unobtrusive experiments, simple and clear in conception yet rich in internal links, *Halloween* is one of the finest horror films ever made. It’s one of the reasons I’m in love with the cinema—and still go the movies all the time. And it’s also one reason why I wanted to make movies myself.” *Tom Tykwer, in: steadycam*

he sliced up three of her friends and is now cowering behind the dark window, eagerly sharpening his blade. Every footstep leads Laurie closer to the monster. She jiggles the knob on the front door—to no avail. She timidly makes her way to the back entrance—it is open. She stands in the kitchen, where just a few minutes earlier a knife plunged into the body of a young man. Moving to the stairs she tentatively begins to climb. Once upstairs she finds her friend lying peacefully in bed, but something is horribly wrong—her friend is dead. A second corpse falls from the closet at her feet, and suddenly the masked murderer is towering ominously behind her. Laurie runs. And she screams.

"Scream Queen"—Jamie Lee Curtis was bestowed this title after her first screen role. As Laurie Strode she manages to elude the lethal grasp of Michael Myers, thanks in large part to the psychiatrist Loomis, who empties an entire clip of bullets into the killer. The fact that Laurie is the one to survive, the outsider who prefers to babysit than make-out on the sly, proved ample ground to criticize the film for moral prudery. In self-defense, Carpenter declared that the psychology of the characters in *Halloween* was of little interest to him—he'd rattled off the screenplay in just two weeks with Debra Hill, who also produced his films *The Fog* (1979) and *Escape from New York* (1981).

Carpenter's aim was to deliver terror to the screen, —unadulterated shock value and gruesome suspense. He hoped to make the true "psychopath film," and he succeeded beyond his wildest dreams. Almost 25 years after his first appearance, Michael Myers continues to slaughter mercilessly on the big screen—he recently appeared in his eighth film. And Jamie Lee Curtis, alias Laurie Strode, is still the most prized victim of the sinister lunatic who seems immune to bullets, knife wounds, and electric shocks. To be continued—you can bet your life on it. NM

1 A bloody encore: Michael Myers, the Bogeyman (Tony Moran). The mask, which was bought at a costume shop, was first used in the horror film, *The Devil's Rain* (1975).

2 You were always on my mind: John Carpenter allegedly named his heroine Laurie Strode (Jamie Lee Curtis) after his first girlfriend.

3 Doctor death: Donald Pleasence was cast as the psychiatrist Samuel Loomis, after Peter Cushing and Christopher Lee had turned down the role.

3

“Yet a lot of people seem to be convinced that *Halloween* is something special—a classic. Maybe when a horror film is stripped of everything but dumb scariness—when it isn’t ashamed to revive the stalest device of the genre (the escaped lunatic)—it satisfies part of the audience in a more basic, childish way than sophisticated horror pictures do.” *The New Yorker*

4 "An audacious hybrid of heterogeneous traditions. Held together by the fluid elegance of its camerawork, it conjures up an atmosphere of subtle terror." (*Die Zeit*)

5 Killer instinct: Donald Pleasence (left) also appeared in John Carpenter's *Escape from New York* (1981) and *Prince of Darkness* (1987).

6 Bedtime stories: Laurie tells Tommy that there's no such thing as the bogeyman, and the little boy discovers that adults really don't know everything.

7 The maxims of murder: Perverts will perish.

ALIEN

1979 – GREAT BRITAIN / USA – 117 MIN.

DIRECTOR

RIDLEY SCOTT (b. 1937)

SCREENPLAY

DAN O'BANNON, RONALD SHUSETT

DIRECTOR OF PHOTOGRAPHY

DEREK VANLINT

EDITING

TERRY RAWLINGS, PETER WEATHERLEY

MUSIC

JERRY GOLDSMITH

PRODUCTION

GORDON CARROLL, DAVID GILER,
WALTER HILL for 20TH CENTURY FOX,
BRANDYWINE PRODUCTIONS LTD.

STARRING

TOM SKERRITT (Dallas), SIGOURNEY WEAVER (Ripley),
VERONICA CARTWRIGHT (Lambert), HARRY DEAN
STANTON (Brett), JOHN HURT (Kane), IAN HOLM (Ash),
YAPHET KOTTO (Parker), BOLAJI BEDEJO (Alien)

ACADEMY AWARDS 1979

OSCAR for BEST SPECIAL EFFECTS (H.R. Giger, Carlo Rambaldi,
Brian Johnson, Nick Allder, Denys Ayling)

a word of warning...

ALIEN

ALIEN
ALIEN
ALIEN
ALIEN

TWENTIETH CENTURY-FOX Presents "ALIEN" A BRANDYWINE-RONALD SHUSETT Production

TOM SKERRITT · SIGOURNEY WEAVER · VERONICA CARTWRIGHT

HARRY DEAN STANTON · JOHN HURT · IAN HOLM

and YAPHET KOTTO as "Parker" Produced by GORDON CARROLL and DAVID GILER

Directed by RIDLEY SCOTT · Screenplay by DAN O'BANNON, WALTER HILL, DAVID GILER

Executive Producer RONALD SHUSETT · Story by DAN O'BANNON and RONALD SHUSETT

PANAVISION® EASTMAN KODAK COLOR®

COMING FROM TWENTIETH CENTURY-FOX

PRINTED IN U.S.A.

ONE SHEET "ALIEN" TEASER

1

"In space no one can hear you scream."

The late 1970s were overrun by the science fiction film, a trend that had begun with George Lucas's *Star Wars* (1977). Consequently, when Ridley Scott's *Alien* was released in theaters in 1979, the producers confidently expected the film to attract attention. But audiences were somewhat surprised: the film did not contain impressive space battles, but centered on the almost futile struggle of average, fallible humans against an eerie being, the like of which had never been seen before. *Alien* was pure horror set in outer space—the logical combination of two film genres.

The story takes place somewhere in the near future on the commercial trade space ship Nostromo, which is on its way back to Earth filled with cargo. The seven-member crew, among them Captain Dallas (Tom Skerritt), his deputy, Ripley (Sigourney Weaver), and helmswoman Lambert (Veronica Cartwright), routinely go about their daily business. No one wastes a minute thinking about the dangers that might be hidden in outer space. But their routine is interrupted by an emergency signal from a planet previously thought to be uninhabited. There, Dallas, Kane (John Hurt), and Lambert find an empty space ship with a hold full of strange eggs. A ghastly being jumps from one of the eggs and attaches itself to Kane's face, where it remains stuck, as though almost welded to his skin. Back on their ship, the crew determine that the strange being can't be removed from the victim's face. But just a short time later it falls off by itself. The danger seems to have been averted. A deadly meal then ensues. As the crew sit down to eat, we initially believe that Kane's hunger is a sign of his recovery, until a disgusting beast pierces its way through his chest and disappears like lightning into the ventilation shafts of the Nostromo. Clearly the "Alien" transforms its outer appearance during its development and the crew realize that they are going to have to kill the monster before it gets them. One crew member after the other falls victim to this mysterious being. When Captain Dallas is also killed, Ripley takes com-

H. R. GIGER The Swiss artist Hans Ruedi Giger was born on February 5, 1940 in Chur. Initially he worked for several years as a construction artist and began studying industrial design at the Zurich School of Arts and Crafts in 1962. After graduating in 1966, Geiger worked as a freelance artist, sculptor, and furniture designer for the renowned production company Knoll. In 1967 he met the actress Li Tobler, with whom he lived until her suicide in 1975. In 1969 he designed his first "biomechanical" monsters for Fredi M. Murer's thirty-minute film *Swissmade—2069.* Erotically sinister machine fantasies would soon become his trademark. At the end of 1977 Giger met his future wife, Mia, whom he divorced in 1982. After contacts with director Alejandro Jodorowsky, for whom he later created the world of the Harkonnen in David Lynch's *Dune* (1984), he was brought aboard the *Alien,* which won an Oscar for Best Special Effects in 1980.

In addition to his work on other films, including David Fincher's *Alien 3* (1992), Roger Donaldson's *Species* (1995), Jean-Pierre Jeunet's *Alien: Resurrection* (1997), and Peter Medak's *Species II* (1998), Giger designed album covers for bands like Blondie, Emerson, Lake & Palmer, and Danzig. He has run the Giger-Bar in Zurich since 1992 for which he even designed the furniture himself. Giger has been together with Carmen Maria Scheifele y de Vega since 1996 and married her in 2006. On May 12, 2014 H. R. Giger died in a Zurich hospital after a fall.

2

1 All systems operational: Second officer Ripley performing a routine maintenance check.

2 Space bait: A member of the Nostromo investigates the alien distress signal and comes down with a case of indigestion.

3 Shoot the moon: Screenwriter Dan O'Bannon is the veritable bard of futuristic space voyages. In addition to working on *Alien 3 & 4*, he chartered the waters for *Screamers* (1995) and John Carpenter's cult classic *Dark Star* (1974).

"It's an old-fashioned scare movie about something that is not only implacably evil but prone to jumping at you when (the movie hopes) you least expect it." *The New York Times*

mand of the ship. She learns the true reason for their mission from the ship's computer, Mother. Their corporation on Earth knowingly misled the crew in order to get their hands on one of the aliens.

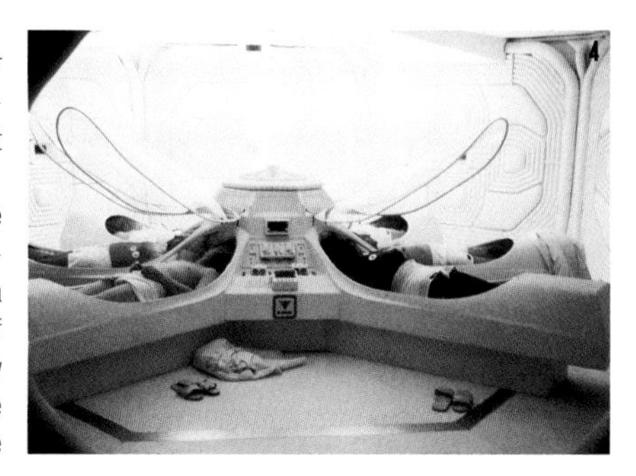

Sigourney Weaver, who also played the main role in the three sequels (1986, 1992, 1997) is initially an unsympathetic figure in *Alien.* Consequently, the camera depicts her from a slightly low angle during the first half of the film. She acts in a "manly" fashion and refuses to allow herself to be governed by her emotions. She has no sense of humor and follows the rules by the book, while the

4 Regaining consciousness: An alien distress signal leads Mother to wake up her Nostromo crew. Only when it is too late does Ripley realize that the "cry for help" is actually an ominous warning…

5 The A-Team's newest warrior: "Its structural perfection is matched only by its hostility."

6 Raising Cain: The baby alien hatches out of Kane's belly. Unfortunately, the proud mother dies during childbirth.

7 Lip locked: Defying Ripley's orders, Kane is brought back on board the Nostromo along with the alien object hugging his face. Interestingly, Walter Hill was originally signed to direct *Alien*, but soon passed the baton on to Ridley Scott.

other crew members behave helpfully and interact harmoniously. When she is left as the lone survivor, she attributes it to her judgment. In what is literally the last minute she finally manages to blow up the Nostromo and thereby destroy the alien.

Alien was Ridley Scott's second feature film after *The Duellists* (1977), and its success instantly catapulted him into the first rank of Hollywood filmmakers. Today his film is regarded as a milestone in the history of horror, applauded with numerous imitations and frequent emulation over the following decades. Scott's recipe for success is based on his preference for subtle horror as opposed to roaring action scenes. In *Alien*, one can detect intimations of the dark, cyber-punk vision the director would demonstrate three years later with *Blade Runner* (1982). From the beginning of the film, Jerry Goldsmith's soundtrack, as rousing as it is oppressive, and Derek Vanlint's slow-motion-like camera movements through the spaceship create a sinister and torturous atmosphere, gradually compressing into pure claustrophobic terror in the last third of the film. The monstrous "Alien," created by H. R. Giger, combines the characteristics of a living organism and a machine—the organic and the inorganic. Blood does not flow through its veins, but corrosive acid. It is surely one of the most terrifying monsters in film history. APO

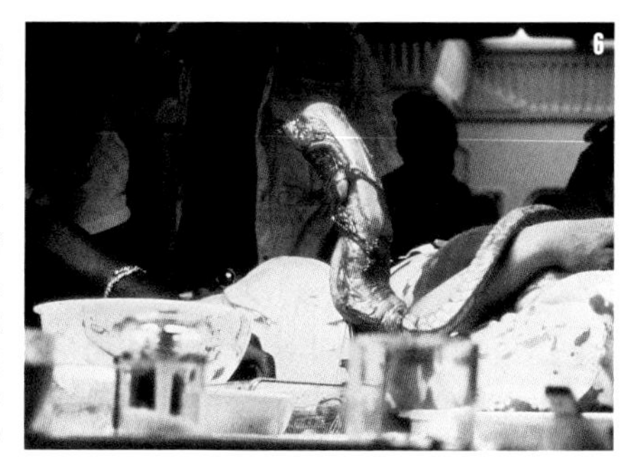
6

"When, as a director, you are offered a project like *Alien*—or any science-fiction-film, really—it is an offer to start with and becomes a confrontation afterwards." *Ridley Scott, in: American Cinematographer*

7

THE SHINING

1980 – USA / GREAT BRITAIN – 144 MIN.

DIRECTOR

STANLEY KUBRICK (1928–1999)

SCREENPLAY

STANLEY KUBRICK, DIANE JOHNSON
based on the novel of the same name by STEPHEN KING

DIRECTOR OF PHOTOGRAPHY

JOHN ALCOTT

EDITING

RAY LOVEJOY

MUSIC

KRZYSZTOF PENDERECKI, GYÖRGY LIGETI,
BÉLA BARTÓK, WENDY CARLOS

PRODUCTION

STANLEY KUBRICK, ROBERT FRYER, MARY LEA JOHNSON, MARTIN RICHARDS for
HAWK FILMS, PRODUCERS CIRCLE, PEREGRINE, WARNER BROS.

STARRING

JACK NICHOLSON (Jack Torrance), SHELLEY DUVALL (Wendy Torrance),
DANNY LLOYD (Danny Torrance), BARRY NELSON (Stuart Ullman),
SCATMAN CROTHERS (Dick Hallorann), PHILIP STONE (Delbert Grady),
JOE TURKEL (Lloyd), ANNE JACKSON (Doctor),
TONY BURTON (Larry Durkin), LIA BELDAM (Young Woman in Bathroom)

A MASTERPIECE OF MODERN HORROR

A STANLEY KUBRICK FILM

STARRING

JACK NICHOLSON SHELLEY DUVALL "THE SHINING"

WITH

SCATMAN CROTHERS, DANNY LLOYD

BASED ON THE NOVEL BY

STEPHEN KING

SCREENPLAY BY

STANLEY KUBRICK & DIANE JOHNSON

PRODUCED AND DIRECTED BY

STANLEY KUBRICK

EXECUTIVE PRODUCER

JAN HARLAN

PRODUCED IN ASSOCIATION WITH THE PRODUCER CIRCLE CO.

R RESTRICTED UNDER 17 REQUIRES ACCOMPANYING PARENT OR ADULT GUARDIAN

From Warner Bros. A Warner Communications Company

1

"Some places are like people: some shine and some don't."

Wendy (Shelley Duvall) slowly bends over the typewriter. Her jaw drops and her widening eyes move from left to right. "All work and no play makes Jack a dull boy." Wendy scrolls down the leaf of paper. The entire sheet is filled with this identical sentence. She looks next to the typewriter and flicks through the bulky manuscript. Line after line the same words, page after page the same sentence. Wendy immediately realizes that Jack (Jack Nicholson) has lost his mind. But it is too late, because in exactly this moment, her husband is standing behind her, resolved to kill her.

Perhaps the most frightening moment in *The Shining* is when Wendy understands she is at the mercy of a madman and cannot escape. For a month Wendy, Jack, and their son, Danny (Danny Torrance) have been looking after the large, empty Overlook Hotel, which lies secluded somewhere in the mountains. They activate the boiler to avoid frost damage from the long winter and idly pass their time: Danny racing toy cars through the halls, Wendy in the kitchen, and Jack at his desk. He is a novelist and is trying to write a new manuscript. But he sinks into lethargy with the first snowfall. And he encounters people who couldn't possibly be present in the hotel: first a bartender who serves him a long-desired drink, then a naked woman who in his embrace transforms into a zombie-like creature. The ultimate hallucination is when an entire ballroom comes alive with party guests from the 1920s and a waiter convinces Jack to call his family to order—with drastic methods.

The Shining is a perfect symphony of horror, composed by Stanley Kubrick, the sublime master of all genres. With his obsessive love of detail, he re-shot some scenes as many as 120 times: one example is the scene in which Dick Hallorann (Scatman Crothers), the chef cook of the hotel, receives a telepathic call for help from Danny. Like the old man, the boy possesses a special ability of the "Shining," which allows him to see traces of the past and images of the future. Hallorann makes his way to the snowed-in hotel and becomes Wendy and Danny's last hope.

The terror in *The Shining* does not stem from shocking special effects, but the inexorable straightforwardness that leads to the deadly finale. Jack's path is predestined, steered by the Overlook Hotel. Like a magnet, it attracts the yellow Volkswagen Beetle as Jack drives through the mountains to interview for a job as caretaker. The hotel empowers him when he complains about his wife, and it

1 It's too late, Baby… By the time Wendy Torrance (Shelley Duvall) acknowledges her marital problems, husband Jack is burning rubber on his hell ride.

2 Writer's block: Jack Torrance (Jack Nicholson) acts out when he can't get his ideas down on paper.

3 Jack the Ripper: "I'm not gonna hurt ya, Wendy. I'm just gonna rip your fuckin' heart out!"

"Stanley Kubrick doesn't do anything by halves. What this diehard perfectionist has created, during the years of postproduction work that went on while tucked away in a British film studio, are exemplary pieces of artistic refinement: *2001, A Space Odyssey* was a masterpiece in science fiction, *Barry Lyndon* set a new standard for historical epics and *The Shining* redefined the meaning of horror altogether."

Der Spiegel

Danny: "What about Room 237?"
Hallorann: "Room 237?"
Danny: "You're scared of Room 237, ain't ya?"
Hallorann: "No, I ain't."
Danny: "Mr. Hallorann, what is in Room 237?"
Hallorann: "Nothin'! There ain't nothin' in Room 237. But you ain't got no business goin' in there anyway. So stay out! You understand? Stay out!"

Film quote: Danny Torrance and Dick Hallorann

4 Victorian Age at the Overlook Hotel: All the interior scenes were shot at a British film studio.

5 Let it shine! Danny Torrance (Danny Lloyd) has a special power, a special friend and runs at the mention of "red rum."

frees him after Wendy zonks him with a baseball bat and locks him up. It is the location itself that comes alive—to assimilate and engulf the living.

Kubrick placed particular importance on the symmetrical construction of the images to intensify the feeling of imprisonment: the characters stick in the middle of the rooms as if caught in the center of a spider web. In contrast to the film's literary forerunner, Kubrick scrapped the psychoanalysis of the family members, preferring to leave wide room for interpretation. And readings of the films were duly divergent. Some saw *The Shining* as a study of writer's block, while others interpreted the piece as a comment on the oppression of Native Americans by white settlers, because the hotel was constructed on an old Indian burial ground.

Stephen King, the author of the novel, made no secret of his dissatisfaction with the Kubrick version, particularly the finale in the labyrinth next to the hotel. But Kubrick's invention of the hedgerow labyrinth is nothing short of ingenious. To find their way out, they are going to have to lay breadcrumbs, says Wendy when she sees the enormous kitchen for the first time. The Overlook Hotel is a labyrinth of endless hallways, forbidden doors, and dead ends like the ballroom. The human brain also resembles a labyrinth. It offers endless possibilities—some paths lead in the wrong direction and one can sometimes get lost. There are ways out, but not everyone is able to find them. Some remain prisoners of their own labyrinth—like Jack.

NM

THE EVIL DEAD

1981 – USA – 85 MIN.

DIRECTOR

SAM RAIMI (b. 1959)

SCREENPLAY

SAM RAIMI

DIRECTOR OF PHOTOGRAPHY

TIM PHILO

EDITING

EDNA RUTH PAUL

MUSIC

JOSEPH LODUCA

PRODUCTION

ROBERT G. TAPERT for NEW LINE CINEMA, RENAISSANCE PICTURES

STARRING

BRUCE CAMPBELL (Ashley "Ash" Williams), ELLEN SANDWEISS (Cheryl Williams), BETSY BAKER (Linda), HAL DELRICH (Scott), SARAH YORK (Shelly)

Starring BRUCE CAMPBELL ELLEN SANDWEISS HAL DELRICH BETSY BAKER SARAH YORK
Make-up Effects by TOM SULLIVAN Photographic Effects by BART PIERCE Photography by TIM PHILO
Music by JOE LoDUCA Produced by ROBERT G. TAPERT Written and Directed by SAM RAIMI
Color by TECHNICOLOR® Renaissance Pictures Ltd. From NEW LINE CINEMA

THE PRODUCERS RECOMMEND THAT NO ONE UNDER 17 BE ALLOWED TO SEE THE EVIL DEAD

1

2

"Ash, I think we ought to get out of here."

A thick fog covers the screen and the silence is palpable. Slowly the clouds begin to lift and a camera glides over a swampy bog, increases its pace, sweeps across the water surface and ultimately races to the shore with a clamorous crescendo, through the thicket of a forest and onto a street. It is this nameless and unidentifiable evil that awaits Ash (Bruce Campbell), Scott (Hal Delrich), Linda (Betsy Baker), Cheryl (Ellen Sandweiss), and Shelly (Sarah York), a group of friends who have rented a vacation home in the thickly forested mountains of Tennessee. While poking around in the basement of their log cabin after nightfall, they discover a book of the dead bound with human skin. Together with the strange book is a tape recording upon which the unemotional voice of a scientist discusses his research and then begins to recite the passages that cause the "Evil Dead" to rise from their deathly slumber. The tense atmosphere and the threatening presence of the reawakened forest grow worse, and become a brutal nightmare—survival at any cost is all one can hope for.

First Cheryl, then Shelly, Linda, and Scott are transformed into zombies with leprous pale-green skin, dead eyes, and foaming mouths. Ultimately, only Ash is left, fighting for his life with spades, shotguns, and even his bare hands. He literally wades through blood, as the only sure victory over these reanimated dead is to dismember them: even headless torsos revivify and continue their bloodthirsty and murderous crusade. Ash's situation seems increasingly hopeless, but when he throws the "Necronomicon" into the fireplace with the last of his strength, the monsters disappear in a long, concluding sequence. Dawn breaks over the trees and Ash drags himself out of the cabin into the open. He is the sole survivor. But in this film, sunlight cannot destroy the evil, and the demon again races through the forest at high speed, closes in on the cabin from behind, breaks through

SPLATTER FILM The splatter film is a sub-genre of the horror film. Its roots lie in the 1960s, with films like *Blood Feast* (1963) and *Night of the Living Dead* (1968). After early classics like *The Texas Chain Saw Massacre* (1974), the genre's real heyday came in the 1980s with productions like *The Evil Dead* (1981) and *Re-Animator* (1985). Peter Jackson's 1992 splatter film persiflage *Braindead* turned into a real cult movie. After the millenium predominantly remakes of classic splatter films entered the theaters: *Wrong Turn* (2003) connects with *The Texas Chain Saw Massacre* and was extended between 2007 and 2014 to two sequels and three prequels. Due to its explicit performance of violence, Eli Roth's *Hostel* (2005) and its sequel two years after also caused quite a stir. The central motif of the splatter film is the use of spectacular special effects. Gallons of artificial blood and innumerable latex masks and wax prosthetics help break bodily boundaries in consistently novel ways. The real aim is not to ignite the fantasies of the audience but to prompt physical reactions like revulsion, laughter, or fear. Most films in this category primarily present comedic features, with a bent for the blackest of humors. The lavish display of violence plays an important role, providing regular ammunition for censorship debates, the likes of which no other genre has experienced.

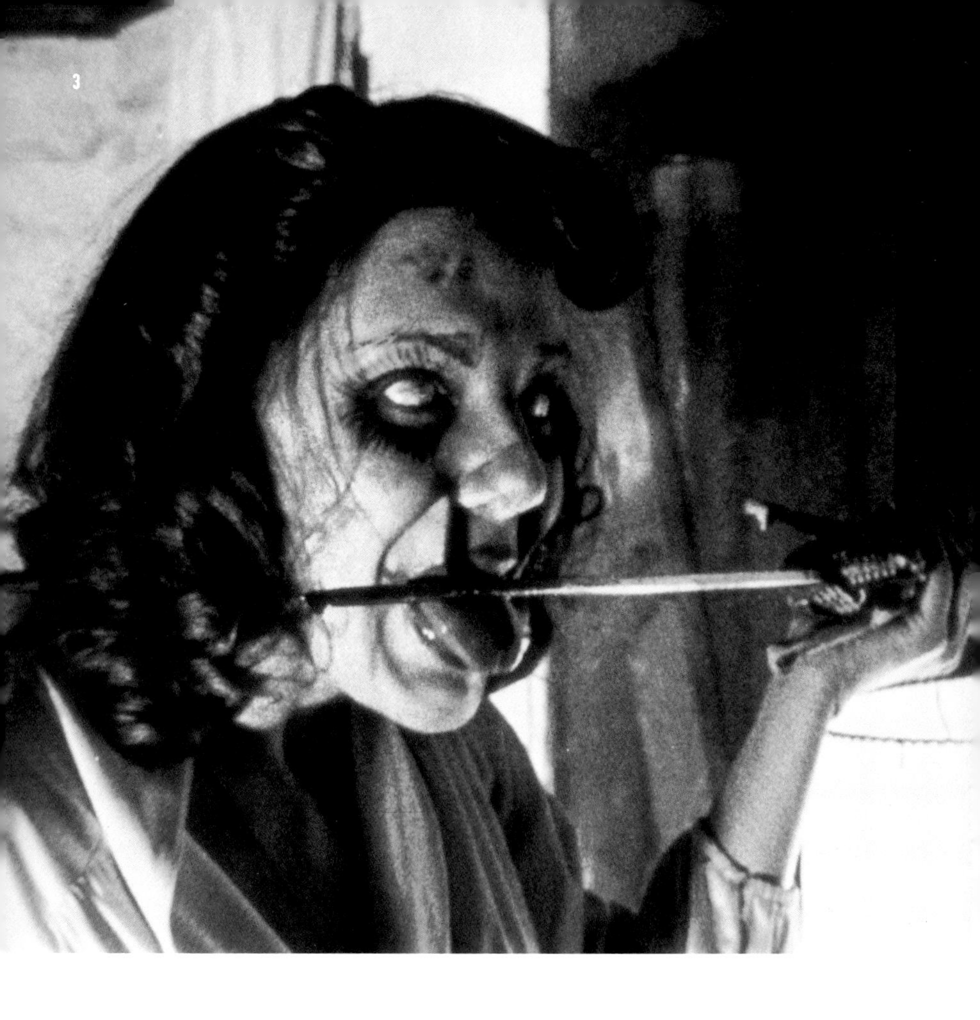
3

several doors, thunders through the entrance, and attacks him.

The Evil Dead was 23-year-old Sam Raimi's first film. This bloody low-budget production has no intellectual aspirations, aiming instead to extract a physical reaction from its audience. The film is like a roller coaster ride: the audience is dragged into the action when the invisible demon—represented exclusively by the "excursions" of a charmingly documentary-like, subjective hand-held camera and special sound effects—races through the undergrowth, splitting and shattering trees in its wake. In view of its graphic and gory excesses, it is hardly surprising that more than any other film of the 1980s, *The Evil Dead* provoked a storm of criticism and demands for the censorship of films which glorify violence. Again and again, blood spurts into the lens of the camera, which at one point is even fitted with a hemoglobin-colored, red filter. However, detractors often overlook the fact that the film—and even more clearly, the sequel, *Evil Dead II* (1987)—plays with horror conventions through its use of comic exaggeration and the blackest humor imaginable.

The Evil Dead also re-introduces multiple citations from well-known horror and splatter films. These sometimes strongly exaggerated genre cliches (such as the theatrical creaking of a basement door) are even occasionally implemented "in reverse" with regard to their precursors. If, for example, after Jamie Lee Curtis's famous appearance in *Halloween* (1978), one could expect the lead female character of a horror film to emit the most bloodcurdling of shrieks, here it is our manly hero Ash who masters the art of hysteria. And as if this were not enough, he also gets doused with gallons of blood, just like the protagonist in *Carrie* (1976). These surreal scenes, primarily shaped by somewhat amateurish special effects, bolster the artificial character of the whole. In addition, the revolting zombies, dripping with slime, blood, and pus, and covering their surroundings with strange fluids, are a defiantly subversive element, mocking their attackers even after their heads have been cut off. These aggressive, eerily cackling creatures are not normal objects of identification, but in ghastly contrast to the ideal bodies that are usually on show in Hollywood movies, they remind the public of undesirable bodily excretions and of the body as a monstrous entity, as it sometimes is in puberty or old age. And it is their disgusting prominence that establishes the feeling of physical revulsion and the actual bodies as the film's central cinematic "instrument," rather than the imagination of the audience. PLB

1 Like in Hitchcock's *Psycho* something wicked is creeping about the basement.

2 Skin turns pale and eyes glow white—hippie Cheryl (Ellen Sandweiss) is the first to be possessed by the demonic forces.

3 No way out—even Ash's pretty girlfriend transforms into a giddy cackling, bloodthirsty zombie.

4 Director Raimi cast friends in all the parts, including Scott (Hal Delrich) and Shelly (Sarah York).

4

A NIGHTMARE ON ELM STREET

1984 – USA – 91 MIN.

DIRECTOR

WES CRAVEN (1939–2015)

SCREENPLAY

WES CRAVEN

DIRECTOR OF PHOTOGRAPHY

JACQUES HAITKIN

EDITING

RICK SHAINE

MUSIC

CHARLES BERNSTEIN

PRODUCTION

ROBERT SHAYE for NEW LINE CINEMA, SMART EGG PICTURES,
MEDIA HOME ENTERTAINMENT

STARRING

ROBERT ENGLUND (Freddy Krueger), RONEE BLAKLEY (Marge Thompson),
HEATHER LANGENKAMP (Nancy Thompson), AMANDA WYSS (Tina Gray),
NICK CORRI (Rod Lane), JOHNNY DEPP (Glen Lantz),
CHARLES FLEISCHER (Dr. King), JOSEPH WHIPP (Sergeant Parker),
LIN SHAYE (The Teacher), JOHN SAXON (Lieutenant Thompson)

IF NANCY DOESN'T WAKE UP SCREAMING
SHE WON'T WAKE UP AT ALL.

WES CRAVEN'S

A Nightmare
ON ELM STREET

NEW LINE CINEMA, MEDIA HOME ENTERTAINMENT, INC. and SMART EGG PICTURES Present
A ROBERT SHAYE Production • A WES CRAVEN Film • "A NIGHTMARE ON ELM STREET"
Starring JOHN SAXON • RONEE BLAKLEY • HEATHER LANGENKAMP • AMANDA WYSS • NICK CORRI • JOHNNY DEPP and ROBERT ENGLUND as Fred Krueger
Music by CHARLES BERNSTEIN • Director of Photography JACQUES HAITKIN • Editor RICK SHAINE • Executive Producers STANLEY DUDELSON and JOSEPH WOLF
R RESTRICTED UNDER 17 REQUIRES ACCOMPANYING PARENT OR ADULT GUARDIAN
Co-Producer SARA RISHER • Produced by ROBERT SHAYE • Written and Directed by WES CRAVEN
FROM NEW LINE CINEMA

1

"God, I look twenty years old!"

15-year-old Tina (Amanda Wyss), already quite brazen in all things sexual, treats herself to a tender interlude with her boyfriend. For extra kicks, they get down to it on her absent mother's bed. But the adventure has a bloody end for Tina. Boyfriend Rob (Nick Corri) is the main suspect in her murder, and is arrested after a brief, frenzied chase.

In reality, the thoroughly distraught Rod is innocent. The true culprit is a man with a face covered in bark-like skin, who wears a striped sweater, and has a razor-sharp steel claw on his hand (Robert Englund). Nancy Thompson (Heather Langenkamp) is aware of his existence and knows what he looks like. For some time the eerie man has been visiting her in her dreams, sporting a vicious grin and seeking her blood. When night falls, her friends are tormented by the same terrifying nightmares. Only while awake are they safe from the clutches of the stranger, for if killed in their dreams, then they also die in reality—just like Tina, the man's first victim.

Nancy is determined to find out more about this human beast, even if it means putting herself in danger. She asks her friend Glen (Johnny Depp) to watch over her while she sleeps. Her desire is fulfilled, and in the midst of a dream she meets the stranger, who is closing in upon Rob in prison. Nancy becomes the next object of his hunt, but she is saved by her shrieking alarm clock at the last possible moment. An ominous feeling prompts her to visit the prison, where her suspicion is confirmed: Rob is dead.

Nancy is admitted to a sleep laboratory, where she has her next encounter with the mysterious murderer. She returns to the real world from her most recent nightmare with a floppy hat and discovers that the name Freddy Krueger is embroidered inside it. The man who owns the hat is no stranger to Nancy's mother: years earlier, Krueger killed several children, was caught, but then quickly released on a technicality. A group of incensed parents banded together, cornered the child molester, and burned him alive, explaining his scarred face. Freddy is dead, but he hasn't disappeared. He has become a "dream walker," seeking revenge against the children of his tormentors.

In the meantime, while she battles her need for sleep with coffee and pills, Nancy plans to lure Freddy into the real world to destroy him once and for all. But just as her scheme begins, Glen also falls asleep and is killed.

WES CRAVEN Born in 1939, Wes Craven taught sociology at Johns Hopkins University in Baltimore before becoming a production assistant and film editor. He captured the hearts of die-hard horror fans in the 1970s with bizarre, low-budget films like *The Hills Have Eyes* (1977). He also did a lot of work for television, before hitting the big time with the *Nightmare on Elm Street* series (1985–94) and the *Scream* trilogy (1996–2000), his greatest successes. In 1999 he unexpectedly changed course with *Music of the Heart*, a film based on the true story of a music teacher who volunteers her services to a group of children in East Harlem. Meryl Streep played the lead role. In 2005, Wes Craven came out successfully with *Red Eye*, a classic suspense thriller. In 2015 he died of a brain tumor in Los Angeles.

2

1 When Freddy's (Robert Englund) around, the term "bedtime" can have deadly connotations.

2 Regardless of what your subconscious would have you believe, Freddy Krueger dictates your dreams.

3 He files his nails with a knife sharpener. Freddy Krueger.

"Marking a significant change in fortune for the moribund horror industry, *A Nightmare on Elm Street* introduced the distinctive presence of Fred Krueger."

Movie Reviews UK

More determined than ever, Nancy sets a handful of traps and goes to sleep. Her plan is a success: after an intense battle, she is able to annihilate the monster. The world can sleep peacefully once again, at least until the call of the obligatory sequel…

On first viewing, the film's most impressive aspect is the wealth of visual stunts: staircases give way like foam rubber, bed clothes transform into deadly nooses, and human tongues slither from telephone receivers. A cunning humor underlies these scenes that introduce the horror into an everyday environment, making it easily intelligible. The Freddy Krueger character fits into this scheme accordingly. He is profoundly evil and he thoroughly enjoys himself in the process! In a perfect cinematic execution, Wes Craven wrenches and teases the nerves of the audience without neglecting milieu or his characters. All his youthful protagonists come from broken homes. Nancy's parents, for example, are divorced—her

4 "You are getting sleepy, very sleepy…" Your eyelids begin to droop, but you must resist if you want to survive Freddy's bloodlust.

5 Nancy's (Heather Langenkamp) clique—all members still present and accounted for.

6 Nancy is not about to take Freddy's assaults sitting down, but her plans are received with juvenile skepticism.

"Here evil has not only captured the real world, but also the unreal one. There's no point in this film in clapping your hands over your eyes. On the contrary: Freddy lives in our dreams, which start of course when our eyes no longer see."

die tageszeitung

mother is an alcoholic, and her father is insensitive to the needs of his daughter. The film says that ultimately children are left to face the problems created by the previous generation. This obviously hit a nerve with many young people in the audience who shared such experiences, and their reactions to this multi-dimensional horror film were correspondingly positive. The film's success spawned eight more movies, of greatly differing quality, as well as a television series, *Freddy's Nightmares* (1988–90).

HK

THE COMPANY OF WOLVES

1984 – GREAT BRITAIN – 93 MIN.

DIRECTOR

NEIL JORDAN (b. 1950)

SCREENPLAY

NEIL JORDAN, ANGELA CARTER from her short stories
The Company of Wolves and *Wolf Alice*

DIRECTOR OF PHOTOGRAPHY

BRYAN LOFTUS

EDITING

RODNEY HOLLAND

MUSIC

GEORGE FENTON

PRODUCTION

CHRIS BROWN for PALACE PRODUCTIONS,
CANNON FILMS, ITC ENTERTAINMENT

STARRING

ANGELA LANSBURY (Grandmother), SARAH PATTERSON (Rosaleen),
DAVID WARNER (Father), GRAHAM CROWDEN (Priest),
BRIAN GLOVER (Father of the Amorous Boy), STEPHEN REA (Bridegroom),
TUSSE SILBERG (Mother), GEORGIA SLOWE (Alice),
SUSAN PORRETT (Mother of the Amorous Boy), SHANE JOHNSTONE (Amorous Boy)

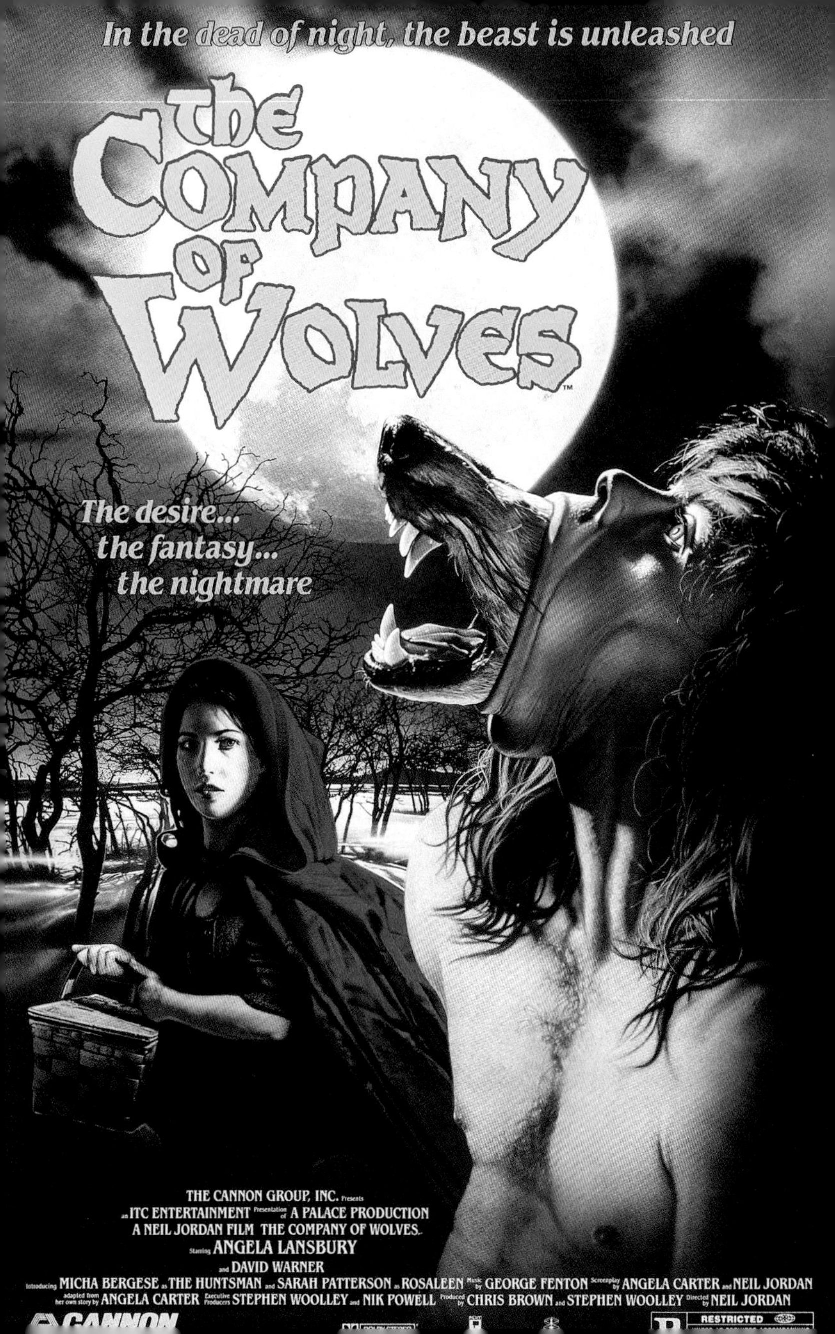
In the dead of night, the beast is unleashed
The Company of Wolves™
The desire...
the fantasy...
the nightmare
THE CANNON GROUP, INC. Presents
an ITC ENTERTAINMENT Presentation of A PALACE PRODUCTION
A NEIL JORDAN FILM THE COMPANY OF WOLVES
Starring ANGELA LANSBURY
and DAVID WARNER
Introducing MICHA BERGESE as THE HUNTSMAN and SARAH PATTERSON as ROSALEEN Music by GEORGE FENTON Screenplay by ANGELA CARTER and NEIL JORDAN
adapted from her own story by ANGELA CARTER Executive Producers STEPHEN WOOLLEY and NIK POWELL Produced by CHRIS BROWN and STEPHEN WOOLLEY Directed by NEIL JORDAN
RESTRICTED

1

2

"... and never trust a man whose eyebrows meet in the middle."

Dream and film are closely affiliated. They pervade one another and speak the same language. Their words consist of images; images that are often both mysterious and familiar at the same time, and which we sometimes understand only intuitively, without the use of reason or intellect.

In *The Company of Wolves*, film and dream are one. In her sleep, the 13-year-old Rosaleen (Sarah Patterson) drifts away into a medieval, fairytale world in which mushrooms grow to be as big as people. The shadowy forest is ruled by wolves with glittering yellow eyes, who tear apart animals and people alike. The wolves, so the girl is told by her grandmother (Angela Lansbury), know no compassion and she must be particularly wary of those who are hairy not on the outside, but on the inside. For this reason, her grandmother warns her that she must never stray from the path, especially not while in the forest.

The forest represents a threat and a temptation at the same time. It is a living thicket of rampant desires, crawling with reptiles, snakes, and toads. But if Rosaleen wants to visit her grandmother, she must walk through the woods. One day, while playing hide and seek with a neighboring boy, she runs off into the forest to hide, wearing a red cloak knitted by her grandmother. On climbing a tall tree, she finds a stork's nest wedged between its branches. At this very moment the babies are hatching from their shells. Rosaleen holds the tiny human embryos in her hands, fascinated.

Just as the visible surface is often deceptive in dreams, appearance masks the true nature of things in this Neil Jordan film. A red apple lying on the ground is riddled with worms, and a beast can lie hidden inside a seemingly friendly man. But there are signs that can help indicate the true nature of things: eyebrows that meet in the middle, says her grandmother, are a characteristic of a wolf in human form. And Rosaleen's red cloak emblematically alludes to her transformation, for the young girl stands at the threshold of sexual maturity and womanhood.

The Company of Wolves is a film about the awakening of sexuality, and the curiosity and fear associated with it. It is not a linear story, but a patchwork of associations related to growing up. The images, replete with poetic

FANTASY FILM Elves, vampires, magicians, and supermen inhabit the land of the fantasy film. Here, the laws of nature do not apply. Instead, there are laser swords, magical rings, journeys through time, and prophecies. The genre includes all films that tell a fantastic story, from George Lucas's *Star Wars* (1977) to John Milius's *Conan the Barbarian* (1981). The fantasy film distinguishes itself from the related horror and science fiction genres by concentrating on myths, legends, and fairy tales. Fantasy films are also often based upon religious themes.

Classics of the fantasy film genre include Raoul Walsh's *The Thief of Bagdad* (1924) and Victor Fleming's *The Wizard of Oz* (1939). The early film *The Cabinet of Dr. Caligari* (1919) by the expressionist Robert Wiene had a great influence on the genre. In order to depict its dream worlds and alternate universes convincingly, the fantasy film makes extensive use of special effects, as for example in Peter Jackson's Tolkien adaptations *The Lord of the Rings—The Fellowship of the Ring* (2001), *The Lord of the Rings—The Two Towers* (2002), and *The Lord of the Rings—The Return of the King* (2003) or in James Cameron's *Avatar* (2009), the most successful movie ever.

3

1 Hunger pangs: At the dinner table, the aristocracy shows us who the real wolves are.

2 The animal inside: Neil Jordan dugs deep into his bag of special effects for the gruesomely vivid man to wolf metamorphosis.

3 Neil Jordan is the son of a painter. Several of his movie images read like artistic tableaux walking the tightrope of kitsch.

4 Thrown to the wolves: A young maiden dressed in white is ripped to shreds in the forest.

5 The mirror as a metaphor of self-discovery… Or is it the portal to a dream world? Jordan's symbolism cleverly eludes simplistic interpretations.

6 Manufactured almost exclusively at the studio to heighten the artificiality of its dream world. All credits to set designer Anton Furst.

beauty and brutality, repulse and fascinate at the same time: a young woman dressed in white is hurried through the forest by wolves, or a wolf's head flying through the air turns into a human face in a milk trough. Although there is no nudity in the film, one female critic denounced the film as "horror porn," perhaps because it depicts archetypical images of sexuality that deal not only with passion, but also with pain, violence, and self-abandon.

Irish director Neil Jordan and British novelist Angela Carter modeled their screenplay on themes from the Grimm Brothers' fairy tale, "Little Red Riding Hood," which, like many of the Grimm stories, can be interpreted as a story about a rite of passage. Just as Red Riding Hood is seduced by the wolf, Rosaleen eventually allows herself to be seduced by a gallant young man in the forest, even though she knows exactly what lurks within him. He kills her grandmother, but when Rosaleen has the chance to shoot the man who has now turned into a wolf, she lets the gun drop to her side. She takes the wounded animal onto her lap and becomes a wolf herself.

Psychoanalysis may claim to be able to unlock the true significance of dreams, but it also robs them of their magic. Any attempt to analyze *The Company of Wolves* down to the last detail, "runs the risk of betraying imagination to psychology, and enslaving the images to an easily transparent symbolism," as one critic poignantly put it.

In any case, the film is immune to conclusive analysis: its complex story telling prevents a one-dimensional interpretation. Thanks to this complexity, the film remains enigmatic and magical, even under close inspection. Despite the fact that Rosaleen now and again makes one detour too many on the road to discovering who she really is, *The Company of Wolves* remains a bewitching, fantastic film. Like Jordan's debut, *Angel* (1982), the film was a huge success at the box-office. NM

5

"The collaboration of feminist writer Angela Carter and Irish novelist, film director Neil Jordan has given us one of the best English films in years, and, quite surprisingly, one of the most commercially successful." *epd Film*

6

THE FLY

1986 – USA – 95 MIN.

DIRECTOR

DAVID CRONENBERG (b. 1943)

SCREENPLAY

CHARLES EDWARD POGUE, DAVID CRONENBERG
based on the short story of the same name by GEORGE LANGELAAN

DIRECTOR OF PHOTOGRAPHY

MARK IRWIN

EDITING

RONALD SANDERS

MUSIC

HOWARD SHORE

PRODUCTION

STUART CORNFELD for BROOKSFILM

STARRING

JEFF GOLDBLUM (Seth Brundle), GEENA DAVIS (Veronica Quaife),
JOHN GETZ (Stathis Borans), JOY BOUSHEL (Tawny),
LESLIE CARLSON (Dr. Cheevers), GEORGE CHUVALO (Marky),
MICHAEL COPEMAN (Second Man in Bar), DAVID CRONENBERG (Gynecologist),
CAROL LAZARE (Nurse)

ACADEMY AWARDS 1986

OSCAR for BEST MAKE-UP (Chris Walas, Stephan Dupuis)

THE FLY
BE AFRAID.
BE VERY AFRAID.

1

"Are you a bodybuilder?"— "Yeah, I build bodies."

Where science fiction meets horror, where the disquiet aroused by unbridled progress becomes sheer, primitive terror; on the tightrope between a technology that's grown beyond our comprehension and an image of human nature whose enlightened optimism can no longer be justified; where science and metaphysics fail equally, where our fear is greatest and no explanations are possible—this is where we find ourselves in *The Fly*. The battlefield is the body of reclusive, eccentric scientist Seth Brundle (Jeff Goldblum), a latter-day Dr. Faust / Mr. Hyde and the inventor of a teleportation machine. When he experiments on himself for the first time, he fails to notice he has company on his trip—a fly has got into the transport capsule. Brundle and the insect "congeal" on a molecular-genetic level, and the consequence is a gradual metamorphosis: the scientist becomes the fly.

Initially, Brundle is assisted by young science journalist Veronica Quaife (Geena Davis), who develops a more-than-academic interest in him. It's only when Veronica awakens Brundle's long-dormant sexual instincts that he achieves an intellectual breakthrough, for her physical desire teaches him to understand "the flesh." Indeed, before his intellect was stimulated by their mutual passion, Brundle's experiments with living material had always failed, leaving nothing in their wake but an unappetizing heap of twitching tissue. Now, he is inspired: sexual desire and the drive for knowledge are intimately bound up with one another.

But just as the sorcerer's apprentice can't control the ghosts he conjures up, Seth and Veronica are at the mercy of the desires they've awakened. Brundlefly, as he calls himself at an advanced stage of transformation, develops animalistic strength as the fly in him gradually "emerges." He becomes insatiably gluttonous and monstrously obsessed with sex. For Veronica, his transformation bears a terrible fruit; she becomes pregnant, and

HORROR REMAKES In 1958, Kurt Neumann made the first version of *The Fly*, in which the scientist emerged from his failed experiment wearing a fly's head, while the fly buzzed off with his. In Cronenberg's remake, the shock of a sudden deformation is replaced by the horror of a gradual metamorphosis. There are two sound economic arguments for remaking classic films: the studio already has the material, and doesn't have to pay a writer to develop it; and, secondly, the material has already proven its popularity. Horror films are favorite subjects for remakes. Lately, box-office magnets include *The Mummy* (directed by Karl Freund in 1933, and by Stephen Sommers in 1999), *The Evil Dead* (directed by Sam Raimi in 1981, and by Fede Alvarez in 2013) while *The Haunting* (Robert Wise, 1962; Jan de Bont, 1999) was among the less successful remake ventures.

1 Between primate and insect: Seth Brundle (Jeff Goldblum) at the start of his transformation.

2 Longevity means fresh meat: Science journalist Veronica Quaife sends Brundle's nerve and brain cells into overdrive.

3 Veronica's boss Stathis Borans (John Getz) is almost as interested in Brundle's invention as he is in Veronica's (Geena Davis) progeny.

4 The cynical scientist archives his body parts for the "Brundle Museum of Natural History."

5 Brundle following his first successful experiment with teleportation.

"*The Fly* is a romance Cronenberg-style, where lovers are transformed by desire into victims of uncontrollable destructive urges, unleashing disaster on themselves and others."

Monthly Film Bulletin

fears only an abortion can save the world from the terrible monster she will bear. But the tragically deformed scientist wants to defend his brood; his animal instincts won't be denied, and a tragic ending is inevitable.

One of the film's main attractions is undoubtedly the metamorphosis, of which we are spared no detail: hair like wire grows on his back, fingers ejaculate pus, and ears drop off. It's not a film for people of a sensitive disposition, and it cemented Cronenberg's reputation as the master of "body horror," the physical terror of mutations and abnormal changes. Brundle's transformation is all the more horrible for taking place so slowly—at first, he doesn't even notice it's happening—and because his body is altered, not by an external act of violence but inexorably from within. Sickness as a consequence of sexual awakening is a theme that rings a bell. When the film first came out, AIDS was just emerging into the public eye, and many critics were quick to jump to conclusions. For him illness is always triggened by a "primal sin"—the thirst for knowledge and sexual craving, always with the awareness that death is unavoidable. Cronenberg himself, however, sees his film in a much broader historical context. As he puts it: "The connection with AIDS is very superficial. I think it's a film about our mortality, our vulnerability and the tragedy of human losses."

MH

4

5

NEAR DARK

1987 – USA – 95 MIN.

DIRECTOR

KATHRYN BIGELOW (b. 1951)

SCREENPLAY

KATHRYN BIGELOW, ERIC RED

DIRECTOR OF PHOTOGRAPHY

ADAM GREENBERG

EDITING

HOWARD E. SMITH

MUSIC

CHRISTOPHER FRANKE, TANGERINE DREAM

PRODUCTION

STEVEN-CHARLES JAFFE, ERIC RED for
F/M, NEAR DARK JOINT VENTURE

STARRING

ADRIAN PASDAR (Caleb Colton), JENNY WRIGHT (Mae),
LANCE HENRIKSEN (Jesse), BILL PAXTON (Severen),
JENETTE GOLDSTEIN (Diamondback), TIM THOMERSON (Loy Colton),
JOSHUA JOHN MILLER (Homer), MARCIE LEEDS (Sarah Colton),
KENNY CALL (Deputy Sheriff), THOMAS WAGNER (Bartender)

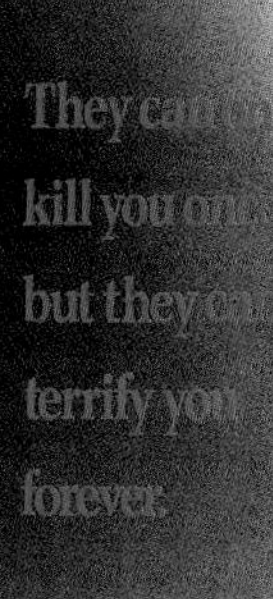

NEAR DARK

...pray for daylight.

F/M ENTERTAINMENT Presents A FELDMAN/MEEKER Production NEAR DARK

Starring ADRIAN PASDAR • JENNY WRIGHT • LANCE HENRIKSEN • BILL PA TON • JENETTE GOLDSTEIN and TIM THOMERSON as Loy Music by TANGERINE DREAM Film Editor HOWARD SMITH

Director of Photography ADAM GREENBERG Executive Producers EDWARD S. FELDMAN and CHARLES R. MEEKER Co-Producer ERIC RED Produced by STEVEN-CHARLES JAFFE Written by ERIC RED & KATHRYN BIGELOW Directed by KATHRYN BIGELOW

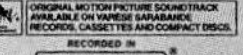

RECORDED IN ULTRA-STEREO

A DEG RELEASE DEG

1

"Listen to the night, it's deafening."

The camera pans over a desolate neighborhood somewhere in Oklahoma. The evening sun dips below the endless fields, which are covered with black power lines that stretch as far as the eye can see. Caleb (Adrian Pasdar) travels through this landscape until he reaches the next nameless small town. Caleb is a cowboy, with the boots and Stetson to match, and he does what cowboys love to do in the evening: he hangs around, drinks beer, and checks out the girls. He approaches a young woman walking the dark streets alone and begins to speak with her. But Mae (Jenny Wright) is not like the other girls: instead of letting him kiss her, she philosophizes about the night, and the white mustang Caleb proudly wants to show her shies from her and gallops away. She succinctly says that horses just don't like her, and if it wasn't apparent at first, we now know that Mae comes from a world that has nothing to do with cowboys.

The film genre Kathryn Bigelow draws upon in this, her second film, becomes clear when Mae ends the goodnight kiss with a bite into Caleb's neck. Mae belongs to a small group of vampires who wander like nomads through the country that was once the expansive frontier that gave rise to the myth of the Wild West. Now, however, it is almost entirely domesticated, with clean farms punctuating the straight–as-a-die fields. It is here that Caleb's family lives. The Coltons are a family we think we know from the American television series, *The Waltons* (1972–81). As Caleb heads home on that morning, he is dragged into a trailer with tinted windows and kidnapped. Strange figures creep from the dark interior of the RV, and express their intention to kill him in no uncertain terms. But suddenly Mae appears and stands in front of him, protecting him from the strangers. She explains to her friends that she has already transformed him. Caleb is ultimately granted a probationary period of one week in which he must become one of them—by killing. His role models include Jesse (Lance Henriksen) and Diamondback (Jenette Goldstein), who murder with a practiced smirk on their lips; or Severen (Bill Paxton), who has mastered the cowboy swagger at least as well as Caleb, but who

GENRE-CROSSING Genre-crossing is a procedure where dissimilar genres are combined to create new associations. There are plenty of examples throughout the history of film. The film classic *King Kong* (1933) used elements of the adventure, fantasy, and horror film, while *Annie Get Your Gun* (1950) combined the Western and the musical. Most notably Film Noir, on its own considered a genre, produced a series of so-called hybrids—films that were melodramas, post-war assimilation stories, and thrillers all rolled into one.

Since the 1980s, genre-crossing has become a form of intertextuality correlating to the postmodern method of story telling. Films refer to earlier as well as contemporary productions, cite genres and mix them together. In this way, a film like *Die Hard* (1987) sends Bruce Willis on a journey through the thriller, the catastrophe film, and the war movie. The teenager movies, *The Lost Boys* (1987) and *Young Guns* (1988) fuse their plots with the vampire genre on the one hand, and the Western on the other. Kathryn Bigelow's films are particularly important examples of genre-crossing: while in *Near Dark* (1987) the Western and the vampire film were combined, *Point Break* (1991) offers a mixture of action thriller and surfer film. The much acclaimed feature-length films *The Hurt Locker* (2008) and *Zero Dark Thirty* (2012) show how expertly Bigelow masters the game of genre-crossing.

1 WANTED: Dead or undead. Caleb (Adrian Pasdar) searches for his blood brothers and sanguinary sisters.

2 Kathryn Bigelow's style thrives on precisely calculated imagery. Turning the Western on its head, she shows her vampires as lone rangers atop the mountain on the horizon, before having them descend to earth.

3 Vampires can't survive in daylight: The sun burns Homer (Joshua John Miller) to a crisp as he crosses over to the realm of the living.

4 Homer has the physique of a boy, but the soul of a man. Driven by love, he desperately tries to win the heart of Caleb's sister Sarah (Marcie Leeds).

5 Sending shivers down your spine: When night falls, the inhabitants of these farm houses put the "wild" back into the West.

seduces women for blood rather than sex. Or Homer (Joshua John Miller), a child on the outside, but a man inside, who uses his illusory helplessness to bait his victims.

But Caleb can't bring himself to kill. As if feeding a child, Mae gives him blood from her arm to drink, thereby inverting the vampire mythology. Caleb is an explorer, like his biblical namesake, a wanderer between the two worlds. Thus he affords us a look into the dark side of civilization, pulling us behind the border where all things excluded from normal life reign supreme. Deviating from the horror norm, Kathryn Bigelow changes perspective and allows us to accompany Caleb on a journey from the interior of the trailer to the dark sides of modernity, a journey reverberant with the legends of the Wild West. Jesse and his friends come across like a group of desperados, not unlike the group of comrades from Sam Peckinpah's *The Wild Bunch* (1969). And they are just as dreadful, as the main scene in a suburban bar shows—a scene in which Kathryn Bigelow's love for dramatization and highly calculated images reaches its zenith. The bizarre battle sequence seems like a uniquely dramatized dance to finally teach Caleb a lesson in killing. But while he is still unable to do it, he saves himself by risking his life to rescue the crew from a motel that has been surrounded by the police. Though Caleb gradually begins to feel comfortable with his new friends, a chance meeting

“When we wrote *Near Dark* we were very conscious of taking a genre and turning it upside down, subverting it in some way—taking the vampire mythology and putting it in the West.”

Kathryn Bigelow in: Film Comment

with his father and little sister convince him that it is their world that he really belongs to. He seizes the opportunity to flee and is transformed back into a normal human being with the help of a blood transfusion. In the end, beautiful Mae receives the same treatment, after all the vampires and the evil that accompanies them have been banished from the world.

Contrary to other representatives of the genre, *Near Dark* unveils the vampire as the protagonist of another life, free from everyday obligations, though forever reproducing its uniformity. This recalls Joel Schumacher's *The Lost Boys* (1987) and firmly locates the film in its 80s context. The same can be said for the fertile mixture of genres: the western and the vampire film are fused, creating a complex and jarringly novel variation on both.

Kathryn Bigelow, who studied art in San Francisco and was active on the New York art scene, presents her audiences with highly original images. When, during a Western-like shoot-out, bullets come flying through the walls of the motel, it is not the bullets but the rays of sunlight streaming through the holes in the wall which injure the undead, burning their vampire skin like lasers, a strange reminder of what films are really made of: light.

KK

5

MISERY

1990 – USA – 107 MIN.

DIRECTOR

ROB REINER (b. 1947)

SCREENPLAY

WILLIAM GOLDMAN based on the novel
of the same name by STEPHEN KING

DIRECTOR OF PHOTOGRAPHY

BARRY SONNENFELD

EDITING

ROBERT LEIGHTON

MUSIC

MARC SHAIMAN

PRODUCTION

ANDREW SCHEINMAN, ROB REINER for
CASTLE ROCK ENTERTAINMENT, NELSON ENTERTAINMENT

STARRING

JAMES CAAN (Paul Sheldon), KATHY BATES (Annie Wilkes),
FRANCES STERNHAGEN (Virginia McCain),
RICHARD FRANSWORTH (J.T. "Buster" McCain),
LAUREN BACALL (Marcia Sindell), GRAHAM JARVIS (Libby),
JERRY POTTER (Pete), TOM BRUNELLE (Anchorman),
JUNE CHRISTOPHER (Anchorwoman), J.T. WALSH (Chief Sherman Douglas)

ACADEMY AWARDS 1990

OSCAR for BEST LEADING ACTRESS (Kathy Bates)

Directed by
ROB REINER

Based on the Novel by
STEPHEN KING

Screenplay by
WILLIAM GOLDMAN

JAMES CAAN · KATHY BATES

MISERY

Paul Sheldon used to write for a living.

Now, he's writing to stay alive.

CASTLE ROCK ENTERTAINMENT in Association with NELSON ENTERTAINMENT Presents A ROB REINER FILM JAMES CAAN KATHY BATES "MISERY"
FRANCES STERNHAGEN and RICHARD FARNSWORTH as "BUSTER" Special Appearance by LAUREN BACALL Co-Produced by STEVE NICOLAIDES and JEFFREY STOTT
Edited by ROBERT LEIGHTON Production Designer NORMAN GARWOOD Music by MARC SHAIMAN Director of Photography BARRY SONNENFELD
Produced by ANDREW SCHEINMAN and ROB REINER Based on the Novel by STEPHEN KING Screenplay by WILLIAM GOLDMAN Directed by ROB REINER

CASTLE ROCK
R RESTRICTED UNDER 17 REQUIRES ACCOMPANYING PARENT OR ADULT GUARDIAN
ORIGINAL SOUNDTRACK RECORDING AVAILABLE ON BAY CITIES CD'S AND CASSETTES
DOLBY STEREO
Read the Signet Paperback
NELSON
Columbia Pictures
A COLUMBIA PICTURES RELEASE

1

"I'm your number one fan."

Popular novelist Paul Sheldon (James Caan) has acquired innumerable devotees with a series of books about the adventures of a heroine called Misery Chastain—and he has no fan more devoted than Annie Wilkes (Kathy Bates). A former nurse, she knows Sheldon's books back-to-front and inside out, and is also familiar with every detail of his private life. Of all people, this "ideal reader" experiences a miracle when the author of her dreams falls right into her lap. Forced off the road by a blizzard, Sheldon lies trapped and unconscious in his wrecked car. Annie finds him, frees him, and carries him back to her lonely farm in the Colorado Mountains. Suddenly the best-selling author is dependent on his reader, as he lies on her guest bed with two broken legs. No one knows that before the accident he had "killed off" Misery Chastain in a final installment which is awaiting publication, clearing the way for his departure from the realm of popular culture and his entry into the literary major league with a new autobiography. When Annie finds out that she's going to have to get by without her heroine, she is aghast; she forces her adored author to think again about killing Misery, and provides him with typewriter and paper, so that the connection between the novels and her life can remain unbroken. This obsessive bookworm mutates into the Muse from Hell, and the writer is a hostage to her happiness. Sheldon finds himself writing for his life, so he awakens the dead and begins a deadly duel with this demonic lector…

Misery is the second Stephen King novel filmed by Rob Reiner. His previous King adaptation, *Stand by Me* (1986), based on *The Body*, also depicts characters who are suddenly confronted with death. Reiner leaves nothing to chance in the treatment of the duel between the author and his reader, with extreme zooms onto tortured, torturing faces, and close-ups of objects like hairpins, which

STEPHEN KING Born in 1947, Stephen King is a new kind of writer, as nearly all of his books have been adapted for the screen. A grand total of forty-one of his fifty novels have now been made into films. His first novel, *Carrie* (1974), was filmed two years later by Brian De Palma. The secret of King's success—and one reason he can demand advances of several million dollars for his novels—lies in the fact that many of his horror stories are designed like film scripts. In addition, King has an extraordinary ability to mix a variety of genres—horror, fantasy, science fiction, and psychological thriller—in a fresh and invariably startling way.

There are other authors of this new species, like the lawyer John Grisham (b. 1955), and the physician Michael Crichton (b. 1942). All three of these "screen writers" enjoy much greater popular acclaim than any of the cinematic *auteurs.*

“Rob Reiner himself is a natural storyteller. A moviemaker not content to tell just a cut and dry story, his film is as much an examination of what it means *to want* to be a storyteller as it is a plot-driven piece of cinema. His approach invariably raises valid questions, questions every director should stop and think about before starting a movie. Rob Reiner has come up with the answers.” *Cahiers du cinéma*

1 Not a stairway to heaven: This nurse is ready to put her patients out of their misery. Kathy Bates as Annie Wilkes.

2 Bed pan hands: He'll behave, but only if he's incapacitated (James Caan).

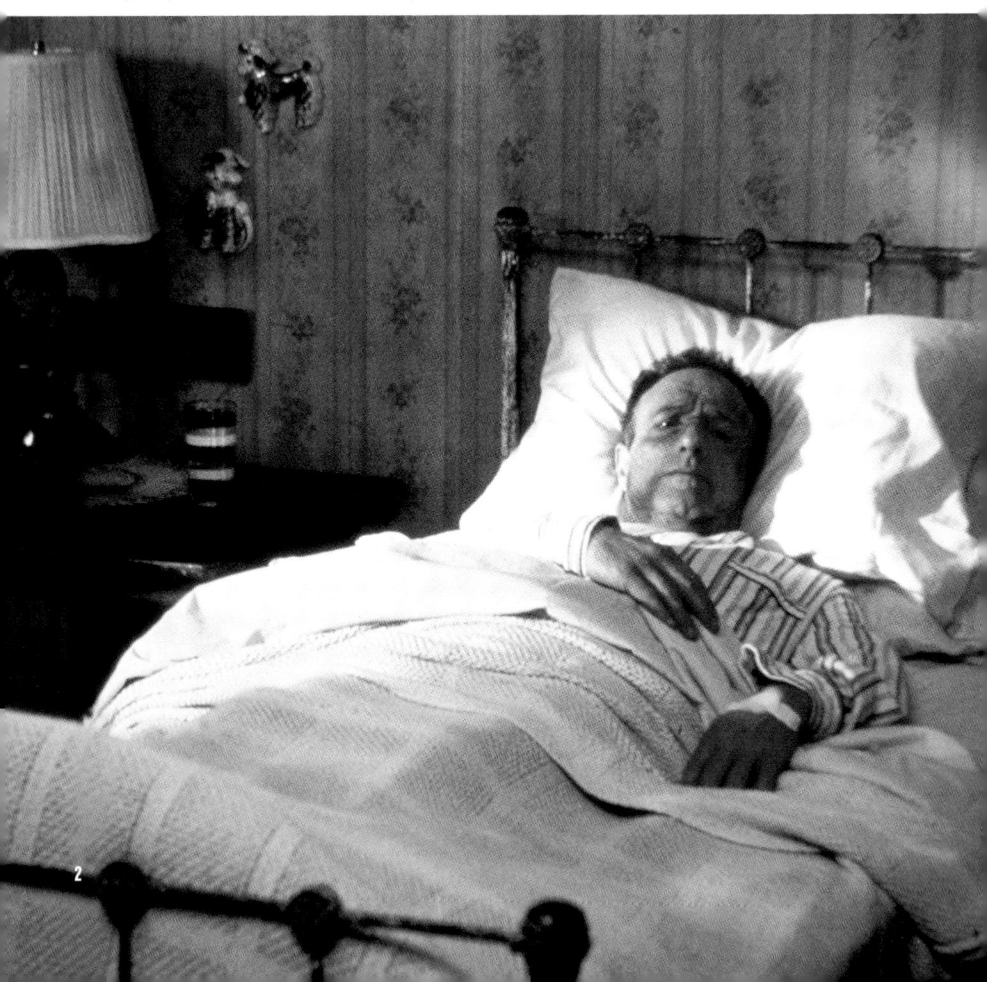

2

3 His new "agent" (Kathy Bates) gives a diligent author the axe. No rush to get back to New York now.

4 Bedtime stories: if the author lets the heroine of this serial die, a serial killer will avenge the guilty party.

5 Samurai sumo wrestling: A neck and neck fight to the bloody finish.

prove to be of vital importance to the development of the plot a few shots later.

This "Kill the Bitch" film-adaptation improves on the book in one way: reading and writing, the main activities of the duelists, are what actually propel the filmic narrative along. The sheriff from the nearest small town picks up on Annie's trail by reading the *Misery* novels; Annie leaves tell-tale clues by buying large amounts of paper; and the typewriter is Sheldon's lifeline: he uses it both to gain time and to keep fit (weightlifting!); and, at the climax, it becomes the writer's weapon in the final showdown with his rabid reader. RV

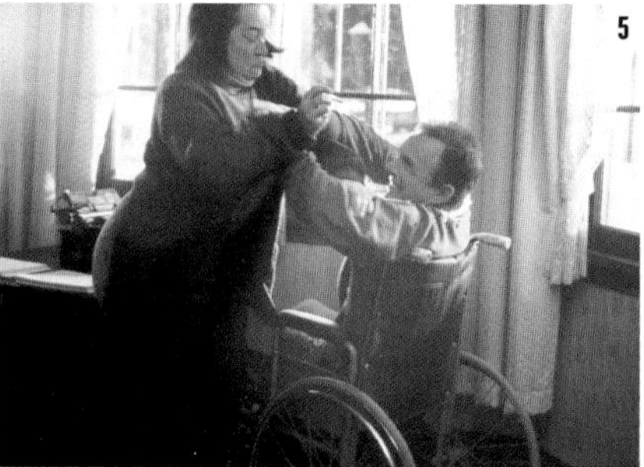

DELICATESSEN

1991 – FRANCE – 99 MIN.

DIRECTORS

JEAN-PIERRE JEUNET (b. 1953),
MARC CARO (b. 1956)

SCREENPLAY

JEAN-PIERRE JEUNET, MARC CARO, GILLES ADRIEN

DIRECTOR OF PHOTOGRAPHY

DARIUS KHONDJI

MUSIC

CARLOS D'ALESSIO

PRODUCTION

CLAUDIE OSSARD for CONSTELLATION,
UGC, HACHETTE PREMIÈRE

STARRING

DOMINIQUE PINON (Louison), MARIE-LAURE DOUGNAC (Julie Clapet),
JEAN-CLAUDE DREYFUS (The Butcher), KARIN VIARD (Miss Plusse),
TICKY HOLGADO (Mr. Tapioca), ANNE-MARIE PISANI (Mrs. Tapioca),
EDITH KER (Grandmother Tapioca), SILVIA LAGUNA (Mrs. Interligator),
HOWARD VERNON (elderly gentleman), MICKAEL TODDE,
BOBAN JANEVSKI (Young Rascals), JACQUES MATHOU (Roger)

“PREPARE TO FEAST ON THIS MOVIE!”
TERRY KELLEHER, NEW YORK NEWSDAY

Claudie Ossard presents

DELICATESSEN

A film by Jeunet and Caro

A MIRAMAX FILMS RELEASE CLAUDIE OSSARD presents “DELICATESSEN” a film by JEUNET AND CARO
with DOMINIQUE PINON MARIE-LAURE DOUGNAC JEAN-CLAUDE DREYFUS KARIN VIARD RUFUS TICKY HOLGADO SILVIE LAGUNA JACQUES MATHOU JEAN-FRANÇOIS PERRIER ANNE-MARIE PISANI HOWARD VERNON CHICK ORTEGA
screenplay by JEAN-PIERRE JEUNET GILLES ADRIEN MARC CARO original music by CARLOS D'ALESSIO director of photography DARIUS KHONDJI line producer MICHÈLE ARNOULD editing by HERVÉ SCHNEID sound by JÉRÔME THIAULT and VINCENT ARNARDI produced by CLAUDIE OSSARD

DOLBY STEREO IN SELECTED THEATRES

MIRAMAX FILMS

"How much do you weigh?"

Something terrible has happened to the world. Everything is in ruins and permanent darkness reigns. Somewhere, a solitary apartment block remains standing. It must have been quite a distinguished residence at some point in the past. Now, the people here are better off than elsewhere—the downstairs of the house is butcher's shop, run by an ingenious master butcher (Jean-Claude Dreyfus) who keeps the occupants supplied with fresh meat. The wares on offer at his "Delicatessen" are the former neighbours, but this no longer seems to bother his customers: in times like these they can't afford to be choosy. When provisions run short at her funeral, Grandmother herself provides the refreshments—giving a whole new meaning to the expression "funeral bake-meats."

Louison (Dominique Pinon), an unemployed clown, strays into this apocalyptic horror-idyll. The butcher, sharpening his knives, takes him on as a caretaker, and the rest of the gruesome crew look forward to a glut of fresh meat.

Despite the difficult times, Louison has retained his sunny character and he entertains the occupants of the house with his tricks—but that isn't enough to get him taken off the menu. Luckily for him the butcher's daughter Julie (Marie-Laure Dougnac) falls in love with him, and she does her utmost to save him from her father's meat grinder. In her hour of need she turns to the archenemies of the house's bizarre inhabitants: the vegetarians, who indulge their repulsive preference for corn and wheat in the Paris sewers...

Delicatessen was the first full-length movie by Jean-Pierre Jeunet and Marc Caro, French directors who had made their names with distinctive shorts. The film is a showcase for comic figures like Mrs. Interligator (Silvia Laguna), who constantly hears voices encouraging her to attempt suicide with a series of daredevil contraptions that are as inventive as they are unsuccessful. Then there's the elderly gentleman (Howard Vernon) who has turned his apartment into a pond to keep himself in frogs and snails: the plot is really just an excuse for the succession of peculiarities and monstrosities that Jeunet and Caro parade before our eyes.

The film's impact also depends on the details of its fairy-tale comic scenery, which is lovingly created. We learn to expect the unexpected from the walls, pipes, and shafts

SURREALISM—CINEMA AS DREAM The poet Guillaume Apollinaire used the term "surréel" for the first time in 1917. Following the ideas of Sigmund Freud, Surrealism tries to make man's internal reality visible. Motifs from dream experiences and intoxicated states distort the Surrealists' view of the world and transform objective reality into a reflection of the soul. As Surrealism coincided with the early days of film, it is not surprising that its images and ideas have influenced cinema history since its very beginnings. An early example is *Der müde Tod* (*Destiny*, 1921) by Fritz Lang. Surrealist set pieces can be found in all movie genres, although not always as explicitly as in Alfred Hitchcock's *Spellbound* (1945), whose dream sequences were designed by Salvador Dalí. Variations on Surrealist themes and motifs have found their way into in a range of different genres, from horror to science fiction.

“There’s nothing remotely like the world of *Delicatessen*. It’s a fragment of childhood miraculously intact. A mirage. A scrap of eternity. It’s heartbreakingly lovely.”

Le Nouvel Observateur

of the house, which, rather than providing shelter for its inhabitants, shifts and stirs like a prehistoric creature and seems to have swallowed them whole. Its crooked staircases and hallways mark it as a surreal motif with many forerunners in the history of the cinema, like the Bates Motel in Hitchcock’s *Psycho* (1960) or the Overlook Hotel in Kubrick’s *The Shining* (1980). But more than anything *Delicatessen* is a slapstick version of Roman Polanski’s apartment house horror film *Le Locataire* (*The Tenant*, 1976) based on the novel by French writer Roland Topor.

Both the “living” house and the hero of the film call to mind Terry Gilliam’s alarming apocalyptic vision *Brazil*. Like the wilful civil servant Sam Lowry, Louison is a naïve revolutionary who has remained human in an inhuman world and is therefore bound to antagonise the people who surround him. Louison forgives his tormentors by constantly reminding himself that it is the circumstances which have turned them to the bad. He respects his fellow men despite their cannibalism, and the fact that they kill his pet ape, who winds up in their stew-pot.

Delicatessen does far more than push back the boundaries of bad taste. It’s also an eloquent plea for humanity, solidarity and—vegetarianism.

SH

2

1 Will that be all, sir? Butcher Clapet (Jean-Claude Dreyfus) always seems to have the welfare of his fellow inhabitants at heart.

2 Living on rabbit food: militant vegetarians barricade themselves in the basement to fight for a meat-free diet.

3 Nobody is safe from the butcher's razor-sharp knife.

4 A Little Night Music… Louison (Dominique Pinon) and Julie (Marie-Laure Dougnac) meet and fall in love.

5 Circus artist Louison tries to survive in an inhuman milieu by using imagination and humanity.

THE SILENCE OF THE LAMBS

1991 – USA – 118 MIN.

DIRECTOR

JONATHAN DEMME (b. 1944)

SCREENPLAY

TED TALLY, based on the novel
of the same name by THOMAS HARRIS

DIRECTOR OF PHOTOGRAPHY

TAK FUJIMOTO

EDITING

CRAIG MCKAY

MUSIC

HOWARD SHORE

PRODUCTION

GARY GOETZMAN, EDWARD SAXON, KENNETH UTT,
RON BOZMAN for STRONG HEART PRODUCTIONS (for ORION)

STARRING

JODIE FOSTER (Clarice Starling), ANTHONY HOPKINS (Dr. Hannibal Lecter),
SCOTT GLENN (Jack Crawford), TED LEVINE (Jame Gumb),
ANTHONY HEALD (Dr. Frederick Chilton), BROOKE SMITH (Catherine Martin),
DIANE BAKER (Senator Ruth Martin), KASI LEMMONS (Ardelia Mapp),
ROGER CORMAN (FBI Director Hayden Burke), GEORGE A. ROMERO (FBI Agent in Memphis)

ACADEMY AWARDS 1991

OSCARS for BEST PICTURE, BEST DIRECTOR (Jonathan Demme),
BEST ACTRESS (Jodie Foster), BEST ACTOR (Anthony Hopkins), and
BEST SCREENPLAY based on material previously produced or published (Ted Tally)

jodie foster / anthony hopkins / scott glenn
the silence of the lambs
from the terrifying best seller
a jonathan demme picture / jodie foster / anthony hopkins / scott glenn / "the silence of the lambs" / ted levine / music by howard shore / production designer kristi zea /
director of photography tak fujimoto / edited by craig mckay, a.c.e. / executive producer gary goetzman / based upon the novel by thomas harris / screenplay by ted tally /
R RESTRICTED
produced by kenneth utt edward saxon and ron bozman / directed by jonathan demme
ORION
MCA

1

"I'm having a friend for dinner."

Clarice Starling (Jodie Foster), daughter of a policeman shot in the line of duty, wants to join the FBI. At the FBI Academy in Woods, Virginia, she races over training courses, pushing herself to the limit. Wooden signs bear the legend "HURT-AGONY-PAIN: LOVE IT"—they're not just there to exhort the rookies to excel, they also reveal the masochism involved. The movie goes through the whole range of this theme, from heroic selflessness to destructive self-hate. Jack Crawford (Scott Glenn), who is Starling's boss and the head of the FBI's psychiatric department, sends her to Baltimore to carry out a routine interview with an imprisoned murderer who is resisting questioning. As well as being a psychiatrist, the prisoner is also an extreme pathological case who attacked people and ate their organs.

For eight years Dr. Hannibal "The Cannibal" Lecter (Anthony Hopkins) has lived in the windowless cellar of a high security mental hospital. Crawford hopes the interview will provide clues to the behavior of a second monster, a killer known as "Buffalo Bill" who skins his female victims and has so far skillfully evaded the FBI. Crawford's plan works, and the professorial cannibal agrees to discuss the pathology of mass murderers with his visitor Clarice—on one condition. Lecter will give her expert advice on Buffalo Bill in exchange for the tale of her childhood trauma. "Quid pro quo"—she lays bare her psyche, he gives her a psychological profile of her suspect. The gripping dialogue that develops between the ill-matched couple can be understood on many levels. On one hand, we see a psychoanalyst talking to his patient, on the other, a young detective interrogating an unpredictable serial killer, and that ambiguity is the determining quality in Lecter and Starling's relationship.

Both follow their own aims unerringly, refusing to give way, and the struggle that results is one of the most brilliant and sophisticated duels in cinema history. The daughter of a U.S. senator falls into the hands of Buffalo Bill, and suddenly the FBI is under increasing pressure to find the murderer. Lecter's chance has come. In return for his help in capturing Jame Gumb alias Buffalo Bill (Ted Levine), he asks for better conditions and is transferred to a temporary prison in Memphis. He kills the warders and escapes in the uniform of a policeman, whose face he has also removed and placed over his own.

His last exchange with Starling takes place over the telephone, when he rings from a Caribbean island to congratulate her on her promotion to FBI agent and bids her farewell with the words: "I'm having a friend for dinner." After hanging up, Lecter follows a group of tourists in which the audience recognize the hated Dr. Chilton (Anthony Heald), director of the secure mental hospital in Baltimore, who clearly will be Lecter's unsuspecting dinner "guest."

The Silence of the Lambs marked a cinematic high point at the beginning of the 1990s. It is impossible to categorize in any one genre as it combines several. There are elements from police movies (where crime does not pay), but it's also a thriller that borrows much from real historical figures: the model for both Gumb and Lecter is

PARALLEL MONTAGE A process developed early in the history of cinema. Editing enables two or more events happening in different places to be told and experienced at the same time. The best-known kind of parallel montage in movies is the "last-minute rescue," where images of an endangered or besieged character are juxtaposed in rapid succession with those of the rescuers who are on their way. Action movies use such sequences over and over as a means of increasing the tension, and the device has remained basically the same from David Griffith's 1916 film *Intolerance* to today's thrillers. Parallel montage allows us to be a step ahead of the figures in a film. We are allowed to know things that the characters do not themselves realize, and we are also in several places at the same time, an experience which is only possible in fiction.

1 The naked man and the dead: "Buffalo Bill" (Ted Levine) uses a sewing machine to make himself a new identity from the skin of his victims; above him are butterflies, a symbol of that metamorphosis.

2 The staring matches between Clarice Starling (Jodie Foster) and Hannibal Lecter (Anthony Hopkins) are a battle for knowledge: Lecter is to help the FBI build a profile of the killer; Starling is to surrender the secret of her childhood.

3 The eyes have it: in the serial killer genre, eyes become a tool for appropriation, destruction, and penetration.

"*The Silence of the Lambs* is just plain scary—from its doomed and woozy camera angles to its creepy Freudian context." *The Washington Post*

4 The cannibal clasps his hands. Cage and pose are reminiscent of Francis Bacon's portraits of the pope.

5 A policeman is disemboweled and crucified on the cage. With his outstretched arms, he looks like a butterfly.

6 The pair meet in the lowest part of the prison system, a basement dungeon from the underworld.

7 The monster is restrained with strait-jacket and muzzle; the powers of the state have the monopoly on violence for the time being.

8 Lecter overpowers the guards with their own weapons: one policeman is given a taste of his own pepper spray.

"It has been a good long while since I have felt the presence of Evil so manifestly demonstrated..." *Chicago Sun-Times*

Edward Gein (1906–1984), who was wearing suspenders made from his victims' skin when arrested in 1957.

But *The Silence of the Lambs* is also a movie about psychiatry. Both murderers are presented as psychopaths whose "relation" to one another forms the basis for criminological research, even though their cases are not strictly comparable. The movie was so successful that it became one of the most influential models for the decade that followed, enriching cinema history to the point of plot plagiarism and quotation.

Hannibal Lecter had already appeared on the silver screen before *The Silence of the Lambs*. In 1986, Michael Mann filmed Thomas Harris's 1981 novel *Red Dragon* under the title *Manhunter*. Five years later, Jonathan Demme refined the material, and the changing perspectives of his camera work give what is fundamentally a cinematic retelling of *Beauty and the Beast* a new twist. Demme films his characters from both within and without.

The director plays with the fluid border between external and internal reality, between memory and the

6

7

present, as when we see Clarice's childhood in two flashbacks for which we are completely unprepared. Jodie Foster's eyes remain fixed on the here and now while the camera zooms beyond her into the past, probing her psychological wounds. During the final confrontation between Clarice and Jame Gumb, the perspective changes repeatedly. We see the murderer through Clarice's eyes but we also see the young FBI agent through the eyes of Jame, who seeks out his victims in the dark using infrared glasses. This changing perspective in the movie's final scenes emphasizes the extreme danger that Clarice is in. Other sequences are straightforward trickery, like the changing perspectives in the sequence which builds up to the finale. A police contingent has surrounded the house where they expect to find Jame Gumb, and a black police officer disguised as a deliveryman rings the bell. On the other side of the door, we hear the bell ring. Jame dresses and answers the door.

The police break into the house, while we see the murderer open the door to find Clarice standing before

8

9

9 In Buffalo Bill's basement lair, Starling is just about to be plunged into total darkness.

10 Jame Gumb aka "Buffalo Bill" once applied for a sex change, but now makes his dream a reality by stalking and skinning women to tailor a "woman suit" for himself.

"I go to the cinema because I feel like being shocked."

Jonathan Demme

him—alone. In the next take, the police storm an empty house. This parallel montage combines two places that are far apart, two actions with the same aim, two houses, of which one is only seen from outside, the other from inside. We are made to think that both actions are happening in the same place. The parallel montage is revealed as a trick and increases the tension: we suddenly realize that Clarice must face the murderer alone.

More than one film critic assumed that this ploy meant that even Hollywood films had moved into an era of self-reflexivity. Instead of consciously revealing a cinematic device, however, the parallel montage serves primarily to heighten the movie's atmosphere of danger and uncertainty. Nevertheless, *The Silence of the Lambs* works on two levels, both as exciting entertainment and as a virtuoso game with key cultural figures and situations. Some critics went so far as to interpret the perverted killer Buffalo Bill as Hades, god of the underworld, and although analyses like that may be interesting, they are not essential to an understanding of the film or its success.

At the 1992 Oscar awards, *The Silence of the Lambs* carried off the so-called Big Five in the five main categories, something which only two films (*It Happened One Night* (1934) and *One Flew Over the Cuckoo's Nest* [1975]) had managed previously. Ten years after his escape, Hannibal Lecter appeared again on the silver screen (*Hannibal*, 2001). Jodie Foster refused to play the role of Clarice for a second time and was replaced by Julianne Moore *(Magnolia)* and Ridley Scott took over from Jonathan Demme as director. RV

SCREAM

1996 – USA – 111 MIN.

DIRECTOR

WES CRAVEN (1939–2015)

SCREENPLAY

KEVIN WILLIAMSON

DIRECTOR OF PHOTOGRAPHY

MARK IRWIN

MUSIC

MARCO BELTRAMI

PRODUCTION

CARY WOODS, CATHY KONRAD for
WOODS ENTERTAINMENT, DIMENSION FILMS, MIRAMAX

STARRING

DREW BARRYMORE (Casey Becker), NEVE CAMPBELL (Sidney Prescott),
DAVID ARQUETTE (Deputy Dewey Riley), COURTENEY COX (Gale Weathers),
JAMIE KENNEDY (Randy), MATTHEW LILLARD (Stewart),
SKEET ULRICH (Billy Loomis), ROSE MCGOWAN (Tatum Riley),
W. EARL BROWN (Kameramann Kenny), LIEV SCHREIBER (Cotton Weary)

Someone has taken their love of scary movies one step too far.
Solving this mystery is going to be murder.
SCREAM
DAVID ARQUETTE
NEVE CAMPBELL
COURTENEY COX
MATTHEW LILLARD
ROSE MCGOWAN
SKEET ULRICH
and
DREW BARRYMORE
DIMENSION FILMS WOODS ENTERTAINMENT WES CRAVEN "SCREAM" MARCO BELTRAMI PATRICK LUSSIER BRUCE ALAN MILLER
MARK IRWIN A.S.C.C.S.C. DIXIE J. CAPP STUART M. BESSER BOB WEINSTEIN HARVEY WEINSTEIN MARIANNE MADDALENA KEVIN WILLIAMSON
WOODS
CARY WOODS CATHY KONRAD WES CRAVEN
DIMENSION
SOUNDTRACK AVAILABLE ON
Visit DIMENSION FILMS on the web at: http://www.dimensionfilms.com
THE HIGHLY ACCLAIMED NEW THRILLER FROM WES CRAVEN

"What's your favorite scary movie?"

It was supposed to be a cozy video evening with popcorn, boyfriend, and a scary movie. It turns into pure horror. Casey (Drew Barrymore) gets an anonymous call. It starts off like a silly boys' trick and ends fatally. The caller draws her into a horror film quiz. What's the name of the killer in *Halloween*? Who's the bloodthirsty murderer in *Friday the 13th*? It turns out that if you get the answer right, you get to stay alive: wrong answers are punishable by death. Casey gets the answer wrong.

The killer's next victim is Sidney Prescott (Neve Campbell), a classmate of the dead girl at Woodsboro High School. Ever since her mother's gruesome murder exactly a year ago, Sidney has been living alone with her father. He goes away on a business trip, and she's left on her own for a few days. The killer calls first, as before, then he stands there in a mask with a knife glinting in his hand. Sidney manages to escape, as her boyfriend Billy (Skeet Ulrich) appears and frightens the psychopath away. But then a hand falls out of Billy's pocket—is he the killer? He is arrested and kept in the local jail overnight. He is released again in the morning: the killer struck again during the night, so it can't be him.

In the meantime all of Woodsboro is in uproar. Camera teams from all over the country have arrived, including the journalist Gale Weathers (Courteney Cox) who reported the death of Sidney's mother a year ago, starting off a media mud fight in the process. The thrill seekers find plenty of trophies as the killer leaves a bloody trail through the town. His next victims are the school director and some more teenagers.

The horror movie genre was dead until Wes Craven awoke it to brilliant new life with *Scream*. "Until now the murderers always acted as if they had just invented killing. Mine knows his predecessors." In *Scream* the killer acts with self-reflective irony, fully conscious of the conventions of the horror movie, and the result is an effective combination of horror and humor. The humor is that of a connoisseur who knows that the dead killer will get up one last time at the end; the humor of Wes Craven who in his short appearance as a caretaker wears Freddy

THE *SCREAM* TETRALOGY "Don't kill me, I want to be in the sequel", one girl says, trying to talk the killer out of his bloody intention. He kills her all the same, but *Scream* has had three sequels. Craven continues the insider jokes: in *Scream 2* (1997) Sidney leaves her hometown and goes to study at a film academy—giving plenty of opportunity to reflect on horror movies and their sequels. The students begin a macabre game—anyone who doesn't die must be the killer. Sidney survives and goes back to Woodsboro in *Scream 3* (2000)—not to the real town, but to a film set where her experiences are being filmed under the title *Stab 3*. That way the number of potential victims is doubled, as each of the protagonists also has an actor playing their part in the movie. The series truly ends in a furious way in part four, which came out in 2011, and which was also Wes Craven's last work as a director.

1 A "slasher" like *Halloween*, with the mask reminiscent of Edvard Munch: Wes Craven draws on a wide range of cultural references.

2 "I don't believe in motives. Did Hannibal Lecter have a reason for wanting to eat people?" (quotation from film)

3 Victim number one: Drew Barrymore starts chatting to a stranger on the phone about horror films, before discovering that she's talking to a lunatic.

4 For reporter Weathers (Courteney Cox) all this is just part of the job—until the killer turns his knife on her.

5 Has Sidney (Neve Campbell) survived everything? Not yet: there are three sequels still to go.

Krueger's striped pullover (from his masterpiece *A Nightmare on Elm Street*) and even that of the bourgeois art connoisseur: the makeup is based on Edvard Munch's *The Scream.* The recognition factor is satisfying. The laughter provides brief pauses in each tense scene—the fundamental suspense, the thrill, the feverish identification with the protagonists still remain. The shock remains too: the resurrection of the killer is not just taken for granted here, it is even announced. And yet we are still shocked when it actually happens. Despite all the quotations and the games with genre conventions *Scream* never becomes a simple parody.

The protagonists are horror movie fans just like normal people, acted by youngsters already familiar from television series, like Neve Campbell from *Party of Five* (1994–98) and Courteney Cox from *Friends* (1994–2004). The only established film actress is Drew Barrymore, but she disappears from the scene within a few minutes—like Janet Leigh in *Psycho* (1960). The characters know what is going on. They know the rules of the teenage horror movie: no sex, no drugs, no booze, and never say you'll be back in a minute. But they don't stick to them—they have sex, they smoke, and they pass round the joints– and they have to pay the consequences. HJK

“People like dying in my films. Even my lawyer asks me when he’ll finally get to play a corpse.” *Wes Craven in: Zeit-Magazin*

THE BLAIR WITCH PROJECT

1999 – USA – 87 MIN.

DIRECTORS

DANIEL MYRICK (b. 1963),
EDUARDO SÁNCHEZ (b. 1968)

SCREENPLAY

DANIEL MYRICK, EDUARDO SANCHEZ

DIRECTOR OF PHOTOGRAPHY

NEAL FREDERICKS

MUSIC

TONY CORA

PRODUCTION

GREGG HALE, ROBIN COWIE, MICHAEL MONELLO for
HAXAN FILMS, ARTISAN ENTERTAINMENT

STARRING

HEATHER DONAHUE (Heather), MICHAEL WILLIAMS (Michael),
JOSHUA LEONARD (Joshua), BOB GRIFFIN (Angler),
JIM KING (Interview Partner), SANDRA SANCHEZ (Waitress),
ED SWANSON (Angler with Glasses), PATRICIA DECOU (Mary Brown),
MARK MASON (Man with the Yellow Hat), JACKIE HALLEX (Interviewee with Child)

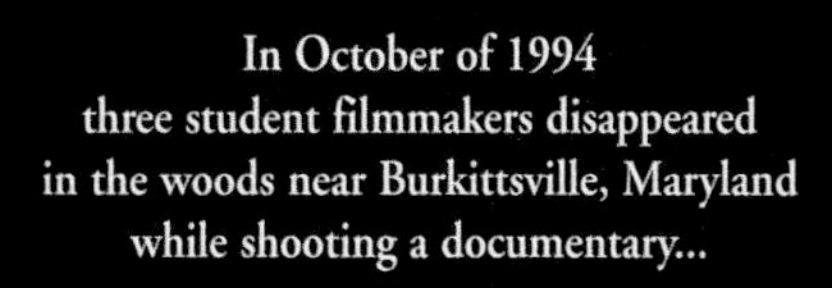

THE BLAIR WITCH PROJECT

ARTISAN ENTERTAINMENT PRESENTS A HAXAN FILMS PRODUCTION HEATHER DONAHUE MICHAEL WILLIAMS JOSHUA LEONARD "THE BLAIR WITCH PROJECT"
PRODUCTION DESIGNER BEN ROCK ART DIRECTOR RICARDO R. MORENO DIRECTOR OF PHOTOGRAPHY NEAL FREDERICKS MUSIC BY ANTONIO CORA EXECUTIVE PRODUCED BY BOB EICK AND KEVIN J. FOXE
CO-PRODUCED BY MICHAEL MONELLO PRODUCED BY GREGG HALE & ROBIN COWIE WRITTEN, DIRECTED AND EDITED BY DANIEL MYRICK & EDUARDO SANCHEZ

COMPANION ALBUM AVAILABLE ON ODEON FILMS www.blairwitch.com DOLBY DIGITAL READ THE ONYX BOOK ARTISAN

"It's very hard to get lost in America these days and even harder to stay lost."

We know the story from the Grimm Brothers: young people get lost in a wood and struggle with a witch. In the contemporary adaptation *The Blair Witch Project* there is however no tempting gingerbread and the witch doesn't get pushed into the oven—instead film students Heather (Heather Donahue), Michael (Michael Williams), and Joshua (Joshua Leonard) set off into the woods in Maryland with their camera to investigate stories of a witch, and they come to a sticky end. First the three youngsters ask people in the village of Blair about the stories, then they go off into the woods to look. It soon becomes ominously clear that they are being watched and they realize too late that they are lost.

The Blair Witch Project cost only a fraction of the cost of a normal Hollywood production. The plot is driven by the movie's own frugal production conditions. A horror movie disguised as a documentary, it begins with a text insert saying that in October 1994 three film students disappeared in the woods near Burkittsville, Maryland while making a documentary film and that their film material was found a year later. This material is what we are about to see. Unlike Danish Dogme films such as *The Celebration* (*Festen*, 1998), which base their stark simplicity on a pseudo-religious creed and a wish to take cinema back to its basics, in this case the movie's lack of technical sophistication is an integral part of its storyline.

Physical movement always has a psychological dimension in cinema: as the three students move further and further away from a normal investigative outing, they penetrate deeper and deeper into the woods and become more and more convinced that they are hopelessly lost. The nearer they get to the witch's house, the closer they are to the darkness within themselves. The would-be filmmakers become increasingly tense. They neither look nor act like future stars, but more like we would imagine ordinary film students: they are not particularly attractive, they're not necessarily very nice and they're ultimately a bit nerdy. This makes it all the more believable that we are seeing the material from their filming expedition: wobbly and unfocused images of a journey with no return, to which the pictures are the only witnesses. Their journey through the woods of Maryland is also an excursion into American history. This wild countryside on the East Coast was where the first settlers arrived, and it was here that James Fenimore Cooper's last Mohican roamed and hunted. It is a sad reflection on today's civilization that the

MARKETING *The Blair Witch Project* cost 35,000 dollars and in the USA alone the movie made 140 million—profit margins which most investors can only dream of. The movie first attracted attention in January 1999 at the Sundance Festival, which is the El Dorado for U.S. independent film. Artisan, a small distribution company, secured the distribution rights to *BWP* and began an unrivalled marketing campaign. Week after week the Internet site www.blairwitch.com published new titbits on the background to the mythology of the Blair Witch. When the movie was released in June 1999 only 27 copies were made, although this number was gradually increased. As copies were kept short, cinema screenings sold out in a few places and the word on the street spread. This is quite unlike the usual Hollywood practice where the market is flooded with as many copies as possible.

3
5 6 7 8 9 10 11 12 13 14 15 16 17 18 19 20 21 22 23 24 25 26
4

1 Face to face with terror—the observer is stuck there with his own fear.

2 Heather (Heather Donahue) in the woods, unaware of the horror to come.

3 Michael (Michael Williams) and Joshua (Joshua Leonard) in the face of horror, which is always located somewhere near the camera.

4 Securing evidence of an expedition into the heart of darkness.

5 Seemingly realistic images of a fictional story.

"*Blair* is the clearest example of a new phenomenon: the film's success was driven not by a conventional publicity campaign, but by a web site combined with word of mouth."

Süddeutsche Zeitung

descendants of this pioneering generation are destroyed by their forefathers' legends. City-dwellers in the wilderness are mostly their own worst enemies, and they fall victim to their own fears rather than to the hostile environment. Trapped in a situation that seems increasingly hopeless, the three students mercilessly document each other's despair and psychic disintegration. Its innovative marketing aside, the movie still basically functions as a relatively old-fashioned horror film. The three students tramp up hill and down dale, and live in terror of what they might find in front of their tent in the morning. But there is actually nothing to be seen—we can't make out anything for sure in the partly blackened pictures and the fear only exists where it is at its worst: in our own heads. MH

THE SIXTH SENSE

1999 – USA – 106 MIN.

DIRECTOR

M. NIGHT SHYAMALAN (Manoj Nelliyattu Shyamalan) (b. 1970)

SCREENPLAY

M. NIGHT SHYAMALAN

DIRECTOR OF PHOTOGRAPHY

TAK FUJIMOTO

MUSIC

JAMES NEWTON HOWARD

PRODUCTION

KATHLEEN KENNEDY, FRANK MARSHALL, BARRY MENDEL
for HOLLYWOOD PICTURES, SPYGLASS ENTERTAINMENT

STARRING

BRUCE WILLIS (Dr. Malcolm Crowe), HALEY JOEL OSMENT (Cole Sear),
TONI COLLETTE (Lynn Sear), OLIVIA WILLIAMS (Anna Crowe),
TREVOR MORGAN (Tommy Tammisimo), DONNIE WAHLBERG (Vincent Grey),
MISCHA BARTON (Kyra Collins), PETER ANTHONY TAMBAKIS (Darren),
JEFFREY ZUBERNIS (Bobby), BRUCE NORRIS (Stanley Cunningham)

BRUCE WILLIS

SIGHT

SOUND

SMELL

TASTE

TOUCH

THE SIXTH SENSE

NOT EVERY GIFT IS A BLESSING.

"I don't want to be scared anymore."

Although death waits for us all, its nature is beyond our knowledge. No film of the 1990s brings this closer to home than *The Sixth Sense.* Little Cole (Haley Joel Osment) has a secret: he has a sixth sense, and he can see the dead. They have chosen him to be their medium. They want to tell him of their torment and reveal the mysterious circumstances of their deaths. Dr. Malcolm Crowe (Bruce Willis) is a child psychologist. He is also dead, shot by a former patient whose treatment failed. The unusual thriller that results from this situation strikes a subtle and moving balance between psychological drama, horror film, buddy movie, and melodrama. In it Bruce Willis, who alongside Sylvester Stallone and Arnold Schwarzenegger is an action star par excellence, demonstrates an unexpected mastery of restrained feeling. The exceptional performance of Haley Joel Osment provides the perfect counterpart as the little boy whose daily encounters with the dead leave painful traces on his body.

Willis portrays the dead psychologist with a combination of melancholy and loneliness, making his vague sense of loss perceptible in every gesture and expression. He's quite unaware that he has joined the ranks of the dead. Only Cole can see him. They meet for the first time in a church near the home that Cole shares with his mother. Cole is tormented by his sixth sense and Crowe offers assistance, not knowing that in fact it is Cole who will be of greater help to him in coming to grips with his past. The exchange between these two characters gives the film emotional plausibility, in spite of its being a ghost story which is not without horrifying moments of subtle terror. *The Sixth Sense* brings a new dimension to the mystery/ghost story horror genre. The nightmarish tale, with its surprise ending, is staged with remarkable creativity and assurance by M. Night Shyamalan. The plot plays with our expectations, exploiting the viewer's assumption that all that is seen is real, and that time, place and causality all correspond to his everyday experience. After Malcolm Crowe is shot in the stomach, the film fades into darkness. It fades in again to the figure of Crowe, who is sitting on a bench and observing a child in the distance. Further deception is provided by a subtitle, fixing the event in space and time. Nothing recalls the previous injury, and

TAK FUJIMOTO The visual power of Tak Fujimoto's images had a lasting influence on the cinema of the 1990s. He trained at the International Film School in London and has left his mark on the style of a generation of cameramen. His impressive debut in 1973 with *Badlands* (director: Terrence Malick) was an early demonstration of his virtuosity and sense of style. *Caged Heat* (1974) was the first of several collaborations with director Jonathan Demme. The originality of this director's American images is largely due to Fujimoto's rich coloring and judicious lighting. Above all, in *The Silence of the Lambs* (1991) Fujimoto developed his virtuoso games with space, with nearness and distance, and with the visible and the invisible to unique perfection.

“The film is so well plotted and the ending so unforeseen that the surprise is complete. This is a film worth seeing several times over to grasp all its nuances.” *M. Night Shyamalan in: Le Figaro*

the world seems to be back in order. From this position of security, the viewer scarcely notices that Crowe no longer has any contact with his fellow humans, with the exception of Cole. Scenes showing Crowe together with other people are staged so cunningly that the audience takes it for granted that he is alive and is still treating Cole's case. In fact, the reverse is true and the film is treating the case of Crowe, but to make the twist at the end of the movie work, the audience must believe that he is still in the world of the living.

In Tak Fujimoto, Shyamalan had one of Hollywood's most distinguished cameramen at his disposal, and it is his artistic mastery that is responsible to a large extent for the great visual power of the film. The calm camerawork together with the subdued coloring of the individual scenes blend to create an atmosphere of morbid foreboding. There

1 Young Cole (Haley Joel Osment) knows what Dr. Malcolm Crowe (Bruce Willis) doesn't know yet.

2 Enough to take your breath away: horrific visions from the realm of the dead.

3 Childish fears and crippling fantasies of death: horror lurks behind the door at the top of the stairs.

is also plenty of visual quotation from other films, like the winding staircase from Hitchcock's *Vertigo*. Shyamalan also follows Hitchcock's lead in making a cameo appearance as a hospital doctor.

Hitchcock's unusual habit of self-portrayal and his subversive brand of psycho-terror are not the only sources of inspiration for this movie. A number of visual shock effects, and the motif of the child's hallucinatory abilities are reminiscent of Stanley Kubrick's horror classic *The Shining* (1980), and the sudden inexplicable opening of kitchen cupboards remind us of Tobe Hooper's *Poltergeist* (1982). *The Sixth Sense* is an illustrious example of the way filmmakers of the 1990s are often masters of the art of quotation. By playing with repetition, ironic refraction, parody, and reversal of meaning, directors open up new perspectives for themselves while at the same time offering audiences a fresh source of entertainment in finding points of comparison with their own knowledge of film. The name of the young protagonist "Cole" for example is a direct reference to the figure played by Bruce Willis in *Twelve Monkeys* (1995) by Terry Gilliam. The characters do much more than share a name—in both films their extraordinary stories are so implausible that they are held to be sane. Both figures find themselves in the same predicament, that they can both see dead people.

The childhood nightmares that make a nightmare of Cole's childhood are dispelled when he accepts his role as go-between and offers the dead his services. When realization of his own death finally catches up with the shocked Crowe, he recalls Cole's words: "I see people—they don't know they're dead." This is the real moment of death for Crowe. The scene is consumed in brilliant white light, and our last visual impression is a short excerpt from his wedding video.

BR

THE OTHERS

2001 – USA / SPAIN / FRANCE / ITALY – 104 MIN.

DIRECTOR

ALEJANDRO AMENÁBAR (b. 1972)

SCREENPLAY

ALEJANDRO AMENÁBAR

DIRECTOR OF PHOTOGRAPHY

JAVIER AGUIRRESAROBE

EDITING

NACHO RUIZ CAPILLAS

MUSIC

ALEJANDRO AMENÁBAR

PRODUCTION

FERNANDO BOVAIRA, JOSÉ LUIS CUERDA, SUNMIN PARK for CRUISE / WAGNER PRODUCTIONS, SOGECINE, LAS PRODUCCIONES DEL ESCORPIÓN, DIMENSION FILMS, CANAL+ ESPAÑA

STARRING

NICOLE KIDMAN (Grace), CHRISTOPHER ECCLESTON (Charles), ALAKINA MANN (Anne), JAMES BENTLEY (Nicholas), FIONNULA FLANAGAN (Mrs. Mills), ERIC SYKES (Mr. Tuttle), ELAINE CASSIDY (Lydia), RENÉE ASHERSON (The Old Lady), KEITH ALLEN (Mr. Marlish), ALEXANDER VINCE (Victor)

SOONER OR LATER THEY WILL FIND YOU.
NICOLE KIDMAN
THE
OTHERS

1

"This house is ours."

The year is 1945; the setting, the island of Jersey in the English Channel. A house looms in the fog, cut off from the rest of the world: the classic haunted house. The Victorian era of great ghost stories seems closer in time than the Second World War. A strict mistress runs her home with military precision. Curtains must be closed at all times, for darkness is of paramount importance—Grace (Nicole Kidman) fears for the health of her children, Anne and Nicholas (Alakina Mann and James Bentley), who suffer from a rare photosensitive allergy. The new servants, led by kind-hearted nanny Mrs. Mills (Fionnula Flanagan), follow her instructions reluctantly. They know more about this house than Grace, who is Catholic and does not believe in ghosts. They worked here "before." The spirits refuse to be locked out. Perhaps they are already there. Doors open themselves; invisible hands play the piano. Little Anne has even seen the intruders. One awful day, the curtains disappear, and Grace is forced to realize that "sometimes the worlds of the living and the dead come together."

What is immediately striking about *The Others* is the dignified elegance of its mise-en-scène. The young Spanish-Chilean director Alejandro Amenábar not only takes his cue from the great models of the Gothic genre such as *Rebecca* (1940), *Gaslight* (1944), and *The Haunting* (1962), but actually directs like an old master. Avoiding any gory shock effects and in true Alfred Hitchcock style, the fear lurks within the mind of the viewer. Hardly innovative, you might think. But there is much in this quiet, elegant ghost film that turns out to be malicious deception. Imperceptibly, normal circumstances become reversed: it is not darkness but light that unleashes the horror, an effect that is carefully constructed by Amenábar, working with the lighting director. Then, of course, there is the final twist in the plot, a narrative device reminiscent of M. Night Shyamalan's

ALEJANDRO AMENÁBAR Alejandro Amenábar was born in Santiago, Chile in 1972 to Spanish-Chilean parents. Just one year later the family fled Pinochet's military dictatorship and settled in Madrid. Amenábar later started a film studies course at Complutense University, though it was not enough to satisfy his penchant for occult and spiritual subjects. To relieve his boredom, he made his first feature film there, *Tesis* (1996): in this cheaply produced horror flick, some students are on the trail of a gang producing snuff films. The very next year came *Open Your Eyes* (*Abre los ojos*, 1997). His surreal treatment of male vanity and humiliation proved Amenábar as a great up-and-coming talent. After decades of Pedro Almodóvar's sole reign, Spanish cinema had a new star.
His next career boost, however, was externally driven. After seeing *Open Your Eyes*, Hollywood star Tom Cruise apparently took a great shine to the female lead, Penélope Cruz. In exchange for the rights to its remake, *Vanilla Sky* (2001), directed by Cameron Crowe and with Cruz reprising her leading role, Amenábar secured finance to film *The Others* (*Los otros*, 2001) as a big Hollywood production, with Cruise's then wife, Nicole Kidman, in the star role. Shortly after, Cruise separated from her. It was not just this publicity, however, that helped to make this superior horror movie a resounding success. With supreme confidence, Amenábar had packed his themes of dreams, identity loss, and the afterlife into a classic ghost story. In addition, as in all his films, he had also provided the music himself, as well as writing the screenplay and directing, thus radically increasing the number of personal awards he received at film festivals. For the rather more sedate film about assisted suicide, *The Sea Inside* (*Mar adentro*, 2004), with Javier Bardem playing a paraplegic sailor, he finally won the Oscar for Best Foreign Language Film. In 2009 his historical epic *Agora*, set in Ancient Egypt, came to the movies; for his latest movie, the psycho thriller *Regression* (2015), Amenábar also wrote the screenplay.

The Sixth Sense (1999), and one that has become diluted in numerous subsequent movies to the point of becoming meaningless. In *The Others* this postmodern playing with increasingly heightened audience expectation is firmly rooted in the narrative. There is a constant refusal to reveal who "the others" really are. In this way, the structure of the movie is not turned on its head by the breathtaking final act, but is rendered plausible from the outset. Completely different levels of meaning open up on repeated viewing—from an economic point of view, a function of the new narrative technique that is quite deliberate.

Seen in the cold light of day, *The Others* is located not so much within the tradition of the ghost or horror movie than as part of a whole series of films such as *The Truman Show* (1998) and *Eternal Sunshine of the Spotless Mind* (2004), which are underpinned by a profound identity crisis in the main character. It is the job of the stars to render such contradictions redundant. The scariest part of this movie by far is the sight of Nicole Kidman (looking like one of Hitchcock's blondes wandering ghost-like through an old-fashioned setting) with a look of terror on her face and holding a shotgun. As white as snow and as delicate as porcelain, she kick-started her second career as a respected

1 Ghostly presence: Nicole Kidman, modeled on Hitchcock's blondes, plays vigilant mother, Grace—the creepiest aspect of the entire film by far.

2 Servants Mrs. Mills, Lydia and Mr. Tuttle (Fionnula Flanagan, Elaine Cassidy, Eric Sykes) "worked here a long time ago." No reassurance whatsoever.

3 Grace resolutely protects her little family. But the ghosts cannot be locked out, and may even be here already.

4 Stricken souls of children: Grace's children Anne (Alakina Mann) and Nicholas (James Bentley) often have contact with the "others."

"We're already so deep in the brave new world of computerized special effects that we hardly notice any more that Hollywood is doing all the imagining for us... In *The Others*, starring Nicole Kidman, we do the imagining, based on sounds that occur beyond the camera's eye, or by the looks on people's faces as they experience the supernatural." *The Washington Post*

3
4

actress and Hollywood's one and only diva with this film. Amenábar's movie itself became the forerunner of a new "Spanish Wave" that brought international acclaim to Latin American and Spanish horror specialists including Guillermo del Toro with *Pan's Labyrinth* (*El laberinto del fauno*, 2006) and Juan Antonio Bayona with *The Orphanage* (*El orfanato*, 2007). In its native country *The Others* (an English-language masterpiece filmed in Spain) won eight Goyas, including the awards for Best Film and Best Music; composed by young prodigy Amenábar himself, the score contributes significantly to the movie's spooky atmosphere. PB

"The most discomfiting thing in *The Others* isn't a human, a ghost, or even a place. It's the otherworldly light." *slate.com*

5 Mysterious light sensitivity: the children themselves are creatures of the night, strictly forbidden to leave the house.

6 Haunted house in the mist: director Amenábar skillfully draws us in with conventions of the genre, only to subvert them in a heart-stopping finale.

7 Dreams and madness: Grace's husband, Charles (Christopher Eccleston), who is believed dead, comes back from the war—but isn't there.

Chronology

1910 The Edison Company's two-reel production of *Frankenstein.* The film is now considered lost.

1919/20 Germany's Expressionistic masterpiece, *The Cabinet of Dr. Caligari.*

1920 *The Golem,* from director-star Paul Wegener.

1922 The greatest of the silent horror pictures, F.W. Murnau's *Nosferatu*, released in Germany.

1925 *The Phantom of the Opera*—Lon Chaney's greatest.

1931 Universal's horror cycle begins—Bela Lugosi in Tod Browning's *Dracula* and Boris Karloff in James Whale's *Frankenstein.* Meanwhile, Fritz Lang's urban (German) thriller *M* introduces the world to Peter Lorre, who engenders sympathy for his pedophilic serial killer.

1932 Hollywood embraces horror: *Island of Lost Souls, The Mummy*, Tod Browning's extraordinary *Freaks,* and Fredric March receives an Academy Award for Best Actor for his title double role in *Dr. Jekyll and Mr. Hyde.*

1933 *King Kong*, the apotheosis of screen fantasy. Also James Whale's H.G. Wells adaptation, *The Invisible Man.*

1935 *Bride of Frankenstein*, Whale and Universal's best.

1941 *The Wolf Man*—Lon Chaney Jr.'s most famous role.

1942 *Cat People*—producer Val Lewton initiates the finest horror cycle of the 1940s. Jacques Tourneur directs.

1943 *I Walked with a Zombie*—classic Lewton-Tourneur.

1951 *The Thing from Another World*—Hollywood's nuclear reaction; Cold War horrors from the Rocket Age.

1 ON THE SET OF "ED WOOD" (1994) Martin Landau as Bela Lugosi in Tim Burton's affectionate biopic of the man often called the worst film director ever. Landau won an Oscar for his dignified portrayal of the drug-addicted fallen horror icon. Lugosi died in 1956 while shooting Wood's *Plan 9 from Outer Space.'*

2 ON THE SET OF "FRANKENSTEIN" (1931) Boris Karloff was over 40 when James Whale selected him to play The Monster. He'd already been acting in films for over a decade.

1954 *Godzilla*. Japan emerges from nuclear disaster with a nuclear monster of its own, and exports it worldwide.

1956 *Invasion of the Body Snatchers*, *The Bad Seed*. Suburbia's dark underbelly.

1957 Hammer Studios begins the second cycle of classic monsters: *The Curse of Frankenstein*; *Horror of Dracula*.

1959/60 *Eyes without a Face*, *The Tingler*. From the Parisian sublime to the Hollywood ridiculous.

1960 Freudian responses to the simmering 1950s begin to emerge: *Psycho* and *Peeping Tom* signal the arrival of "realist horror"; Mario Bava arrives with *Mask of the Demon* from Italy; England licks its wounds and shows its backbone with *Village of the Damned*; and Roger Corman begins his Edgar Allan Poe cycle with *House of Usher*.

3 ON THE SET OF "GREMLINS" (1984) Bringing little monsters to life, here using techniques originally developed for *The Muppet Show.*

4 ON THE SET OF "JAWS" (1975) Steven Spielberg and rubber friend.

1962 Hollywood begins to replay itself. Robert Aldrich's "Grand Dame Guignol" classic, *What Ever Happened to Baby Jane?*

1963 Sensibilities are rapidly changing. Hitchcock's *The Birds*, Herschell Gordon Lewis's *Blood Feast*, and Robert Wise's *The Haunting* are all harbingers (in very distinct ways) of the morally ambiguous and psychosexual horror films to come.

1965 Female fury (and psychosis) in Roman Polanski's quite brilliant *Repulsion.*

1968 The innocence of the Summer of Love gives way to the raw viscera of George A. Romero's *Night of the Living Dead* and the urban paranoia of Roman Polanski's *Rosemary's Baby.*

1972 Wes Craven arrives with *The Last House on the Left.* Arguably the most popular and successful horror filmmaker ever, Craven presents the extreme violence of a nation raped and adrift. Meanwhile, with the arrival of *Blacula*, blaxploitation plays the horror card.

1973 Hollywood gets back in the act, shocking the world with *The Exorcist.* Brian De Palma arrives with *Sisters.* Along with Dario Argento, De Palma makes "Hitchcockian" work for a younger generation. Robin Hardy's singular *The Wicker Man* proves England's not out of the game.

1974 *The Texas Chain Saw Massacre.* Tobe Hooper lifts the covers off the family bed that America's made for itself. Horror cinema will never be the same.

1975 With *Jaws* and *Shivers*, Steven Spielberg and David Cronenberg arrive—two of the greatest of their generation.

4

1976 De Palma introduces the world to Stephen King with *Carrie*. *The Omen* proves there's life (and death) after *The Exorcist* in Hollywood.

1977 Dario Argento goes gothic with *Suspiria*.

1978 John Carpenter's *Halloween* initiates the "slasher cycle" and becomes the biggest indie hit of them all.

1979 *Dawn of the Dead*, *Alien*, *The Brood*. Horror's gotten so big, there's room for satire, sci-fi, and psychodrama.

1980 *Dressed to Kill*, *Friday the 13th*, *The Shining*. The effects of King's rise and *Halloween*'s explosive success. Italian bloodbath *Cannibal Holocaust* offends and compels.

1981 Twin lycanthrope pics, *The Howling* and *An American Werewolf in London*. Sam Raimi arrives on the scene with *The Evil Dead*.

1982 *The Thing*, *Poltergeist*—horror shock effects reach new heights.

1984 *A Nightmare on Elm Street*. Craven strikes again with this high-concept supernatural/surreal slasher hit. *Gremlins*—Joe Dante's greatest.

1986 *The Fly*, David Cronenberg's unforgettable parlor piece. John McNaughton's chilling *Henry: Portrait of a Serial Killer* introduces videotape to the killer's menu.

1987 *Hellraiser*. Clive Barker's S and M fetish horror.

1991 *The Silence of the Lambs*—Hannibal Lecter arrives.

1996 *Scream*. Screenwriter Kevin Williamson and director Wes Craven revive the slasher genre by giving it a much-needed dose of self-reflexive humor.

1998 Hideo Nakata's *Ringu* introduces "J-horror" to the world.

1999 *The Blair Witch Project*, mock-doc horror for the digital generation. Takashi Miike tortures us (in a good way) with *Audition*.

2001 The critical and financials success of supernatural Gothic horror films *The Others*, directed by Spaniard Alejandro Amenábar, and *The Devil's Backbone*, directed by Mexican Guillermo del Toro, opened the door to further Gothic movies like *The Orphanage* (*El orfanato*, 2007), *The Woman in Black* (2012) and *Crimson Peak* (2015).

2002 *The Ring* bursts open the door for Hollywood remakes of Asian horror hits. *28 Days Later* and *Resident Evil* kickstart a new interest in zombie movies, that leads to the comic (since 2003) and TV series (since 2010) of *The Walking Dead*, as well as new movies from zombie king George A. Romero, *Land of the Dead* (2005), the *[REC]* series (since 2007), *World War Z* (2013), and *Train to Busan* (*Busanhaeng*, 2016).

2003 Remakes of 1970s horror classics abound with, among others, *The Texas Chainsaw Massacre* (2003), *The Hills Have Eyes* (2006), *Halloween* (2007) *Friday the 13th* (2009), *A Nightmare on Elm Street* (2010), and *Evil Dead* (2013).

2004 James Wan's *Saw* establishes the "torture porn" subgenre and becomes horror's biggest franchise, with seven sequels and a worldwide gross of over $873 million at the box office.

2007 The success of *Paranormal Activity* reignites the independent (i.e. low budget) found footage supernatural horror movie and has spawned five sequels so far.

2008–present The established means of expression of the different horror subgenres are being reinvented and subverted by films such as *Let the Right One in* (2008), *Black Swan* (2010), *We Are What We Are* (2010), *You're Next* (2011), *Kill List* (2011), *Cabin in the Woods* (2012), *The Babadook* (2014), *It Follows* (2014), and *Under the Skin* (2014).

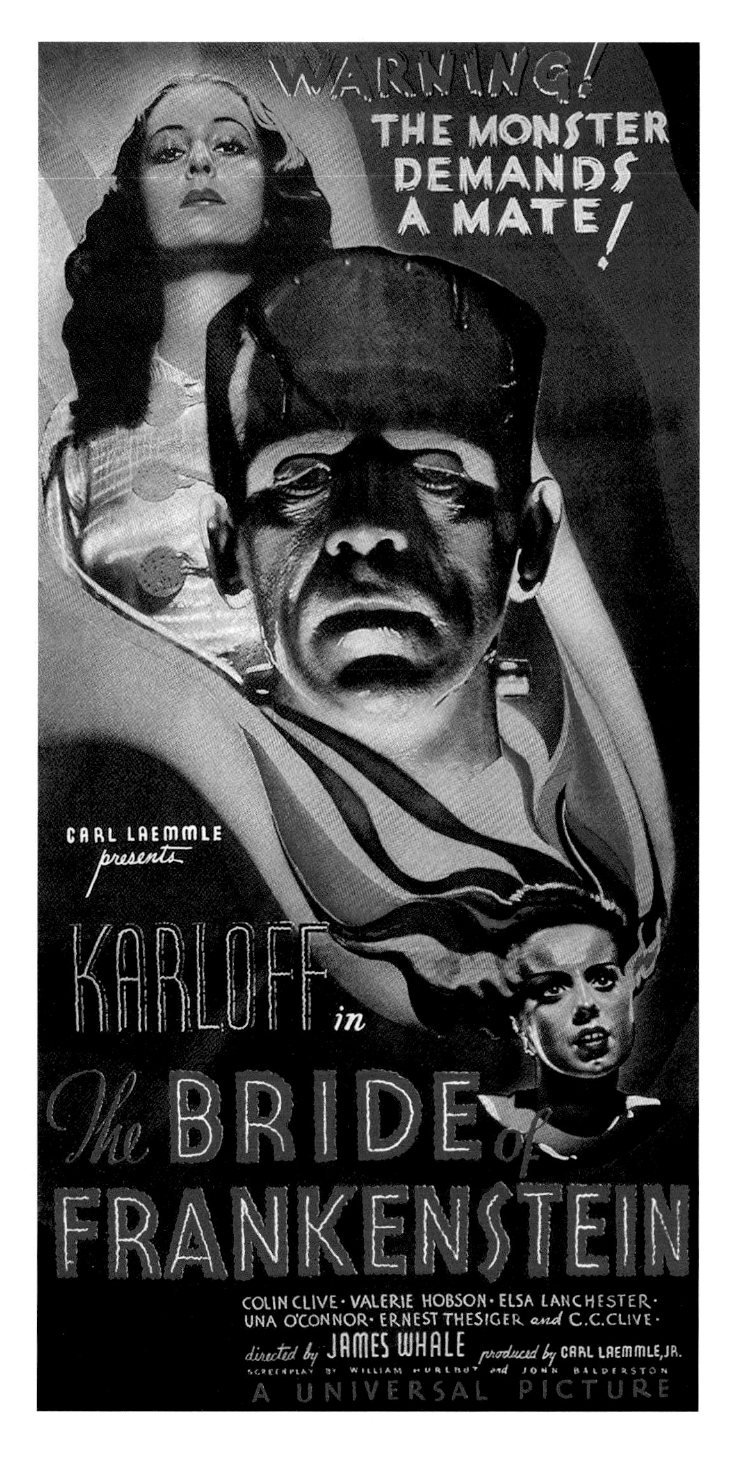
WARNING!
THE MONSTER DEMANDS A MATE!
CARL LAEMMLE presents
KARLOFF in
The BRIDE of FRANKENSTEIN
COLIN CLIVE · VALERIE HOBSON · ELSA LANCHESTER ·
UNA O'CONNOR · ERNEST THESIGER and C.C.CLIVE ·
directed by JAMES WHALE produced by CARL LAEMMLE, JR.
SCREENPLAY BY WILLIAM HURLBUT and JOHN BALDERSTON
A UNIVERSAL PICTURE

Bibliography

Arkoff, Sam: *Flying through Hollywood by the Seat of My Pants.* Birch Lane Press, 1992.

Beck, Calvin Thomas: *Heroes of the Horrors.* Macmillan, 1975.

Bojarski, Richard & Kenneth Beals: *The Films of Boris Karloff.* Citadel Press, 1974.

Bouzereau, Laurent: *The De Palma Cut.* Dembner Books, 1988.

Britton, Andrew, Richard Lippe, Tony Williams & Robin Wood (eds.): *The American Nightmare: Essays on the Horror Film.* Festival of Festivals, 1979.

Brunas, Michael, John Brunas & Tom Weaver: *Universal Horrors: The Studio's Classic Films, 1931–1946.* McFarland, 1990.

Carroll, Noël: *The Philosophy of Horror; or, Paradoxes of the Heart.* Routledge, 1990.

Clarens, Carlos: *An Illustrated History of the Horror Film.* Capricorn Books, 1967.

Clover, Carol: *Men, Women, and Chain Saws: Gender in the Modern Horror Film.* Princeton University Press, 1992.

Corman, Roger: *How I Made a Hundred Movies in Hollywood and Never Lost a Dime.* Delta Books, 1990.

Crane, Jonathan Lake: *Terror and Everyday Life: Singular Moments in the History of the Horror Film.* Sage Publications, 1994.

Creed, Barbara: *The Monstrous-Feminine: Film, Feminism, Psychoanalysis.* Routledge, 1993.

Curtis, James: *James Whale: A New World of Gods and Monsters.* Faber and Faber, 1998.

Derry, Charles: *Dark Dreams: A Psychological History of the Modern Horror Film.* A.S. Barnes, 1977.

Dika, Vera: *Games of Terror: Halloween, Friday the 13th, and the Films of the Stalker Cycle.* Farleigh Dickinson University Press, 1990.

Donald, James (ed.): *Fantasy and the Cinema.* British Film Institute, 1989.

Gifford, Denis: *A Pictorial History of Horror Movies.* Hamlyn, 1973.

Gifford, Denis: *The Dread of Difference: Gender and the Horror Film.* University of Texas Press, 1996.

Golden, Christopher (ed.): *Cut! Horror Writers on Horror Film.* Berkley Books, 1992.

Grant, Barry Keith (ed.): *Planks of Reason: Essays on the Horror Film.* Scarecrow Press, 1984.

Hardy, Phil (ed.): *The Aurum Film Encyclopedia Volume 3—Horror.* Aurum Press, 1985.

Hendershot, Cyndy: *I Was a Cold War Monster: Horror Films, Eroticism and the Cultural Imagination.* Bowling Green State University Press, 2001.

Hoberman, J. & Jonathan Rosenbaum: *Midnight Movies.* Harpers and Row, 1983.

Humphries, Reynold: *The American Horror Film: An Introduction.* Edinburgh University Press, 2002.

Huss, Roy & T.J. Ross (eds.): *Focus on the Horror Film.* Prentice-Hall, 1972.

Hutchings, Peter: *Hammer and Beyond: The British Horror Film.* Manchester University Press, 1993.

Hutchings, Peter: *Terence Fisher.* Manchester University Press, 2002.

Jancovich, Mark: *American Horror from 1951 to the Present.* Keele University Press, 1994.

Jancovich, Mark: *Horror.* Batsford, 1992.

Jancovich, Mark (ed.): *Horror: The Film Reader.* Routledge, 2002.

Juno, Andrea & V. Vale (eds.): *RE/Search #10—Incredibly Strange Films.* RE/Search Publications, 1986.

Kermode, Mark: *The Exorcist.* British Film Institute, 1997.

Lindsay, Cynthia: *Dear Boris: The Life of William Henry Pratt a.k.a. Boris Karloff.* Alfred A. Knopf, 1975.

Mank, Gregory William: *It's Alive!: The Classic Cinema Saga of Frankenstein.* A.S. Barnes, 1980.

McCarthy, Kevin & Ed Gorman (eds.): *"They're Here…": Invasion of the Body Snatchers: A Tribute.* Berkley Boulevard, 1999.

McDonagh, Maitland: *Broken Mirrors/Broken Minds: The Dark Dreams of Dario Argento.* Sun Tavern Fields, 1991.

Newman, Kim: *Nightmare Movies: A Critical History of the Horror Film, 1968–88.* Bloomsbury, 1988.

Pirie, David: *A Heritage of Horror: The English Gothic Cinema 1946–1972.* Gordon Fraser, 1973.

Polanski, Roman: *Roman*. William Morrow, 1984.
Prawer, S.S.: *Caligari's Children: The Film as Tale of Terror*. Oxford University Press, 1980.
Rodley, Chris (ed.): *Cronenberg on Cronenberg*. Faber and Faber, 1992.
Schneider, Steven Jay (ed.): *100 European Horror Films*. BFI, 2007.
Schneider, Steven Jay (ed.): *Fear Without Frontiers: Horror Cinema Across the Globe*. FAB Press, 2003.
Schneider, Steven Jay (ed.): *Horror Film and Psychoanalysis: Freud's Worst Nightmares*. Cambridge University Press, 2004.
Schneider, Steven Jay & Daniel Shaw (eds.): *Dark Thoughts: Philosophic Reflections on Cinematic Horror*. Scarecrow Press, 2003.
Schneider, Steven Jay & Tony Williams (eds.): *Horror International*. Wayne State University Press, 2004.
Senn, Bryan: *Golden Horrors: An Illustrated Critical Filmography, 1931–1939*. McFarland, 1996.
Siegel, Don: *A Siegel Film*. Faber and Faber, 1993.
Silver, Alain & James Ursini (eds.): *Horror Film Reader*. Limelight Editions, 2000.
Skal, David J.: *The Monster Show: A Cultural History of Horror*. W.W. Norton, 1993.
Tohill, Cathal & Pete Tombs: *Immoral Tales: Sex and Horror Cinema in Europe, 1956–1984*. Primitive Press, 1994.
Truffaut, François: *Hitchcock*. Touchstone, 1983.
Tudor, Andrew: *Monsters and Mad Scientists: A Cultural History of the Horror Movie*. Basil Blackwell, 1989.
Twitchell, James B.: *Dreadful Pleasures: An Anatomy of Modern Horror*. Oxford University Press, 1995.
Waller, Gregory (ed.): *American Horrors: Essays on the Modern American Horror Film*. University of Illinois Press, 1987.
Williams, Tony: *Hearths of Darkness: The Family in the American Horror Film*. Farleigh Dickinson University Press, 1996.
Wood, Robin: *Hollywood from Vietnam to Reagan*. Columbia University Press, 1986.

Photo credits / Copyright

The publishers would like to express their thanks to the archives and collections for their kind support in the production of this book and for making their pictures available: Bibliothèque du Film, Paris; British Film Institute, London; ddp images, Hamburg; defd and CINEMA, Hamburg; Deutsche Kinemathek, Berlin; Filmbild Fundus Robert Fischer, Munich; Heritage Auctions/HA.com; The Del Valle Archives, David Del Valle, Los Angeles; The Kobal Collection, London/New York; The Joe Dante Collection

ON THE SET OF "HORROR OF DRACULA" (1958) Even the undead stop for tea occasionally.

THE NORTH AMERICAN
INDIAN
TASCHEN

TASCHEN

BURTON HOLMES
TRAVELOGUES
TASCHEN

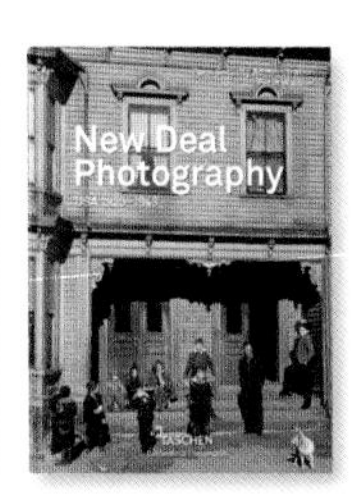
New Deal
Photography
TASCHEN

Lewis W. Hine
America
at
Work
TASCHEN

PHOTO ICONS
TASCHEN

THE DOG
IN PHOTOGRAPHY
1839–TODAY
TASCHEN

1000
TATTOOS
TRUE LOVE
TASCHEN

SVEN A. KIRSTEN
TIKI
POP

HARRY SEIDLER
THE GRAND TOUR
Travelling the World with an Architect's Eye
TASCHEN

MODERN
ARCHITECTURE
A–Z

100
INTERIORS AROUND THE WORLD
TASCHEN

100
CONTEMPORARY
HOUSES
TASCHEN

SMALL
ARCHITECTURE
TASCHEN

GREEN
ARCHITECTURE
TASCHEN

100 CONTEMPORARY
WOOD
BUILDINGS

CONTEMPORARY
CONCRETE
BUILDINGS

CABINS
TASCHEN

tree houses
TASCHEN

FASHION
HISTORY
TASCHEN

Fashion
TASCHEN

100
CONTEMPORARY
FASHION
DESIGNERS
TASCHEN

LIVING IN
ASIA
TASCHEN

LIVING
IN PROVENCE
TASCHEN

LIVING
IN TUSCANY

M

Must-see movies

Get to know cinema's greats

Take a journey through the makers and shapers of celluloid history. From horror to romance, noir to slapstick, adventure to tragedy, Western to new wave, this selection gathers the greats of 20th-century cinema into one indispensable guide to movie gold.

"A masterpiece of picture research and attractive design."
— *The Times*, London

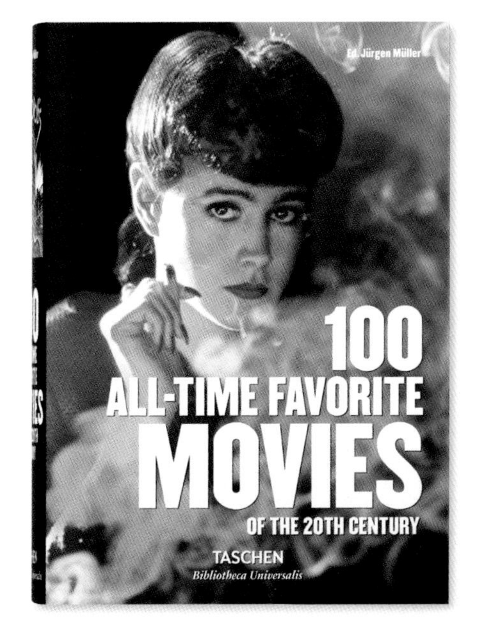

100 All-Time Favorite Movies of the 20th Century
Jürgen Müller
832 pages

YOU CAN FIND TASCHEN STORES IN

Berlin
Schlüterstr. 39

Beverly Hills
354 N. Beverly Drive

Brussels
Place du Grand Sablon /
Grote Zavel 35

Cologne
Neumarkt 3

East Hampton
26 Park Place

Hollywood
Farmers Market,
6333 W. 3rd Street, CT-10

Hong Kong
Shop 01-G02 Tai Kwun,
10 Hollywood Road,
Central

London
12 Duke of York Square

Madrid
Calle del Barquillo, 30

Miami
1111 Lincoln Rd.

"If browsing is considered an art form, the TASCHEN store is a masterpiece."
—Dwell
Milan
Via Meravigli 17
Paris
2 rue de Buci

Imprint

EACH AND EVERY TASCHEN BOOK PLANTS A SEED!
TASCHEN is a carbon neutral publisher. Each year, we offset our annual carbon emissions with carbon credits at the Instituto Terra, a reforestation program in Minas Gerais, Brazil, founded by Lélia and Sebastião Salgado. To find out more about this ecological partnership, please check: *www.taschen.com/zerocarbon*
Inspiration: unlimited. Carbon footprint: zero.

To stay informed about TASCHEN and our upcoming titles, please subscribe to our free magazine at *www.taschen.com/magazine*, follow us on Instagram and Facebook, or e-mail your questions to *contact@taschen.com.*

PAGE 1 STILL FROM "DRACULA" (1931) Transylvanian triage: Having determined which of his prey will most benefit from an eternity of twisted immortality, Dracula (Bela Lugosi) moves in for the kill.

PAGE 2 STILL FROM "THE BLAIR WITCH PROJECT" (1999) Heather (Heather Donahue) alone in the woods.

PAGE 7 STILL FROM "THE TEXAS CHAINSAW MASSACRE 2" (1986)
Modern horror is often so extreme as to be cartoonish. Bill Johnson plays mass murderer Leatherface as loveable clown… to viewers if not to his victims.

Hohenzollernring 53, D–50672 Köln
www.taschen.com

Introduction and texts on the genre:
Steven Jay Schneider and Jonathan Penner
Texts on the individual movies:
Ulrike Bergfeld (UB), Philipp Bühler (PB), Paul Duncan (PD), Malte Hagener (MH), Steffen Haubner (SH), Jörn Hetebrügge (JH), Harald Keller (HK), Katja Kirste (KK), Heinz-Jürgen Köhler (HJK), Petra Lange-Berndt (PLB), Nils Meyer (NM), Anne Pohl (APO), Stephan Reisner (SR), Burkhard Röwekamp (BR), Rainer Vowe (RV)

Translations: Monika Bloxam, Caroline Durant, Isabel Varea, and Karen Waloschek, for Grapevine Publishing Services Ltd., London; Ann Drummond in association with First Edition Translations Ltd, Cambridge; Deborah Caroline Holmes; Katharine Hughes; Daniel A. Huyssen, Patrick Lanagan, and Shaun Samson for English Express, Berlin

Printed in Bosnia–Herzegovina
ISBN 978–3–8365–6185–3

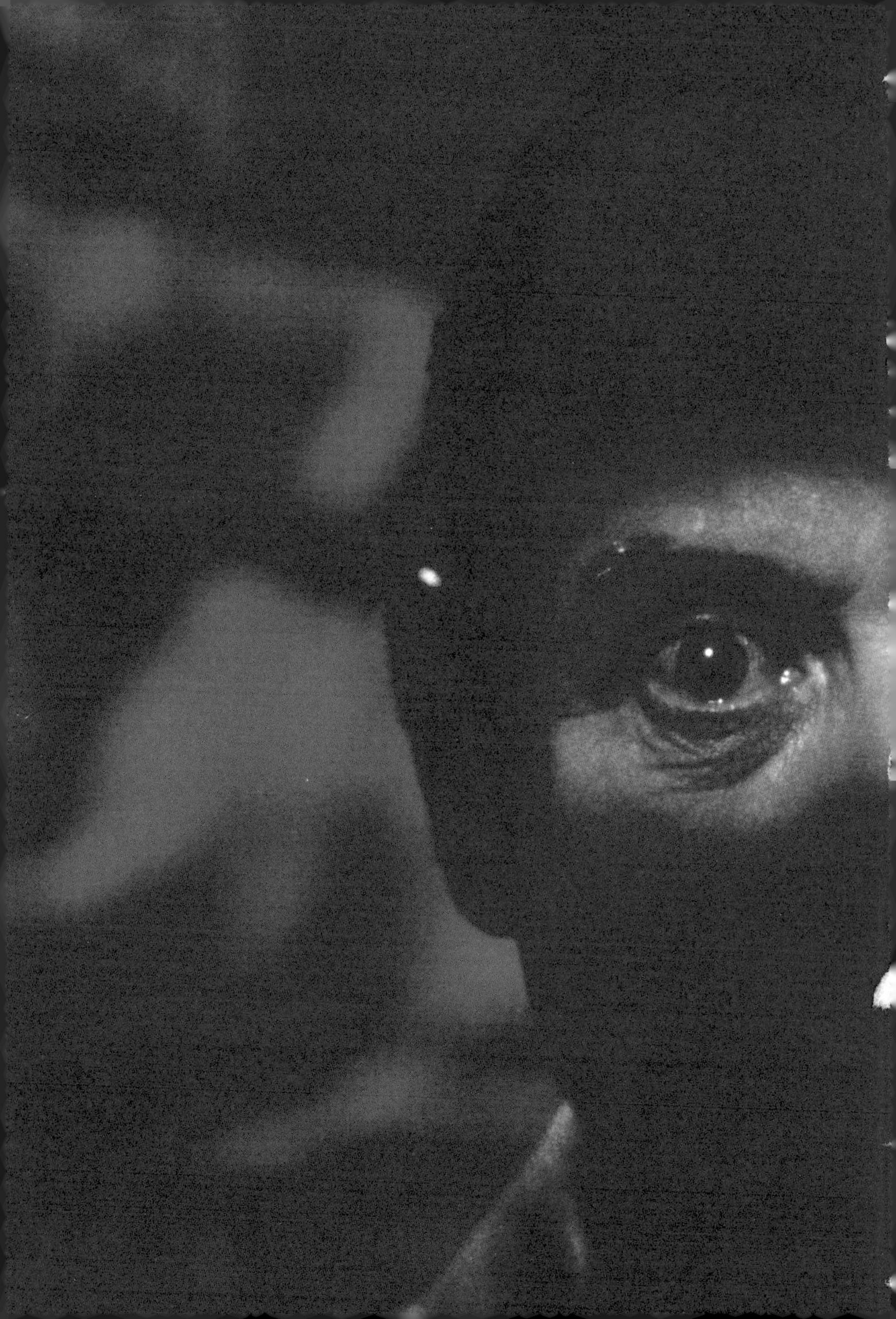